Contributors

CHARLES R. ADRIAN, *University of California at Riverside*
ROBERT R. ALFORD, *New York University*
DAVID S. ARNOLD, *International City Management Association*
BRIAN J. L. BERRY, *University of Chicago*
TERRY N. CLARK, *University of Chicago*
ROBERT FIRESTINE, *Syracuse University*
DOUGLAS JEFFREY, *University of New South Wales*
LESLIE J. KING, *McMaster University*
DAVID R. MEYER, *University of Massachusetts at Amherst*
ROBERT A. MURDIE, *York University*
D. MICHAEL RAY, *State University of New York at Buffalo*
PHILIP H. REES, *Leeds University*
SEYMOUR SACKS, *Syracuse University*
LEO F. SCHNORE, *University of Wisconsin at Madison*
BENJAMIN WALTER, *Vanderbilt University*
HAL H. WINSBOROUGH, *University of Wisconsin at Madison*
FREDERICK M. WIRT, *University of California at Berkeley*

Series Preface

American cities are attracting more public attention and scholarly concern than at perhaps any other time in history. Traditional structures have been seriously questioned and sweeping changes proposed; simultaneously, efforts are being made to penetrate the fundamental processes by which cities operate. This effort calls for marshaling knowledge from a number of substantive areas. Sociologists, political scientists, economists, geographers, planners, historians, anthropologists, and others have turned to urban questions; interdisciplinary projects involving scholars and activists are groping with fundamental issues.

The Wiley Series in Urban Research has been created to encourage the publication of works bearing on urban questions. It seeks to publish studies from different fields that help to illuminate urban processes. It is addressed to scholars as well as to planners, administrators, and others concerned with a more analytical understanding of things urban.

TERRY N. CLARK

Contents

INTRODUCTION: THE GOALS OF CITY CLASSIFICATION 1
BRIAN J. L. BERRY

PART ONE METHODOLOGICAL UNDERPINNINGS: DIMENSIONS OF VARIATION AND DERIVATION OF CLASSES 9

1. Latent Structure of the American Urban System, with International Comparisons 11
BRIAN J. L. BERRY

2. Classification of U.S. Metropolitan Areas by the Characteristics of Their Nonwhite Populations 61
DAVID R. MEYER

PART TWO USES OF CITY CLASSIFICATIONS IN SOCIAL AND POLITICAL RESEARCH 95

3. Social and Political Dimensions of American Suburbs 97
BENJAMIN WALTER AND
FREDERICK M. WIRT

4. Functional Classification and the Residential Location of Social Classes 124
LEO F. SCHNORE AND
HAL H. WINSBOROUGH

5. Urban Typologies and Political Outputs 152
TERRY N. CLARK

ix

PART THREE   ALTERNATIVE MODES OF CLASSIFICA-
              TION AND TYPES OF CITIES   179

              6.   Canadian and American Urban Dimen-
                   sions   181
                   D. MICHAEL RAY AND ROBERT A. MURDIE

              7.   City Classification by Oblique-Factor
                   Analysis of Time-Series Data   211
                   LESLIE J. KING AND DOUGLAS JEFFREY

              8.   Dimensions and Classification of British
                   Towns on the Basis of New Data   225
                   SEYMOUR SACKS AND ROBERT FIRESTINE

              9.   A Comparative Typology of Urban Gov-
                   ernment Images   247
                   CHARLES R. ADRIAN

PART FOUR   STRENGTHS AND WEAKNESSES OF
              ALTERNATIVE CLASSIFICATORY PRO-
              CEDURES   263

              10. Problems of Classifying Subareas within
                   Cities   265
                   PHILIP H. REES

              11. Critical Evaluation of the Principles of
                   City Classification   331
                   ROBERT R. ALFORD

PART FIVE   OVERVIEW   360

              12. Classification as Part of Urban Manage-
                   ment   361
                   DAVID S. ARNOLD

INDEX   379

CITY CLASSIFICATION HANDBOOK:
METHODS AND APPLICATIONS

Introduction   The Goals of City Classification

BRIAN J. L. BERRY
University of Chicago

Why should anyone be interested in classifying cities? To those of an unremittingly scientific frame of mind classificatory exercises are at best limited, a primitive beginning beyond which, they feel, social science has developed. Yet it is equally true that we would never have learned anything if we had never thought how objects resemble each other, and whether they manifest the same properties. If every object in the world were taken as distinct and unique, our perception of the world would disintegrate into complete meaninglessness. The purpose of classification is to give order to the things we experience. We classify things so that we may learn more about them.[1]

This volume begins with the premise that much may yet be gained by city classification. Indeed, few urban research workers are so presumptive as to argue that the need for city classifications is now passed. To quote a recent review of Latin American urban research:

A firm foundation for future Latin American urban research requires the development of more explicit notions of relevant types of cities . . . on dimensions along which urban experiences can be classified for different purposes.[2]

Such a need has been reiterated by many other urban analysts and policy-makers in the United States, Canada, and overseas.

The essence of the continuing need is to recognize dimensions of varia-

---

[1] Ronald Abler, John S. Adams, and Peter Gould, *Spatial Organization* (Englewood Cliffs, N.J.: Prentice-Hall, Inc., 1971), p. 149.
[2] Francine F. Rabinowitz and Felicity M. Trueblood, Eds., *Latin American Urban Research*, Vol. 1 (Beverly Hills, Calif.: Sage Publications, 1970), p. 20.

tion, to facilitate purposive classification, and this is what this handbook is about. Yet the purposes are manifold. To some classification is a means of data exploration, either to determine convenient ways of summarizing information, to find new and potentially useful hypotheses, or to produce a universally true typology. To others classification provides a means of facilitating hypothesis-testing or model-fitting. Yet others are concerned with developing improved modes of prediction, using subgroups rather than an entire population as guides to an efficient sampling plan, elements for which predictions are made, or guides to the selection of analogs or other forms of strategic comparative cases.

Clearly many such purposes are incompatible, unless there is some universally true typology, which hardly seems to be the case for cities. If such a true typology existed, there has surely been enough urban research in the past century for it to have revealed itself by now. Hence the orientation of this book—to emphasize methods of city classification flowing from identification of the dimensions of variation of cities and following from the selection of dimensions relevant to a stated purpose. The essays exemplify several methodologies and outline their results and their limitations. They also show how classifications or dimensions of variation (or both) can be used in more systematic social and political research, and they consider some of the many policy implications. The whole is an illustrated methodological handbook on city classification.

OVERVIEW OF THE ESSAYS

This handbook contains 12 essays in all, grouped into five sections, as follows: (a) methodological underpinnings: dimensions of variation and derivation of classes; (b) uses of city classification in social and political research; (c) alternative modes of classification and types of city; (d) strengths and weaknesses of alternative classificatory procedures; (e) a final overview dealing with classification as part of urban management.

To understand this organization one has to appreciate something of the history of the project leading to its creation. On June 24, 1965 a small group of geographers, political scientists, and sociologists met in Chicago under the sponsorship of the International City Management Association to explore the feasibility of developing an entirely new approach to city classification—an approach that would be comprehensive, flexible, expandable, and as valid as the input variables would permit. The group was convened at the suggestion of Victor Jones, who, with Andrew Collver and Richard L. Forstall, had coauthored the classification of cities section in *The Municipal Year Book 1963*.

The group quickly agreed that significant advances had taken place in concepts and methods since the pioneering economic classification of American cities was made by Chauncy D. Harris in 1943. The group further agreed on the necessity of commissioning a group of papers that would take advantage of the much wider availability of statistical data, refined statistical methodologies, and computer technology for processing extremely large volumes of data on a multivariate basis. Following up on this meeting, the International City Management Association (ICMA) and Resources for the Future (RFF) agreed to the joint funding of committee meetings and the preparation of papers.

The executive committee for the ICMA–RFF Project on Concepts, Techniques, and Applications of the Classification of Cities was formed with Brian J. L. Berry as chairman. Other committee members (affiliation noted if not an author of this book) included Robert L. Alford, David S. Arnold, Richard L. Forstall (Rand McNally), Cyril McC. Henderson (City Manager, Halifax, Nova Scotia), Victor Jones (Department of Political Science, University of California, Berkeley), Leslie J. King, Harold M. Mayer (Department of Geography, Kent State University), Robert H. T. Smith (Department of Geography, Queens University, Kingston, Ontario), and Frederick M. Wirt. Help to the committee was provided by Rand McNally and Company—clerical help and key-punching of the 97 input variables for 1762 cities of 10,000 or more inhabitants as well as other staff services; and the Center for Urban Studies, University of Chicago—programming and computer services, composition of tabular materials, and drafting of maps and illustrations.

Meetings of the executive committee were held in January 1968 and in September 1968, at the time a one-day conference on city classification was held at the University of Maryland. The intent of the group was to help provide a better understanding of the American urban system, both internally and in relation to other countries, to point out directions for the future exploration of city characteristics, to show the factors that are influential in community development, and, above all, to provide a conceptual framework for the continual development of typologies to provide a better understanding of local data within the framework of national data.

The organization of this handbook reflects these purposes. The first chapter is the point of departure. In it I suggest that each city in the American urban system can be characterized by latent dimensions analogous to the educators' characterization of students by their verbal and quantitative abilities, and that, if exposed, these dimensions reveal the different types of cities in the nation and their correlates—or, more generally, the variety of America's urban landscapes. A particular mode of investigation —factor analysis—is used to extract the dimensions from the variables that traditionally have been used in city classification. It is also suggested that similar studies in other parts of the world show similar latent dimensions, although the nature of the dimensionality may change with the level of economic and cultural development.

Richard L. Forstall has complemented this chapter in papers published by the International City Management Association in *The Municipal Year Book 1970* and in *Urban Data Service 1971*, by taking the results of the factor analyses and preparing several new social and economic groupings of American cities.

In these papers Forstall points out that factor scores created for cities from the original data with respect to the latent dimensions (such as socio-economic status) themselves provide a wide-ranging statistical description of each individual city. Since they are usually standardized to zero mean and unit variance, this description is in terms of the profile of each city's position on the principal factors with respect to all other cities in the nation.

Given such evidence, it might seem unnecessary to proceed further and produce a grouping of cities into classes or categories. However, a grouping has the advantage of identifying whether a given city is unique, whether it is a member of a small or large class of generally similar cities, and whether the cities in a given group tend to be alike with respect to many factors or only a few. Factor analysis isolates uncorrelated dimensions of variation and hence suggests that on a national basis these factors operate essentially independently of one another. However, this does not preclude a significant correlation of given factors within specific smaller groups of cities, for example, within one region. Indeed, if no such limited paralleling occurs, there would seem to be little possibility for a grouping on more than one factor at a time.

Of course, any grouping should (as Forstall argues) cast light on the universe, or system of cities, as a whole by indicating to what extent there is a clustering of cities into like groups, and if so whether these are associated with regional location or other variables. Such a grouping can be expected to aid in the comprehension of the vast array of data represented by the 170,000-odd items of input data and the more than 24,000 factor scores produced by the analysis summarized in Chapter 1. It is characteristic of cities as an academic and popular concern that most people, both lay and specialist, have direct knowledge of a few of them, but only of a few. It is natural for generalizations about cities to begin with familiar cities, but the cities familiar to a given person may be unusual or even unique among all cities. A grouping of cities may provide an objective background against which more subjective impressions can be checked and tested.

Any really useful grouping should be based on several factors. A classification or grouping based on only one or two factors, such as size or racial breakdown, is of course perfectly possible and may in fact be of greater value for some types of analysis than any scheme likely to result from the proposal in Chapter 1. However, the more factors a grouping can reflect, the closer it may be to reflecting the complex actuality of city conditions. However useful for analytical purposes, single-factor classifications tend to bypass other salient characteristics of cities, their complexity and the ease and naturalness with which many cities, especially the larger ones, fulfill multiple functions and roles. For example, Boston can be described as one of the largest American cities; a wholesaling and distribution center, of national significance and dominant in the New England region; a major industrial center (with certain manufacturing specialties); a major educational center, also of national significance; a tourist center, especially for its historic associations; and a cultural center with a long and individual tradition. The list could be readily extended to such additional specialties as the city's role as a headquarters for religious denominations, or its port, naval, and fishing activities. All of these are accurate conclusions from possible single-factor approaches—yet it is one city that is being described, not a half dozen different cities.

Too much attention to this multiplicity of characteristics will lead to a situation in which there will be almost as many groups as there are cities—no other city has precisely the same combination of characteristics as Boston. Any grouping should therefore represent a reasonable compromise between a few very large and internally diverse groups and a breakdown so fine as to add little beyond what the individual city scores already provide. If factor analysis is thus a logical procedure for reducing the complexity of many variables to the relative simplicity of the underlying latent dimensions, grouping and classification are the logical means of gathering the observations into their latent subsets.

This complementary nature of factorial procedures and grouping methods is illustrated in Chapter 2, in which David R. Meyer rounds out the picture of American cities by repeating my analysis of the 1960 standard metropolitan statistical areas (SMSAs) in regard to the characteristics of their *nonwhite* populations and then developing a classification by the stepwise clustering procedures of numerical taxonomy.

The chapters in Part Two ask whether the classifications are related to those other characteristics of American cities that are of central concern to social and political analysts. Frederick M. Wirt and Benjamin Walter focus on the variety of suburbs and the correlation between suburban characteristics and voting behavior. Leo F. Schnore and Hal H. Winsborough find that the residential location of social classes within cities is a function of type of city, and Terry N. Clark shows that a range of political outputs, including expenditure patterns of various kinds, differs by community type.

Part Three explores a broad range of alternative modes of classification and of differing classes arising in different situations. D. Michael Ray and Robert A. Murdie find an essential similarity in American and Canadian city types. Leslie J. King and Douglas Jeffrey show that groups of cities can be established on the basis of their reactions to short-term changes in the nation's economy and that such types may be of real importance in urban economic forecasting. Seymour Sacks and Robert Firestine explore the international potentialities of using land-use and valuation data in city classifications, and Charles R. Adrian looks for new variables relating to cities' political images.

The strengths and weaknesses of the wide range of classificatory methods are the concern of Part Four. In one extensive chapter Philip H. Rees adds a further perspective by thoroughly reviewing the concepts, methods, and findings of studies that have attempted to classify subareas within cities. Robert R. Alford then discusses the limitations of the factorial methods used in several of the preceding chapters and calls for more and better data of a political kind, with explicit purposive orientations.

The final chapter by David S. Arnold looks to applications and potential extensions of city classifications. It calls for new classifications that are responsive to change and to the needs of management in an increasingly complex urban society. Most day-to-day users want classifications that will help them accomplish their present tasks and assignments more efficiently. They need independent variables that predict more accurately the values of the dependent variables in which they are interested. If classifications can do this easily, all to the good; if some other method does it better, then effort involved in classification is of little value.

In focusing on the relationships between dependent and independent variables in classifications, users express two general kinds of concern. The first involves developing improved measures of the purposes for which agency or official programs are undertaken in respect to cities or communities. For example, there is a reiterated desire for measures of "local competence" to deal with community problems. Such measures include such concepts as "community will" or "style" (especially "capacity to innovate") in dealing with local problems. The second concern is for more effective indicators of actual needs for services, whether these be for facilities, human resources, or even architectural design.

A corollary need of many users is for "dynamic" typologies that might give some hint as to the future shape and characteristics of cities. It would seem that the methodological problem in creating such classifications is no different from that of establishing more efficient urban typologies for the present urban community, as King and Jeffrey point out. The necessary ingredient would appear to be more substantive knowledge concerning present urban trends. The payoff is in terms of federal users, for what could emerge would be classifications developed in relation to federal programs that assess cities in terms of their needs and capacities, emphasizing either administrative policy and programs relative to cities or the requirements for the development of general definitions of urban regions.

The chapters in this book do not provide classifications that meet such user needs, but they do suggest methodologies whereby these goals can be achieved as better understanding of the appropriate input variables is developed. Indeed, if the volume provides insights and guidelines for the development of the kinds of new classifications that Arnold envisages while revealing some of the systematic bases of variety in American urban landscapes and a few of the consequences of urban differentiation in the nation's social and political life, it will have served its purpose.

ACKNOWLEDGMENTS

Many individuals have contributed to the individual essays in this book. The authors want to recognize in particular the help of Robert Ferber, Henri Theil, Michael Aiken, Elizabeth Balcer, Jenny Rensch, Ann Wallace, Yeu Man Yeung, Yehoshua Cohen, Pat Blair, Robert Van der Linde, David Sterrett, Dyke MacInnes, David Mongees, Satya Pabuwal, and Martin Mattes.

The chapter by Terry N. Clark is research paper No. 21 of the Comparative Study of Community Decision-Making, supported by grant GS-1904 from the National Science Foundation. D. Michael Ray and Robert A. Murdie acknowledge financial support from the Central Mortgage and Housing Corporation. Leo F. Schnore and Hal H. Winsborough's chapter is one of a series of papers in a research program directed by the senior author, focused on ecological patterns in American cities, and supported by the National Science Foundation (grant GS-921) and the Graduate School of the University of Wisconsin. The facilities of the Center for Demography and Ecology, University of Wisconsin, were used. Robert R. Alford notes that his research was supported in part by funds granted to the Institute for Research on Poverty, University of Wisconsin, pursuant to provisions of the Economic Opportunity Act of 1964 and that the Institute is not responsible for errors of fact or interpretation. Many of the chapters were revised as a result of the comments and suggestions of other contributing authors.

Finally, the authors wish as a group to express their thanks to Victor

Jones, who conceived the project and provided continuing support. This interest has been in the development of more efficient tools for urban policy-making and management. It is hoped that this handbook, by illustrating methodologies for transcending the barriers of complex voluminous mounds of urban data, has provided the means whereby less time need be spent on data processing and correspondingly more on diagnosis, inference, strategy evaluation, and policy determination and assessment.

PART ONE

Methodological Underpinnings: Dimensions of Variation and Derivation of Classes

. . . Latent structure of the American urban system, with international comparisons

. . . Classification of U.S. metropolitan areas by the characteristics of their nonwhite population

CHAPTER 1

Latent Structure of the American Urban System, with International Comparisons

BRIAN J. L. BERRY
University of Chicago

Cities differ in many ways. The literature is replete with efforts to reduce the complexity of the differences by classifying urban centers into relatively uniform types, in the belief that a typology aids in sampling and in generalization and prediction from sample evidence. Best known and most frequently used are the so-called functional classifications, developed from data on the economic specialties of cities.[1] Not unexpectedly each functional classification has ended up by differentiating between mining towns, manufacturing cities, service centers, college towns, and the like.

The cynic is inclined to say: "So what?" As Smith points out, the classifiers all too often fail to answer the question: "Classification for what

---

[1] The seminal contribution to functional classification was that of Harris. Chauncy D. Harris, "A Functional Classification of Cities in the United States," *Geographical Review,* Vol. 33, No. 1 (January 1943), pp. 86–99. More recent studies include the following: L. L. Pownall, "The Functions of New Zealand Towns," *Annals of the AAG,* Vol. 45, No. 4 (December 1953), pp. 332–350; Howard J. Nelson, "A Service Classification of American Cities," *Economic Geography,* Vol. 31, No. 3 (July 1955), pp. 189–210; John Fraser Hart, "Functions and Occupational Structures of Cities of the American South," *Annals of the AAG,* Vol. 45, No. 3 (September 1955), pp. 269–286; William Steigenga, "A Comparative Analysis and Classification of Netherlands Towns," *Tijdschrift voor Economische en Sociale Geografie,* Vol. 46, No. 6/7 (June–July 1955), pp. 105–119; Victor Jones and Richard L. Forstall, "Economic and Social Classification of Metropolitan Areas," *The Municipal Year Book 1963* (Chicago: International City Managers' Association, 1963), pp. 31–44; Richard L. Forstall, "Economic Classification of Places Over 10,000, 1960–1963," *The Municipal Year Book 1967* (Chicago: International City Managers' Association, 1967), pp. 30–65.

purpose?"[2] To compound the brute empiricism of classification for classification's sake, consumers often have used the resulting classifications uncritically. They have frequently sought explanation of some phenomenon of interest in *a priori* class differences, without asking whether similarities and differences between classes of cities have any relevance to the questions they want answered.

This chapter was prepared in the belief that some rethinking of the city-classification problem would provide a framework within which the consumer might be induced to address the issue of theoretical relevance more directly. As such, the intent was to challenge, to provide an alternative point of departure, rather than to assert that there now exists some superior scheme for typifying the diverse elements in the American urban landscape.

METHODOLOGY

The Classical Taxonomic Approach

The decision to place cities in the same class has usually been based on observed or "manifest" similarities. To take an example, avoiding for the moment the most fundamental questions of *what* similarities for *which* units of observation, any one or a combination of the 97 variables listed in the appendix to this chapter could qualify as providing this manifest evidence when measured for such units of observation as the 1762 urban places in the United States that had 10,000 or more inhabitants within their legal city limits in both 1950 and 1960.

The traditional city classifier would approach the resulting 1762×97 data matrix in a special way, developing a series of criteria for class membership and allocating cities to classes on their basis. Most frequently he would work with the variables one at a time, splitting the cities into relatively uniform subsets in a series of steps.

Consider a classification based on the percentages of the city's labor force in various sectors of the economy. After studying the frequency distributions of cities on each of the variables, the taxonomist might decide that it is important to separate towns with more than 20% of their workers employed in mining from those with less. Similarly he finds a 40% "break" in

[2] R. H. T. Smith, "Method and Purpose in Functional Town Classification," *Annals of the AAG,* Vol. 55, No. 3 (September 1965), pp. 539–548, and "The Functions of Australian Towns," *Tijdschrift voor Economische en Sociale Geografie,* Vol. 56, No. 3 (May–June 1965), pp. 81–92.

manufacturing and 25% in retailing employment "significant." On reflection, he also decides that manufacturing is "more important" than mining, and mining is "more important" than retailing. Thus he first splits towns into subsets based on manufacturing, then on mining, and finally on retailing, so that his taxonomic "tree" takes the form illustrated in Figure 1. A relatively straightforward set of mutually exclusive types of town results.

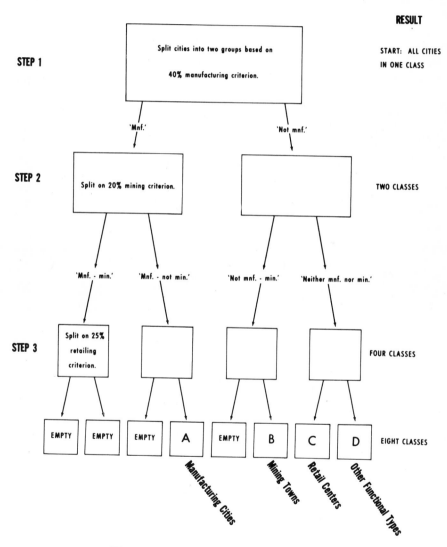

Figure 1 A traditional taxonomic process.

The Search for Latent Dimensions

Clearly the traditional approach will not suffice when a large number of variables are available. If 97 variables are each used to split cities into two groups, as in Figure 1, the number of classes possible is 2^{97}. In practice, of course, many of the combinations will not be realized because many of the variables differentiate towns in the same ways. For example, high-income communities also have populations with high educational levels, large proportions of white-collar and professional workers, and, more fundamentally, all of the outward symptoms of high social status. We might therefore postulate that the manifest similarities of cities are due to certain fundamental "latent" traits, tendencies, or progenitors like social status, resulting from basic cultural traits and processes, such as the aggressive pursuit of economic achievement and related "success." A particular method of analysis, factor analysis, provides a means of searching for these causal factors, by separating and identifying clusters of closely interdependent variables whose interpretation is keyed to latent structure and processes.

Take the 1762×97 city-data matrix D and its 97 separate column vectors $d_1, d_2, d_3, \ldots, d_{97}$ (one for each variable). The fundamental hypothesis of factor analysis is that each of these columns is a product of different combinations of the same underlying factors or common causes and that these latent factors are substantially fewer than the manifest variables. To change the example for a moment, if a column of the d terms were to represent the scores of 1762 students on a test, one would be able to predict these scores on the basis of the underlying verbal and quantitative abilities of the students and the "mixture" of these latent abilities tested by the particular test, also taking into account a random-error term:

$$d_i = \Lambda \Theta_i + \Sigma_i$$

where d_i is the manifest (test) vector (1762×1), Λ contains the coefficients measuring each student's latent verbal-ability and quantitative-ability scores (1762×2), Θ_i identifies the verbal–quantitative "mixture" of test i (2×1), and Σ_i is a vector of random errors and other "disturbance" terms for the test (1762×1). Obviously Λ is unchanged for different tests, but Θ_i and Σ_i vary.

Educational psychologists determine the Λ for students and the Θ_i for tests by factor analysis. In the same way, therefore, factor analysis of the 1762×97 city-data matrix should produce *factor scores for cities* (coefficients measuring each city's rating on the latent urban dimensions) and *factor loadings for manifest variables* (coefficients measuring the mixture of latent dimensions present in each manifest variable). This output should in turn enable the fundamental dimensions of the American urban system to be interpreted and new city classifications to be built *on the basis of those latent traits that bear usefully on the purposes for which the classifications are to be used.* The purposive orientation is critical.

Likewise the full output of scores of the 1762 urban places on each of the latent dimensions should enable users[3] to focus more clearly on the central issues in city classification as they bear on their subsequent analytic use:

1. What dimensions of variation are relevant to the analysis, that is, which structural features are of explanatory significance?
2. Are they of equal relevance, or should they receive different weights, that is, what is the relative explanatory power of the dimensions?
3. How many classes, or types, of cities are needed?

When these questions have been satisfactorily answered, it is possible to prepare a classification that minimizes within-group differences, producing classes containing cities that are as much alike as possible.[4] The frame is then set for sampling, for cross-tabulation, or for covariance analysis and other forms of hypothesis-testing or estimation.

AMERICAN URBAN DIMENSIONS, 1960

To provide factorial output of the type described above principal-axis factor analysis was applied to the 1762×97 data matrix after the 97 variables had been normalized by using the transformations outlined in the Appendix. Only factors whose eigenvalues were greater than unity were extracted. Factor scores were produced after rotating the principal axes to orthogonal simple structure by using the normal varimax criterion.

The complete output of a factor analysis usually includes a correlation matrix for all variables, unrotated and varimax-rotated factor loadings indicating correlations of the primary variables with the latent dimensions, eigenvalues telling the amount of original variance accounted for by the underlying dimensions, and factor scores for each city on each dimension. Obviously not all of these can be presented here. Nor is it appropriate to

[3] See Terry N. Clark, "Community Structure, Decision-Making, Budget Expenditures, and Urban Renewal in 51 American Communities," *American Sociological Review,* Vol. 33, No. 4 (August 1968), pp. 576–593. Robert C. Wood, *1400 Governments* (New York: Doubleday–Anchor, 1964).
[4] Brian J. L. Berry, "A Method for Deriving Multi-Factor Uniform Regions," *Przeglad Geograficzny,* Vol. 33 (1961), pp. 263–279.

divert attention from the substantive features of the urban dimensions by reviewing the method, which has been effectively described elsewhere.[5] Instead we focus on the 14 latent dimensions of variation of American cities in 1960 that resulted from the analysis, presenting only those elements of the output that are necessary for purposes of illustration and identification. Together the dimensions account for 77% of the original variance of the 97 primary variables. Table 1 summarizes the dimensions that were identified.

Table 1. Latent dimensions of the American urban system in 1960

Factor No.	Factor Description
1	Functional size of cities in an urban hierarchy
2	Socioeconomic status of the city residents
3	Stage in family cycle of the city residents
4	Nonwhite population and home ownership
5	Recent population growth experience
6	Economic base: college towns
7	Population proportion that is foreign-born or of foreign stock
8	Recent employment expansion
9	Economic base: manufacturing
10	Extent of female participation in the labor force
11	Economic base: specialized service centers
12	Economic base: military
13	Economic base: mining
14	Extent to which elderly males participate in labor force

An important feature of factor analysis is that the latent dimensions are uncorrelated. They thus contribute additively to the character of each urban place. A first finding is therefore very significant. The elements of the urban economic base traditionally built into functional classifications are largely *independent* of the position of centers in the urban hierarchy, socioeconomic dimensions, and growth behavior. There is much more to urban character than can be explained on the basis of simple economic differences. This being so, we divide what follows into two parts, the first dealing with the system-wide sociocultural factors and the second more briefly with the better known differences in economic base. Some recent evidence on the declining significance of the traditional categories of economic functions is then introduced, examples of composite community profiles and the multi-

[5] See, for example, D. Michael Ray and Brian J. L. Berry, "Multivariate Socioeconomic Regionalization: A Pilot Study in Central Canada," in S. Ostry and T. Rymes, Eds., *Regional Statistical Studies* (Toronto: University of Toronto Press, 1965).

variate classification problem are discussed, and the question of the universality of the latent structure of urban systems is addressed by comparing our results with those of other studies.

SYSTEM-WIDE FACTORS

Functional Size of Centers in the Urban Hierarchy

A substantial number of variables—such as the number of inhabitants, size of the urban labor force, and employment levels—are highly correlated reflections of the total "functional size" or aggregate economic power of cities, or more generally of the status of towns within the nation's urban hierarchy. It was this dimension that was identified first by the factor analysis (see Table 2). That increasing numbers and types of economic functions are now distributed according to size of center has been observed by other research workers.[6] For retail and service activities this is of course perfectly consistent with central-place theory.[7]

Not unexpectedly therefore the highest scoring cities on the dimension are almost all "national business centers" according to Rand McNally's hierarchical ratings.[8] There is, however, also a close relationship of total manufacturing employment to size of city, consistent with the increasing significance of market orientation for industry and location of various types of manufacturing according to the relative scale economies and externalities afforded by different-sized cities.[9] Not surprisingly, then, the International City Managers' Association's (ICMA)[10] 1960–1963 economic classification of cities with the highest scores on this factor was either diversified manufacturing (MR) or diversified retailing (RM).[11]

The only other variable to correlate with this hierarchical pattern was

[6] Colin Clark, "The Economic Functions of a City in Relation to Its Size," *Econometrica,* Vol. 13, No. 2 (April 1945), pp. 97–113. Stanford Research Institute, *Costs of Urban Infrastructure for Industry as Related to City Size in Developing Countries* (Menlo Park, Calif.: Stanford Research Institute, 1968). Thomas M. Stanback, Jr., and Richard V. Knight, *The Metropolitan Economy* (New York: Columbia University Press, 1970).

[7] Brian J. L. Berry, *Geography of Market Centers and Retail Distribution* (Englewood Cliffs, N.J.: Prentice-Hall, Inc., 1967).

[8] *City Rating Guide* (Chicago: Rand McNally and Co., 1964).

[9] Brian J. L. Berry and Frank Horton, *Geographic Perspectives on Urban Systems* (Englewood Cliffs, N.J.: Prentice-Hall, Inc., 1970).

[10] Now the International City Management Association.

[11] Forstall, "Economic Classification of Places Over 10,000."

Table 2. Functional size of centers in the urban hierarchy

Loadings on Constituent Variables: Factor One

No.	Name	Loadings
79	Population 1960	0.968
78	Population 1965	0.958
74	Total labor force 1960	0.963
65	Retail labor force 1960	0.974
66	Service labor force 1960	0.943
64	Wholesale labor force 1960	0.909
68	Transportation labor force 1960	0.911
69	FIRE labor force 1960	0.912
70	Public Administration labor force 1960	0.888
71	HEWO labor force 1960	0.889
73	Miscellaneous labor force 1960	0.930
63	Manufacturing labor force 1960	0.777
44	Service employment 1963	0.853
43	Retail employment 1963	0.826
42	Wholesale employment 1963	0.817
41	Manufacturing employment 1963	0.616
48	Service employment 1958	0.704
47	Retail employment 1958	0.643
46	Wholesale employment 1958	0.730
45	Manufacturing employment 1958	0.571
21	Area of city	0.493
16	Date city passed 100,000 population	-0.433

Hierarchy Rating of Largest Centers

Rank	Code	City	Scores	RANALLY City Rating	ICMA Economic Class
1	189	New York, N.Y.	6.24	1AAAA	MR
2	659	Chicago, Ill.	5.40	1AAA	MR
3	1663	Los Angeles, Calif.	5.21	1AA	MR
4	437	Philadelphia, Pa.	4.69	1AA	MM
5	769	Detroit, Mich.	4.45	1AA	MR
6	1416	Houston, Tex.	4.32	1A	MR
7	504	Cleveland, Ohio	4.17	1AA	MM
8	1396	Dallas, Tex.	3.92	1A	MR
9	1028	Baltimore, Md.	3.86	1A	MR
10	1719	San Francisco, Calif.	3.76	1AA	RM
11	851	Milwaukee, Wis.	3.65	1A	MM
12	1455	San Antonio, Tex.	3.65	2AAA	RM
13	1342	New Orleans, La.	3.64	1A	RM
14	965	St. Louis, Mo.	3.62	1AA	MR
15	1570	Seattle, Wash.	3.61	1A	MR
16	1038	Washington, D.C.	3.58	1AA	G
17	30	Boston, Mass.	3.57	1AA	MR
18	951	Kansas City, Mo.	3.50	1A	MR
19	1504	Denver, Colo.	3.48	1A	RM
20	1249	Memphis, Tenn.	3.40	2AAA	MR
21	439	Pittsburgh, Pa.	3.39	1AA	MR
22	1135	Atlanta, Ga.	3.39	1A	MR
23	890	Minneapolis, Minn.	3.35	1AA	MR
24	1533	Phoenix, Ariz.	3.31	2AAA	RM
25	1717	San Diego, Calif.	3.31	2AA	MM
26	613	Indianapolis, Ind.	3.29	1A	MR
27	1366	Oklahoma City, Okla.	3.29	2AAA	RR
28	506	Columbus, Ohio	3.20	2AAA	MR
29	1586	Portland, Ore.	3.18	1A	RM
30	502	Cincinnati, Ohio	3.17	1A	MR
31	1404	Fort Worth, Tex.	3.17	2AA	MR
32	145	Buffalo, N.Y.	3.11	1A	MR

NOTES: The names of variables contain the following abbreviations: FIRE—finance, insurance, and real estate; HEWO—health, education and welfare.

The list of cities contains all Rand McNally (RANALLY) class 1 "national business centers" except Miami, Fla. (1A) and Newark, N.J. (1B). Their factor scores are 2.78 and 2.84, respectively.

the date that a city passed 100,000 population, indicating that the largest cities were those places that were fortunate enough to achieve earliest eminence, a position maintained by self-sustaining growth as they progressed to higher levels of the urban size ratchet.[12]

Figure 2a shows the spatial distribution of the nation's metropolitan centers as indicated by our factorial results, and Figure 2b shows their commuting areas, or zones of daily contact.[13] Such daily urban systems are the real metropolitan areas of the country.

Socioeconomic Status

Communities also vary in socioeconomic status (see Table 3). The notion that a social mobility process affects individuals during their lifetime is well known. People are born into particular families from which they achieve initial status, and they are first socialized in the physical and social environment provided by the neighborhood within which the family's residence is located. Education affords the opportunity for upward (or lack of it the reason for downward) mobility from that initial status through access to different occupations and therefore incomes. In turn financial resources provide access to residential environments of varying quality and to different levels and standards of consumption. These levels and standards represent the base any individual provides for the next generation.

Because developers prefer to build homes in particular price ranges for a market made up of families of similar resources and because individual purchasers prefer to buy homes in areas that will be occupied by others of similar social status and life style, small communities tend to be relatively homogeneous in terms of the type and quality of housing they provide and the families residing in them.[14] Thus size and quality of homes, educational levels, occupations, and incomes are all highly intercorrelated, each indexing one facet of the differentiation of communities according to socioeconomic status.

The complete range of community types according to social status is clouded by the use of city data, however, for such statistics are affected by the fragmented overlay of political units on urban systems. The nation's highest status, politically independent communities are therefore suburbs of the largest and richest metropolitan areas (Figure 3). On the other

[12] Wilbur Thompson, *A Preface to Urban Economics* (New York: John Wiley & Sons, Inc., 1965).
[13] Brian J. L. Berry, *Metropolitan Area Definition: A Re-evaluation of Concept and Statistical Practice* (U.S. Department of Commerce, Bureau of the Census, 1968).
[14] Berry and Horton, *Geographic Perspectives.*

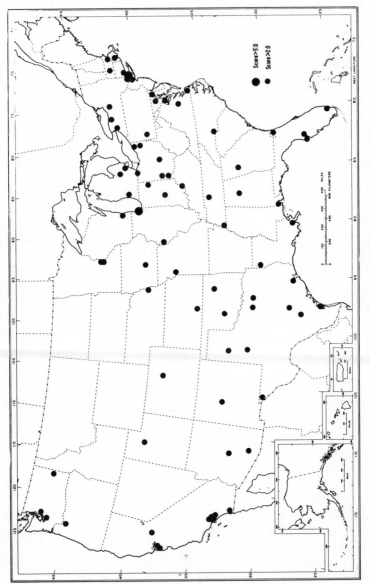

Figure 2a The metropolitan network in 1960.

20

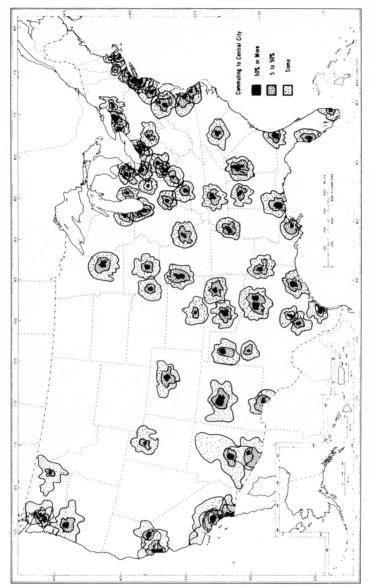

Figure 2b Commuting areas of the nation's metropolitan-level centers in 1960.

21

Table 3. Socioeconomic status of community residents

Loadings on Constituent Variables: Factor Two

No.	Name	Loadings
59	Median income	0.876
56	Per cent incomes exceeding $10,000	0.897
55	Per cent incomes below $3,000	-0.747
28	Per cent with high-school education	0.834
3	Median school years	0.805
38	Value occupied housing units	0.676
58	Median rent	0.534
11	Per cent housing units sound	0.755
10	Per cent housing units owner-occupied	0.413
35	Median rooms/housing unit	0.557
61	Per cent white collar	0.783
32	Unemployment rate	-0.514

The Highest Status Communities

Rank	Code	City	Scores	Sample Median Incomes
1	208	Scarsdale, N.Y.	4.05	22,177
2	752	Winnetka, Ill.	4.03	20,166
3	683	Glencoe, Ill.	3.60	20,136
4	1415	Highland Park, Tex.	3.53	13,707
5	1276	Mountain Brook, Ala.	3.26	14,689
6	157	Garden City, N.Y.	3.21	13,875
7	282	Millburn, N.J.	3.00	
8	1724	San Marino, Calif.	2.98	
9	1698	Piedmont, Calif.	2.97	
10	734	River Forest, Ill.	2.93	
11	751	Wilmette, Ill.	2.91	
12	1020	Prairie Village, Kan.	2.85	
13	578	Upper Arlington, Ohio	2.81	
14	868	Whitefish Bay, Wis.	2.80	
15	413	Lower Merion Twp., Pa.	2.77	
16	566	Shaker Heights, Ohio	2.73	

The Lowest Status Communities

Rank	Code	City	Scores	Sample Median Incomes
1	1434	Mercedes, Tex.	-4.42	2,395
2	1400	Eagle Pass, Tex.	-4.25	2,436
3	1473	Weslaco, Tex.	-3.98	2,604
4	1426	Laredo, Tex.	-3.50	
5	1456	San Benito, Tex.	-3.45	
6	1401	Edinburg, Tex.	-3.37	
7	1449	Pharr, Tex.	-3.33	
8	1389	Brownsville, Tex.	-3.21	
9	1438	Mission, Tex.	-2.98	
10	1453	Robstown, Tex.	-2.92	
11	1166	Belle Glade, Fla.	-2.82	
12	1397	Del Rio, Tex.	-2.62	
13	1468	Uvalde, Tex.	-2.59	
14	1311	Helena, Ark.	-2.43	
15	1457	San Marcos, Tex.	-2.38	
16	1279	Prichard, Ala.	-2.28	

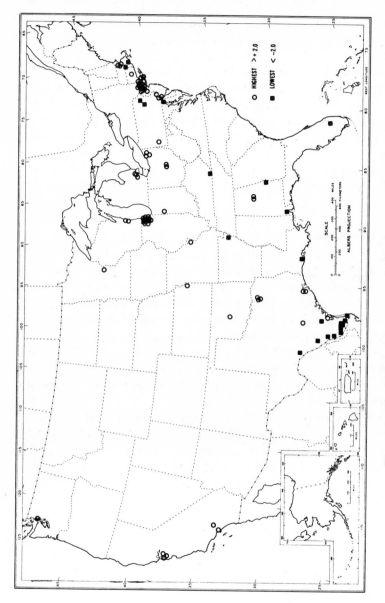

Figure 3 The nation's highest and lowest status communities.

23

hand, the lowest status communities lie in the nation's isolated poverty regions. The greatest cluster occurs in Texas along the Rio Grande border with Mexico.

The lowest status, politically independent communities within the more affluent larger metropolitan areas are somewhat better off than small towns in areas of rural poverty, although they too suffer from the same deficiencies of unsound small housing units, low levels of education, inferior job opportunity, high unemployment, and low incomes. On the other hand, major central cities all have average status scores because they are very large polities spanning a wide range of community areas of all status levels within them, and because they have a diversified economic structure with a broad range of job types.

Stage in Life Cycle

There is variability not simply according to social status but also according to the stage in the life cycle of community residents (Table 4). If there were no geographic mobility, a community would age naturally along with its residents. Initially, perhaps, it would house new, young families actively engaged in child-rearing. Later it would reach a stage in which family sizes were at their maximum. Thereafter it would experience increasing median ages, diminishing family sizes, and a declining population as children leave home. Final dissolution of the original families with death of the partners would lead to regeneration of the community. Another cycle would begin as new families move in.

Another reason for life-cycle differentiation is found, however. If a community specializes in providing the kinds of housing units and residential environments that are appropriate to families at a particular stage of the life cycle, and if there is mobility, with people moving in and out as their housing needs change, the specialized character of the community can be maintained over a long period of time.

In actuality any community experiences a mixture of these two patterns, but communities do differ according to the stage in the life cycle of their residents: by age levels and mixes, fertility rates, family sizes, and population-growth characteristics.

Many of the nation's young-family communities in 1960 were bedroom suburbs within large metropolitan areas (Figure 4). At the other extreme were the retirement communities of Florida and California. The older family communities of the large central cities, being specific apartment neighborhoods (e.g., along Chicago's North Shore) cannot, of course, be identified in a study of legal cities.[15]

[15] Berry and Horton, *Geographic Perspectives.*

Table 4. Stage in the life cycle of community residents

Loadings on Constituent Variables: Factor Three

No.	Name	Loadings
12	Median age	-0.806
13	Per cent population under 18	0.869
62	Per cent population over 65	-0.838
22	Fertility rate	0.775
23	Population per household	0.906
36	Persons per dwelling unit	0.869
54	Per cent homes built 1950-1960	0.627
57	Rate of growth 1950-1960	0.484

Youthful Child-rearing Communities

Rank	Code	City	Scores
1	654	Carpentersville, Ill.	3.59
2	1514	Thornton, Colo.	3.47
3	1656	La Puente, Calif.	3.19
4	738	Rolling Meadows, Ill.	3.12
5	1463	Weslaco, Tex.	3.09
6	875	Brooklyn Center, Minn.	3.02
7	873	Bloomington, Minn.	2.91
8	1401	Edinburg, Tex.	2.91
9	1449	Pharr, Tex.	2.91
10	879	Crystal, Minn.	2.90
11	494	Brook Park, Ohio	2.89
12	777	Garden City, Mich.	2.87
13	876	Brooklyn Park, Minn.	2.81
14	705	Markham, Ill.	2.77
15	714	Mundelein, Ill.	2.76
16	943	Florissant, Mo.	2.74

Communities with Many Elderly Residents

Rank	Code	City	Scores
1	1192	Miami Beach, Fla.	-4.87
2	1606	Beverly Hills, Calif.	-3.55
3	1187	Lake Worth, Fla.	-3.51
4	1692	Palm Springs, Calif.	-3.36
5	1415	Highland Park, Tex.	-3.23
6	1168	Bradenton, Fla.	-3.02
7	1206	St. Petersburg, Fla.	-2.95
8	1649	Huntington Park, Calif.	-2.91
9	1731	Santa Cruz, Calif.	-2.72
10	1183	Hollywood, Fla.	-2.64
11	1734	Santa Monica, Calif.	-2.54
12	1740	South Pasadena, Calif.	-2.54
13	1169	Clearwater, Fla.	-2.46
14	1208	Sarasota, Fla.	-2.40
15	1173	De Land, Fla.	-2.37
16	1467	University Park, Tex.	-2.35

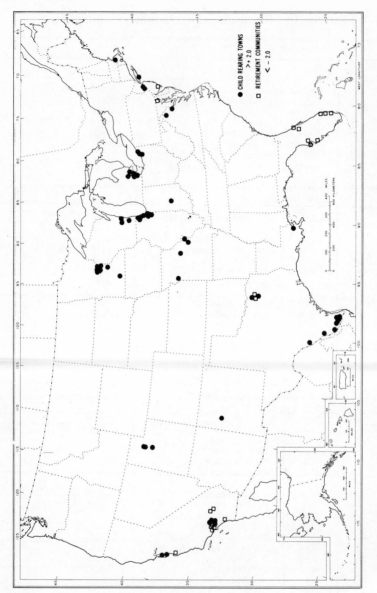

Figure 4 The extremes of stages in the life cycle: child-rearing towns and retirement communities.

Nonwhite and Foreign-Born Populations

Apart from size, social status, and stage in life cycle, two other cultural components important in differentiating American cities were revealed by the analysis: patterns of the nonwhite population and of the population that is foreign-born or of foreign stock (see Tables 5 and 6). The regional variations are quite familiar, the one emphasizing the cities of the South and the Manufacturing Belt, and the other the peripheral points of entry (see Figures 5 and 6).

Recent Population Growth and Recent Increase in Employment

Population growth and employment expansion operate independently of other structural features and of each other (see Tables 7 and 8). This of course reflects the fact that the highest growth rates will represent extension of development into new areas. However, the broad regional differentiation of population growth in the nation's southern and western "rimland" (Figure 7) contrasts with the largely intrametropolitan differ-

Table 5.   Nonwhite population in communities

Loadings on Constituent Variables: Factor Four

No.	Name	Loadings
60	Per cent population nonwhite	0.850
37	Per cent housing units nonwhite	0.848
75	Per cent housing units nonwhite with over 1.01 persons per room	0.831
76	Nonwhite housing units owned	0.826
77	Median income nonwhite	0.798
29	Per cent married couples without own household	0.465

Substantially Nonwhite Communities

Rank	Code	City	Scores	Sample Per cent Nonwhite
1	1268	Fairfield, Ala.	2.80	53
2	248	Englewood, N.J.	2.60	27
3	745	Urbana, Ill.	2.59	6
4	1174	Delray Beach, Fla.	2.59	44
5	1181	Hallandale, Fla.	2.59	42
6	655	Centerville, Ill.	2.51	56
7	773	Ecorse, Mich.	2.43	
8	1213	Winter Park, Fla.	2.34	
9	1761	Hilo, Hawaii	2.34	
10	1303	Yazoo City, Miss.	2.31	
11	1204	Riviera Beach, Fla.	2.30	
12	284	Montclair, N.J.	2.27	
13	393	Farrell, Pa.	2.25	
14	1117	Aiken, S.C.	2.25	
15	788	Inkster, Mich.	2.24	
16	1261	Bessemer, Ala.	2.22	

Table 6.   Foreign-born or foreign-stock population

Loadings on Constituent Variables: Factor Seven

No.	Name	Loadings
25	Per cent population foreign-born	0.822
26	Per cent population foreign stock	0.755
1	Per cent population foreign-born; mother tongue not English	0.567
53	Per cent elementary school children in private school	0.480
9	Per cent housing units 1-unit	-0.463
34	Per cent using public transport	0.390

Communities with Greatest Foreign Component

Rank	Code	City	Scores	Sample Per cent Foreign-born
1	1192	Miami Beach, Fla.	3.74	33
2	1400	Eagle Pass, Tex.	3.50	28
3	1473	Weslaco, Tex.	3.38	17
4	1648	Huntington Beach, Calif.	3.17	8
5	1449	Pharr, Tex.	3.01	15
6	1434	Mercedes, Tex.	2.92	
7	252	Garfield, N.J.	2.83	
8	1401	Edinburg, Tex.	2.69	
9	301	Passaic, N.J.	2.68	
10	783	Hamtramck, Mich.	2.67	
11	1181	Hallandale, Fla.	2.66	
12	1438	Mission, Tex.	2.66	
13	352	Ambridge, Pa.	2.58	
14	95	Central Falls, R.I.	2.57	
15	251	Fort Lee, N.J.	2.55	
16	601	East Chicago, Ind.	2.55	

"Native American" Communities

Rank	Code	City	Scores
1	576	Troy, Ohio	-4.01
2	1444	Palestine, Tex.	-2.88
3	1392	Cleburne, Tex.	-2.80
4	489	Bellefontaine, Ohio	-2.46
5	1418	Hurst, Tex.	-2.46
6	580	Van Wert, Ohio	-2.42
7	1409	Garland, Tex.	-2.42
8	1390	Brownwood, Tex.	-2.35
9	706	Mattoon, Ill.	-2.32
10	1411	Greenville, Tex.	-2.30
11	1398	Denison, Tex.	-2.25
12	461	Sunbury, Pa.	-2.19
13	1413	Haltom City, Tex.	-2.19
14	496	Bucyrus, Ohio	-2.17
15	1433	Marshall, Tex.	-2.17
16	508	Coshocton, Ohio	-2.15

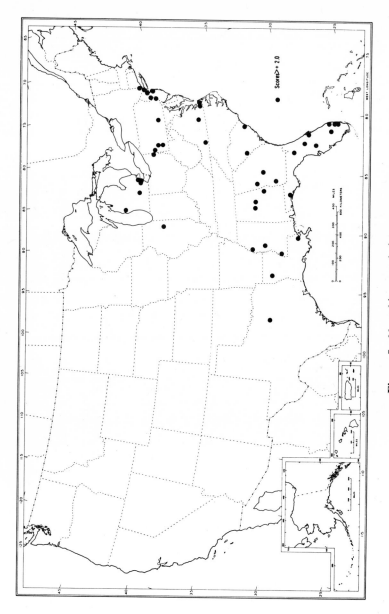

Figure 5 Nonwhite population.

29

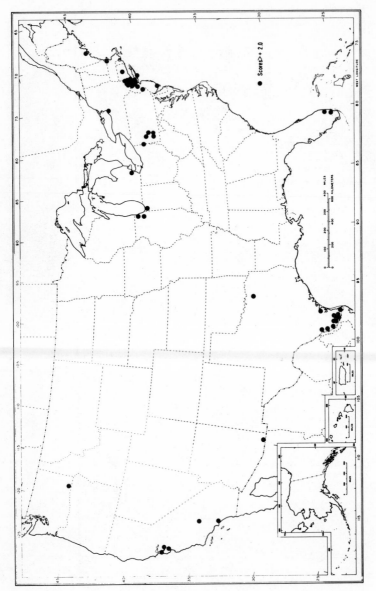

Figure 6 Foreign-born or foreign-stock population.

Table 7.   Recent population growth

Loadings on Constituent Variables: Factor Five		
No.	Name	Loadings
2	Per cent population residing in state of birth	-0.685
39	Vacancy rate, owner-occupied units	0.674
96	Growth rate 1960-1965	0.609
27	Per cent moved after 1958	0.600
52	Per cent population over 5 years old who are migrants	0.574
40	Vacancy rate, rental units	0.551

New Communities: Rapid Post-1960 Growth			
Rank	Code	City	Scores
1	1535	Scottsdale, Ariz.	6.36
2	1648	Huntington Beach, Calif.	5.72
3	1181	Hallandale, Fla.	4.88
4	1201	Pinellas Park, Fla.	4.66
5	1183	Hollywood, Fla.	4.60
6	1192	Miami Beach, Fla.	4.55
7	1175	Eau Gallie, Fla.	4.45
8	1692	Palm Springs, Calif.	4.39
9	1167	Boynton Beach, Fla.	4.30
10	1187	Lake Worth, Fla.	3.95
11	1548	Las Vegas, Nev.	3.80
12	1169	Clearwater, Fla.	3.79
13	1658	Livermore, Calif.	3.57
14	1203	Pompano Beach, Fla.	3.45
15	1208	Sarasota, Fla.	3.45
16	1633	Escondido, Calif.	3.45

Most Stable Communities Since 1960			
Rank	Code	City	Scores
1	290	New Hanover Twp., N.J.	-2.35
2	407	Lansdowne, Pa.	-2.29
3	187	New Hyde Park, N.Y.	-2.21
4	1761	Hilo, Hawaii	-2.21
5	461	Sunbury, Pa.	-2.11
6	277	Maplewood, N.J.	-2.07
7	202	Rensselaer, N.Y.	-2.06
8	56	Medford, Mass.	-1.96
9	40	Fall River, Mass.	-1.91
10	28	Belmont, Mass.	-1.89
11	64	Newton, Mass.	-1.86
12	370	Carnegie, Pa.	-1.86
13	386	Dunmore, Pa.	-1.86
14	217	Watervliet, N.Y.	-1.84
15	433	North Braddock, Pa.	-1.81
16	577	University Heights, Ohio	-1.81

entiation of employment expansion around the peripheries of the largest metropolitan areas (Figure 8).

Female Participation in the Labor Force

Table 9 reveals differences in the percentages of women in the labor force, in labor-force participation rates, and inversely in fertility rates.

Table 8. Recent growth in employment

Loadings on Constituent Variables: Factor Eight

No.	Name	Loadings
82	Growth in manufacturing employment 1958-1963	0.798
83	Growth in wholesale	0.757
81	Growth in retail	0.724
80	Growth in service	0.707

Growth Centers

Rank	Code	City	Scores
1	689	Hinsdale, Ill.	4.72
2	1147	Forest Park, Ga.	3.91
3	859	South Milwaukee, Wis.	3.74
4	935	Berkeley, Mo.	3.71
5	1755	Westminster, Calif.	3.48
6	712	Mount Prospect, Ill.	3.42
7	586	Whitehall, Ohio	3.35
8	875	Brooklyn Center, Minn.	3.18
9	716	Niles, Ill.	3.02
10	589	Willowick, Ohio	2.98
11	494	Brook Park, Ohio	2.90
12	878	Coon Rapids, Minn.	2.87
13	583	Warrensville Heights, Ohio	2.77
14	478	Yeadon, Pa.	2.75
15	392	Falls Twp., Pa.	2.73
16	879	Crystal, Minn.	2.65

Textile towns in the American South have the highest female-employment levels, whereas retirement communities, mining towns, heavy industrial complexes, and young-family suburbs have the lowest (Figure 9).

Elderly Males in the Labor Force

Table 10 separates out a group of communities in which a relatively high number of males remain employed past the normal retirement age of 65. Interestingly, most of these communities are metropolitan suburbs housing high proportions of independent businessmen; a few are isolated towns in peripheral regions from which many individuals in the active younger age groups have emigrated (Figure 10).

FUNCTIONAL TOWN TYPES

American cities are also differentiated according to the nature of their economic bases. Fine distinctions of functional types were not possible in this study because of the somewhat gross input variables used, but five functional types were isolated. In every case the towns displaying high de-

Table 9.   Female participation in the labor force

Loadings on Constituent Variables: Factor Ten			
No.	Name		Loadings
5	Females over 14 in labor force		−0.808
31	Married women in labor force		−0.805
4	Cumulative fertility rate		0.652
30	Nonworker/worker ratio		0.576

Towns with Greatest Participation

Rank	Code	City	Scores
1	1166	Belle Glade, Fla.	−4.97
2	1149	Griffin, Ga.	−3.45
3	1154	Milledgeville, Ga.	−3.32
4	1257	Alexander City, Ala.	−3.17
5	1277	Opelika, Ala.	−2.93
6	1760	Fairbanks, Alaska	−2.88
7	1566	Pullman, Wash.	−2.87
8	137	Willimantic, Conn.	−2.68
9	1292	Greenwood, Miss.	−2.60
10	48	Lawrence, Mass.	−2.59
11	1087	Concord, N.C.	−2.55
12	1151	La Grange, Ga.	−2.52
13	1037	Takoma Park, Md.	−2.44
14	1122	Gaffney, S.C.	−2.39
15	1491	Moscow, Idaho	−2.39
16	1029	Cambridge, Md.	−2.37
17	1125	Greenwood, S.C.	−2.31
18	1084	Burlington, N.C.	−2.30
19	1106	Reidsville, N.C.	−2.30
20	1113	Thomasville, N.C.	−2.30

Towns with Least Participation

Rank	Code	City	Scores
1	422	Monessen, Pa.	3.19
2	1206	St. Petersburg, Fla.	2.99
3	383	Donora, Pa.	2.96
4	1187	Lake Worth, Fla.	2.73
5	387	Duquesne, Pa.	2.58
6	402	Johnstown, Pa.	2.56
7	1724	San Marino, Calif.	2.52
8	780	Grosse Pointe Farms, Mich.	2.52
9	592	Youngstown, Ohio	2.38
10	1183	Hollywood, Fla.	2.38

grees of functional specialization tended to be quite small, as the ensuing tables indicate.

Manufacturing Towns

Table 11 identifies the variables separating towns according to manufacturing specialization and gives examples. The map is a very familiar one of the northeastern Manufacturing belt and a few cities on the southern and western peripheries (Figure 11).

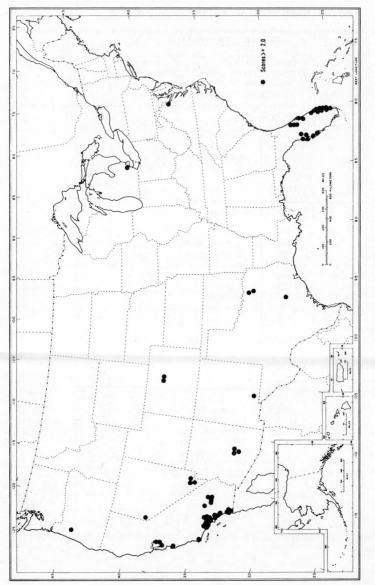

Figure 7 Recent population growth.

34

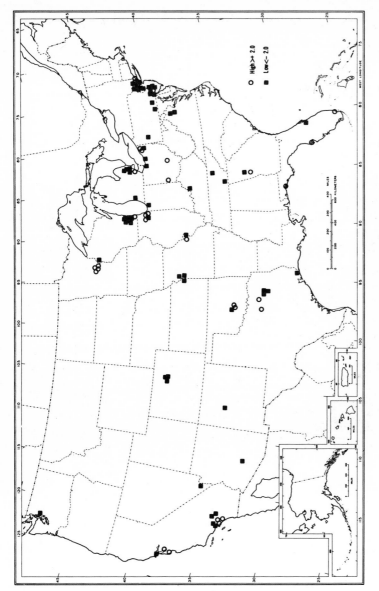

Figure 8 Recent growth in employment.

35

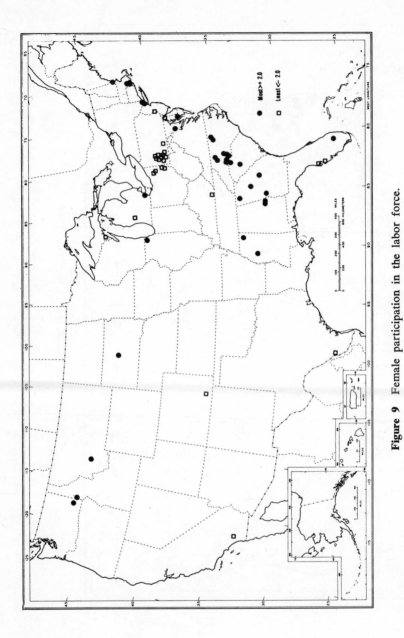

Figure 9 Female participation in the labor force.

36

Table 10. Elderly working males (+) and interstate commuting (—)

Loadings:	Factor Fifteen	
No.	Name	Loadings
33	Per cent working outside county of residence	-0.628
6	Males over 65 in labor force	0.406

Positive-scoring Communities

Rank	Code	City	Scores
1	701	Lincolnwood, Ill.	3.90
2	1606	Beverly Hills, Calif.	3.32
3	1449	Pharr, Tex.	2.88
4	115	Groton, Conn.	2.86
5	1623	Culver City, Calif.	2.75
6	1568	Renton, Wash.	2.71
7	758	Alpena, Mich.	2.51
8	577	University Heights, Ohio	2.46
9	788	Inkster, Mich.	2.38
10	1554	Bellevue, Wash.	2.38
11	1607	Brawley, Calif.	2.36
12	683	Glencoe, Ill.	2.35

Negative-scoring Communities

Rank	Code	City	Scores
1	1147	Forest Park, Ga.	-4.79
2	1064	Vienna, Va.	-3.86
3	1039	Alexandria, Va.	-3.82
4	1163	Warner Robins, Ga.	-3.59
5	276	Maple Shade, N.J.	-3.40
6	478	Yeadon, Pa.	-3.37
7	1046	Fairfax, Va.	-3.30
8	1648	Huntington Beach, Calif.	-3.14
9	1043	Chesapeake, Va.	-3.13
10	1047	Falls Church, Va.	-3.12
11	1355	Del City, Okla.	-3.04
12	1037	Takoma Park, Md.	-3.00

Mining Towns

Small mining towns also separate clearly, as in previous classifications (Table 12). In studying Figure 12 one should note that the inclusion of extraction of petroleum and natural gas in the mining category leads to the particular spatial pattern.

College Towns

A well-dispersed set of relatively small towns is supported by colleges and universities (see Table 13 and Figure 13).

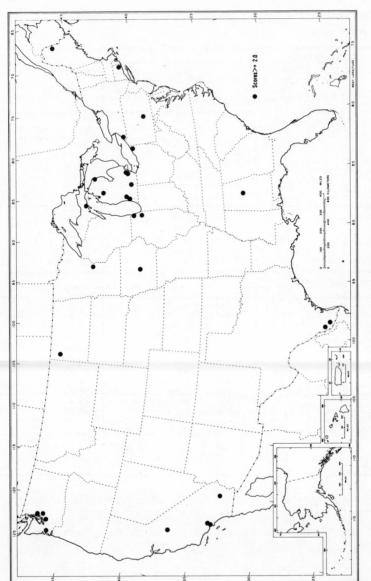

Figure 10 Elderly males in the labor force.

38

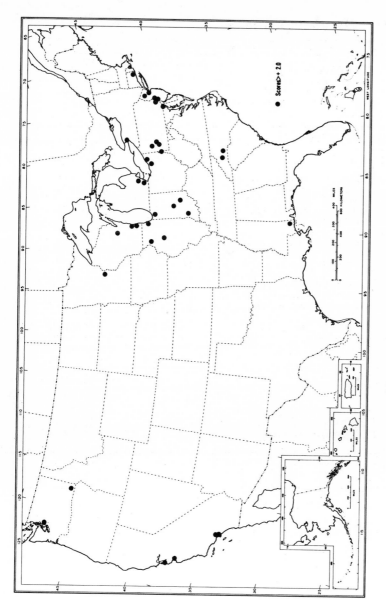

Figure 11 Manufacturing towns.

Scores > + 2.0

Table 11. Manufacturing towns

Loadings on Constituent Variables: Factor Nine

No.	Name	Loadings
8	Manufacturing ratio	0.812
85	Per cent labor force engaged in manufacturing	0.671
51	Employment/residence ratio	0.388

The Manufacturing Towns

Rank	Code	City	Scores	Sample ICMA Economic Classes
1	1721	San Jose, Calif.	6.44	MR
2	1632	El Segundo, Calif.	3.83	MM
3	115	Groton, Conn.	3.13	MM
4	494	Brook Park, Ohio	2.98	MM
5	672	East Peoria, Ill.	2.91	MM
6	1080	Weirton, W. Va.	2.65	
7	587	Wickliffe, Ohio	2.64	
8	1096	Hickory, N.C.	2.59	
9	773	Ecorse, Mich.	2.58	
10	820	Trenton, Mich.	2.54	
11	601	East Chicago, Ind.	2.52	
12	349	Aliquippa, Pa.	2.37	
13	212	Tonawanda, N.Y.	2.35	
14	1568	Renton, Wash.	2.33	
15	473	West Mifflin, Pa.	2.28	
16	275	Manville, N.J.	2.27	

Table 12. Mining towns

Loadings on Constituent Variables: Factor Fourteen

No.	Name	Loadings
89	Per cent labor force engaged in mining	-0.835
67	Total mining employment	-0.741

The Mining Towns

Rank	Code	City	Scores	ICMA Economic Class
1	1524	Grants, N. Mex.	-9.78	MG
2	1378	Andrews, Tex.	-7.38	MG
3	1420	Kermit, Tex.	-7.34	MG
4	1520	Carlsbad, N. Mex.	-7.14	MG
5	1436	Midland, Tex.	-6.24	MG
6	1525	Hobbs, N. Mex.	-6.12	MG
7	886	Hibbing, Minn.	-5.79	MG
8	904	Virginia, Minn.	-5.57	MG
9	1352	Bartlesville, Okla.	-5.41	MG
10	1442	Odessa, Tex.	-5.18	RR/MG
11	1522	Farmington, N. Mex.	-5.13	RR/MG
12	1013	Liberal, Kans.	-4.77	RR/MG

40

Table 13. College towns

Loadings on Constituent Variables: Factor Six		
No.	Name	Loadings
50	College population 1963	0.821
49	College population 1960	0.809
84	Change in college population 1960-1963	0.783
24	Population living in group quarters	0.734
93	Per cent population employed in HEWO	0.652

The College Towns			
Rank	Code	City	Scores
1	458	State College, Pa.	5.09
2	1085	Chapel Hill, N.C.	4.84
3	484	Athens, Ohio	4.71
4	772	East Lansing, Mich.	4.60
5	639	West Lafayette, Ind.	4.20
6	1393	College Station, Tex.	4.11
7	1566	Pullman, Wash.	4.05
8	1260	Auburn, Ala.	3.92
9	597	Bloomington, Ind.	3.84
10	1372	Stillwater, Okla.	3.77
11	530	Kent, Ohio	3.73
12	802	Mount Pleasant, Mich.	3.70
13	309	Princeton, N.J.	3.64
14	492	Bowling Green, Ohio	3.60
15	922	Iowa City, Iowa	3.59

Table 14. Military installations

Loadings on Constituent Variables: Factor Twelve		
No.	Name	Loadings
94	Per cent labor force in armed forces	0.845
72	Total armed forces employment	0.648

The Bases				Sample ICMA
Rank	Code	City	Scores	Economic Class
1	290	New Hanover Twp., N.J.	13.58	AF
2	732	Rantoul, Ill.	7.63	AF
3	245	Eatontown, N.J.	6.60	AF
4	1313	Jacksonville, Ark.	6.60	AF
5	98	Newport, R.I.	6.44	AF
6	1286	Biloxi, Miss.	6.22	AF
7	1620	Coronado, Calif.	6.14	AF
8	1086	Charlotte, N.C.	5.58	MR
9	1701	Port Hueneme, Calif.	5.21	AF
10	115	Groton, Conn.	5.10	MM
11	1591	Alameda, Calif.	5.06	AF
12	1422	Killeen, Tex.	4.68	AF
13	1098	Jacksonville, N.C.	4.53	AF
14	1350	Altus, Okla.	4.48	AF
15	1650	Imperial Beach, Calif.	4.24	
16	1684	Novato, Calif.	4.02	
17	1759	Anchorage, Alaska	3.96	
18	1055	Norfolk, Va.	3.94	
19	1676	Monterey, Calif.	3.91	
20	1760	Fairbanks, Alaska	3.78	

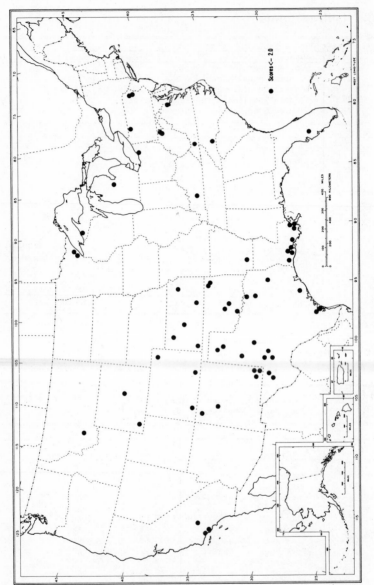

Figure 12 Mining towns.

42

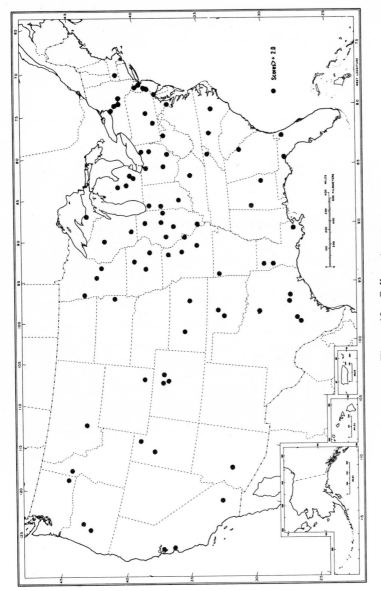

Figure 13 College towns.

43

Military Installations

Military installations also provide a source of support for many small towns, as shown in Table 14 and Figure 14.

Service Centers

Finally, relatively uniformly distributed throughout the West and South are towns functioning primarily as local service centers. Conversely, the midwestern and northeastern sections of the country, along with the Piedmont area, are characterized by towns of specialized function (see Table 15 and Figure 15).

GENERAL DIMENSIONS VERSUS ECONOMIC TYPES

An increasing number of economic activities are now market-oriented. Locationally these activities tend to be differentiated according to access to national markets and position in the urban hierarchy rather than by class-

Table 15. Service centers

Loadings on Constituent Variables: Factor Eleven

No.	Name	Loadings
87	Per cent labor force in retail occupations	0.746
88	Per cent labor force in service	0.691
90	Per cent labor force in transport	0.620
95	Per cent labor force in miscellaneous	0.610
86	Per cent labor force in wholesale	0.505
91	Per cent labor force in FIRE	0.505
92	Per cent labor force in public administration	0.432

The Centers

Rank	Code	City	Scores	Sample ICMA Economic Class
1	1548	Las Vegas, Nev.	2.33	X
2	1240	East Ridge, Tenn.	2.19	S
3	222	Atlantic City, N.J.	1.90	RR/X
4	994	North Platte, Neb.	1.89	RR/T
5	1523	Gallup, N. Mex.	1.79	RR
6	1482	Havre, Mont.	1.70	RR/T
7	1538	Yuma, Ariz.	1.70	
8	1392	Cleburne, Tex.	1.67	
9	1551	Sparks, Nev.	1.66	
10	1312	Hot Springs, Ark.	1.61	
11	1549	North Las Vegas, Nev.	1.61	
12	1710	Roseville, Calif.	1.60	
13	861	Superior, Wis.	1.59	
14	956	Moberly, Mo.	1.58	
15	1194	North Miami, Fla.	1.55	

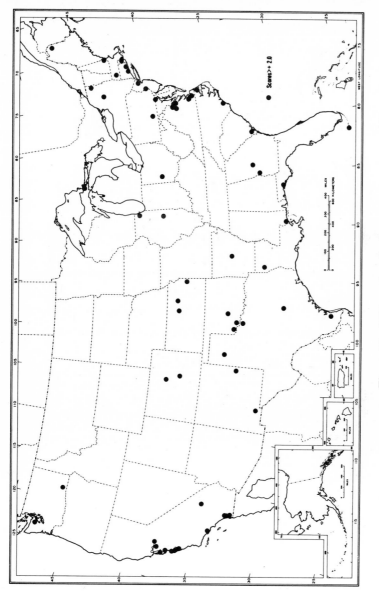

Figure 14 Military installations.

45

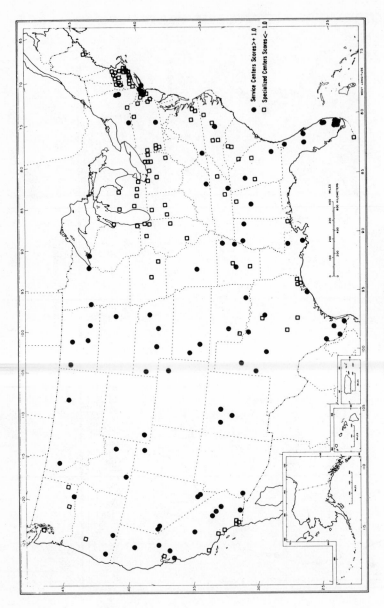

Figure 15 Service centers.

46

ical location factors. Moreover, although there are broad regional patterns according to which the lowest status communities are found in regions of rural poverty and retirement communities are located in the West and South, and more important elements of socioeconomic differentiation are increasingly *intra*metropolitan in a nation that is fully metropolitanized.

The metropolitan centers are multifunctional, and much of their growth is self-generative. Hence the traditional approach to classification based on economic functions today tends to separate only relatively small communities in terms of the following:

1. The few remaining economic activities for which traditional non-metropolitan location factors still prevail; among these are cases of raw-materials orientation (generally mining and agricultural processing) and labor orientation (textiles in poverty regions).

2. Activities located by noneconomic determinants (colleges, military bases).

It follows that the traditional economic approach to city classification is of minimal and declining relevance.

Another question follows: Why mix intermetropolitan and intrametropolitan differences by using legal cities as units of observation, rather than the "real" urban systems revealed in Figure 2*b*? Might not the structural dimensions be confounded by this mixture? Parallel analyses at the intermetropolitan and intrametropolitan levels do not suggest this.[16] The principal dimensions of intermetropolitan and intrametropolitan differentiation appear to be the same: size,[17] socioeconomic status, stage in life cycle, recent growth behavior, and the like, as Philip H. Rees shows in Chapter 10. These dimensions also spill over to the differentiation of nonwhite populations, as David R. Meyer shows in Chapter 2.

COMMUNITY PROFILES

One outcome of the analysis is a set of scores for each town. Together these scores enable "community profiles" to be developed.

For example, if one looks at the sample output in Table 16, New York

[16] Brian J. L. Berry and Elaine Neils, "Location, Size, and Shape of Cities as Influenced by Environmental Factors," in Harvey S. Perloff, Ed., *The Quality of the Urban Environment* (Baltimore: Johns Hopkins Press, in press).

[17] In intrametropolitan studies it is useful to suppress size as a variable, since it is usually measured for fragmented political units that bear a discordant relationship to community areas and neighborhood units within the metropolis.

Table 16. Sample community profiles

	1 Size	2 Status	3 Family Cycle	4 Nonwhite Population	7 Foreign-born	5 Population Growth	9 Mfg.	14 Mining	6 College	12 Military
189 New York City	6.24	-0.30	-0.24	-0.61	1.63	-0.03	-0.32	-0.12	-0.73	0.32
208 Scarsdale, N.Y.	-0.65	4.05	-0.35	1.71	0.70	-0.01	1.01	0.28	0.45	0.34
1473 Weslaco, Tex.	-0.34	-3.98	3.09	-0.83	3.38	-1.17	-3.27	0.59	0.05	-0.59
1692 Palm Springs, Cal.	-0.81	1.16	-3.36	0.33	1.22	4.39	-0.46	0.44	-1.03	-0.42
1268 Fairfield, Ala.	-0.94	-0.47	0.48	2.80	-0.48	-0.91	0.34	0.15	-0.43	-0.82
1535 Scottsdale, Ariz.	-0.56	1.17	0.18	-0.48	0.68	6.36	-0.19	1.82	-0.50	-2.10
1761 Hilo, Hawaii	0.25	-0.34	1.45	2.34	1.39	-2.21	-1.06	-1.07	-0.42	0.21
1122 Gaffney, S.C.	-1.00	-0.70	0.39	1.59	-0.09	-0.40	0.15	0.05	0.81	-0.55*
701 Lincolnwood, Ill.	-0.61	2.25	0.77	0.30	0.93	-1.49	0.41	0.75	-0.44	-0.90**
672 East Peoria, Ill.	-0.97	-0.80	0.00	-0.62	-0.41	0.13	2.91	-0.26	-0.19	0.29
1520 Carlsbad, N. Mex.	-0.19	-0.09	0.68	-0.48	0.31	0.94	-0.72	-7.14	-0.64	-0.56
458 State College, Pa.	-1.17	1.34	-0.72	-0.11	0.36	1.17	-1.27	0.16	5.09	0.30
98 Newport, R.I.	-0.13	-0.20	-0.55	0.74	0.46	-0.22	-0.93	0.97	0.91	6.44

Note: The scores have been standardized for each factor to zero arithmetic average and unit standard deviation.

*Female labor force score of -2.39
**Elderly male labor force score of 3.90

City scores high on size, slightly below average on status and family structure, and has a high concentration of foreign-born residents. Weslaco, Texas, is a very-low-status community with large families, many foreign-born residents, and a low growth rate. Palm Springs, California, which is above average in status, has small families, a substantial foreign-born element, and a high growth rate. East Peoria, Illinois, is a small, low-status, manufacturing town. State College, Pennsylvania, is a small college town with above average growth.

Classification of the Cities

Any research worker has in such community profiles the basic data needed for analytically meaningful city classification, because the redundancies of overlapping variables have been eliminated by factor analysis. With such materials in hand, the questions to be answered by the user remain, to reiterate:

1. Which of the structural dimensions are relevant to this study? Which afford explanation?
2. Are they of equal relevance, or should they be weighted differentially, according to external criteria?
3. How many classes of cities are needed?

Several classifications based on the factor scores and community profiles discussed above for each of the 1762 urban places have been published in *The Municipal Year Book* and in *Urban Data Service* by Forstall.[18] Other classifications appear in other chapters of this volume, as do extended presentations of the classificatory process.

GENERALITY OF THE LATENT STRUCTURE

How general are the dimensions described above? Are they latent in systems of cities elsewhere? Have they been consistent through time? One author (Gerald Hodge) argues for complete universality:

1. Common structural features underlie the development of all centers within a region.

---

[18] Richard L. Forstall, "A New Social and Economic Grouping of Cities," *The Municipal Year Book 1970* (Washington, D.C.: International City Managers Association, 1970), pp. 102–159, and "Applications of the New Social and Economic Grouping of Cities," *Urban Data Service*, June 1971.

2. Structural features of centers tend to be the same from region to region regardless of the stage or character of regional development.

3. Urban structure may be defined in terms of a set of "independent" dimensions covering at least (a) size of population, (b) quality of physical development, (c) age structure of population, (d) education level of population, (e) economic base, (f) ethnic and/or religious orientation, (g) welfare, and (h) geographical situation.

4. Economic base of urban centers tends to act independently of other urban structural features.[19]

Clearly we need to review other studies that have been completed to see if Hodge's assertions are valid. If they are, considerable economy in urban studies is suggested, enabling the developing science to pass beyond the easily perceived structural entities of city classifications by supplementing and ultimately superseding them in attention by organizational and developmental ideas.

To move beyond morphology, however, one needs to be sure that there are certain time-constant aspects of the system, an enduring architecture whose physiology and organization, reversible changes in time, and adaptive or homeostatic adjustments to environmental pressure can be described and then explained by the development or evolution of the system—the irreversible secular changes that accumulate in time.[20]

In effect we are only at the beginning of what must be a long-term effort to describe the processes giving rise to the structural organization and orderly functioning of urban activities and the innovations giving rise to periodic transformations in the structural arrangements. A first step is to determine whether urban systems have common latent structures.

Other Studies of the United States

There has been a long history of multivariate studies of American cities, largely overlooked until recently. These include Price's study of American metropolitan centers in 1930,[21] reanalyzed comparatively by Perle in 1960,[22] Hofstaetter's study (based on work by Thorndike) of American

[19] Gerald Hodge, "Urban Structure and Regional Development," paper presented at the 14th Annual Meeting of the Regional Science Association, Harvard University, 1967.

[20] Berry and Neils, "Location, Size, and Shape of Cities."

[21] Daniel O. Price, "Factor Analysis in the Study of Urban Centers," *Social Forces*, Vol. 20 (1941–1942), pp. 449–461.

[22] Sylvia M. Perle, "Factor Analysis of American Cities" (M.A. dissertation, University of Chicago, 1964).

cities of 30,000 to 50,000 inhabitants in 1930,[23] Kaplan's 1950 study of 370 selected cities with populations exceeding 25,000,[24] Hadden and Borgatta's equivalent 1960 investigation,[25] and Mayer's analysis of the 1960 standard metropolitan statistical areas (SMSAs).[26]

Using 15 variables, Price found four dominant dimensions of metropolitan centers: size, nonservice occupational specialization, socioeconomic status, and trade-center orientation. Perle confirmed these factors for 1960, using the same set of input variables. Hofstaetter, using 23 variables that he thought indexed the quality of urban environments, found the principal dimensions to be socioeconomic status, degree of industrialization, and prevalence of slum conditions. Kaplan's factors in a 47-variable study were size, socioeconomic status, population stability and growth, relative ethnic and racial homogeneity, and age–sex structure (life cycle). Hadden and Borgatta, in a study closely corresponding to the one reported in this chapter, produced 16 factors in all from data comprising 65 variables for 644 cities: socioeconomic status, nonwhite population, age composition, educational centers, residential mobility, population density, foreign-born concentration, total population, wholesale concentration, retail concentration, manufacturing concentration, durable manufacturing concentration, communication centers, public administration centers, high-school education, and transportation centers. Mayer's factors (data 212 SMSAs $\times$ 66 variables) were similar: socioeconomic status, age and size of city, family structure, growth 1950–1960, commercial versus manufacturing orientation, foreign population, nonwhite population, unemployment and male labor force (inversely with female employment), institutional or military population, relative isolation, use of public transport, and low-density development.

Clearly Hodge's generalizations hold in the United States for the period 1930–1960. Differences in the output of the various studies simply reflect differences in the subset of variables, and the larger scale Hadden–Borgatta

[23] Peter R. Hofstaetter, "Your City Revisited—A Factorial Ecology of Cultural Patterns," *American Catholic Sociological Review*, Vol. 13 (October 1952), pp. 159–168. Based on E. L. Thorndike, *Your City* (New York: Harcourt, Brace and Co., 1939).

[24] Howard B. Kaplan, "An Empirical Typology for Urban Description" (Ph.D. dissertation, New York University, 1958).

[25] J. K. Hadden and E. F. Borgatta, *American Cities: Their Social Characteristics* (Chicago: Rand McNally and Co., 1965). See also John E. Tropman, "Critical Dimensions of Community Structure. A Reexamination of the Hadden–Borgatta Findings," *Urban Affairs Quarterly*, Vol. 5, No. 2 (December 1969), pp. 215–232.

[26] Harold M. Mayer, study in progress. Results reported in Berry and Neils, "Location, Size, and Shape of Cities."

work and ours embrace the data subsets and variety of results of the other research workers.

Canada

The first multivariate studies of Canada were completed by King for the years 1951 and 1961.[27] Subsequently Ray et al[28] restudied the Canadian urban scene in a broader framework of variables from the 1961 census and a wider interpretive context.

King (106 cities × 52 variables) found dimensions of socioeconomic status (related also to differences between English and French Canada), relative isolation with primary industry orientation, smaller specialized manufacturing towns, etc. Ray and his associates (113 cities × 95 variables) reiterated the basic socioeconomic significance of English–French contrasts in Canada and identified several functional types of city mining, service centers, manufacturing, and metropolitan growth poles.

A separate postwar growth pattern emerged, as did British Columbian and Prairie city types based on distinctive Asiatic and Slavic cultural components. Since a comparison of our United States study and these Canadian materials appears in Chapter 6, all that need be said here is that the similarities in latent structure are substantial.

Britain

One of the best presentations of results of multivariate urban studies is *British Towns* by Moser and Scott.[29] In a path-breaking study the authors examined 157 towns in England and Wales with respect to 60 different variables. The main object of their work was "to classify British towns into a few relatively homogeneous categories, or to see whether such a classification makes sense."[30] They used eight main categories of variable: population size and structure (7 variables), population change (8), households and housing (10), economic functions and employment characteristics (15), social class (4), voting behavior (7), health (7), and education (2).

[27] Leslie J. King, "Cross-Sectional Analysis of Canadian Urban Dimensions, 1951 and 1961," *Canadian Geographer,* Vol. 10 (1966), pp. 205–224.
[28] D. Michael Ray et al. "The Socio-Economic Dimensions and Spatial Structure of Canadian Cities," unpublished paper, University of Waterloo, 1968.
[29] C. A. Moser and Wolf Scott, *British Towns: A Statistical Study of Their Social and Economic Differences* (Edinburgh and London: Oliver and Boyd, 1961).
[30] Moser and Scott, *British Towns.*

Prior to classification the authors found it necessary to isolate the basic patterns according to which the towns varied, ". . . because the many series that describe towns are not independent; they overlap in the story they tell . . . Towns with a high proportion of heavy industry tend, on the whole, to have low 'social class' proportions, a substantial Labor vote, high infant mortality, and so on."[31] Four common factors were found to account for the correlations among the primary variables: social class; age of the area, including growth in 1931–1951, recent (1951–1958) growth, and housing conditions, including overcrowding. "The essence [of the analysis was] to investigate how much of the total variability of towns exhibited in the primary variables [could] be accounted for and expressed in a smaller number of new independent variates, the principal components."[32]

Notable in these results is the correlation in the Moser and Scott "social status" dimension of North American socioeconomic status and age-structure elements. In Britain higher status is accompanied by higher proportions of older, smaller families, lower birth rates, etc. In turn the highest status communities represent a combination of resorts and retirement communities, exclusive residential suburbs, and professional administrative centers. The universal validity of factorial results postulated by Hodge is thus called into question.

Since the common factors summarized the essential differences among towns contained in the entire set of original primary variables, Moser and Scott could simplify the classification problem. Each town was given a score on each common factor, and towns were then allocated to groups on the basis of relative scores on the four factors. The 14 groups of towns that were identified fall into three major categories:

1. Resort, administrative, and commercial centers
   a. Seaside resorts
   b. Spas; professional and administrative centers
   c. Commercial centers

2. Industrial towns
   a. Railway centers
   b. Ports
   c. Textile centers of Yorkshire and Lancashire
   d. Industrial centers of the northwest and Welsh mining towns
   e. Metal-manufacturing centers

---

[31] Moser and Scott, *British Towns.*
[32] Moser and Scott, *British Towns.*

3. Suburbs and suburban-type towns
   a. Exclusive residential suburbs
   b. Older mixed residential suburbs
   c. Newer mixed residential suburbs
   d. Light industrial suburbs, national defense centers, and towns within the influence of large metropolitan conurbations
   e. Older working-class industrial suburbs
   f. Newer industrial suburbs

In the grouping "the general aim [was] to minimize within-group [differences] and to maximize those between groups."[33]

Yugoslavia

Moving beyond the North Atlantic context, Fisher,[34] using 1961 data, analyzed 55 selected urban centers in Yugoslavia with respect to 26 variables. He interpreted the most important latent dimension as comprising an index of relative development in which status and proportion of population in the economically active child-rearing age groups are highly related. This factor indicated a broad difference between the "developed" and the "underdeveloped" regions of Yugoslavia.

Fisher also found several functional types (construction and transportation; traditional cultural, commercial, and administrative centers; industrial towns) and a factor identifying recent growth and change, but these he felt were secondary to the principal dimension.

Chile

Several analyses of Chilean data have been completed:[35] employment structure of 105 communes with populations exceeding 15,000 in both 1952 and 1960; 59 social, economic, political, and demographic variables for 80 urban communes in 1960; and exploration of data on transportation and traffic flows for 94 urban places in 1962–1965.

The principal factors in the first analysis were the functional sizes of centers in the urban hierarchy and a contrast between traditional towns of the agricultural heartland of the country and mining towns on the periph-

[33] Moser and Scott, *British Towns.*
[34] Jack C. Fisher, *Yugoslavia. A Multinational State* (San Francisco: Chandler Publishing Co., 1966).
[35] Brian J. L. Berry, "Relationships between Regional Economic Development and the Urban System: The Case of Chile," *Tijdschrift voor Economische en Sociale Geografie,* Vol. 60 (1969), pp. 283–307.

ery. The larger analysis reiterated the factors of size and traditionalism versus modernism. The latter factor represented, as in Yugoslavia, a combination of socioeconomic status and age structure. In addition, separate factors were identified for recent growth, mineral exploitation, manufacturing, and certain elements of voting behavior.

India

Ahmad's 102-city, 62-variable analysis of the largest Indian cities in 1966[36] identified as factors certain by now already familiar themes: size, recent change, and economic specialization (commercial, industrial). In addition, certain broad regional differences were also noted—between northern and southern India in the sex composition of cities and the position of women in the labor force, between eastern and western India in migration patterns, etc., each reflecting broad regional differences in India's cultures. Types of town were shown to be highly differentiated by region within the country.

Nigeria and Ghana

Studies of the urban systems of Nigeria and Ghana have been completed by Mabogunge[37] and McNulty,[38] respectively.

McNulty found a principal factor differentiating urban populations according to age structures and sex ratios. This factor, he felt, reflected the migration of males in the active age groups to growing commercial and service centers, leaving behind high proportions of poorly educated young, old, and females in areas of primary occupational specialization. A similar dimension was found by Mabogunge in Nigeria. These dimensions are not unlike Fisher's "modernism–traditionalism" scale for Yugoslavia.

A second factor found by McNulty related to functional type: highly specialized mining towns were distinguished from centers offering diversified employment in commerce, services, and manufacturing. Both McNulty and Mabogunge argued that these dimensions are structural correlates of

---

[36] Qazi Ahmad, *Indian Cities: Characteristics and Correlates,* University of Chicago Department of Geography Research Paper No. 102 (1965).

[37] Akin Mabogunge, "Economic Implications of the Pattern of Urbanization in Nigeria," *Nigerian Journal of Economic and Social Studies,* Vol. 7 (1965), pp. 9–30, and "Urbanization in Nigeria—A Constraint on Economic Development," *Economic Development and Cultural Change,* Vol. 13 (1965), pp. 413–438.

[38] Michael L. McNulty, "Urban Structure and Development: The Urban System of Ghana," *Journal of Developing Areas,* in press; "Dimensions of Urban Structural Change in Ghana: 1948–1960," unpublished manuscript, 1969.

the development process, particularly as overlaid on the countries by colonial capital, and that urban structural change, in turn, is attendant on development through the interrelated processes of migration and increasing economic diversification.

CONCLUSIONS

Extending and modifying Hodge's arguments, several conclusions about the latent structure of urban systems follow:

1. The economic base of urban centers tends to act independently of other urban structural features (with the exception of hierarchical organization of market-oriented activities; see item 2 below), and, to the extent that there is geographic specialization based on locational factors other than market orientation, each broad economic function will lead to its own distinctive economic town type. Public activities—military bases, educational centers, public administration—act as any other specialized economic base.

2. Every urban system is organized system-wide into a hierarchy of centers based on aggregate economic power. The functional size of centers in an urban hierarchy is a universal latent dimension.

3. In every society the principal dimensions of socioeconomic differentiation are those of social status and age structure, or stage in life cycle. However, only at the highest levels of development do these factors appear to operate independently. At somewhat lower levels of welfare (Britain) there remains a correlation between income and family structure, and only the rich elderly can segregate themselves in retirement resorts and spas; at lower income levels there is a great mixture of family types in the same residential areas. Further down the scale still (Yugoslavia, Chile, West Africa), status and age-structure differences combine in broad regional patterns of development versus underdevelopment or modernism versus traditionalism, often expressed spatially in the differences between the national core region, or heartland, and the periphery, or hinterlands. In India, lacking a single heartland, the pattern is one of relative accessibility to the national metropolises of Bombay, Calcutta, Delhi, and Madras. In both the United States and Canada the factor of relative accessibility at the national level is independent of status and life-cycle variations but remains correlated with manufacturing as an economic specialization.

4. A culturally heterogeneous society will be characterized by separate ethnic or racial dimensions if the cultural groups are clustered in particu-

lar cities. If the groups occupy different status levels and have different family structures, the cultural differences may override other socioeconomic dimensions, as in the case of English–French contrasts in Canada.

5.   Generally each new stage of growth will act independently of prior structural features if it is based on innovations giving rise to structural transformations. Thus distinct phases or stages of growth should each result in a separate latent dimension indexing a distinct pattern of variation of urban centers.

Such are the latent bases of manifest urban differences—the proximate underlying causes of distinctive town types. Their recognition and use can provide the much needed basis for a systematic comparative classification of cities.

APPENDIX List of Variables

Number	Mnemonic	Name	Transformation
1	P/FOR.B/NENG	Per cent foreign-born with mother tongue not English	None
2	P/POP/SOB	Per cent native population residing in state of birth	None
3	MDSYO.25	Median school years for persons over 25	None
4	CUMFERTRATE	Cumulative fertility rate	None
5	FOVR14LF	Females over 14 in labor force	None
6	MOVR65LF	Males over 65 in labor force	None
7	P/MNF	Per cent in manufacturing	None
8	MNF TOTEMP	Manufacturing ratio, 1958: manufacturing employment as per cent of "aggregate employment"	None
9	P/HV 1-UNT	Per cent of all housing units in one-housing-unit structures, 1960	None
10	P/HVOWN	Per cent of occupied housing units which are owner-occupied, 1960	None
11	P/HV-SOUND	Per cent of all housing units sound and with all plumbing facilities, 1960	None
12	M AGE	Median age, 1960	None
13	P/U. 18	Per cent of population under 18, 1960	None
14	1st CENSUS	Year place first appeared in census	None
15	PASS 2-5TH	Year place passed 2-5,000	None
16	PASS 10TH	Year place passed 10,000	None
17	PASS 25TH	Year place passed 25,000	None
18	PASS 50TH	Year place passed 50,000	None
19	PASS 100TH	Year place passed 100,000	None
20	PASS 10TH R	Year place first over 10,000 and in Rand Metro Area	None
21	AREA	Area, 1960	None
22	FERT. RATE	Fertility Ratio	Sq. root
23	POP/HH	Population per household	Sq. root
24	P/GP Q	Per cent living in group quarters	Sq. root
25	P/FOR. BORN	Per cent foreign-born	Sq. root
26	P/FOR. ST	Per cent foreign stock	Sq. root
27	P/MVED 58+	Per cent moved in after 1958	Log
28	P/HS 4 YRS	Per cent completing over 4 years high school	Sq. root
29	P/MWHH	Per cent married couples without own household	Sq. root
30	NW/W	Nonworker/worker ratio	Sq. root
31	MWINLF	Married women in the labor force	Sq. root
32	P/UNEM	Per cent unemployed	Log
33	P/W. OUT	Per cent working outside county of residence	Sq. root
34	P/PB. TRANS	Per cent using public transport	Sq. root

APPENDIX   List of Variables

Number	Mnemonic	Name	Transformation
35	MD. ROOMS	Median rooms of all housing units	Sq. root
36	PERS/D.U.	Median persons per dwelling unit	Log
37	P/HV NW	Per cent housing units occupied by nonwhites	Sq. root
38	VAL. OCC. UN	Median value owner-occupied units	Log
39	VAC. RAT. OCU	Vacancy rate owner-occupied units	Log
40	VAC. RAT. RNT	Vacancy rate rentals	Sq. root
41	MNF63	Manufacturing employment, 1963	Log
42	WHL 63	Wholesaling employment, 1963	Log
43	RET 63	Retail employment, 1963	Log
44	SERV 63	Services employment, 1963	Log
45	MNF 58	Manufacturing employment, 1958	Log
46	WHL 58	Wholesaling employment, 1958	Log
47	RET 58	Retail employment, 1958	Log
48	SERV 58	Services employment, 1958	Log
49	COLL 60	College enrollment 1960 in 100s	Log
50	COLL 63	College enrollment 1963 in 100s	Log
51	E/R RAT 58	Employment/residence ratio, 1958	Sq. root
52	P/Of MIGR	Per cent of persons 5 and over who are migrants, 1960	Sq. root
53	P/ELMPRIV	Per cent of elementary school children in private school, 1960	Sq. root
54	P/HV 50-60	Per cent of all housing units in structures built 1950-1960, 1960	Sq. root
55	P/V 3,000	Per cent of families with incomes under $3,000, 1959	Sq. root
56	P/O 10,000	Per cent of families with incomes over $10,000, 1959	Log
57	P/50-60	Per cent change in population 1950-1960	Sq. root
58	MDRENT	Median gross rental of renter-occupied housing units, 1960	Sq. root
59	MDINC	Median income of families, 1959	Log
60	P/NW	Per cent of population which is nonwhite, 1960	Sq. root
61	P/WC	Per cent of employed persons in white-collar occupations, 1960	Sq. root
62	P/O.65	Per cent of population 65 and over, 1960	Sq. root
63	MNF.LF	Manufacturing, 1960	Log
64	WHL.LF	Wholesale trade, 1960	Log
65	RET.LF	Retail trade, 1960	Log
66	SERV.LF	Services, 1960	Log
67	MIN.LF	Mining, 1960	Log

59

APPENDIX List of Variables

Number	Mnemonic	Name	Transformation
68	Tran.LF	Transport and communications, 1960	Log
69	FIRE.LF	FIRE, 1960	Log
70	PUBAD.LF	Public administration, 1960	Log
71	HEWO.LF	HEWO, 1960	Log
72	ARMED.LF	Armed Forces, 1960	Log
73	MISCELL.	Miscellaneous, 1960	Log
74	TOT.LF	Total employed labor force, 1960	Log
75	NW HU 1.01+	Per cent of nonwhite housing units with over 1.01 persons per room	Log
76	NW HU OWN	Per cent of nonwhite housing units which are owner-occupied	Log
77	MED. INC. NW	Median income of nonwhite families	Log
78	POP 65	1965 estimated population	Log
79	POP 60	1960 population	Log
80	63/58 MANU	Manufacturing employment growth, 1958-1963	Log
81	63/58 WHL	Wholesaling employment growth, 1958-1963	Log
82	63/58 RET	Retail employment growth, 1958-1963	Log
83	63/58 SERV	Services employment growth, 1958-1963	Log
84	63/58 COLL	College enrollment growth, 1958-1963	Log
85	PR MANU	Per cent employed in manufacturing, 1960	Log/Log
86	PR WHL	Per cent employed in wholesaling, 1960	Log/Log
87	PR RET	Per cent employment in retail trade, 1960	Log/Log
88	PR SERV	Per cent employed in services, 1960	Log/Log
89	PR MINING	Per cent employed in mining, 1960	Log/Log
90	PR TRAN	Per cent employed in transport and communications, 1960	Log/Log
91	PR FIRE	Per cent employed in FIRE, 1960	Log/Log
92	PR PUB AD	Per cent employed in public administration, 1960	Log/Log
93	PR HEWO	Per cent employed in HEWO, 1960	Log/Log
94	PR ARMED SRV	Per cent employed in Armed Forces, 1960	Log/Log
95	PR MISC	Miscellaneous, 1960	Log/Log
96	PR GROWTH	Per cent growth 1960-1965	Log/Log
97	DENSITY	Population density	None

CHAPTER 2

Classification of U.S. Metropolitan Areas by Characteristics of Their Nonwhite Populations

DAVID R. MEYER

University of Massachusetts at Amherst

Nonwhites, though a minority, are significant elements in the social and economic life of American cities. A classification of cities from a nonwhite perspective should therefore impart to the differentiation of American cities an important insight that is not provided in Chapter 1.

This chapter has hence a fourfold purpose:

1. To set forth a multidimensional analysis of standard metropolitan statistical areas (SMSAs) based on the characteristics of their nonwhite inhabitants.

2. To suggest some implications of the dimensions for understanding the intermetropolitan differentiation of nonwhites.

3. To briefly relate these dimensions to the material presented in Chapter 1.

4. To propose a classification of SMSAs based on the characteristics of nonwhites, a step not taken in Chapter 1.

The data consist of 40 variables for each of the 145 SMSAs in 1960 for which the U.S. Bureau of the Census compiled separate data for nonwhites[1] in the census-tract volumes. The statistical technique is factor analysis with orthogonal rotation according to the normal varimax criterion.[2]

---

[1] Since the black population comprises 91.4% of the nonwhites in the 145 SMSAs, the following discussion refers primarily to blacks except where otherwise indicated.

[2] The technique employed in this study is the same as that used in Chapter 1 by Berry. Also see Harry H. Harmon, *Modern Factor Analysis* (Chicago: University of Chicago Press, 1967), pp. 304–313.

Studies of the intermetropolitan differentiation of nonwhites (almost exclusively referring to black Americans) have tended to focus on patterns of segregation[3] or city-to-city variations in measures of socioeconomic status.[4] Generally cities have been classified according to their regional location (e.g., northern, southern, and border). Since only a few characteristics of nonwhites have been employed in any one study, a complete picture of nonwhite intermetropolitan differentiation has not been produced. The present research is an attempt to fill this gap.

The variables employed primarily relate to the nonwhite population's characteristics and housing.[5] Total population size is the only general city characteristic employed other than the characteristics of nonwhites.

SEVEN INDEPENDENT DIMENSIONS OF THE SMSAs

An examination of the factor-analysis output led to a decision to use a seven-factor matrix for the analysis.[6] As Table 1 shows, the two most im-

Table 1.   Variance accounted for by factors

No.	Name	% of Total Variance	% of 7-Factor Variance
1	Socioeconomic status	19.6	23.2
2	Variations among nonwhite groups in socioeconomic status levels	16.5	19.4
3	Stage in life cycle	13.3	15.7
4	Size of housing and unemployment	10.7	12.6
5	Housing type	10.3	12.2
6	Position in urban hierarchy	8.5	10.0
7	Service workers	5.9	6.9
	Totals	84.8	100.0

[3] Charles S. Johnson, *Patterns of Negro Segregation* (New York: Harper and Brothers, 1943), pp. 8–12; Karl E. Taeuber and Alma F. Taeuber, *Negroes in Cities* (Chicago: Aldine Publishing Company, 1965); and T. J. Woofter, Jr., ed., *Negro Problems in Cities* (Garden City, N.Y.: Doubleday, Doran and Company, Inc., 1928), pp. 37–77.
[4] E. Franklin Frazier, "Occupational Classes Among Negroes in Cities," *American Journal of Sociology,* Vol. 35 (1930), pp. 718–738; and Leo F. Schnore, "Social Class Segregation Among Nonwhites in Metropolitan Centers," *Demography,* Vol. 2 (1965), pp. 126–133.
[5] See the appendix to this chapter for a description of each of the 40 variables.
[6] The factor descriptions, along with the percentage for which each factor accounts of the total variance of the 40 variables and of the variance of the seven factors, are shown in Table 1.

portant factors relate to socioeconomic status and together account for 36.1% of the total variance of the variables. They are followed by a stage-in-life-cycle factor, two housing factors, population size, and a service-worker factor. Taken together, the seven factors account for a substantial proportion (84.8%) of the city-to-city variation among nonwhites.

Factor 1: Socioeconomic Status of Black Americans

The most important factor (19.6% of total variance) is a general measure of socioeconomic status. It comprises such traditional indices of status as income, education, occupation, value of home, and rent (see Table 2).

Table 2. Factor 1: socioeconomic status of black Americans

No.	Name	Loadings
1	Median family income	0.811
2	Median rent	0.796
3	Per cent male laborers	−0.773
4	Median value of owner-occupied units	0.749
5	Median school years completed	0.712
6	Per cent sound occupied units	0.648
7	Per cent female private household workers	−0.612
8	Per cent male clerical workers	0.559
9	Per cent female clerical workers	0.555
10	Ratio of nonrelatives of heads of households to heads of households	0.493
33	Per cent single-family dwelling units	−0.492
23	Per cent heads of household with wife present	0.463
30	Per cent total population Black American	−0.447
25	Median number of rooms	0.409

In terms of occupation this factor distinguishes between nonwhites employed in "high-status" occupations (clerical workers) and low-status occupations (male laborers and female private-household workers).

The negative correlation of two variables with factor 1, the percentage of population of black Americans (−.447) and the percentage of single-family dwellings (−.492), provides some clue to the characteristics of the cities whose nonwhite families have higher socioeconomic status. High-socioeconomic-status cities tend to have relatively few single-family dwellings available to nonwhites. Furthermore, the black American population is a very small percentage of the total population.

An examination of the SMSAs with factor scores lower than −1.00 (see Table 3) and a corresponding map of the same SMSAs (Figure 1) reveals that the SMSAs with the lowest socioeconomic status are primarily southern cities. Thus factor 1 has an important regional component.

Table 3.   Low-socioeconomic-status SMSAs

Rank	SMSA	Scores
1	Texarkana, Tex.-Ark.	-2.27
2	Stockton, Calif.	-2.24
3	Bakersfield, Calif.	-2.15
4	Charleston, S.C.	-2.13
5	Monroe, La.	-2.04
6	Phoenix, Ariz.	-1.74
7	Fresno, Calif.	-1.70
8	Augusta, Ga.-S.C.	-1.64
9	Orlando, Fla.	-1.63
10	Gadsden, Ala.	-1.60
11	Shreveport, La.	-1.55
12	Montgomery, Ala.	-1.54
13	Macon, Ga.	-1.45
14	Greenville, S.C.	-1.42
15	Tucson, Ariz.	-1.41
16	Waco, Tex.	-1.37

The southern cities also have a very high percentage of single-family dwellings. Thus this association between low socioeconomic status and a high percentage of single-family dwellings in southern cities probably accounts for the inverse relationship between these variables.

Although the socioeconomic status of blacks is inversely related to their relative proportion in the total population, this does not imply that there necessarily is a causal relationship between the two; that is, we cannot infer that black Americans will have greater opportunities for attaining a higher socioeconomic status if they are a relatively small proportion of the total population.[7] Rather, the factor identifies the southern, low-socioeconomic-status SMSAs, in which, because of various historical circumstances, black Americans comprise a relatively large percentage of the total population. Traditional southern social and economic institutional constraints on black Americans probably have had more to do with the low socioeconomic status of the southern urban black than the mere fact that black Americans are a relatively large percentage of the total population.

Factor 2: Status Differentiation of Nonwhite Groups

Factor 2 reveals a second element of status differentiation, showing that different nonwhite groups have substantially different status levels (see Table 4). The most important variable in factor 2 is the percentage of

---

[7] The writer does not mean to deny the possibility of a causal relationship between black socioeconomic status and their relative proportion of the total population. However, this relationship remains to be demonstrated or disproved through a careful control of many factors.

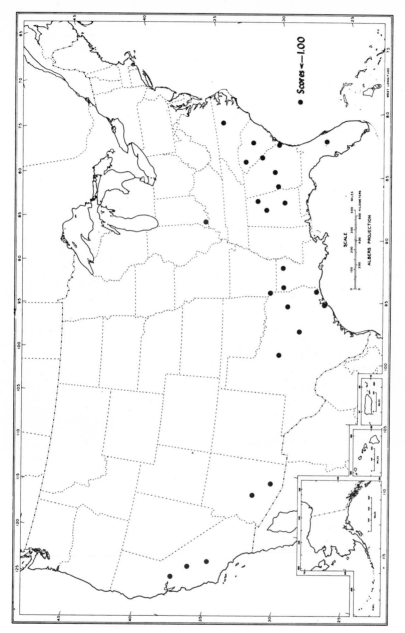

Figure 1 Low-socioeconomic-status SMSAs.

Table 4.   Factor 2: status differentiation of nonwhite groups

No.	Name	Loadings
11	Per cent nonwhite population Black American	-0.919
12	Per cent male managers	0.845
13	Ratio of married women not separated from husband to separated and divorced women	0.703
14	Other races population size	0.628
15	Per cent male operatives	-0.616
16	Per cent male professional workers	0.607
17	Ratio of males to females	0.568
37	Per cent living in different house in SMSA who moved into SMSA since 1955	0.504
9	Per cent female clerical workers	0.495
5	Median school years completed	0.478
40	Ratio of other relatives of heads of households to heads of households	-0.446
18	Taeubers' segregation index for 207 cities	-0.415

blacks among the nonwhite population (loading —.919). The list of SMSAs with high positive factor scores (examples in Table 5) reveals that SMSAs with a relatively high nonwhite socioeconomic status on some measures also have a low percentage of blacks and large proportions of "other races" (loading .628) in their nonwhite populations.[8] Such cities are all in the West, especially along the Pacific Coast (Figure 2), where large numbers of Japanese, Chinese, and Filipinos live.

The presence of large Japanese and Chinese populations is probably the most important factor in explaining the high socioeconomic status of the SMSAs along the Pacific Coast. Both groups tend to have a higher socio-

Table 5.   High-socioeconomic-status SMSAs

Rank	SMSA	Scores
1	San Jose, Calif.	3.92
2	Stockton, Calif.	3.25
3	Honolulu, Hawaii	3.16
4	Fresno, Calif.	2.92
5	Sacramento, Calif.	2.88
6	Salt Lake City, Utah	2.76
7	Tacoma, Wash.	2.54
8	Santa Barbara, Calif.	2.49
9	Spokane, Wash.	2.21
10	Seattle, Wash.	2.18
11	Tucson, Ariz.	2.00
12	Bakersfield, Calif.	1.93
13	San Diego, Calif.	1.86
14	San Bernardino-Riverside-Ontario, Calif.	1.82
15	Phoenix, Ariz.	1.79
16	Albuquerque, N. Mex.	1.66

[8] The term "other races" includes Japanese, Chinese, and Filipinos.

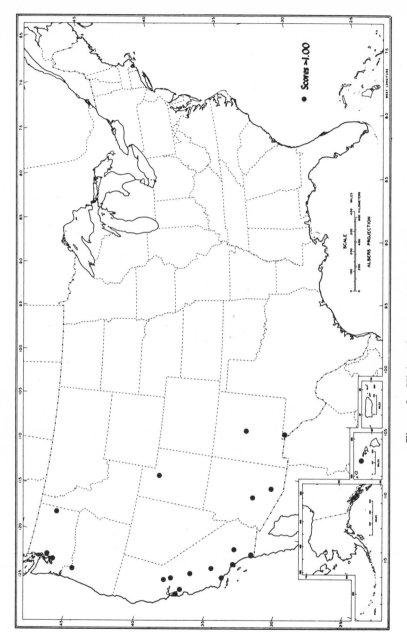

Figure 2 High-socioeconomic-status SMSAs.

67

economic status than black Americans.[9] Furthermore, few Japanese and Chinese live in SMSAs outside the West. Where their numbers are large, in such cities as Chicago and New York, the black American population is much larger. Thus the range of socioeconomic status among nonwhites in SMSAs outside the West covers mainly the black American population.

The same explanation holds for the finding that the percentages of male managers and male professionals (loadings .845 and .607, respectively) are highly correlated with factor 2. The Chinese and Japanese tend to be highly represented in the above occupations compared with black Americans.[10]

Unfortunately the data cannot answer the question whether black Americans in SMSAs whose nonwhite populations have high proportions of other races have a higher socioeconomic status than black Americans in SMSAs outside the West.

The relationship of the Taeubers' segregation index ($-.415$) to factor 2 suggests that the western SMSAs also are relatively less segregated than other cities in the United States. This finding partially agrees with the Taeubers' regional mean segregation indices, which are lower for the Northeast and the West than they are for the North Ceneral States and the South.[11] Of course, as the Taeubers rightly emphasize, the *relatively* lower segregation indices of some cities (e.g., in the Northeast and West) are inconsequential since these same cities still have high segregation indices.[12]

Factor 3: Stage in Life Cycle

Variables measuring family characteristics like age and size of family (variables 19 through 22) have high correlations with factor 3, indicating that this factor is an index of stage in life cycle (see Table 6).

Variables 26 and 29, measures of room-crowding and female participation in the labor force, respectively, add further evidence that factor 3 represents stage in life cycle. The fact that room-crowding tends to occur with young families seems reasonable since these families have extensive demands on their resources while the head of the household is just begin-

---

[9] See, for example, Calvin F. Schmid and Charles E. Nobbe, "Socio-Economic Differentials Among Nonwhite Races in the State of Washington," *Demography,* Vol. 2 (1965), pp. 549–566. Although the conclusions in the Schmid and Nobbe study apply only to the state of Washington, the writer is assuming that they are equally applicable to California and Oregon.

[10] Schmid and Nobbe, "Socio-Economic Differentials."

[11] Taeuber and Taeuber, *Negroes in Cities,* p. 37.

[12] Taeuber and Taeuber, *Negroes in Cities,* pp. 35–37.

Table 6.   Factor 3: stage in life cycle

No.	Name	Loadings
19	Female median age	-0.874
20	Per cent population under age 18	0.866
21	Population per household	0.816
22	Male median age	-0.745
23	Per cent heads of household with wife present	0.581
24	Per cent male craftsmen	0.522
26	Per cent occupied units with 1.01 or more persons per room	0.515
29	Per cent females in the labor force	-0.413
15	Per cent male operatives	0.326

ning to attain seniority and thus is at a relatively low position on the wage scale. In addition, the lower degree of female participation in the labor force in young families is anticipated since the female in American society is generally expected to stay home with the children.

Age and size of family are definitely the most important characteristics of factor 3. However, an additional aspect is revealed by the correlation of the percentages of male craftsmen (.522) and of male operatives (.326) with this factor. These two variables are measures of the relative male participation in manufacturing. Thus we have a pattern of young black families with a relatively large male participation in manufacturing.

The list of SMSAs with factor scores greater than +1.00 in Table 7 and the map of the same SMSAs (Figure 3) add further support for the existence of this pattern. About half the SMSAs in Figure 3 are small industrial cities in the Manufacturing Belt. The lower participation of females

Table 7.   Young-family SMSAs

Rank	SMSA	Scores
1	Muskegon-Muskegon Heights, Mich.	2.41
2	Erie, Pa.	2.39
3	Charleston, S.C.	2.29
4	Saginaw, Mich.	2.27
5	Tacoma, Wash.	1.99
6	Honolulu, Hawaii	1.94
7	Gary-Hammond-East Chicago, Ind.	1.82
8	Rockford, Ill.	1.78
9	Waterloo, Iowa	1.66
10	El Paso, Tex.	1.56
11	Milwaukee, Wis.	1.53
12	Utica-Rome, N.Y.	1.51
13	Lubbock, Tex.	1.48
14	Columbia, S.C.	1.47
15	Lorain-Elyria, Ohio	1.45
16	Mobile, Ala.	1.30

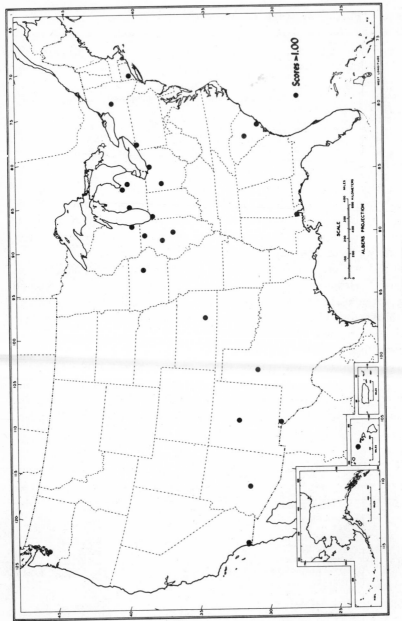

Figure 3 Young-family SMSAs.

in the labor force in these SMSAs,[13] in addition to being related to the high incidence of young large families, may also result from fewer job opportunities for women. The female-employment situation is most acute in the smallest industrial SMSAs. Larger SMSAs have a more diversified employment base even when manufacturing is important.[14]

Factor 4: Old Housing and High Unemployment in Northern Industrial Cities

Housing characteristics, such as the median number of rooms (—.749), units with 1.01 or more persons per room (.664), construction prior to 1939 (—.663), and male unemployment (—.603) are highly associated with factor 4 (see Table 8). The interpretation of this factor is aided by

Table 8. Factor 4: age and size of housing, and unemployment

No.	Name	Loadings
25	Median number of rooms	-0.749
26	Per cent occupied units with 1.01 or more persons per room	0.664
27	Per cent occupied units built 1939 or earlier	-0.663
28	Per cent male unemployment	-0.603
7	Per cent female private household workers	0.526
29	Per cent females in the labor force	0.488
30	Per cent total population Black American	0.455

examining the list of SMSAs whose factor scores are lower than —1.00 (Table 9) and the corresponding map (Figure 4). The SMSAs that have low negative scores are characterized by a high median number of rooms, a low percentage of occupied units with 1.01 or more persons per room, a high percentage of the occupied units built before 1939, and a high percentage of male unemployment.

From Table 9 and Figure 4 we deduce that these SMSAs are northern industrial cities. These are not the same cities as those identified by factor 3, however. Those cities appeared to be important sources of manufacturing employment for black workers. The SMSAs identified in factor 4 have high unemployment among black males.

[13] The percentage of females in the labor force' correlated (—.413) with factor 3.
[14] There are exceptions. Thompson cites two large cities, Pittsburgh and Detroit, as examples of cities in which there are few job opportunities for women because the economy is heavily industrial. Wilbur R. Thompson, *A Preface to Urban Economics* (Baltimore: Johns Hopkins Press, paperback ed., 1968), p. 65.

Table 9.   SMSAs with old housing and high unemployment

Rank	SMSA	Scores
1	Jackson, Mich.	-2.82
2	Erie, Pa.	-2.29
3	Buffalo, N.Y.	-2.02
4	Grand Rapids, Mich.	-1.68
5	Stockton, Calif.	-1.66
6	Waterloo, Iowa	-1.61
7	Canton, Ohio	-1.58
8	Harrisburg, Pa.	-1.58
9	Des Moines, Iowa	-1.53
10	Albany-Schenectady-Troy, N.Y.	-1.52
11	Youngstown-Warren, Ohio	-1.51
12	Detroit, Mich.	-1.46
13	Pittsburgh, Pa.	-1.39
14	Toledo, Ohio	-1.39
15	Portland, Ore.-Wash.	-1.35
16	Providence-Pawtucket, R.I.-Mass.	-1.28

Factors 3 and 4 identify two different types of industrial city: (a) cities with stable or growing industries—factor 3; and (b) cities with declining industries—factor 4. The SMSAs in factor 4 have a disproportionate share of declining industries and hence decreasing manufacturing employment, and since black workers are frequently low-skilled and have low seniority, unemployment is further compounded among them.[15]

In terms of housing, units constructed in the northern industrial cities prior to 1939 probably tend to be larger than more modern units. Since black Americans in these cities tend to live in the old housing, they are less crowded than black Americans living in newer housing in other SMSAs.

Factor 5: Multifamily Housing in the Northeast

Factor 5 distinguishes another set of housing characteristics, the housing type. Owner occupancy (.797), multifamily dwelling (—.763), and single-family dwelling (.732) have the highest correlations with the factor (see Table 10). The negative correlation of the median value of owner-occupied units (—.424) with the factor means that high rates of single-family-dwelling occupancy are partially related to lower values of owner-occupied dwellings. Possibly an important contributor to this relationship is the presence of high rates of low-value single-family black American housing in many southern cities.

At the opposite extreme are the SMSAs with a low percentage of owner-

---

[15] Thompson, *Urban Economics*, p. 113.

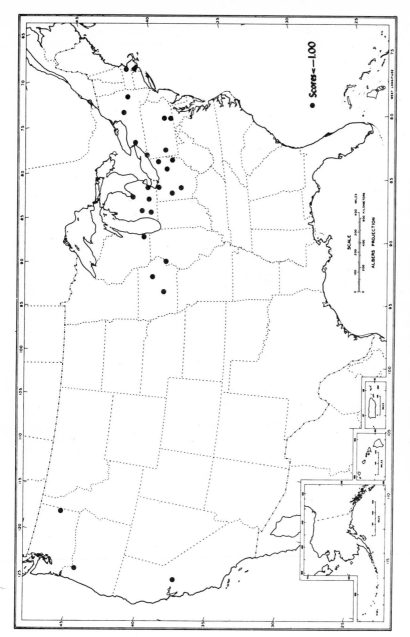

Figure 4 SMSAs with old housing and high unemployment.

73

Table 10. Factor 5: multifamily-dwelling occupancy

No.	Name	Loadings
31	Per cent owner-occupied units	0.797
32	Per cent multifamily dwelling units (5 or more units in structure)	-0.763
33	Per cent single-family dwelling units	0.732
34	Per cent female operatives	-0.649
39	Per cent female service workers	0.447
4	Median value of owner-occupied units	-0.424

occupied units, a high percentage of multifamily dwellings, a low percentage of single-family dwellings, and a high percentage of female operatives. These SMSAs, with factor scores less than —1.00, are listed in Table 11 and mapped in Figure 5.

Figure 5 demonstrates that the above SMSAs are found predominantly in the Northeast: southern New England, New York, and northern New Jersey. The core characteristic of housing for blacks in these cities is multi-family-dwelling occupancy. Examination of white occupancy within the central cities of the same SMSAs reveals the same pattern of multifamily housing.

The multidwelling characteristic of housing results from the fact that these cities were early centers of industrial growth, before transportation improvements made dispersed living feasible on a large scale.[16] Blacks, then, are merely the "new" occupants to whom the multifamily buildings have "filtered down."

Table 11. Multifamily-dwelling SMSAs

Rank	SMSA	Scores
1	Jersey City, N.J.	-3.28
2	Utica-Rome, N.Y.	-2.76
3	Waterbury, Conn.	-2.67
4	New York, N.Y.	-2.39
5	Boston, Mass.	-2.36
6	New Haven, Conn.	-2.28
7	Hartford, Conn.	-2.22
8	Chicago, Ill.	-2.11
9	Providence-Pawtucket, R.I.-Mass.	-2.04
10	Bridgeport, Conn.	-2.01
11	Syracuse, N.Y.	-1.95
12	Norwalk, Conn.	-1.88
13	Newark, N.J.	-1.83
14	Stamford, Conn.	-1.79
15	Springfield-Chicopee-Holyoke, Mass.	-1.60
16	Rochester, N.Y.	-1.49

[16] Harvey S. Perloff et al., *Regions, Resources, and Economic Growth* (Baltimore: Johns Hopkins Press, 1960), pp. 112–121, present a brief discussion of the early rise of the New England and Middle Atlantic cities to industrial prominence before 1870.

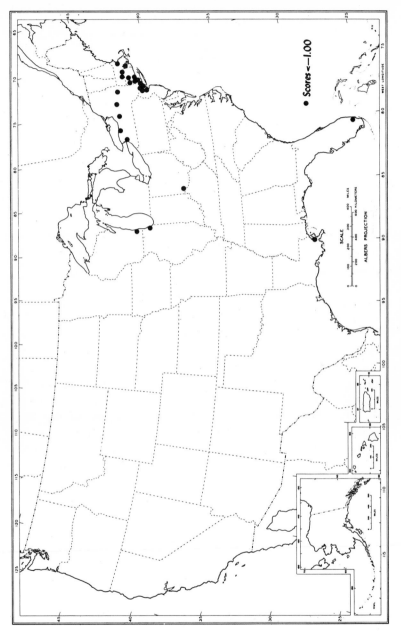

Figure 5 Multifamily-dwelling SMSAs.

An additional characteristic of the northeastern cities is that black females tend to be employed as operatives. This pattern is a reflection of black-female employment in the apparel and electrical machinery industries.[17]

Factor 6: The Black Urban Hierarchy

Factor 6 measures the position of cities in a hierarchy. Black population size (.835) and total population size (.723) have the highest correlations with the factor (see Table 12). The negative correlation of variable 37 (—.579) with factor 6 suggests that the larger SMSAs have lower rates of inmigration.[18]

Table 12. Factor 6: position in urban hierarchy

No.	Name	Loadings
35	Black American population size	0.835
36	Total population size	0.723
37	Per cent living in different house in SMSA who moved into SMSA since 1955	-0.579
8	Per cent male clerical workers	0.498
14	Other races population size	0.492
30	Per cent total population Black American	0.430

Cities whose factor scores are greater than 1.00, the large SMSAs, are listed in Table 13 and mapped in Figure 6. As-expected, some of the nation's largest SMSAs in terms of total population appear on the list. However, since factor 6 is more importantly a measure of black American population size, certain SMSAs that are smaller in terms of *total population* appear because they have large black American populations. The SMSAs at the opposite extreme, large in terms of total population but small black populations, do not appear on the list.

Factor 7: Service Workers in Farming States

The most important variable of factor 7 (Table 14) is the percentage of male service workers (—.746). The SMSAs whose factor scores are below —1.00 (i.e., those with high proportions of service workers) are listed in Table 15 and mapped in Figure 7.

[17] U.S. Bureau of the Census, *U.S. Census of Population: 1960,* Vol. 1, *Characteristics of the Population* (Washington, D.C.: U.S. Government Printing Office, 1963), Parts 8, 23, 32, and 34; Table 129.

[18] The assumption is, however, that all SMSA mobility rates are the same.

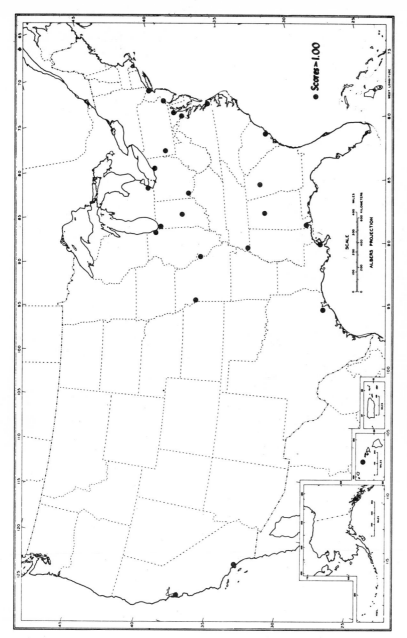

Figure 6 SMSAs in the upper levels of the urban hierarchy.

Table 13. SMSAs in the upper levels of the urban hierarchy

Rank	SMSA	Scores
1	Chicago, Ill.	2.39
2	Washington, D.C.-Md.-Va.	2.32
3	New York, N.Y.	2.31
4	Los Angeles-Long Beach, Calif.	2.29
5	Detroit, Mich.	2.19
6	Philadelphia, Pa.-N.J.	2.15
7	St. Louis, Mo.-Ill.	1.94
8	San Francisco-Oakland, Calif.	1.94
9	New Orleans, La.	1.74
10	Honolulu, Hawaii	1.68
11	Baltimore, Md.	1.66
12	Memphis, Tenn.	1.49
13	Birmingham, Ala.	1.44
14	Cleveland, Ohio	1.43
15	Cincinnati, Ohio-Ky.	1.30
16	Pittsburgh, Pa.	1.29

Table 14. Factor 7: service workers

No.	Name	Loadings
38	Per cent male service workers	-0.746
39	Per cent female service workers	-0.470
40	Ratio of other relatives of heads of households to heads of households	0.464
10	Ratio of nonrelatives of heads of households to heads of households	0.453
21	Population per household	0.406

Table 15. SMSAs with high proportions of service workers

Rank	SMSA	Scores
1	Las Vegas, Nev.	-3.24
2	Colorado Springs, Colo.	-2.67
3	El Paso, Tex.	-2.37
4	Wichita Falls, Tex.	-1.80
5	Lubbock, Tex.	-1.65
6	Oklahoma City, Okla.	-1.63
7	Wichita, Kans.	-1.62
8	Abilene, Tex.	-1.56
9	Peoria, Ill.	-1.51
10	San Antonio, Tex.	-1.51
11	Topeka, Kans.	-1.48
12	Denver, Colo.	-1.47
13	Spokane, Wash.	-1.36
14	Minneapolis-St. Paul, Minn.	-1.34
15	Des Moines, Iowa	-1.32
16	Tulsa, Okla.	-1.29

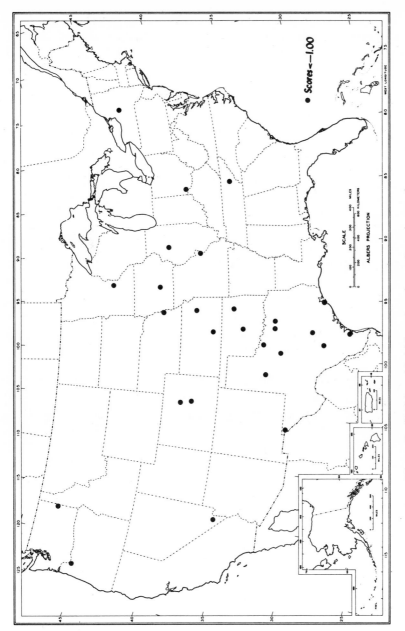

Figure 7 SMSAs with high proportions of service workers.

A large share of these SMSAs are located in farming states: Iowa, Nebraska, Kansas, Oklahoma, and Texas. Two mutually reinforcing conditions explain this factor. First, severe discrimination against black Americans, especially in Texas and Oklahoma, has restricted employment opportunities.[19] Second, many of the SMSAs in the farming states have few industrial employment opportunities since they function primarily as service centers for the surrounding rural areas and small towns. Thus the only employment open to blacks is in the low-status service occupations.

An additional element is the presence of American Indians (also classified as nonwhite) in the farming-state SMSAs. Since American Indians face the same patterns of discrimination in education and employment as black Americans, service occupations are the only ones open to them in the farming-state SMSAs.

COMBINED EFFECTS OF THE FACTORS

Status and Life Cycle

Since black Americans comprise 91.4% of the nonwhite population in the 145 SMSAs, the analysis mainly characterizes them. The significant exception is factor 2, which identifies variations in socioeconomic status among nonwhite groups. The two most important differentiating factors are socioeconomic status (factor 1) and stage in life cycle (factor 3). By plotting the factor scores of the stage in life cycle along the abscissa and those of the socioeconomic status along the ordinate in Figure 8, additional patterns in the differentiation of black Americans are revealed in the four quadrants of the graph. Northern industrial SMSAs[20] with under one million total population are in quadrant I, a function of their relatively high socioeconomic status and young families, arising because wage rates in manufacturing are relatively high for black males in these cities and therefore attractive to the mobile young families.

The SMSAs whose populations exceed one million are chiefly found in quadrant II, ranking high in socioeconomic status and containing older families. Greater employment and educational opportunities for black Americans within the large SMSAs, especially compared with those in the

[19] Gunnar Myrdal, *An American Dilemma* (New York: Harper and Brothers, 1944), p. 188.
[20] "North" is loosely defined as east of the Mississippi and north of a line extending from the southern border of Illinois and Indiana east to the Atlantic Ocean.

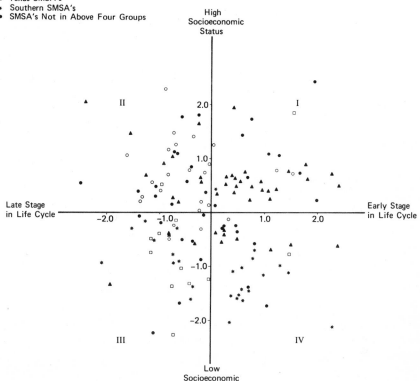

Figure 8   Socioeconomic (factor 1) versus stage in life cycle (factor 3).

smaller southern SMSAs, probably account for the high socioeconomic status. The older age of the population may derive from the fact that the large SMSAs have had sizable black populations for many years. They were the primary foci of the great migrations out of the South from 1910 to 1930.[21] Thus they tend to have large numbers of middle-aged and older

[21] Myrdal, *An American Dilemma,* p. 183, and Woofter, *Negro Problems,* pp. 26–33. For accounts of the impact of the great migrations on the two largest American cities, Chicago and New York, see Gilbert Osofsky, *Harlem: The Making of a Ghetto* (New York: Harper Torchbooks, 1968; first published in 1966 by Harper and Row), pp. 127–149; and Allan H. Spear, *Black Chicago: The Making of a Negro Ghetto, 1890–1920* (Chicago: University of Chicago Press, 1967), pp. 129ff.

people, who either arrived in the cities in migrations preceding the extensive movements of the 1950s or were born of parents who moved to the large cities during and just after World War I.

Quadrant III contains Texan SMSAs with low socioeconomic status and old families. The low socioeconomic status is probably a product of the same southern constraints on black educational and employment opportunities as exist in southern states east of the Mississippi plus the additional factor of competition from Mexicans for the lowest status occupations.[22]

The SMSAs with a low socioeconomic status and young families are found in quadrant IV. Southern SMSAs in Louisiana, Alabama, Georgia, and South Carolina comprise the largest group with these characteristics.[23] The low socioeconomic status results from the system of constraints on black Americans mentioned previously. The young-family characteristic is a product of the movement of large rural families with many young children to these SMSAs[24] and the high fertility of the women in these SMSAs —women with a farm background and low levels of educational achievement.[25]

Housing and Stage in Life Cycle

The variables measuring stage in life cycle, size of housing, and type of housing were allocated by the factor analysis to separate independent factors.[26] Among black Americans, therefore, the intermetropolitan distribution of housing is unrelated to the intermetropolitan distribution of family types, which differs from findings related to the majority white population.

The reasons are not clear. Previous studies have suggested that inadequate income and discrimination are important factors at the *intra*metropolitan scale.[27] Inadequate income as the sole factor in the lack of

[22] Myrdal, *An American Dilemma,* p. 188.

[23] Atlanta, Georgia, the only SMSA from the four southern states with over one million population, is not listed in Figure 9 as being part of the fourth pattern.

[24] Due to the emphasis on the migration of southern rural blacks to large northern cities the equally important movement of rural blacks to the southern cities is often ignored. For a discussion of this latter movement see T. Lynn Smith, "The Redistribution of the Negro Population of the United States, 1910–1960," *The Journal of Negro History,* Vol. 51 (1966), pp. 155–173.

[25] Otis Dudley Duncan, "Farm Background and Differential Fertility," *Demography,* Vol. 2 (1965), pp. 240–249.

[26] Stage in life cycle—factor 3; size of housing—factor 4; and housing type—factor 5.

[27] The literature at the intrametropolitan scale is quite large. The focus has tended to be on black segregation. See Beverly Duncan and Philip M. Hauser, *Housing a Metro-*

correspondence between housing stock occupied and housing needs also has been rejected by some writers.[28] However, results from the intrametropolitan scale may not be totally applicable to the intermetropolitan one. For example, the variation from SMSA to SMSA in the type and quality of available housing stock is probably a factor in the differences in housing occupied by black Americans—a factor that is independent of their socioeconomic status and stage in life cycle. Other factors that have been suggested as contributing to differences in housing occupancy are the economy and social climate of the city and the structure and quality of life in the black community.[29] These factors are probably independent of the family characteristics of the black population.

Position in the Urban Hierarchy

The location and existence of factor 6 (position in the urban hierarchy) in the classification is significant in two respects. First, the urban hierarchy has a *minor* role in the differentiation of nonwhites, especially black Americans. Factor 6 accounted for only 8.5% of the total variance and 10.0% of the variance common to the seven factors.

Second, position in the urban hierarchy is independent of socioeconomic status, stage in life cycle, and housing characteristics.[30] This renders inappropriate simple generalizations in which the size of the black ghetto is claimed to be a factor in socioeconomic opportunities, family patterns, pathological relationships, and the like.

polis—*Chicago* (Glencoe, Ill.: Free Press, 1960); Nathan Glazer and David McEntire, Eds., *Studies in Housing and Minority Groups* (Berkeley and Los Angeles: University of California Press, 1960); Davis McEntire, *Residence and Race* (Berkeley and Los Angeles: University of California Press, 1960); Taeuber and Taeuber, *Negroes in Cities;* and Robert C. Weaver, *The Negro Ghetto* (New York: Harcourt, Brace and Company, 1948).

[28] See, for example, Duncan and Hauser, *Housing a Metropolis—Chicago;* Karl E. Taeuber, "The Effect of Income Redistribution on Racial Residential Segregation," *Urban Affairs Quarterly,* Vol. 4 (1968), pp. 5–14; and Taeuber and Taeuber, *Negroes in Cities.*

[29] Robert A. Thompson, Hylan Lewis, and Davis McEntire, "Atlanta and Birmingham: A Comparative Study in Negro Housing," in Glazer and McEntire, Eds., *Housing and Minority Groups,* p. 80.

[30] Black population size and total population size were the two major variables in the urban-hierarchy factor. Of these two, and excluding factor 2, only total population size showed moderate correlations with some of the factors. Total population size was correlated (.339) with factor 1 (socioeconomic status) and (−.370) with factor 5 (housing type).

RELATIONSHIP TO BERRY'S FINDINGS

Further insight into nonwhite differentiation can be gained by comparing the present analysis with Berry's findings reported in Chapter 1.

The major congruity between the two studies is that in both position of city in the urban hierarchy, socioeconomic status, and stage in life cycle were important independent dimensions differentiating cities.

However, in the present study the urban-hierarchy dimension was sixth in importance, whereas in Berry's analysis it was first, a discrepancy resulting from (a) fundamental differences between nonwhite and white inter-metropolitan differentiation,[31] (b) the fact that fewer variables related to the urban hierarchy were included in the nonwhite analysis, and (c) because Berry dealt with legal cities whereas we dealt with a more limited subset of SMSAs.

The close correspondence between the position of socioeconomic status and stage in life cycle in both studies[32] suggests that these factors identify fundamental dimensions of the differentiation of cities. The dimensions apply not only to the white majority but also to the nonwhite minority.

CLASSIFICATION

Up to this point we have analyzed the multidimensional character of SMSAs on the basis of the characteristics of nonwhites. The factor scores for each SMSA will now be employed as a basis for developing a classification according to logical rules.

Methodology

We begin with a 145 × 7 matrix of factor scores.[33] Thus each SMSA is treated as a point in seven-dimensional space. The problem is to systematically allocate the 145 SMSAs to distinct groups. The method used here is the *neighborhood-limited algorithm* developed by Neely.[34] However, before

[31] Since Berry dealt mainly with the average characteristics of the total population, his classification chiefly applies to the white population.

[32] In Berry's study socioeconomic status and stage in life cycle were second and third, respectively, in importance, whereas in the present study they were first and third, respectively, in importance.

[33] Data on 145 SMSAs; seven factor scores for each SMSA corresponding to the 7 factors analyzed.

[34] For a discussion of several grouping algorithms, including Neely's neighborhood-

the neighborhood-limited algorithm can be employed, a "neighborhood" must be defined for each point (SMSA). In the present analysis a program developed by Neely to define "relatively close neighbors" was used to define the neighborhoods.[35]

There were 144 steps in the grouping procedure, progressively clustering the cities into larger groups by a sequential classificatory process.[36] For interpretative purposes, however, one works backward as if the classes had been produced by logical division.[37]

The Classification

The dominant pattern in steps 81 through 144 is one large group, to which relatively isolated cities are added in the grouping process. At step 71 the large group breaks down into three groups, excluding isolates. By step 54 there are six groups, and at step 28, six groups.[38]

Figure 9 presents a tree diagram of the classification of SMSAs at two steps, 71 and 54.[39] For the sake of simplicity, groups with less than three

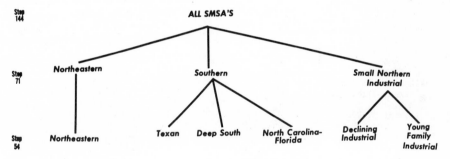

Figure 9 Tree diagram of SMSA classification.

limited algorithm, see Philip M. Lankford, "Regionalization: Theory and Alternative Algorithms," *Geographical Analysis,* Vol. 1 (1969), pp. 196–212. The writer owes special thanks to Mr. Lankford for his assistance in using the neighborhood-limited algorithm and associated computer programs.
[35] *Ibid.* pp. 201–202.
[36] David Grigg, "The Logic of Regional Systems," *Annals of the Association of American Geographers,* Vol. 55 (1965), pp. 466–468.
[37] Grigg, "Logic of Regional Systems," p. 468.
[38] Of course as we move backward from step 144 to step 1 the total number of SMSAs included in the classification declines. We do *not* attempt to allocate to groups SMSAs not allocated by the algorithm. Thus the groups at any one step might be considered cores of larger groups.
[39] Step 144 is not counted since all of the SMSAs are in one group.

Table 16. SMSA classification at step 71

Northeastern

Bridgeport, Conn.
Hartford, Conn.
New Haven, Conn.
Rochester, N.Y.
Springfield-Chicopee-Holyoke, Mass.
Syracuse, N.Y.
Waterbury, Conn.

Southern

Augusta, Ga.-S.C.
Austin, Tex.
Baton Rouge, La.
Beaumont-Port Arthur, Tex.
Birmingham, Ala.
Charlotte, N.C.
Chattanooga, Tenn.-Ga.
Columbia, S.C.
Columbus, Ga.-Ala.
Columbus, Ohio
Corpus Christi, Tex.
Dallas, Tex.
Dayton, Ohio
Durham, N.C.
Evansville, Ind.-Ky.
Fort Worth, Tex.
Gadsden, Ala.
Galveston-Texas City, Tex.
Greensboro-High Point, N.C.
Greenville, S.C.
Indianapolis, Ind.
Jacksonville, Fla.
Knoxville, Tenn.
Lexington, Ky.
Little Rock-North Little Rock, Ark.
Louisville, Ky.-Ind.
Macon, Ga.
Memphis, Tenn.
Mobile, Ala.
Monroe, La.
Montgomery, Ala.
Nashville, Tenn.
Norfolk-Portsmouth, Va.
Orlando, Fla.
Raleigh, N.C.
Richmond, Va.
San Antonio, Tex.
Savannah, Ga.
Shreveport, La.
Tampa-St. Petersburg, Fla.
Waco, Tex.
Winston-Salem, N.C.

Small Northern Industrial

Akron, Ohio
Canton, Ohio
Davenport-Rock Island-Moline, Iowa-Ill.
Decatur, Ill.
Flint, Mich.
Fort Wayne, Ind.
Grand Rapids, Mich.
Hamilton-Middletown, Ohio
Harrisburg, Pa.
Kalamazoo, Mich.
Lima, Ohio
Lorain-Elyria, Ohio
Muskegon-Muskegon Heights, Mich.
Peoria, Ill.
Saginaw, Mich.
South Bend, Ind.
Steubenville-Weirton, Ohio-W. Va.
Toledo, Ohio
York, Pa.
Youngstown-Warren, Ohio

Table 17.   SMSA classification at step 54

Northeastern

Bridgeport, Conn.
Hartford, Conn.
New Haven, Conn.
Rochester, N.Y.
Springfield-Chicopee-Holyoke, Mass.
Syracuse, N.Y.
Waterbury, Conn.

Texan

Austin, Tex.
Corpus Christi, Tex.
Dallas, Tex.
Fort Worth, Tex.
Galveston-Texas City, Tex.
Knoxville, Tenn.
Nashville, Tenn.
San Antonio, Tex.
Waco, Tex.

Deep South

Augusta, Ga.-S.C.
Baton Rouge, La.
Beaumont-Port Arthur, Tex.
Birmingham, Ala.
Chattanooga, Tenn.-Ga.
Columbia, S.C.
Columbus, Ga.-Ala.
Gadsden, Ala.
Greenville, S.C.
Little Rock-North Little Rock, Ark.
Macon, Ga.
Memphis, Tenn.
Mobile, Ala.
Monroe, La.
Montgomery, Ala.
Norfolk-Portsmouth, Va.
Raleigh, N.C.
Savannah, Ga.
Shreveport, La.

North Carolina-Florida

Durham, N.C.
Greensboro-High Point, N.C.
Jacksonville, Fla.
Orlando, Fla.
Richmond, Va.
Tampa-St. Petersburg, Fla.
Winston-Salem, N.C.

Declining Industrial

Canton, Ohio
Harrisburg, Pa.
Steubenville-Weirton, Ohio-W. Va.
Youngstown-Warren, Ohio

Young Family Industrial

Akron, Ohio
Davenport-Rock Island-Moline, Iowa-Ill.
Decatur, Ill.
Flint, Mich.
Fort Wayne, Ind.
Grand Rapids, Mich.
Hamilton-Middletown, Ohio
Kalamazoo, Mich.
Lorain-Elyria, Ohio
South Bend, Ind.

members are ignored. The SMSAs at steps 71 and 54 are listed in Tables 16 and 17, respectively. At step 71 there are three subgroups, the northeastern, southern, and small northern industrial cities.[40]

Thus at the first stage in the classification the southern SMSAs, the most commonly identified group of SMSAs in the literature on the black American, form the largest subset. This result is merely support for the accepted view that black Americans who live in the South participate in a similar set of social and economic institutions, whose most distinguishing characteristic is low socioeconomic status.

Although the southern SMSAs form a distinct group at step 71 of the grouping process, the nonsouthern SMSAs are divided into what the writer has loosely termed the northeastern and small northern industrial groups. The description of factor 5 indicated that the northeastern SMSAs have in common a high rate of multifamily-dwelling living and female employment as operatives. All seven SMSAs in the Northeast had very low negative factor scores on factor 5.

The small northern industrial SMSAs, on the other hand, were prominent on factors 3 or 4. The factor scores of the SMSAs are graphed in Figure 10, and, as is evident, the small northern industrial SMSAs tend to have young families with males employed as craftsmen and operatives, and old housing and high unemployment.

These characteristics of black Americans and their housing are reflections of the industrial nature of the SMSAs in which they live. The small northern industrial SMSAs have been important centers of manufacturing since the period 1870–1910.[41] Since in the North black Americans are frequently limited to housing in the oldest parts of the cities, substantial amounts of the housing available to them in the small northern industrial SMSAs probably date from the period 1870–1910. Hence the old-housing characteristic.

The employment of males as craftsmen and operatives is readily understandable. The reason for the high unemployment has already been discussed. Briefly, the curious occurrence of high unemployment with high employment in manufacturing exists in cities with stable or declining manufacturing establishments and expanding black populations. Since they face job discrimination and are usually low in seniority, black males have high rates of unemployment.

Further breakdown of the classification is possible. At step 54 we see that the southern and small northern industrial groups divide into three and two

[40] "Northeastern" includes SMSAs in New York and New England. "Southern" refers to SMSAs south of the southern border of Kentucky. "Small northern industrial" includes SMSAs in Illinois, Indiana, Ohio, and Michigan.
[41] Perloff et al., *Regions, Resources, and Economic Growth*, pp. 174–175.

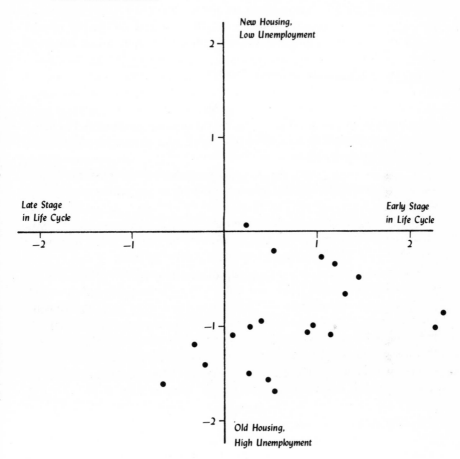

Figure 10 Small northern industrial SMSAs: stage in life cycle (factor 3) versus age of housing and unemployment (factor 4).

groups, respectively (see Figure 9). The northeastern group remains the same. From Table 17 we suggest that the southern SMSAs can be classified into Texan, "Deep South,"[42] and North Carolina–Florida types.

Texas is a special case because its growth occurred after the Civil War. In this frontier situation black Americans had to compete with white

[42] The writer is using the term "Deep South" in a very broad sense to include Arkansas, Louisiana, Alabama, Georgia, South Carolina, and Tennessee.

migrants to Texas for a place in the social and economic system while being handicapped by discrimination. Furthermore, black Americans have had to compete with Mexican Americans for the low-status occupations.[43] Since employment opportunities are unattractive and the supply of rural migrants is limited, young families are unlikely to move to, or remain in, Texan SMSAs.

Texan SMSAs can be contrasted with those in the Deep South, which are centers of inmigration of rural black families. Hence their age structure is skewed toward the lowest age groups. Black Americans in the Deep South have traditionally been assigned the lowest position in the social system,[44] though since there is no need to compete with other groups for employment, more jobs are available to them. Yet because of the more structured social system in the Deep South, the occupations open to them are still low-status ones. New occupations only become available when whites are not displaced.[45]

The North Carolina–Florida subgroup identifies two subsets of SMSAs: industrial SMSAs in North Carolina with textile and furniture industries[46] and SMSAs in Florida with an important tourist function.

The small northern industrial group divides into declining industrial and young-family industrial types (see Table 17). The declining industrial subgroup includes the SMSAs in Ohio along the border with Pennsylvania together with Harrisburg, Pennsylvania. The young-family industrial subgroup includes small SMSAs important in light manufacturing, especially that associated with the automobile industry.

The two subgroups are graphed in Figure 11 on the basis of scores for factors 3 and 4. Therefore the axes are the same as those in Figure 10. As

[43] Myrdal, *An American Dilemma,* pp. 187–188.
[44] For two classic statements about the position of the black in southern society see Allison Davis, Burleigh B. Gardner, and Mary R. Gardner, *Deep South* (Chicago: University of Chicago Press, 1941), and John Dollard, *Caste and Class in a Southern Town* (New Haven: Yale University Press, 1937).
[45] Richard L. Simpson and David R. Norsworthy, "The Changing Occupational Structure of the South," in John C. McKinney and Edgar T. Thompson, Eds., *The South in Continuity and Change* (Durham, N.C.: Duke University Press, 1965), p. 211.
[46] See Rupert B. Vance, *Human Geography of the South* (Chapel Hill: University of North Carolina Press, 1932), pp. 275–315, for a discussion of the rise of the Piedmont Crescent as an industrial center in the South. North Carolina is a prominent part of the Piedmont Crescent. For a discussion of the nature of the developing urban system in North Carolina see F. Stuart Chapin, Jr., and Shirley F. Weiss, Eds., *Urban Growth Dynamics in a Regional Cluster of Cities* (New York: John Wiley & Sons, Inc., 1962).

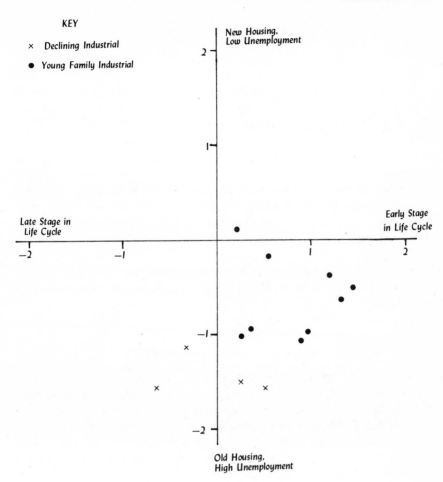

Figure 11 Declining industrial and young-family industrial SMSAs: stage in life cycle (factor 3) versus age of housing and unemployment (factor 4).

can be seen, old housing and high unemployment are characteristic of the declining industrial SMSAs, and young families with males employed as craftsmen and operatives are characteristic of the young-family industrial SMSAs. Thus we see that black Americans are highly differentiated even among small industrial SMSAs in the North.

Contrary to their clearly identifiable position on factor 2, Pacific Coast SMSAs do not form a distinct group in the classification. All Pacific Coast SMSAs were grouped after step 79, and only a few formed a separate group.

Generally most of them were added to the main group one by one. There-fore the close similarity among the Pacific Coast SMSAs applies only to a few characteristics of nonwhites, in particular the proportion of black Americans.

Another significant group missing from the classification is the group containing SMSAs with more than one million inhabitants. The implica-tion of this is that black American populations in these large SMSAs *do not* closely resemble each other on the set of characteristics employed in this study. Hence assumptions that all large black "ghettos" are the same are inaccurate.

Perhaps of some significance is the fact that New York and Chicago, the cities with the largest black populations in the United States, were joined at step 122 and not joined to the rest of the SMSAs until step 136. They are thus dissimilar to most SMSAs but share some characteristics with each other.

Finally, the most "isolated" SMSA in the grouping was Honolulu, Hawaii. Its uniqueness has been reaffirmed by inspection of the factor scores in Berry's study.

CONCLUSIONS

The intermetropolitan differentiation of nonwhites, especially black Americans, is complex. The necessity of using seven dimensions to describe the variation among SMSAs underscores the importance of caution in generalizing about black Americans from studies of single cities.

In the classification most of the SMSAs were placed in one group from steps 81 through 144. Some people might point to this and assert that black Americans are *not* very highly differentiated among SMSAs. Such an in-terpretation reiterates a common theme in studies of black Americans, who are, of course, "excused" for being homogeneous because of slavery and surviving forms of racial discrimination that appear in countless guises. Most black Americans, according to this interpretation, are characterized by low socioeconomic status and "disorganized" families, constituting "problems" in some form or another. These characterizations are not only inaccurate but also a reflection of a persistent one-sided emphasis by scholars studying black Americans.[47]

[47] See Andrew Billingsley, *Black Families in White America* (Englewood Cliffs, N.J.: Prentice-Hall, Inc., 1968), pp. 197–215, for a perceptive critique of scholarship on the black family. The ideas expressed by Billingsley formed a basis for part of the discussion in this section.

Our understanding of black Americans will be greatly enhanced by the purposeful examination of the diversity existing within the black population. In terms of a classification of SMSAs according to the characteristics of nonwhites (mainly black Americans) we see that there is in fact a great deal of complexity, and it is difficult to interpret with our present knowledge because of the traditional interpretive bias. A variety of possible interpretations of the groups has been suggested, but more research is needed before a definitive classification can be developed.

APPENDIX   List of Variables

No.	Name
1	Median family income
2	Median rent
3	Per cent male laborers
4	Median value of owner-occupied units
5	Median school years completed
6	Per cent sound occupied units
7	Per cent female private household workers
8	Per cent male clerical workers
9	Per cent female clerical workers
10	Ratio of nonrelatives of heads of households to heads of households
11	Per cent Black American of nonwhite population
12	Per cent male managers
13	Ratio of married women not separated from husband to separated and divorced women
14	Other races population size
15	Per cent male operatives
16	Per cent male professional workers
17	Ratio of males to females
18	Taeubers' segregation index for 207 cities, 1960
19	Female median age
20	Per cent population under age 18
21	Population per household
22	Male median age
23	Per cent heads of household with wife present
24	Per cent male craftsmen
25	Median number of rooms
26	Per cent occupied units with 1.01 or more persons per room
27	Per cent occupied units built 1939 or earlier
28	Per cent male unemployment
29	Per cent females in the labor force
30	Per cent total population Black American
31	Per cent owner-occupied units
32	Per cent multifamily dwelling units (5 or more units in structure)
33	Per cent single-family dwelling units
34	Per cent female operatives
35	Black American population size
36	Total population size
37	Per cent living in different house in SMSA who moved into SMSA since 1955
38	Per cent male service workers
39	Per cent female service workers
40	Ratio of other relatives of heads of households to heads of households

PART TWO

Uses of City Classifications in Social and Political Research

... Social and political dimensions of American suburbs

... Functional classification and the residential location of social classes

... Urban typologies and political outputs

CHAPTER 3

Social and Political Dimensions of American Suburbs

BENJAMIN WALTER

Vanderbilt University

FREDERICK M. WIRT

University of California at Berkeley

This chapter has two major aims. The first is to show by means of factor analysis, in the spirit of the preceding two chapters, that American suburbs are not as socially homogeneous as folklore would have it. The second and more important task will be to connect the suburban differences that emerge from the factor analysis to observed variations in recent presidential and congressional elections.[1]

MEASURING SUBURBAN DIFFERENCES

One way to chart the diversity among American suburbs would be to show how they vary on several standard census measures taken one at a time. The census data show immediately how misleading the stereotype can be. For example, in 1960 the median family income for Chelsea, Massachusetts was $5300. The corresponding figure for families living in Needham, also a suburb of Boston, was nearly $9300. Only 8% of the families

---

[1] An early use of this perspective may be found in Frederick M. Wirt, "The Political Sociology of American Suburbia: A Reinterpretation," *Journal of Politics*, Vol. 27 (1964), pp. 647–666. Also see Joseph Zikmund, "Suburban Voting in Presidential Elections: 1948–1964," *Midwest Journal of Political Science*, Vol. 12 (1968), pp. 239–258.

living in Grosse Pointe Park, Michigan, could be classified as poor, but nearly a quarter of the families inhabiting nearby River Rouge had incomes of less than $3000 a year.

Slightly more than 30% of the labor force in Chester, Pennsylvania, was engaged in white-collar occupations. In Dormont, Pennsylvania, on the other hand, almost two of every three gainfully employed persons filled such positions. Over two-thirds of the adults living in Brookline, Massachusetts, had completed at least 4 years of high school, but almost two-thirds of Attleboro's citizens had left high school before receiving a diploma.

Census measures show the wide range of living conditions that differentiate American suburbs. If we looked at measures of income, education, occupation, and housing separately, we would have a general image of the diversity of American suburbs. In the end, however, there would be as many different pictures as there are variables.

Fortunately the variables we might use in comparing different suburbs are related to one another. As one increases in value, others frequently tend to rise (or fall) with it. In statistical language, the variables are *correlated*. The first step in this study therefore was to compute the degree of correlation of 29 selected census variables with each of the others, using data for 407 American suburbs.

As shown in Part One of this volume, factor analysis can be used to reduce a mass of interrelated but distinct primary variables to a smaller number of abstract indices called factors. This was the second step taken in the study, in the belief that the conceptual simplification that factorial classification helps to attain will make it easier to isolate the links joining the social characteristics of American suburbs to electoral data.

THE DATA

Electoral Data

The principal goal of the study was to join the factors to various measures of electoral performance. Hence only those suburbs for which reliable and reasonably complete election data could be assembled were used.

Abundant voting data are available at the county level, but securing election information for governmental units below this level is extremely difficult. Local election officials were canvassed to obtain authenticated copies of election returns. Some responded; others did not. Where local officials failed to respond, the legislative manuals that most states publish annually were consulted. Some contained no data at all bearing on elections held in the separate municipalities.

Equally troublesome was the fact that the election returns reported in the manuals of various states refer to different kinds of areas. Some states report data for entire rural townships, but not for the separate municipalities they contain. Others present data ward by ward for the entire state. In some cases the ward votes could be combined to produce citywide totals; in others, it was impossible to determine exactly what combination of wards coincided with municipality boundaries. Some states present the vote in gubernatorial elections and omit the vote for congressmen; in other states, it is the other way around.

It took 3 years to accumulate data for congressional elections in 166 suburbs and for presidential elections in 407. A state-by-state distribution is presented in Table 1.

The sample contains some obvious regional biases. Most of the suburbs are situated in New England and the North Central States. Outside these two regions only a handful of California's many suburbs appear. Even so, the 15 states represented in this sample account for over half the votes cast in the electoral college. Eight of the most populous ten states are included; only Texas and Florida are absent. Apart from having many inhabitants, every state in the sample has had a history of alternating between the two major parties in presidential elections, however, assuring that the analysis would not be biased by including predominantly one-party constituencies.

These difficulties stated, it should also be noted that this sampling of

Table 1. State-by-state distribution of suburbs

State	Type of Election	
	Presidential	Congressional
Maine	2	
Massachusetts	46	
Rhode Island	9	
Connecticut	14	14
New York	27	2
New Jersey	104	104
Pennsylvania	69	9
Ohio	56	
Illinois	1	1
Missouri	2	1
Minnesota	18	19
Michigan	23	
Virginia	1	
Wisconsin	15	
California	20	16
N =	407*	166

*Congressional and presidential totals do not agree for a number of reasons. Some states do not report votes for congressional elections, and other election results arrived too late to be included in our analysis.

American suburbs is broader and deeper than any survey so far compiled. As of 1960, *The Municipal Year Book* listed 736 suburbs.[2] This study covers 55.3% of that total. Many of the suburbs omitted are located in thinly populated states that regularly vote for either Democrats or Republicans in statewide or congressional elections.

Social Characteristics

Data bearing on the social and economic characteristics of the suburbs were drawn from the 1960 Census of Population and the 1960 Census of Housing. Taken together, they yield a wide variety of measures that can be used to differentiate suburbs. From the vast array of available data 29 primary variables were chosen (see Table 2). The list could have been expanded beyond 29, but we felt that it covered most of the determinants of voting behavior needed for the purposes of analysis.

THE INTERCORRELATION MATRIX

The matrix of intercorrelations among the 29 primary variables is presented as Table 2. Coefficients in excess of $\pm.60$ have been underscored. These correlations are based on individual suburbs rather than suburban individuals. Correlations based on the many millions of individuals living in suburbs would almost certainly have diverged from those reported in Table 2, as Robinson has shown.[3] It is often hazardous to make inferences about the behavior of individuals on the basis of measures that refer to whole communities; individual and aggregate correlations are not the same thing. Therefore it is important to show how the ecological correlations in Table 2 coincide with the results of studies in which individual voters have been used as the basic units of analysis, a step we take later in this chapter.

Even though the bulk of the matrix makes it unwieldy for precise analysis, certain correlation patterns do emerge. The highest coefficient is $+.95$, between the two educational measures. The measures are of course technically dependent; the way they are defined compels one to vary with the other. A high proportion of high-school graduates automatically pushes up the median school age. Similarly school-attendance laws guarantee that

[2] Orin F. Nolting and David S. Arnold, Eds., *The Municipal Year Book 1963* (Chicago: International City Managers' Association, 1963), p. 97.
[3] W. S. Robinson, "Ecological Correlations and the Behavior of Individuals," *American Sociological Review*, Vol. 15 (1950), pp. 351–357.

Table 2. Intercorrelation matrix: 407 suburbs

Variable	1 SY25	2 HS4	3 MINC	4 3TH	5 1OTH	6 VOCC	7 WC	8 MANU	9 FIRE	10 MWLF	11 UNEM	12 RET	13 AGE	14 FERT	15 U.18	16 0.65	17 MWHH	18 H50S	19 P50S	20 VACO	21 VACR	22 MV58	23 HU1	24 HUOW	25 FRST	26 FENE	27 NW	28 POP
1. Adults, Median School Yrs.																												
2. Adults, % Completing H.S.	.95																											
3. Median Annual Family Income	.71	.73																										
4. % Families Earning < $3,000	-.64	-.59	-.61																									
5. % Families Earning > $10,000	.72	.78	.93	-.56																								
6. Median Value, Owner-occupied	.69	.72	.86	-.54	.90																							
7. % White-collar	.62	.88	.77	-.54	.86	.75																						
8. % in Manufacturing	-.60	-.62	-.40	-.10	-.50	-.48	-.65																					
9. % in FIRE*	-.62	-.65	.63	-.45	.50	.62	.77	-.58																				
10. % Married Women in Labor Force	.61	.65	.42	-.17	-.37	.45	.47	-.44	.45																			
11. % Unemployed	.34	.38	-.30	.06	-.20	-.36	-.50	.87	-.48	-.51																		
12. % in Retailing	-.48	-.49	-.21	.16	-.25	-.22	.00	-.19	-.08	-.02	-.18																	
13. Median Age	.00	-.04	.20	.22	-.33	.24	-.18	-.19	.36	-.43	-.16	-.04																
14. Fertility Ratio	-.09	-.03	.20	-.24	-.30	-.22	.00	.20	-.24	-.39	.17	.03	-.82															
15. % Under 18	.12	.07	.06	-.24	-.08	-.05	.06	.16	-.14	-.36	.15	.16	-.86	.81														
16. % Over 65	.26	.23	-.18	-.41	.01	-.06	.00	.18	-.19	.32	-.17	.03	.82	-.68	-.87													
17. % Married without Own Hsehold.	-.23	-.19	-.11	.49	-.19	-.25	.06	-.19	.07	-.09	.09	.16	.39	-.40	-.46	.39												
18. % Housing Built, 1950-1960	-.48	-.46	-.25	.43	.18	.12	.00	-.02	-.08	-.24	.00	-.19	-.50	.65	.81	-.83	-.52											
19. % Pop. Growth, 1950-1960	.45	.42	.27	-.62	.07	.06	-.36	-.03	-.08	-.16	.00	-.11	-.42	.53	.58	-.57	-.36	.71										
20. Vacancy Rate: Owner-occupied	.25	.26	.14	-.16	-.02	-.25	.25	-.03	-.08	-.17	-.07	.00	-.43	.47	.44	-.38	-.17	.50	.43									
21. Vacancy Rate: Rental	.19	.18	-.23	.06	-.27	.25	.24	.07	-.15	-.30	-.15	-.03	-.46	.40	.39	-.28	-.30	.27	.28	.37								
22. % Moved in After 1958	-.08	-.08	-.23	-.20	-.14	.12	.14	-.19	-.04	-.20	.00	-.07	-.44	.38	.65	-.25	-.20	.31	.23	.54	.38							
23. % Housing in Single Dwelling	-.13	-.13	-.11	-.14	.23	.06	.01	.00	.18	-.13	.02	-.07	.39	.41	.67	-.56	-.13	.63	.37	.34	.34	.03						
24. % Housing, Owner-occupied	.40	.40	.29	.06	.33	-.30	.00	.01	.13	-.09	.12	.05	.43	-.36	.65	-.59	.10	.70	.41	.29	.29	-.11	.82					
25. % Foreign-stock	.48	.46	.41	-.38	.06	-.05	.21	.15	-.15	.08	.18	-.10	.15	-.17	.67	.20	-.09	.63	.41	.29	.29	-.48	-.41	-.19				
26. % Foreign-born, Nat. Tongue Not English	-.18	-.19	.01	-.63	-.08	.09	.31	.26	.08	-.05	-.08	-.12	.06	-.12	.35	.00	.01	.10	.10	.29	.29	.03	.82	-.12	.39			
27. % Nonwhite	-.28	-.27	-.21	.06	-.15	.24	-.05	-.01	.00	.12	-.09	.06	.05	-.06	.15	.17	.12	.03	.16	.07	.07	-.11	-.41	-.32	-.19	-.07		
28. Pop. Size	.01	.02	.00	.42	.03	.16	-.18	-.09	.08	.06	.00	-.12	.18	-.12	-.20	.04	.12	-.03	-.04	-.07	-.07	.00	-.29	-.21	.20	-.06	.04	
29. Density	-.07	-.07	-.02	.15	.02	-.04	.04	.02	.00	.00	.06	.09	.18	-.20	-.24	.13	.00	-.23	-.07	-.23	-.23	-.08	-.16	-.22	.05	.06	.22	.05

most adults growing up in the United States will have had schooling at least through the tenth grade. The magnitude of the correlation suggests that the two measures are interchangeable for most purposes, an inference further strengthened by the similar pattern of correlation between each of these measures and the remaining 27 in the matrix.

The intercorrelations sort out the education, income, and occupation measures as a well-defined cluster. The percentage of white-collar workers correlates at absolute values equal to, or greater than, .54 with all income and education measures, an indication that the best paying jobs with high prestige tend to be filled by the better educated segment of the labor force.

Some indices, on the other hand, show small correlations with all the others. Of these, the most important are population size and density. Only two of the coefficients pairing population size with other variables exceed an absolute value of .20.[4] Population size correlates at —.29 with the percentage of all housing in single units, and at —.21 with the percentage of owner-occupied housing. In short, patterns of residential construction and ownership change only slightly as one goes from small to large suburbs. Also important is the lack of any correlation between population size and density; increasing population size does little to alter the ratio between man and land.

The share of housing stock built in the 1950s correlates substantially with a number of variables. This measure shows high positive correlations with both fertility ratio and youth, and high negative correlations with median and old age. Taken individually, each of these correlations is ambiguous. Seen together, they indicate that the suburbs experiencing the most ebullient growth contain a high proportion of young married people with small children. The tenuous correlations between housing growth in the 1950s and every income variable suggest that many of the new homes were built for people of moderate means. The .70 correlation between new housing and owner occupancy indicates that the new young suburbanites can at least afford the down payment on their new homes in the suburbs.[5]

---

[4] Conceivably the actual population figures could have been transformed into their logarithmic equivalents, to dampen the effects of averaging together percentages from very large and medium-size cities. Such transformations act to depress the overall correlation between two variables when the extreme values are correlated with one another, and to raise them when they are uncorrelated. Such log transformations were not used for two reasons. First, they had little effect in other studies. Second (and more important), the distribution of population size is not nearly as sharply skewed as it would have been if all American cities had been used in the analysis.

[5] William Michelson's analysis of a survey conducted by the University of Michigan's Survey Research Center shows that about 65% of the people living in metropolitan areas would prefer a private, single-family house if they had the opportunity. See

FACTOR ANALYSIS OF THE INTERCORRELATION MATRIX

Factor analysis is a statistical technique devised to winnow down a large set of primary variables into a much smaller set of "factors," or underlying dimensions to which the original set of primary variables is related. As shown in Chapters 1 and 2, factor analysis reassembles a large array of basic indicators into a few clusters of intercorrelated variables. Each cluster is considered as a separate factor. Then, to secure valuable economies in presentation, correlations *among* the basic variables can be expressed as correlations *between* each of the measures and the underlying factor that groups them together.

The first factor analysis of the 29×29 correlation matrix undertaken in this study was designed to produce an unrotated principal-components factor pattern. Such a pattern has two major properties. The first is that the factor axes are uncorrelated with one another. The second characteristic is that it summarizes as much variation as possible with the fewest factors.

The second step of the study was to rotate the factor axes to normal varimax position. Although the axes generated by a principal-components solution are always uncorrelated with one another, it sometimes occurs that many of the original variables load highly on more than one factor, making interpretation uncertain guesswork. Interpretation is easiest for a matrix where each variable loads significantly on only one factor, with zero loadings on all others. Such results are seldom if ever reached in actual work, but normal varimax rotation can be shown to approximate the situation as closely as possible.

The Principal-Components Analysis

Table 3 portrays the outcome of the analysis. Three-fifths of all the variation among the suburbs (as measured by the set of 29 primary variables) was summarized by four underlying factors, a significant reduction in complexity.[6] Of the four highest ranking factors, the first two are especially

"Most People Don't Want What the Architects Want," *Transaction,* Vol. 5 (July–August 1968), pp. 37–43.

[6] The variance associated with each factor is:

$$100 \times \frac{1}{N} \left(\sum_{j=1}^{N} \right) f_j^2$$

where f_j stands for the correlation of the jth primary variable with the fth factor and N is the total number of primary variables. It is clear from the formula that it is an average multiple-correlation coefficient between the designated factor and all primary variables.

important because they contain over three-fourths (77.9%) of the variation held in common by the four, and almost half (48.4%) of all the variance in the entire set of 29 primary variables.

A few communalities are worth noting. The factors do especially well in collecting the variability in the education and income measures. Only one communality falls below .800. The occupational variables are more diverse. For some the variance summarized by the four factors is considerable, but for others the communalities dwindle significantly, going down to .091 for the proportion of the labor force employed in retailing. The communalities for the age and growth groups also exhibit large differences, going all the way from .376 for the vacancy rate in nonrental housing to .875 for new housing constructed between 1950 and 1960.

Interpreting the Components

What sensible meaning can be assigned the factors? Factor 1 gathers the variables traditionally used to differentiate social classes, correlating positively with (a) years of schooling, (b) three measures associated with high income, (c) the percentage of the labor force in white-collar occupations, and (d) the percentage of the labor force employed in finance, insurance, and real estate (FIRE). It correlates negatively with poverty, as measured by (a) the proportion of families earning less than $3000 a year, (b) the percentage of the labor force employed in manufacturing, and (c) the percentage of the labor force unemployed. The first factor, then, may be viewed as a measure of *affluence*. It will carry this name throughout this chapter, although Berry labels it "socioeconomic status" in Chapter 1.

The second factor summarizes all the variables that signify rapid growth, presumably in new suburbs. Also of interest are the high vacancy rates, both for rental and owner-occupied housing. New suburbs are characterized by young married people starting off on their own, as indicated by the sizable negative correlations between this factor and median age, old age, and percentage of married couples without their own households. The contrast with the affluence factor is particularly sharp, for all the age variables change signs between factors 1 and 2. That the wives stay home and take care of the children is shown by (a) the high loadings associated with fertility and youth and (b) the negative correlation between factor 2 and the proportion of married women gainfully employed. This dimension of suburban life is completely dissociated from affluence; we call it the *recent-growth* factor. In Berry's terminology it represents a particular "stage in the life cycle."

VARIABLE	FACTOR				Communalities
	1	2	3	4	
Education Variables:					
1. Adults, median school years	.858	.322	-.147	-.061	.865
2. Adults, per cent completing high school	.891	.275	-.165	-.071	.902
Income Variables:					
3. Median annual family income	.857	.072	.193	-.156	.801
4. Per cent families earning less than $3,000	-.599	-.488	-.396	.164	.781
5. Per cent families earning more than $10,000	.924	-.056	-.148	-.115	.892
6. Median value owner-occupied housing	.865	.057	-.224	.058	.805
Occupational Variables:					
7. Per cent white-collar	.934	.027	-.268	.080	.951
8. Per cent in manufacturing	-.688	.120	.524	-.222	.811
9. Per cent in finance, insurance, and real estate	.790	-.121	-.038	-.029	.641
10. Per cent married women in labor force	.553	-.366	-.059	.078	.455
11. Per cent unemployed	-.574	.147	.519	-.183	.654
12. Per cent in retailing	-.071	-.026	-.280	.082	.091
Age Variables:					
13. Median age	.279	.859	.185	.065	.854
14. Fertility ratio	-.224	.818	-.144	-.069	.748
15. Per cent under 18	-.058	.884	-.062	-.319	.787
16. Per cent over 65	.023	.862	-.130	.200	.800
17. Per cent married without own household	-.310	.587	.093	-.117	.463
Growth Variables:					
18. Per cent housing built, 1950-1960	.221	.891	.054	-.171	.875
19. Per cent population growth, 1950-1960	.112	.667	-.009	-.018	.458
20. Vacancy rate: owner-occupied housing	.011	.568	-.224	-.058	.376
21. Vacancy rate: rental housing	-.276	.392	-.404	-.008	.393
22. Per cent moved in after 1958	-.058	.472	-.440	.417	.594
Amenities Variables:					
23. Per cent housing in single dwelling units	.193	.493	-.197	-.762	.900
24. Per cent housing owner-occupied	.320	.538	.063	-.728	.926
Ethnicity Variables:					
25. Per cent foreign stock	.026	-.326	.670	.157	.581
26. Per cent foreign-born, native tongue not English	-.166	-.120	.390	.053	.197
27. Per cent nonwhite	-.241	-.271	-.268	.079	.210
Physical Variables:					
28. Population size	.079	-.016	.085	.336	.127
29. Density	-.032	-.231	.005	.054	.184
Per cent all variance	25.6	22.8	7.4	6.2	= 62.0%
Per cent common variance	41.2	36.7	11.9	10.0	= 99.8%*

*Totals do not equal 100.0% because of rounding

105

Factor 3 is more difficult to interpret. The only variable with which it correlates substantially is the percentage of foreign stock, with employment in manufacturing and unemployment trailing not far behind. This configuration of variables probably indexes ethnically homogeneous suburban enclaves with a labor force employed in heavy industry. The difficulty is that as a primary measure the percentage of foreign stock does not exhibit very much discriminatory potential, and this is why interpretation is not easy. However, factor 3 accounts for only 7.4% of the variability in the set of primary indices and hence is not of major importance as a summary index.

Factor 4 is easier to interpret. Both the percentage of housing in single-family units and the percentage of owner-occupied housing have high negative correlations with this factor; in fact, over half the variance in each of these measures is absorbed by it. Of the 12 suburbs with the highest rankings on this factor, 11 are located in the "inner ring" of Metropolitan New York Region (the twelfth is Central Falls, Rhode Island). Because these suburbs filled up long ago, land is scarce in relation to the population, and much of the resident population is housed in rental apartment buildings.[7]

Oblique Rotation

Principal-components analysis will always produce factors that are orthogonal to one another. If the factors are actually correlated, the principal-components resolution may arbitrarily make it appear that there are independent factors where none exists. To check this possibility an oblique rotation was designed to detect the presence of correlated factors. The results are shown in Table 4, with coefficients greater than ±.055 being emphasized.

The results were much the same as in the varimax case. Although the oblique rotation slightly changes the magnitude of the loadings on the affluence factor, both solutions rank the variables in the same order of importance. For the recent-growth factor the oblique rotation alters the rankings, but not by very much. Table 5 gives the correlation among the four factors obtained by the oblique rotation. There is virtually no correlation between the two dominant factors, and very little between each of them and the other two. The a priori assumption of statistical independence clearly was appropriate. The factors do represent distinct dimensions of intersuburb variability.

[7] For details see Edgar M. Hoover and Raymond Vernon, *Anatomy of a Metropolis* (New York: Anchor Books, 1962), p. 154.

Table 4. Oblique factor matrix

VARIABLE	FACTOR			
	1	2	3	4
Education Variables:				
1. Adults, median school years	.856	.219	-.201	-.083
2. Adults, per cent completing high school	.886	.164	-.225	-.102
Income Variables:				
3. Median annual family income	.850	.011	.134	-.140
4. Per cent families earning less than $3,000	-.609	-.495	-.385	.066
5. Per cent families earning more than $10,000	.915	-.128	.079	-.119
6. Median value owner-occupied housing	.884	.045	.217	.129
Occupational Variables:				
7. Per cent white-collar	.931	-.068	-.136	-.049
8. Per cent in manufacturing	-.691	.244	.584	-.105
9. Per cent in finance, insurance, and real estate	.790	-.180	-.018	.008
10. Per cent married women in labor force	.549	-.421	-.112	.023
11. Per cent unemployed	-.572	.267	.576	.065
12. Per cent in retailing	-.090	-.084	-.296	-.140
Age Variables:				
13. Median age	.267	-.859	.136	.020
14. Fertility ratio	-.212	.819	-.099	-.020
15. Per cent under 18	-.067	.848	-.042	-.264
16. Per cent over 65	.015	-.877	-.165	.106
17. Per cent married without own household	-.336	-.574	.079	-.149
Growth Variables:				
18. Per cent housing built, 1950-1960	.231	.876	.073	-.094
19. Per cent population growth, 1950-1960	.130	.668	.015	.037
20. Vacancy rate: owner-occupied housing	.026	.547	-.201	.069
21. Vacancy rate: rental housing	-.278	.349	-.385	-.044
22. Per cent moved in after 1958	-.015	.471	-.399	.393
Amenities Variables:				
23. Per cent housing in single dwelling units	.122	.334	-.257	-.793
24. Per cent housing owner-occupied	.263	.422	.012	-.707
Ethnicity Variables:				
25. Per cent foreign stock	.055	-.189	.696	.262
26. Per cent foreign-born, native tongue not English	-.151	-.029	.418	.123
27. Per cent nonwhite	-.012	-.013	-.038	-.003
Physical Variables:				
28. Population size	.116	.043	.110	.362
29. Density	-.033	-.224	.000	.037
Per cent all variance	25.5	21.4	8.0	5.1 = 60.0%
Per cent common variance	42.6	35.7	13.4	8.5 = 100.2%*

*Totals do not equal 100.0% due to rounding

Table 5. Correlation coefficients among the four principal factors*

FACTORS	1	2	3	4
1		-.0489	-.0373	.1042
2	.0024		-.1796	-.2127
3	.0013	.0323		-.2146
4	.0109	.0452	.0461	

*The coefficients listed above the diagonal are zero-order product-moment correlations. Below the major diagonal are the squared r's, often called coefficients of determination. Coefficients of determination give the proportion of variance shared in common by any given pair of factors.

107

SUBURBAN VOTING: 1956–1964

Are these factors helpful in explaining differences in recent electoral performance in the suburbs? This is the question that must now be answered.

Two Election Series

Two separate series of elections are examined. One is the string of three consecutive presidential elections spanning the years from 1956 to 1964. In 1956 Dwight D. Eisenhower defeated Adlai E. Stevenson with an impressive nationwide majority, capturing many normally Democratic states. The election of 1960 is the midpoint of the series, both chronologically and in a broader political sense. In that year John F. Kennedy barely defeated Richard M. Nixon. The first two elections thus depict a Republican avalanche and a razor-thin Democratic victory. In 1964 Lyndon B. Johnson trounced Barry M. Goldwater as decisively as Eisenhower had defeated Stevenson 8 years before. He also captured many states traditionally regarded as opposition strongholds. The third election is therefore the mirror image of the first. This trio of presidential elections thus exhibits as much heterogeneity as one can achieve outside the confines of the small group laboratory where the experimenter can manipulate his design to attain the heterogeneity he desires.[8]

The other series consists of three consecutive congressional elections held between 1958 and 1962. Two of the three congressional elections were held in off years, and the other was held concurrently with the presidential election of 1960, presenting another useful opportunity to contrast elections occurring *within* the same series.

Affluence and the Presidential Vote: 1956–1964

A first step is to analyze whether the Republican or the Democratic candidate won an absolute majority of all votes cast. Relevant data can be seen in Table 6.

As in the nation, so there was in the suburbs a precipitous decline in the

---

[8] As David Gold has shown, students of elections often succumb to the fallacy of selection. The fallacy lies in the (often tacit) assumption that the single election being studied is "characteristic" of all. See "Some Problems in Generalizing Aggregate Associations," *The American Behavioral Scientist,* Vol. 8 (December 1964), pp. 16–18.

Table 6.   Suburbs and electoral majorities in presidential elections: 1956–1964

Election Years	56	60	64	56	60	64	56	60	64	56	60	64
Majority Party:	D	D	D	R	D	D	R	R	D	R	R	R
		70			141			160			36	

fortunes of the Republican party. In 1956 Eisenhower had electoral majorities in all but 70 of the 407 suburbs.[9] In 1960, 141 suburbs abandoned the Republican party to vote for Kennedy, leaving Nixon with fewer than half the total. The attrition between 1960 and 1964 was even more pronounced. Of the 196 suburbs casting majorities for Nixon in 1960, only 36 remained faithful to the Republican party 4 years later.

The steepness of the gradient can be seen by comparing Republican percentages at the beginning and at the end of the series. Where the republicans had conquered 83% of the 407 suburbs in 1956, by 1964 Goldwater was able to obtain electoral majorities in only 8%.

What social characteristics differentiate among the four types of suburbs divided according to their electoral behavior? The data bearing on this question appear in Table 7.

The more affluent suburbs voted Republican in all three presidential elections. At the other extreme, the least prosperous never deserted the Democratic party. Of the groups that alternated between the parties, the 141 suburbs that went Democratic in both 1960 and 1964 were somewhat less prosperous than the 160 that voted Democratic only in 1964.

Table 7 presents the means for the variables composing the affluence factor as well as the affluence-factor scores. The paths that the means describe all tilt in the expected direction, ascending across the columns for the two education measures, and for the income and occupation indices associated with increasing prosperity. The steadfast Democratic suburbs have the highest means on measures of unemployment and poverty. Beginning with the first column, the averages taper off steadily until the bottom is reached in the 36 uniformly Republican suburbs.

---

[9] After this election scholars and journalists alike rushed into print with fanciful explanations of how "suburban social pressures" finally converted migrating Democrats into Republicans. Those displeased by the fragility of some of the assumptions underlying this explanation rejected it. Far from being converted, they said, the people settling in the suburbs were Republican to begin with. In addition to the blunders painstakingly cataloged by Gold in his anatomy of errors, the Republican share of the big-city vote increased from 1948 to 1952, and again from 1952 to 1956. This fact was ignored in fashioning both explanations and tends to confound them.

Table 7. Affluence and the suburban Republican vote in presidential elections: 1956–1964*

	ELECTORAL PATTERN: 1956–1964				
	DDD (n=70)	RDD (n=141)	RRD (n=160)	RRR (n=36)	Suburban Mean (n=407)
Mean Affluence Factor Scores	-0.798	-0.345	+0.325	+1.308	+0.000
Education Variables:					
1. Adults, median school years	10.5	11.0	11.8	12.6	11.4
2. Adults, per cent completing high school	39.6	44.2	53.4	67.2	49.2
Income Variables:					
3. Median annual family income	$6,372	$6,769	$7,745	$9,762	$7,369
4. Per cent families earning less than $3,000	12.1	9.6	8.5	7.2	9.3
5. Per cent families earning more than $10,000	15.2	19.1	27.9	44.7	24.3
6. Median value of owner-occupied housing	$12,336	$14,361	$17,250	$22,242	$15,912
Occupation Variables:.					
7. Per cent white-collar	38.9	44.4	54.1	67.4	49.4
8. Per cent in manufacturing	42.8	40.0	32.9	28.6	36.5
9. Per cent in FIRE	3	4	6	8	5
10. Per cent married women in labor force	21.1	29.0	34.2	35.5	30.3
11. Per cent unemployed	4.1	3.9	3.3	3.3	3.6

*All figures are means
The highest value in each row has been underlined

Affluence and the Congressional Vote: 1958–1962

For the biennial congressional elections the array of alternatives confronting citizens varies with the district in which the election is held. For this reason there has not been any attempt to isolate distinct patterns of alternation, as with the presidential series. Rather, the number of times Republican candidates for Congress received electoral majorities has been noted, suburb by suburb. The results are shown in Table 8.

The congressional subset is not a random sample of the 407 suburbs. Because of the limitations inherent in the data, certain states are sharply overrepresented and other states are not represented at all. Indeed, as the last column in Table 8 shows, the congressional subset comprises a somewhat more prosperous portion of the entire collection of suburbs.

However, the general pattern of presidential elections holds for congres-

Table 8.   Affluence and the suburban vote for Republican congressmen: 1958–1962*

NUMBER OF REPUBLICAN VICTORIES	0 (n=58)	1 (n=19)	2 (n=17)	3 (n=72)	Suburban Mean (n=166)
Mean Affluence Factor Score	-0.451	+0.189	+0.299	<u>+0.706</u>	+0.168
Education Variables:					
1. Adults, median school years	10.6	11.5	11.4	<u>12.0</u>	11.4
2. Adults, per cent completing high school	40.9	50.7	48.6	<u>57.3</u>	49.9
Income Variables					
3. Median annual family income	$6,748	$7,620	$7,664	<u>$8,523</u>	$7,711
4. Per cent families earning less than $3,000	<u>9.2</u>	6.8	7.7	7.3	7.9
5. Per cent families earning more than $10,000	17.6	25.6	27.8	<u>34.3</u>	26.8
6. Median value of owner-occupied housing	$12,356	$14,647	$15,336	<u>$17,960</u>	$17,087
Occupation Variables:					
7. Per cent white-collar	42.6	50.5	52.6	<u>58.7</u>	51.5
8. Per cent in manufacturing	<u>39.7</u>	34.9	32.9	31.2	34.8
9. Per cent in FIRE	5	5	<u>7</u>	<u>7</u>	6
10. Per cent married women women in labor force	25.5	32.3	<u>34.1</u>	34.0	30.8
11. Per cent unemployed	3.9	3.5	3.3	3.1	3.4

*All figures are means
The highest value in each row has been underlined

sional ones as well. The Republicans fared best in the most affluent suburbs, and the Democrats in the least affluent. As before, the overall affluence-factor scores increase as one goes from the least to the most Republican group. Also, the highest average values for all the constituent variables appear in either the completely Democratic or the completely Republican suburbs. The distinctions noted between the extreme groups are somewhat muted for the collection of 36 suburbs that wavered between the two parties. The predominantly Republican suburbs were slightly more wealthy than the suburbs that went Democratic in two elections of three, but they contained a slightly smaller portion of high-school graduates.

The Recent-Growth Factor and the Presidential Vote: 1956–1964

The recent-growth factor scores presented in Table 9 show that the uniformly Democratic suburbs had a higher score than the suburbs that

Table 9.   Recent growth and the suburban Republican vote in presidential elections: 1956–1964*

Electoral Pattern: 1956-1964

	DDD (n=70)	RDD (n=141)	RRD (n=160)	RRR (n=36)	Suburban Mean (n=407)
Mean Factor 2 Score	+.308	-.052	-.093	-.039	+0.000
Age Variables:					
1. Median age	29.0	31.5	32.3	33.5	31.6
2. Fertility ratio	510.2	473.6	452.4	416.4	466.9
3. Per cent under 18	37.4	35.0	34.4	35.2	35.2
4. Per cent over 65	7.4	8.8	9.2	9.2	8.7
5. Per cent married without own household	2.5	2.3	2.2	1.6	2.2
Growth Variables:					
6. Per cent housing: 1950-1960	34.4	28.7	31.5	38.9	31.9
7. Per cent population increase: 1950-1960	66.2	44.4	53.3	72.4	54.3
8. Vacancy rate: owner-occupied housing	1.2	1.1	1.2	1.4	1.2

*All figures are means
 The highest value in each row has been underlined

consistently supported the Republican party. One reaction is that both affluence and recent-growth factors sort out the suburbs in about the same way. A closer examination belies this hasty inference.

In the first place, the range of the affluence (factor 1) scores is considerably greater than the spread of the recent-growth (factor 2) scores. On the affluence factor an absolute difference of 2.106 divided the homogeneously Republican suburbs from the uniformly Democratic ones. This figure is much greater than the corresponding difference of 0.617 on factor 2, a sign that the prosperity of a suburb provides a more reliable clue to its voting behavior than the age of its population or the rate of its growth. The distribution of the affluence scores (Table 8) shows that the low socioeconomic profiles of the least prosperous suburbs have weighted down the means in the first two columns of the table and that the high profiles of the more prosperous have boosted them in the third and fourth columns. The distribution of the recent-growth component is more even, as can be further seen in the very small differences in the factor 2 scores appearing in the second, third, and fourth columns of Table 9.

The recent-growth factor compresses both age and growth variables into a single unified dimension. A high score on this factor signifies a quickly growing suburb with a predominantly young population; a low score, a stable community with many elderly people and relatively few children.

Suburbs with scores near zero may be slowly growing communities with young populations or, what seems more likely, mature, settled suburbs that have been invaded by people with young children.[10] Table 9 shows that suburbs with a younger age distribution are uniformly or predominantly Democratic. They have a lower median age, a higher fertility ratio, more children, and fewer aged.

The Recent-Growth Factor and the Congressional Vote: 1958–1962

As Table 10 shows, the mean growth–youth score for the congressional subset was closer to the average for all the suburbs than was the corresponding affluence score. Once more, the Republican suburbs have a higher median age, a smaller proportion of children, and a larger fraction of adults

Table 10.   Recent growth and the suburban vote for Republican congressmen: 1958–1962*

NUMBER OF REPUBLICAN VICTORIES	0 (n=58)	1 (n=19)	2 (n=17)	3 (n=72)	Suburban Mean (n=166)
Mean Factor 2 Score	+0.211	+0.369	-0.201	-0.880	+.063
Age Variables:					
1. Median age	30.3	29.8	33.3	32.8	31.6
2. Fertility ratio	480.7	506.5	419.1	433.0	456.7
3. Per cent under 18	35.6	36.5	34.1	34.5	35.1
4. Per cent over 65	7.8	7.2	8.8	8.8	8.3
5. Per cent married without own household	2.2	2.1	2.4	2.1	2.2
Growth Variables:					
6. Per cent housing: 1950-1960	35.1	39.0	33.5	34.9	35.3
7. Per cent population growth: 1950-1960	66.8	79.8	62.3	58.2	64.0
8. Vacancy rate: owner-occupied housing	1.2	1.1	1.2	1.1	1.1

*All figures are means
The highest value in each row has been underlined

[10] William T. Dobriner has called these "reluctant" suburbs. See his *Class in Suburbia* (Englewood Cliffs, N.J.: Prentice-Hall, Inc., 1963), pp. 127–140. Small, quiet communities are invaded by young families with children. In the early stages of new growth the rates of population and housing expansion are rapid because the community is small to begin with, and the high average age of the old-timers, few of whom have children present in the home, helps keep the median age high for the entire community. In later stages the increasing numbers of *arrivistes* pulls down the median age and sharply increases the proportion of people under 18.

than the Democratic ones. This time, however, it is the Democratic suburbs that grew faster in the decade between 1950 and 1960. The means for both housing and population growth are highest of all for the predominantly Democratic suburbs and next highest for the 58 suburbs that never gave the Republicans a majority in a single congressional election.

EVALUATION: THE UTILITY OF THE AGGREGATE ANALYSIS

The aggregated voting returns we have used so far are but one set of the materials that might be explored in understanding voting behavior. Aggregate data are useful for several reasons. They are more readily available than opinion surveys for broad segments of the entire population, cheaper to secure, and easier to manipulate over a lengthy series of elections. Also, they are the *only* source of data for elections before surveys came on the scene.

As data, however, they do present problems. Because of honest mistakes or outright fraud, the reported vote may not be exact. Since precincts and census tracts rarely match, larger units of aggregation often have to be used than is statistically desirable. Voting data tell little about how individual voters performed their most important civic responsibility or why they voted the way they did. To explain the behavior of individuals, surveys are the more appropriate instrument.

Despite these deficiencies, aggregate analysis has its uses. It permits generalizations about the behavior of electorates over time, from homogeneous units as small as an individual precinct to those as heterogeneous as the entire nation. Where aggregate data and surveys corroborate one another, they can be used together to remedy the deficiencies of each taken alone. Aggregate analysis permits location of spectacular deviant cases from broad generalizations, and surveys help explain the deviancy.[11] Furthermore, aggregate studies through time are reasonable facsimiles of more expensive panel survey studies, which follow a sample of individuals through numerous elections. With panel studies, the sample is really not always the same, election to election. Among other problems, some people move, the old die, the adolescents become voters, and some blue-collar workers achieve white-collar status. The people in the sample are the same, but the composition of

[11] Seymour M. Lipset, *Union Democracy* (Glencoe, Ill.: Free Press, 1956), illustrates the relationship.

the sample changes as the social characteristics of the people change. Despite their other weaknesses, aggregate data present no such problems.[12]

These two instruments and the data they generate, then, may well be mutually corroborative. To illustrate, Tables 6 through 10 suggest a close relationship between affluence and voting among a sizable number of suburbs. That relationship has also been attested to in almost all studies of individual behavior that rely on surveys.[13] Without reviewing the findings, it is sufficient to show that conclusions about whole communities coincide and therefore reinforce those of studies based on individual behavior.

A further feature of aggregate electoral analysis should be noted. Survey data are bound to a given time and place, telling how the voters, but not electoral units, reacted. The degree to which these findings can be retrojected to explain the past—or even projected into the future—is quite limited. It is possible to use polls over a period of time, but consistent use of the same question form is not common, making longitudinal analysis very hazardous.[14]

The use of voting returns does provide such data, most importantly in the form of a population of elections, either in a given year or over a number of years. Key was correct in saying that, despite the considerable insight provided political science by survey data, "if the specialist in electoral behavior is to be a student of politics, his major concern must be the population of individual voters. One does not gain an understanding of elections by the

---

[12] Robert C. Tryon has shown for San Francisco that its precinct–census tract components, when carefully matched, showed remarkably little change from 1940 to 1950, either electorally or socially. This stability seems to be much greater than that encountered in typical panel surveys. See Robert C. Tryon, "Predicting Group Differences in Cluster Analysis: The Social Area Problem," *Multivariate Behavioral Research,* Vol. 2 (1967), pp. 453–475. Fuller treatment is given by Robert C. Tryon and D. E. Bailey in *Cluster and Factor Analysis* (New York: McGraw-Hill Book Co., 1970).

[13] Angus Campbell et al., *The American Voter* (New York: John Wiley & Sons, Inc., 1960); Heinz Eulau, *Class and Party in the Eisenhower Years* (New York: Free Press, 1962); Robert Alford, *Party and Society* (Chicago: Rand McNally and Co., 1963); Angus Campbell et al., *Elections and the Political Order* (New York: John Wiley & Sons, Inc., 1966), Part 1. However, none of these scholars is a strict social determinist, as they all point to forces that mediate between status and voting under specified circumstances.

[14] Examination of the inventory of surveys on a given topic, found in the *Public Opinion Quarterly,* will show how question wording shifts in a fashion that raises serious questions about the comparability of findings. However, the Survey Research Center of the University of Michigan has been quite consistent in question wording on partisan affiliation. See Campbell et al., *The American Voter.*

simple cumulation of the type findings from the microscopic analysis of the individuals in the system."[15]

The need to deal with a population of elections, and not a single contest, should be emphasized. Without it there is no way of knowing whether any single election is "characteristic" of the system under study. Despite such a narrow focus, analysts of the single election too often seek to generalize to a larger population as if the current election were a carefully drawn sample— when it is only a convenient one.[16]

Presumed associations between the voting outcome and some purported set of causal factors based on such a narrow base are highly suspect. The 1956 Eisenhower landslide in the suburbs caused many commentators to conclude that the suburbs were converting to the Republican party. Yet closer analysis revealed that all kinds of electorates besides suburbs were voting for Eisenhower by larger margins than they had in 1952 and that Republicans running for other offices were not receiving the benefits of this alleged switch. Furthermore, longitudinal studies showed that even the increased presidential vote for Republicans was far from permanent, either nationally or in the suburbs—as witness 1960 and 1964.[17]

A further indication of the unrepresentative nature of a single election is found in the fact that each contest is subject to short-run impacts. An issue, a personality, or an event moves some segments of the electorate, often on reciprocal courses, in each election. The affection that Eisenhower attracted from voters was not a constant that could be transferred to Nixon in later elections. More dramatically, the issues that moved voters in 1964 were quite different 4 years later in one of the most abrupt reversals of electoral opinion in our history. Single elections, then, are poor indicators of the total political system over time.[18] One election may in fact be highly critical in reversing long-run party fortunes, but longitudinal data from a population of elections are still necessary to determine whether the election was critical.[19]

[15] V. O. Key, Jr., "The Politically Relevant in Surveys," *Public Opinion Quarterly,* Vol. 24 (1960), pp. 54–61.

[16] For an elaboration of the statistical errors involved see Gold, "Generalizing Aggregate Associations."

[17] A fuller analysis of this phenomenon is found in Wirt, "Political Sociology of Suburbia."

[18] Donald Stokes, "Party Loyalty and the Likelihood of Deviating Elections," *Journal of Politics,* Vol. 24 (1962), pp. 689–702, and Angus Campbell, "Voters and Elections, Past and Present," *Journal of Politics,* Vol. 26 (1964), pp. 745–757.

[19] The point is made emphatically by V. O. Key, Jr., in "A Theory of Critical Elections," *Journal of Politics,* Vol. 17 (1955), pp. 3–18. See also Charles Sellers, "The Equilibrium Cycle in Two-Party Politics," *Public Opinion Quarterly,* Vol. 29 (1965), pp. 16–38.

LIMITATIONS OF TRADITIONAL CORRELATION ANALYSIS

The degree of association between the social and political aspects of electoral units has traditionally been measured by the use of correlational techniques. The logic of these techniques permits the evaluation of the relative importance of several independent variables in accounting for the dependent variable. Thus one might wish to judge whether occupation or education is more important in explaining the suburban Republican vote. Typically one tries to control for the effects of one while measuring the relationship of the other to the dependent variable.

Yet a basic flaw arises in such an analysis when variables purportedly independent of one another are actually related. The technical name for this problem is "multicollinearity." Its presence is detected when the variables assumed to be "independent" actually show high correlations among themselves. When this condition exists, partial correlation measures yield misleading coefficients.[20] To illustrate, take the 1960 Republican presidential percentage of the vote in our 407 suburbs as the dependent variable and as explanatory variables the percentage of white-collar workers, housing value, and the percentage of high school graduates. Inspection of the correlation matrix in Table 2 shows that all three variables are highly intercorrelated, with coefficients ranging from .72 to .88. Table 11 displays the partials. Both occupation and education show a modest relationship with the vote when the housing value is controlled, implying that the first two should correlate highly when one or the other is controlled. But the fact is that neither occupation nor education shows any relationship when the other is controlled; both partial correlations shrink sharply when the other is controlled.

FACTORS AS SOLUTIONS TO MULTICOLLINEARITY

When one is faced by multicollinearity, there is merit in using whole factors as independent variables. A factor is a weighted aggregate of partial correlations among primary variables. The intercorrelations among these variables have already been taken into account in extracting the factor. As Cattell has explained:

In partial correlation it is our aim to eliminate the effect of one (or more) contributory influences to a correlation to see how much remains due to the

[20] For one study of the unsuspected consequences of multicollinearity see Hugh D. Forbes and Edward R. Tufte, "A Note of Caution in Causal Modelling," *American Political Science Review*, Vol. 62 (1968), pp. 1262–1264.

Table 11. Partial coefficients of the Republican percentage in the 1960 presidential election

Variables Correlated	Simple Coefficient	Variable(s) Controlled	Partial Coefficient
Vote-WC	.56	VOCC	.42
Vote-HS 4	.53	VOCC	.36
Vote-VOCC	.42	WC	+.00
Vote-HS 4	.53	WC	-.09
Vote-WC	.56	HS 4	.02
Vote-VOCC	.42	HS 4	.06
Vote-WC	.56	VOCC-HS 4	.23
Vote-VOCC	.42	WC-HS 4	+.00
Vote-HS 4	.53	VOCC-WC	.09

NOTE: The names of variables are abbreviated as follows: WC—percentage of white-collar employees; HS 4—high school graduates; VOCC—median value of owner-occupied home.

influence which most interests us. . . . Factor analysis achieves the same end as partial correlation [in that it] gives the correlation of a particular performance separately with *each* of a number of factors when the others are held constant. It differs from partial correlation in that this procedure holds whole *factors* constant where the former holds *variables* constant.[21]

Any problem of multicollinearity among the factors has been eliminated by orthogonalizing the original set of factors, so that the resultant factors are independent. Even when obliquely rotated, the major factors of affluence and recent growth, for example, correlate at —.05 with an R^2 of about .0024, close enough to zero to constitute independence. Used as independent variables, whole factors avoid the pitfall of multicollinearity and also possess the advantage of automatically collecting a group of primary variables so closely related that their relative independent effect cannot possibly be estimated.

Table 12 relates the factors to the variance in the percentage of Republican votes. Only factor 1, affluence, shows any association with the variation in the Republican vote over six elections; the degree of correlation is quite consistent. Factors 2, 3, and 4, on the other hand, though discriminating among suburbs in a sociological sense, are virtually meaningless in differentiating among voting patterns.

[21] Raymond B. Cattell, *Factor Analysis* (New York: Harper, 1952), p. 18.

Table 12.   Partial coefficients of factor scores with the suburban Republican vote

Factors	Presidential			Congressional		
	1956	1960	1964	1958	1960	1962
1	.53	.54	.42	.50	.51	.52
2	.15	.12	.04	.16	.21	.16
3	-.03	.26	.14	.18	.26	.16
4	-.02	.20	.19	.09	.12	.25
R^2	.29	.34	.22	.32	.36	.39

NOTES: The factor score here refers to affluence.

Data on ethnic groups are from census reports. Yiddish measure from tables on the mother tongue of foreign-born population. Other ethnic measures from tables on the country of origin of foreign stock. Slavic origin here refers to persons of Polish, Czechoslovakian, and Yugoslavian descent.

It is the affluence factor, then, that best relates social and electoral patterns. The relative closeness of that relationship may be indicated in ways other than the partial coefficient. Some graphic sense is provided by Figure 1, which plots the position of each of the 407 suburbs on two measures, the mean Republican percentage of the vote in the three presidential elections combined and the affluence-factor score. Each suburb is assigned a factor score whose weightings are a function of that suburb's position on the variables constituting the factor. If the correlation were perfect, all would lie on the least squares regression line. Instead, there is a clustering around that diagonal. Many of the suburbs hug the line, but some are spread further away. The central tendency is that increasing Republicanism accompanies increases in the affluence score.

OTHER EXPLANATIONS OF ELECTORAL BEHAVIOR

Yet this relationship leaves much to be explained. Referring again to Table 12, and considering the wide range of variables measuring the diversity of the 407 suburbs in 1960, the explained variance is surprisingly low. Although it is true that affluence is the most impressive explanatory variable of all, in no election is more than 39% of the variance explained. In some cases it runs much lower, as in the 22% in the 1964 presidential contest. By itself, the affluence factor accounts for only 18 to 29% of the variance in the vote.

Similar evidence of the failure of the affluence factor to explain as much as one might think may be seen in Figure 1. Note the dots furthest removed from the general cluster. These are of two kinds. Those in the upper left-

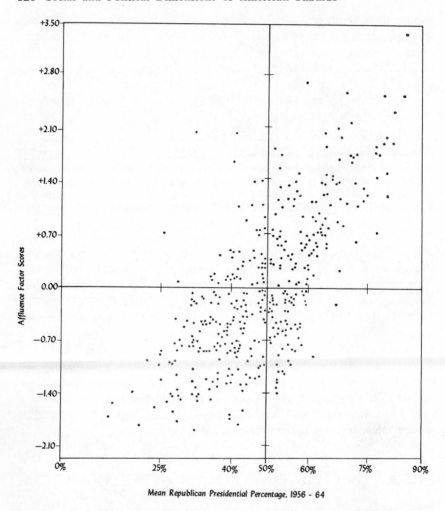

Figure 1   Scattergram plotting affluence scores against the mean Republican vote in three presidential elections, 1956–1964.

hand quadrant are more Democratic than their high factor scores would predict, whereas those in the lower right-hand quadrant are more Republican. These deviating cases can tell us something about society.

One hypothesis that might explain their deviation relates to ethnicity. Political scientists have recently rediscovered the power of ethnic or cultural ties, despite the popular belief that the melting pot homogenizes emigrants into "average" Americans.[22] The ethnic variables in the factor analysis conceal too much to be of much value.[23] To determine whether different ethnic complexions of these deviant suburbs are associated with different electoral behaviors, it is necessary to examine ethnicity in greater detail.

The five most incongruent suburbs in the upper left-hand quadrant provide a chance to test this proposition. The major ethnic subgroups are shown for these municipalities in 1970 in Table 13. Several inferences may be drawn. The Jewish vote, as other research has consistently reported, tends to be Democratic, and where there are many suburban Jews, there

Table 13.   Characteristics of most incongruent and Italian suburbs

Suburb	Factor Score	Pres. % Rep.	Origin				
			[Yiddish	Slav.	Ital.	Germ.	Ire.]
University Heights, Ore.	2.07	33	31	21	4	5	1
Brookline, Mass.	1.69	42	21	7	2	4	13
South Euclid, Ore.	1.10	43	24	22	19	9	2
Long Beach, N.Y.	.74	26	20	15	7	5	6
South San Francisco, Cal.	.09	29	--	3	30	7	5
Barrington, R.I.	.58	55	--	2	36	4	5
South San Francisco, Cal.	.09	29	--	3	30	7	5
Norristown, Pa.	-1.08	44	1	7	54	6	9
Bristol, R.I.	-1.41	31	--	10	26	1	4
Aliquippa, Pa.	-1.65	28	1	37	34	3	1

[22] The most publicized and emphatic statement of the potency of ethnicity in political behavior, focusing on New York City, is that of Nathan Glazer and Daniel P. Moynihan, *Beyond the Melting Pot* (Cambridge: M.I.T. Press and Harvard University Press, 1963). A technical survey of specialized research on this theme is found in Lawrence H. Fuchs, Ed., *American Ethnic Politics* (New York: Harper Torchbooks, 1968). A close view of the Jewish vote is found in Lawrence H. Fuchs, *The Political Behavior of American Jews* (Glencoe, Ill.: Free Press, 1956), and Milton Himmelfarb, "Is American Jewry in Crisis?" *Commentary,* March 1969, pp. 33–42. See also Raymond E. Wolfinger, "The Development and Persistence of Ethnic Voting," *American Political Science Review,* Vol. 59 (1965), pp. 896–908, and "Some Consequences of Ethnic Politics," in Harmon Zeigler and Kent Jennings, Eds., *The Electoral Process* (Englewood Cliffs, N.J.: Prentice-Hall, Inc., 1966); James Q. Wilson and Edward C. Banfield, "Public-Regardingness as a Value Premise in Voting Behavior," *American Political Science Review,* Vol. 58 (1964), pp. 882–887; Lucy C. Davidowicz and Leon T. Goldstein, *Politics in a Pluralist Democracy* (New York: Institute of Human Relations Press, 1963).

[23] The chief census measure is percentage of foreign stock. Its major weakness is its failure to discriminate among different countries of origin.

is also a large Democratic vote. As a measure of the proportion of Jews in a given suburb, the percentage of people speaking Yiddish is used; this clearly understates the number of Jews. Although there is no single country of origin common to all Jews, a significant proportion came from Slavic countries, primarily Russia and the old Austro-Hungarian Empire. However loose the index, the percentage speaking Yiddish sharply sets off the four suburbs that deviate most markedly from the relationship in Figure 1; although their affluence scores are high, the percentage voting Republican is low. Thus the congruency between a suburb's affluence and Republicanism does not operate when the Jewish population is substantial. But in the first four suburbs the relationship is not totally linear; Brookline and Long Beach have similar proportions speaking Yiddish, but there are many more Republican voters in the former than the latter, just as the former has a higher affluence factor score than the latter. This suggests that with a larger sample, analysts might try to determine whether, when the Jewish proportion is held constant, increasing affluence accompanies increasing Republicanism.

The data for South San Francisco suggest that its incongruity stems from its high proportion of Italians. However, when it is compared with four other suburbs with relatively large proportions of this ethnic group, as in the lower portion of Table 13, the inference appears to be less certain. The contrast between Barrington and Aliquippa in affluence and Republicanism is totally unrelated to their common Italian proportion. The anomalous position of South San Francisco stems from another ethnic consideration. It contains rather large minorities of Spanish-speaking and Chinese populations, groups with a strongly Democratic orientation. The presence of Italians, Mexicans, and Chinese outside the ethnic enclaves of San Francisco suggests they have done well enough to get out of the city but have retained their Democratic affiliation.

Of course ethnicity does not exhaust alternatives to status in explaining voting patterns. Concern has recently developed among some political scientists about the power of regionalism to create distinctive beliefs, political or otherwise, which override the influence of status. Suggestive of this possibility is southern polarization over race, which lumps together poor and rich alike in their voting. At least one analysis demonstrates not merely the existence of regional differences in a host of moral, political, and economic ideas but also the possibility that the differences are diverging even more in recent years.[24]

[24] The last study is found in Norval D. Glenn and J. L. Simmons, "Are Regional Cultural Differences Diminishing?" *Public Opinion Quarterly,* Vol. 31 (1967), pp. 176–193. For differences in politics, cf. Samuel C. Patterson, "The Political

The foregoing are suggestions stemming from the major finding of this chapter—namely, that, despite the use of the powerfully inclusive device of factor analysis, the qualities usually subsumed under the heading of status, or affluence, explain only a part of the variance in suburban electoral behavior. That income, education, and occupation imprint social and political life there is no doubt. But there is much doubt that these marks alone provide a sufficient portrait of the nexus between the social and the political life of American citizens.[25]

Cultures of the American States," *Journal of Politics*, Vol. 30 (1968), pp. 187–209; Bernard Cosman, *Five States for Goldwater* (University, Ala.: University of Alabama Press, 1966). Daniel J. Elazar has given much emphasis to the ignored role of regionalism, e.g., in *American Federalism: A View from the States* (New York: Cromwell, 1966). Differences in the structural characteristics of American cities (including measures appearing in our factors) have been detailed by Leo F. Schnore in *The Urban Scene* (New York: Free Press, 1965), *passim;* the political significances of such interurban differences are revealed in Joseph Zikmund, "A Comparison of Political Attitudes and Activity Patterns in Central Cities and Suburbs," *Public Opinion Quarterly*, Vol. 31 (1967), pp. 69–75.

[25] Gerhard Lenski, in *The Religious Factor* (Garden City, N.Y.: Doubleday, Anchor Books, 1961), argues that there is evidence that religious differences muffle those of status; cf. also Morris Janowitz and David R. Segal, "Social Cleavage and Party Affiliation: Germany, Great Britain and the United States," *American Journal of Sociology*, Vol. 72 (1967), pp. 601–619.

CHAPTER 4

Functional Classification and the Residential Location of Social Classes

LEO F. SCHNORE
HAL H. WINSBOROUGH

University of Wisconsin at Madison

Functional classification schemes have been developed and applied to American cities for over 30 years. The first such effort was that of William F. Ogburn in a 1937 pioneering study[1] sponsored by the International City Managers' Association (ICMA).[2] The latter group has continued to support this line of work and has published five related functional classifications over the years, those by Kneedler[3] in 1945, Jones[4] in 1953, Jones and Collver[5] in 1960, Jones, Collver, and Forstall[6] in 1963, and Forstall[7] in

[1] William F. Ogburn, *Social Characteristics of Cities* (Chicago: International City Managers' Association, 1937).
[2] Now the International City Management Association.
[3] Grace Kneedler, "Economic Classification of Cities," *Municipal Year Book 1945* (Chicago: International City Managers' Association, 1945), pp. 30–38 and 48.
[4] Victor Jones, "Economic Classification of Cities and Metropolitan Areas," *The Municipal Year Book 1953* (Chicago: International City Managers' Association, 1953), pp. 49–57 and 69.
[5] Victor Jones and Andrew Collver, "Economic Classification of Cities and Metropolitan Areas," *The Municipal Year Book 1960* (Chicago: International City Managers' Association, 1960), pp. 67–79 and 89–90.
[6] Victor Jones, Richard L. Forstall, and Andrew Collver, "Economic and Social Characteristics of Urban Places," and "Economic and Social Classification of Metropolitan Areas," *The Municipal Year Book 1963* (Chicago: International City Managers' Association, 1963), pp. 31–37 and 85–113.
[7] Richard L. Forstall, "Economic Classification of Places Over 10,000, 1960–1963," *The Municipal Year Book 1967* (Chicago: International City Managers' Association, 1967), pp. 30–48.

1967. Other noteworthy efforts by scholars grappling with the same problems of functional classification include those of Harris[8] in 1943, Nelson[9] in 1955, Duncan and Reiss[10] in 1956, Alexandersson[11] in 1956, Duncan et al.[12] in 1960, Hadden and Borgatta[13] in 1965, and Atchley[14] in 1967.

As a result the student of the American city has a variety of classifications by geographers, political scientists, and sociologists from which to choose; fully a dozen classifications are available. These classificatory schemes have been sadly underemployed in urban research. The determinants, concomitants, and consequences of city functions have *not* been carefully explored by scholars in the field of urban studies. In fact the present authors know of only three such efforts. Nelson[15] has shown a selected array of 1950 census characteristics of American cities grouped according to his own classification. Galle[16] has used the scheme developed by Duncan et al. in their study of metropolitan occupational composition. Pinkerton[17] has employed the Jones–Collver types in a sociological study of 200 standard metropolitan statistical areas (SMSAs) for 1950 and 1960. The impression, then, is that we are faced with what might be called a taxonomic dead end, or classification for the mere sake of classification. No matter

[8] Chauncy D. Harris, "A Functional Classification of Cities in the United States," *Geographical Review,* 30 (January 1943), pp. 86–99; reprinted in Harold M. Mayer and Clyde F. Kohn, Eds., *Readings in Urban Geography* (Chicago: University of Chicago Press, 1959), pp. 129–138.

[9] Howard J. Nelson, "A Service Classification of American Cities," *Economic Geography,* Vol. 31 (July 1955), pp. 189–210; reprinted in Mayer and Kohn, Eds., *Urban Geography,* pp. 139–160.

[10] Otis Dudley Duncan and Albert J. Reiss, Jr., *Social Characteristics of Urban and Rural Communities, 1950* (New York: John Wiley & Sons, Inc., 1956), Part IV.

[11] Gunnar Alexandersson, *The Industrial Structure of American Cities* (Lincoln: University of Nebraska Press, 1956).

[12] Otis Dudley Duncan, Richard W. Scott, Stanley Lieberson, Beverly Duncan, and Hal H. Winsborough, *Metropolis and Region* (Baltimore: Johns Hopkins Press, 1960).

[13] Jeffrey K. Hadden and Edgar F. Borgatta, *American Cities* (Chicago: Rand McNally and Co., 1965).

[14] Robert C. Atchley, "A Size-Function Typology of Cities," *Demography,* Vol. 4, No. 2 (1967), pp. 721–733.

[15] Howard J. Nelson, "Some Characteristics of the Population of Cities in Similar Service Classifications," *Economic Geography,* Vol. 33 (April 1957), pp. 95–108; reprinted in Mayer and Kohn, Eds., *Urban Geography,* pp. 167–179.

[16] Omer R. Galle, "Occupational Composition and the Metropolitan Hierarchy: The Inter- and Intra-Metropolitan Division of Labor," *American Journal of Sociology,* Vol. 69 (November 1963), pp. 260–269.

[17] James R. Pinkerton, *The Residential Redistribution of Socioeconomic Strata in Metropolitan Areas* (unpublished doctoral dissertation, Department of Sociology, University of Wisconsin, 1965), Chapter III.

how carefully developed, once it is completed, the work tends to gather dust on the library shelf.

This chapter is a modest effort in the direction of correcting this unfortunate tendency not to have made use of the traditional functional classifications. It comprises a test of the predictive power of a city's broad economic function in understanding and explaining the residential location of the various socioeconomic strata, or "social classes." The latter is a problem that has long intrigued sociologists, geographers, and urban land economists, and it seems that an investigation of city function as an independent variable with respect to ecological patterns is long overdue.

We have chosen to use the classification developed and reported by Forstall in the 1967 edition of *The Municipal Year Book*. Some of our reasons for making this choice should be obvious. The initial impetus for this volume argues for it. More persuasive is the relative simplicity and ease of understanding this particular scheme; there is a certain advantage, for example, in dealing with a city as if it were representative of one and only one functional class, as contrasted with the Duncan–Reiss and Hadden–Borgatta typologies, where a given city can simultaneously appear in more than one category. The availability of the basically similar ICMA schemes over the years also makes for possible historical analysis of changes in a city's functions. Finally, the most powerful consideration of all in our decision to select the classification by Forstall is the fact that his types are developed on the basis of workplace rather than residence. A city is thus characterized according to the distribution of jobs it contains rather than the jobs that happen to be held by the residents of the city, as in the Nelson and Atchley schemes. Many vexing analytical problems that arise out of the fact of widespread commuting into and out of cities are thus avoided. A classification based on workplace data is far more suitable to our immediate purposes than any other alternative.

We also employ the "manufacturing ratio" that is regularly reported in *The Municipal Year Book*. There are two reasons for this decision. First, we were curious about the correlation or degree of overlap between these two bases of classification, especially given the operational definitions of the four main types in the functional classification: manufacturing centers (MM), diversified centers with a predominance of manufacturing (MR), diversified centers with a predominance of retail trade (RM), and retail-trade centers per se (RR). Second, we wished to assess the comparative predictive utility of the two measurement approaches on the strong suspicion that the manufacturing ratio alone is a better predictor in this instance than the more complex functional classification yielded by the detailed typology.

KEY HYPOTHESES: HOW CITY FUNCTION CAN INFLUENCE THE RESIDENTIAL LOCATION OF SOCIAL CLASSES

This chapter tests a whole series of widespread "common-sense" notions, most especially the frequently expressed idea that the dirt, noise, odors, physical hazards, residential crowding, and traffic congestion associated with a concentration of industry within the central city have driven out the social elite and the broad "middle classes," who have increasingly taken up suburban residence, abandoning the central city to Negroes and other groups with low socioeconomic status. This factor—the concentration of industry—is obviously only one of many that may be operating to yield such selective suburbanization. Others include the aging housing stock of the central city, the evolving system of available transportation, and the changing ethnic composition of the city (especially the mounting proportion of nonwhites).

We take up these matters in the course of our analysis, attempting to measure them as best we can. The main focus, however, remains on the city's economic function as an independent variable with respect to the ecology of social class. What is the relative standing of cities and their suburbs in centers dominated by industry as against those in which manufacturing has a lesser role? What is the comparative importance of a city's economic base in influencing the class composition of cities and suburbs when other relevant factors are taken into account? Operationally we are testing *two* main hypotheses:

1. Manufacturing cities exhibit a greater degree of concentration of low-status people than do diversified cities or retail-trade centers. Moreover, this class differentiation between city and suburb follows a predictable gradient, ranging from manufacturing (MM) cities, through diversified (MR and RM) centers, to retail-trade (RR) centers in that order. (Because of their small numbers, this phase of the analysis ignores "unusual" types—government centers like Washington, D.C., educational centers like Ann Arbor and Champaign–Urbana, and resort and recreation centers like Reno and Las Vegas.)

2. Similarly, the greater the importance of manufacturing in a city's economy—as measured by the manufacturing ratio—the greater the preponderance of low-status people within its political limits. (In this portion of the analysis a somewhat larger number of cities can be examined, for those with "unusual" specializations are included for the sake of complete coverage.)

INDEPENDENT AND CONTROL VARIABLES: THE LESSONS OF PRIOR RESEARCH

The Variables

Research already accomplished has suggested the importance of a number of variables. These were discovered by the senior author in the course of two studies entitled "The Socioeconomic Status of Cities and Suburbs" (1963) and "Urban Structure and Suburban Selectivity" (1964).[18] Both analyses were based mainly on 1960 census data and yielded the suggestion that the following six broad "structural" or "morphological" features were very important in explaining differences between cities and suburbs in social class composition:

1. *The population size of the urbanized area within which the central city is located.* Although its predictive ability was attenuated when other factors were held constant by regression techniques, we have retained the size factor in this investigation, transforming it via logarithms in order to reduce the skewed distribution of sizes that results from the existence of a few very large places.

2. *The age of the central city,* as indicated by the number of decades that have passed since the census first reported it as having at least 50,000 inhabitants. This is a crude measure of "age," of course, and a number of alternative treatments are possible,[19] but it was retained in this fashion in order to facilitate direct comparisons with earlier results.

3. *Regional location of the city.* The earlier study of "Urban Structure and Suburban Selectivity" showed sharp differences between census divisions (New England, Middle Atlantic States, etc.). In order to adapt this factor to a regression analysis we have treated it here by means of "dummy variables."[20]

4. *The percentage of the urbanized area's population found within the*

---

[18] Leo F. Schnore, "The Socioeconomic Status of Cities and Suburbs," *American Sociological Review,* Vol. 28 (February 1963), pp. 76–85, and "Urban Structure and Suburban Selectivity," *Demography,* Vol. 1 (1964), pp. 164–176. Both articles are reprinted in Leo F. Schnore, *The Urban Scene: Human Ecology and Demography* (New York: Free Press, 1965), Chapters 11 and 12.

[19] See Leo F. Schnore and Philip C. Evenson, "Segregation in Southern Cities," *American Journal of Sociology,* Vol. 72 (July 1966), pp. 58–67, for a number of alternative measures of age.

[20] Daniel B. Suits, "Use of Dummy Variables in Regression Equations," *Journal of the American Statistical Association,* Vol. 52 (December 1957), pp. 548–551.

political limits of the central city. In "The Socioeconomic Status of Cities and Suburbs" this item was treated as a "proxy variable" representing the relative success of the city in the legal annexation of outlying territory. It seemed to be a fairly important factor, but it now appears that this was an overly simplistic interpretation. Nevertheless we have retained it in the present analysis for the sake of comparability with the earlier research.

5. *The percentage of the 1960 city population found in areas annexed between 1950 and 1960.* This is a *direct* measure of the annexation factor and thus superior to item 4. It was not available at the time the analysis of "The Socioeconomic Status of Cities and Suburbs" was conducted, but it was subsequently employed in the study of "Urban Structure and Suburban Selectivity." It has been retained in the present analysis since city–suburb status comparisons over a number of cities at one point in time (say, 1960) may merely reflect differential success in annexing high-status residential areas at the outskirts of cities.

6. *The percentage of 1960 housing units in the urbanized area that were built between 1950 and 1960.* This "new housing" measure was previously interpreted in "Urban Structure and Suburban Selectivity" as a surrogate, or proxy, variable, reflecting the recent population growth of the entire area within which the city is situated.[21] Again, it appears that this interpretation was not entirely appropriate, but we have kept it in the present analysis for the sake of comparability with earlier results.

What did we learn from previous research employing the above variables? We can summarize the results of our earlier work by means of a brief quotation from "The Socioeconomic Status of Cities and Suburbs":

Sheer age of settlement has emerged as the best predictor of the direction of city-versus-suburb differences in socioeconomic status. Older urbanized areas tend strongly to possess peripheral populations of higher socioeconomic standing than found in the central cities themselves. In contrast, newer cities tend to contain populations ranking higher on education, occupation, and income than their respective suburbs. To some extent, these differences are also revealed when urbanized areas are classified by size, but control of the latter factor does not eliminate the apparent importance of age as a factor in residential structure.[22]

The follow-up study—"Urban Structure and Suburban Selectivity"—continued to work with the gross distinction between "city" and "suburbs,"

[21] Direct measures of population growth are not possible for urbanized areas, but new housing is highly correlated with population growth for standard metropolitan statistical areas. Hence we conceived new housing as a growth measure.
[22] *Ibid.*, pp. 212–213.

but we turned to a single indicator of socioeconomic status. Rather than simply comparing the proportions of adults who had at least 12 years of schooling, however, we examined the residential distributions of eight detailed educational classes. We found that all of the independent variables used in the study—divisional location, size, age, new housing, and annexation—showed definite associations (on a cross-tabular basis) with the residential location of educational classes. Moreover, the same general patterns were revealed in even sharper fashion when attention was confined to the locational behavior of the white population alone; in other words, as we noted then, " 'control' of color seems to bring out even more clearly the operation of the second principle of residential segregation, viz., socioeconomic status."[23]

The present analysis considers the impact of *four additional factors,* conceived here as independent and/or "control" variables. We indicate briefly the reasons for their inclusion.

7. *The gross population density of the central city;* that is, the residential population per square mile. This is a crude measure of density, of course, and other alternatives might be preferred if appropriate data were fully available.[24] Other things being equal, however, it might be expected that high densities exert an influence on the suburbanization of the "middle class," encouraging at least younger families with children to move to the suburbs.[25]

8. *The percentage of all work trips that were made via mass transportation by the employed residents of the central city.* This variable, available for the first time in the 1960 census, has been the subject of prior research, where it was treated as the dependent variable.[26] In the context of the present analysis, however, it represents an attempt to characterize the available transportation system and is treated as a potential independent variable with respect to the residential location of the various social classes. Where center-oriented public transportation is accessible to all, it might be surmised that the upper "white-collar" strata (whose workplaces have been traditionally concentrated in the urban core) might be encouraged to take up suburban residence.[27]

23 Schnore, *The Urban Scene,* p. 237.
24 Hal H. Winsborough, "An Ecological Approach to the Theory of Suburbanization," *American Journal of Sociology,* Vol. 68 (March 1964), pp. 565–570, and "City Growth and City Structure," *Journal of Regional Science,* Vol. 4 (Winter 1962), pp. 35–49.
25 Peter Rossi, *Why Families Move* (Glencoe, Ill.: Free Press, 1955).
26 Leo F. Schnore, "The Use of Public Transportation in Urban Areas," *Traffic Quarterly,* Vol. 16 (October 1962), pp. 488–498.
27 Beverly Duncan, "Intra-urban Population Movement," in Paul K. Hatt and Albert J. Reiss, Jr., Eds., *Cities and Society* (Glencoe, Ill.: Free Press, 1957), pp. 297–309.

9. *The percentage of nonwhite population in the central city.* This measure, which varies substantially from place to place, is included in order to provide a rough test of the widely held notion that an influx of Black Americans and other nonwhites plays a large role in "driving out" the white middle class from the city.[28] Perhaps no factor is more often cited than this one in current discussions of urban and suburban America.

10. *The percentage of housing units in the city that have been classified as sound and have plumbing facilities.* We have included this measure in an attempt to assess the common-sense notion that it is the aging and otherwise undesirable character of much central-city housing that supplies the impetus for the exodus of the middle class to the suburbs. Although this variable may also reflect uncontrolled area-to-area variations in income, it seemed worth including as a kind of intervening variable. Whatever other factors (such as size, age of city, density, etc.) may be operating to influence the ecology of the social classes, it might be expected that they exert a joint effect on the quality of the city's available housing stock. The latter, in turn, might be regarded as an intermediate or proximate cause of selective suburbanization. In cities with relatively large quantities of sound housing, for example, there is no obvious necessity for an outward shift on the part of middle-class families seeking "appropriate" quarters.

As already noted, we employ the manufacturing ratio and the functional classifications reported by Forstall:

11. *The manufacturing ratio of the central city.* This is simply "the percentage that manufacturing employment forms of aggregate employment [in] manufacturing, wholesale trade, retail trade, and [selected] services. . . ."[29] It should be noted that not all services provided in cities are included in the base, nor are government-operated manufacturing establishments and employment. These omissions are probably not significant for most cities.

12a. In our first treatment of *functional classification of the central city* we treated the scheme (MM through RR) as an ordered series, scoring MM or M as 4, MR as 3, RM as 2, RR as 1, and all other places (only nine in number) as 0. We subsequently abandoned this treatment in favor of a dummy-variable approach, in which the statistical assumptions are less restrictive.

12b. The *functional classification of the central city* was ultimately treated as follows: each city was successively scored 1 or 0: 1 if MM or M and 0 if any other type; then it was scored as 1 if MR and 0 if any other type; and so on through the "all other" category. (In the regression

[28] Schnore, *The Urban Scene,* Chapters 14 and 15.
[29] Forstall, "Economic Classification," p. 38.

analysis the MM and M combined type was dropped in order to yield a matrix of intercorrelations among the independent variables which was of full rank.)

The Interrelations among the Independent Variables

Some of the 12 variables we have used are known to be highly correlated with each other, especially the complex of age, size, density, and annexation. Older and larger places tend to be densely settled and to find annexation of new territory difficult because they are surrounded by established incorporated suburbs able to resist pressures in the direction of political assimilation by the central city. And there are undoubtedly other high correlations between these variables, at least at the zero-order level. In any case disentangling the effects of these potential independent variables seems to be an eminently worthwhile enterprise. A large part of the prior exploratory research on the topic of residential location of the social classes has utilized a simple cross-tabular approach, wherein the limited number of cases for analysis has prevented the proper exercise of relevant controls.[30] This chapter therefore depends heavily on the use of regression analysis. Before we report our results, however, we must (a) clarify the nature of the spatial units employed in this study and (b) describe our treatment of the dependent variables.

SPATIAL UNITS OF ANALYSIS

We have worked throughout this analysis with "urbanized areas," census units consisting of (a) politically defined central cities and (b) their suburbs and rural–urban fringes. We make no distinction between the various subparts outside the central city limits, as in the work of some other investigators.[31]

The Nature of the Urbanized Area

The urbanized area is fundamentally delineated on the basis of population density. It is the physical city, so to speak, in contrast with the legally bounded city. It is also not to be confused with the standard metropolitan statistical area, a more territorially extensive unit built up of whole towns

---

[30] Schnore, *The Urban Scene,* Chapter 12.
[31] See Joel Smith and Herbert Collins, "Another Look at Socioeconomic Status Distributions in Urbanized Areas" (unpublished mimeographed manuscript, not dated).

and counties. A brief quotation should convey the essential character of
our unit:

Urbanized areas.—Although the major objective of the Bureau of the Census
in delineating urbanized areas was to provide a better separation of urban and
rural population in the vicinity of the larger cities, individual urbanized areas
have proved to be useful statistical areas. They correspond to areas called
"conurbations" in some other countries. An urbanized area contains at least
one city of 50,000 inhabitants or more in 1960, as well as the surrounding
closely settled incorporated places and unincorporated areas that meet the
criteria listed below. An urbanized area may be thought of as divided into the
central city or cities, and the remainder of the area, known as the urban fringe.
All persons residing in an urbanized area are included in the urban population.
For the 1960 Census, urbanized areas were delineated in terms of the census
results rather than on the basis of information available prior to the census, as
was done in 1950. A peripheral zone was drawn around each 1950 urbanized
area and around cities that were presumably approaching a population of
50,000. Within the unincorporated parts of this zone small enumeration districts
were established, usually including no more than 1 square mile of land area and
no more than 75 housing units.
Arrangements were made to include within the urbanized area those enumeration districts meeting specified criteria of population density as well as
adjacent incorporated places. Since the urbanized area outside incorporated
places was defined in terms of enumeration districts, the boundaries for the most
part follow such features as roads, streets, railroads, streams, and other clearly
defined lines which may be easily identified by census enumerators in the field
and often do not conform to the boundaries of political units.
In addition to its central city or cities, an urbanized area also contains the
following types of contiguous areas, which constitute its urban fringe:

(1) Incorporated places with 2,500 inhabitants or more.
(2) Incorporated places with less than 2,500 inhabitants, provided each has a
closely settled area of 100 housing units or more.
(3) Towns in the New England states, townships in New Jersey and Pennsylvania, and counties elsewhere which are classified as urban.
(4) Enumeration districts in unincorporated territory with a population
density of 1,000 inhabitants or more per square mile. (The areas of large nonresidential tracts devoted to such urban land uses as railroad yards, factories,
and cemeteries were excluded in computing the population density of an
enumeration district.)
(5) Other enumeration districts in unincorporated territory with lower
population density provided that they served one of the following purposes:
(a) To eliminate enclaves,
(b) to close indentations in the urbanizzed areas of 1 mile or less across the
open end, and

(c) to link outlying enumeration districts of qualifying density that were no more than 1½ moles from the main body of the urbanized area.

Contiguous urbanized areas with central cities in the same standard metropolitan statistical area are combined. Urbanized areas with central cities in different standard metropolitan statistical areas are not combined, except that a single urbanized area was established in the New York–Northeastern New Jersey Standard Consolidated Area, and in the Chicago–Northwestern Indiana Standard Consolidated Area.[32]

One problem that we faced in this analysis is the existence of a number of multiple central cities, including such "twin cities" as Minneapolis–St. Paul, Minnesota, and Allentown–Bethlehem, Pennsylvania. In some phases of the present study we combined data for multiple central cities and treated them as if they represented a single city. In other parts of our analysis, however, we eliminated all multiple central cities and worked only with data for 160 urbanized areas with single central cities, since there are both technical and theoretical grounds for adopting such a decision.

THE MEASUREMENT OF SOCIOECONOMIC STATUS AND THE RESIDENTIAL LOCATION OF "SOCIAL CLASSES"

The use of census sources permits three measures of socioeconomic status: education, occupation, and income. In "The Socioeconomic Status of Cities and Suburbs" we simply compared central cities and suburbs on three bases: (a) the proportion of high school graduates among adults aged 25 years and older, (b) the proportion of the employed population in white-collar occupations, and (c) the median family income. *Suburb-to-city ratios* of these values were then computed and used in a regression analysis. We have continued to use these three ratios in this study. As a fourth indicator, we simply scored each area according to its consistency vis-à-vis the three ratios—suburbs consistently higher, a mixed pattern, or cities consistently higher.

In "Urban Structure and Suburban Selectivity" we employed a somewhat different approach. Attention was solely confined to educational data, and city-versus-suburb comparisons were made on a much more detailed basis. Our technique is illustrated in Table 1, where data for the Detroit urbanized area are employed.

Table 1 shows the detailed distribution of educational categories for the

---

[32] U.S. Bureau of the Census, *County and City Data Book, 1962* (Washington, D.C.: U.S. Government Printing Office, 1962), pp. xiii–xv.

Table 1.   Educational data for the Detroit urbanized area, 1960

EDUCATIONAL DATA FOR DETROIT CITY AND URBANIZED AREA, 1960

School Years Completed		Number in Urbanized Area	Number in City	Per Cent in City	Index of Centralization
TOTAL		1,967,153	991,818	50.4	100
None		36,410	25,773	70.8	141
Grade:	1-4	97,133	66,360	68.3	136
	5-6	126,607	80,167	63.3	126
	7	110,203	63,503	57.6	114
	8	333,943	185,981	55.7	111
High:	1-3	458,677	228,727	49.9	99
	4	508,681	219,227	43.1	86
College:	1-3	159,649	69,229	43.4	86
	4+	135,870	52,861	38.9	77

Source: U.S. Bureau of the Census, U.S. Census of Population: 1960, General Social and Economic Characteristics, Michigan, Final Report PC(1)-24C (Washington: U.S. Government Printing Office, 1962), Table 73.

city of Detroit and its urbanized area. The percentage of each subgroup found in the city is shown, and a series of index values is then reported in the last column. This index is formed by dividing each subgroup value (e.g., 70.8% for those with no formal schooling) by the comparable value (50.4%) for the population taken as a whole. It will be seen that these index values, which range above and below the "expected value" of 100, tend to fall regularly as we move up the educational ladder. This is the pattern that might be anticipated if the well-known Burgess hypothesis is fundamentally correct—the product of a systematic sifting and sorting of the population according to socioeconomic status, with higher status groups progressively more concentrated in the suburbs.

But the outstanding result of our study of "Urban Structure and Suburban Selectivity" was that there are *three* basic configurations, only one of which represents the Burgess pattern shown in the Detroit case. These three patterns are illustrated in Table 2.

Like Detroit, New York shows the expected pattern of regularly descending values in the index of centralization. Tucson, however, exhibits precisely the opposite pattern; as one goes up the educational scale, the values rise from one subclass to the next. Finally, Los Angeles represents an intermediate type, in which the largest index values are found at the extremes, in the very highest and lowest educational classes. In "Urban Structure and Suburban Selectivity" these three configurations were interpreted as representing sequential stages in an "evolutionary" cycle, from the Tucson

Table 2. Patterns of the residential distribution of educational classes based on indices of centralization, 1960

School Years Completed		Highest Educational Classes are Overrepresented in the City	Both Highest and Lowest Educational Classes are Overrepresented in the City	Lowest Educational Classes are Overrepresented in the City
None		90	131	129
Grade:	1-4	93	113	119
	5-6	96	110	111
	7-8	99	99	107
High:	1-3	100	94	100
	4	101	97	91
College:	1-3	102	102	87
	4+	103	106	84
Area used in Example:		Tucson	Los Angeles	New York
Number of Areas Represented by Example Shown		24	70	90

Source: Adapted from Leo F. Schnore, The Urban Scene (New York: Free Press, 1965), Table 4, p.228.

type, through the Los Angeles type, to the New York type. This is the sequence that would appear over time if cities first displayed a concentration of the socioeconomic elite at the center, and if they were subsequently joined, and ultimately displaced, by the lowest socioeconomic strata. We used the three "evolutionary stages" as a fifth indicator in the regression analysis. Finally, we distinguished between those areas exhibiting the Burgess pattern (à la Detroit) and all others. We were thus able to work with six separate but related dependent variables.

CROSS-TABULAR FINDINGS

First, we link the results of the present analysis to those previously reported. Our first question concerned the extent to which different *functional types* of city display status differences between city and suburb. Table 3 shows our first results. The four main types of city (manufacturing, diversified with manufacturing predominant, diversified with retail trade predominant, and retail trade) are quite clearly differentiated, and the differences are in the predicted direction. Manufacturing centers show clearly a higher suburban status, but this suburban superiority is progressively attenuated from one type to the next until, in the case of retail-trade centers,

Table 3. Proportions of urbanized areas with higher status popu-lations in suburbs, by functional classification of central city, 1960

	Manufacturing	Diversified, with Manufacturing Predominant	Diversified, with Trade Predominant	Retail Trade	Other	N
Education	76.3	70.7	70.3	40.0	44.4	200
Occupation	61.8	56.9	40.5	15.0	33.3	200
Income	80.3	80.0	78.4	35.0	44.4	200
Education	78.7	74.5	67.3	46.7	33.3	160
Occupation	65.6	59.6	32.3	20.0	33.3	160
Income	83.6	85.1	77.4	33.3	33.3	160

the cities themselves show higher socioeconomic status. [The two "samples" shown—with $N = 200$ and $N = 160$, respectively—include (a) all those urbanized areas for which 1960 data are available and (b) those with single central cities only. Both groups show the same patterns.]

Similarly Table 4 compares cities of different functional classification with respect to their positions in terms of the three evolutionary stages mentioned above. It will be seen that the four main types of city exhibit the predicted differences. Manufacturing cities tend to be chiefly inhabited by lower status educational groups. Diversified cities show a mixed pattern. Finally, retail-trade centers more often exhibit a concentration of higher status educational groups.

Our second set of questions concerned *the manufacturing ratio*. We divided the urbanized areas into quartiles on this measure and repeated the cross-tabular analysis. The first results are presented in Table 5, which shows that this measure is a somewhat less adequate predictor of city-

Table 4. Breakdown of the three evolutionary stages, by functional classification of central city (160 single central cities only), 1960

	Manufacturing	Diversified, with Manufacturing Predominant	Diversified, with Trade Predominant	Retail Trade	Other
High Educational Groups in City	6.6	8.5	12.9	40.0	50.0
Both in City	29.5	34.0	58.1	33.3	16.7
Low Educational Groups in City	63.9	57.5	29.0	26.7	33.3
TOTAL	100.0	100.0	100.0	100.0	100.0
N	61	47	31	15	6

Table 5. Proportions of urbanized areas with higher status populations in suburbs, by manufacturing ratio in central city, 1960

	Manufacturing Ratio: Quartiles				
	Low (6-30)	(31-43)	(44-57)	High (58-78)	N
Education	50.0	62.7	80.4	80.0	200
Occupation	29.2	45.1	62.7	64.0	200
Income	54.2	72.5	84.3	84.0	200
Education	50.0	65.0	85.4	80.5	160
Occupation	29.9	45.0	65.8	65.8	160
Income	52.6	75.0	90.2	85.4	160

suburb status differences than the functional classification scheme. The higher the manufacturing ratio, the greater the likelihood that suburban status measures will be higher than those of the cities. Nevertheless there are minimal differences between the two highest quartiles.

Similarly Table 6 shows that the manufacturing ratio is a less effective predictor of evolutionary stage than the functional classification scheme. In particular, the two highest quartiles do not show the predicted differences in a sharp and unambiguous fashion. Up to this point, then, the functional typology would seem to be superior as a predictive device. We would do better, however, to suspend judgment in this matter until we examine the results of the regression analysis. We turn now to that phase of the inquiry.

MULTIVARIATE ANALYSIS

Let us begin this section by recapitulating the main proposition in this investigation: the dirt, noise, odors, physical hazards, residential crowding,

Table 6. Breakdown of the three evolutionary stages, by manufacturing ratio of central city (160 single central cities only), 1960

	Manufacturing Ratio: Quartiles			
	Low (6-30)	(31-43)	(44-57)	High (58-78)
High Educational Groups in City	31.6	10.0	9.8	2.4
Both in City	44.7	45.0	19.5	36.6
Low Educational Groups in City	23.7	45.0	70.7	61.0
TOTAL	100.0	100.0	100.0	100.0
N	38	40	41	41

and traffic congestion associated with a concentration of industry within the central city have driven out the social elite and the broad middle class, who have increasingly taken up suburban residence. More generally this notion suggests that the economic functions performed in the central city may be variously inimical to co-occupancy of the area for residential purposes, at least by economically favored status groups.

The previously presented cross-tabular analysis shows that the functional type of a city has a fairly pronounced zero-order association with selective suburbanization. Does this association hold up when we control certain other variables, those whose effects on selective suburbanization are suspected or known from prior research?

A somewhat subsidiary question from the point of view of our research, but of great interest for this volume, is the issue of how best to index the functional types of city for our specific problem. Does the Forstall classification show effects on selective suburbanization independently of the manufacturing ratio?

Initial Explorations: Regression Equations

We may begin by addressing ourselves to the last question first. Table 7 presents the coefficients of determination (R^2) for two regression equations for each dependent variable. The equations for which coefficients are presented in the first column include dummy variables indexing the Forstall classification scheme as well as the manufacturing ratio and most of the variables previously mentioned as affecting suburban selectivity. The variables included in the equations are listed in the first footnote to Table 7. The second column presents the coefficients for the same equations but *excludes* the dummy variables for the typology. The increment in the proportion of variance explained by adding the Forstall types is very small in every case—so small as to be judged not statistically significant by the value of the F-ratio, which is shown in the third column. Our conclusion, therefore, is that for our specific problem the detailed functional classification has few advantages over the simple manufacturing ratio in indexing the functional type of city.

But does functional type, as indexed by the manufacturing ratio, have anything to do with selective suburbanization in the face of many possible "control" variables? Table 8 presents some answers to this question. This table presents standardized regression coefficients (beta values) for the aforementioned equations, excluding the dummy variables indexing the classification scheme.

As can be seen from the last row of this table, the manufacturing ratio has comparatively large and statistically significant regression coefficients

Table 7.   Coefficients of determination for regressions[a] including and excluding the Forstall classification, for 160 selected urbanized areas, 1960

Dependent Variable	Coefficient Including Classification	Coefficient Excluding Classification	F-Value for Significance of Difference[b]
Education Ratio	.460	.459	.636
Occupational Ratio	.461	.457	.267
Income Ratio	.440	.437	.178
Consistency Index	.425	.412	.810
Evolutionary Type	.401	.400	.419
Burgess Index	.394	.381	.821

[a]The regression excluding the classification contains the following variables: the Logarithm of Population Size; Age of the Central City; dummy variables for Region separating South, West, and Northeast-North Central taken together; Per Cent of Urbanized Area Population in the Central City; Per Cent of Population in Areas Annexed between 1950 and 1960; Per Cent of Housing Units Built between 1950 and 1960; Gross Population Density of the Central City; Per Cent of Housing Units Sound with All Plumbing; and the Manufacturing Ratio. The regression including the classification has the above variables plus four dummy variables indexing the five classes in the Forstall typology. The correlation matrix of independent variables for the latter model is ill-conditioned, having a determinant of approximately .00006. Experience with our regression program run on a CDC 3600 having a 64-bit word suggests that the problem of rounding errors is not massive in such a circumstance and the value of the coefficient of determination is accurate to at least three places.

[b]The F-value is computed from the following equation:

Let: SSI be the sum of squares due to regression
          including the dummies for the classification,
      SSE be the sum of squares due to regression
          excluding the dummies for the classification,
      SSR be the sum of squares for the residuals
          excluding the dummies for the classification.

Then:

$$F = \frac{(SSI - SSE)}{SSR} \cdot \frac{148}{4} \; .$$

for each equation. The higher the manufacturing ratio, the higher the status of the suburb in comparison with the central city.

Two other variables have relatively high and significant beta values for most equations. They are the percentage of housing units classified as sound, with all plumbing, and the percentage of the urbanized area's population living in the central city. The results with respect to the first of these variables seem to be consistent with the general proposition that higher status people are "driven out" of the central city by unattractive features in the area, in this case higher proportions of unsatisfactory housing units.

The size and significance of the coefficient for the percentage of the

Table 8.   Standardized regression coefficients for indices of selective suburbanization on all independent variables for 160 selected urbanized areas, 1960

Standardized Regression Coefficient of Index on:[a]	Indices of Selective Suburbanization					
	Education Ratio	Occupation Ratio	Income Ratio	Consistency Index	Evolutionary Type	Burgess Index
Population Size	.1013	.0962	-.0247	.0467	.1919	-.2418[b]
Age--Central City	.2192	.1933	.2397	.3652[c]	.2736[b]	.2340
Region						
Northeast & North Central	.0058	-.0504	-.1454	-.1193	.1241	-.0195
West	-.0297	.0202	.0210	.1022	.0219	.0424
% Population in Central City	-.2226[c]	-.2782[c]	-.2858[c]	-.1985[c]	-.1932[c]	-.2280[c]
% Population in Annexed Areas	-.1133	-.0865	-.0094	-.0854	-.1327	-.0535
% of Housing Units "New"	.1212	.0817	.0585	.2320[b]	.1680	.1235
Gross Density of Central City	.0949	.0246	.0352	-.0163	-.1016	-.0269
% Nonwhite in Central City	.0097	.1011	.1737[b]	.0000	-.0768	-.1677[b]
% of Housing Units Sound with All Plumbing	-.1497[b]	-.1493[b]	-.1960[b]	-.1974[b]	-.1654[b]	-.0815
Manufacturing Ratio	.3190[c]	.3068[c]	.2491[c]	.3036[c]	.2636[c]	.2197[c]

[a]Variables are defined in the text
[b]Significantly different from zero at the .05 level
[c]Significantly different from zero at the .01 level

urbanized area's population living in the central city represent an example of serendipity at work. This variable was used previously by the senior author as a surrogate variable, a proxy measure of annexation. In these equations (Table 8) we find that when annexation is measured directly and included in the equation with the percentage of the area's population in the central city, it is the latter variable that retains its effect. As the percentage of the urbanized area's population living in the central city goes up, indices of selective suburbanization go down. This finding seems to say that, other things being equal, as the boundaries of the central cities vary to include more of the urbanized area's population, the percentage of the city's population that is higher in status rises more rapidly than does that of the suburbs.

A third variable, the age of the central city, has quite high beta values for all equations but fails by a small margin to reach significance in four out of six equations. In assessing the predictive utility of this variable we attribute more importance to its high beta values than to the statistical tests pertaining to it, because we believe that the standard errors of the regression coefficients are inflated by near-collinearity problems.

Other variables show occasional large beta values that reach significance. The size of the population seems to have an impact on the evolutionary type and the Burgess index, but it shows no direct effect on the various ratio indices. A greater proportion of new housing seems to be indicative of "consistency" but shows no marked relationship with the other indices.

The percentage of the central city's population that is nonwhite exhibits surprisingly little partial association with selective suburbanization, and—in the two instances in which its effect is notable—the sign of the relationship varies, showing a positive association with suburban selectivity for the income ratio but a negative one with the Burgess index.

What do we conclude from Table 8? First, some structural variables (size, age, and region) previously found to be related to suburban selectivity now show a rather unimpressive direct effect on the phenomenon when other variables are controlled. Second, variables conceived as "controls" (annexation, density, and percentage of housing units that are new) show little effect on the dependent variable, although they seem to be useful in sorting out the effects of certain other variables. Third, the variables that *do* seem to have a direct effect on selective suburbanization are (a) those that we take to indicate the relative unattractiveness of the central city to higher status persons (the manufacturing ratio and the percentage of housing units classified as sound, with all plumbing) or (b) those that indicate the relative possibility of a location outside the central city for higher status persons (percentage of the area's population living in the central city).

The Second Stage of the Multivariate Analysis: Constructing a Model

From Table 8 we have proceeded to derive a somewhat more complicated model than that with which we began the analysis. We would now hold that the "structural" characteristics of an urbanized area (i.e., its size, regional location, and age) affect the degree to which conditions incompatible with higher status residence are found in the central city. Variables indicating these conditions, in turn, exert a direct effect on selective suburbanization. We may begin exploring these ideas by regressing the "intermediate" variables on the "structural" ones.

Experience with the prior regressions suggested that we have inadequately indexed the regional effects for this more detailed analysis through our failure to separate the Deep South from the Middle South. We felt that the "percentage of sound housing, with all plumbing" variable might be better predicted if the Deep South and the Middle South were separated. Furthermore, the effect of the percentage of nonwhites in the central city on the income ratio might be discounted if this distinction were made.[33]

The regional variables used henceforth in this analysis are dummy variables scored in a rather unusual way. Table 9 lists the regions in its stub and the variable names in the column headings. The body of the table shows the scoring on each variable for an urbanized area located in the region indicated in the stub.

When used in a zero-order correlation, regional variable 1 indicates a distinction between the Deep South and the rest of the country. The r^2 indicates the proportion of variance in the continuous variable "explained" by the difference in means between the Deep South and the rest of the country. Region 2 indicates a distinction between *all* of the census South and the rest of the country. Region 3 indicates a comparison of the northeastern and north central region with the rest of the country. When all three variables are used in a multiple regression, the mean value of the dependent variable in the South (net of the effect of other independent variables) is taken as a base line. The coefficient for region 1 expresses the net increment or decrement in the Middle South over the Deep South. The coefficient for region 2 expresses the net increment or decrement in the West over the net mean value of the dependent variable in the Middle South. Region 3 shows the difference in net means between the West and the combined northeastern and north central region.

---

[33] An additional observation on the curious behavior of the percentage of nonwhites is worth noting. One might have expected this variable to behave like our other indicators of the unattractiveness of the central city to high-status persons. In fact, however, no marked effect of this kind was noted. We then reasoned that this effect might show up if selective suburbanization scores were derived for the white population only. Constructing such indices and rerunning the equations in Table 8 yielded a little clarification in the effect of this variable but required a good deal of rearrangement of values for other variables (such as the percentage of housing units new, and the percentage of housing units sound, with all plumbing). We intend to report on these regressions at a later date. For the present let it suffice to say that we now feel that selective suburbanization and nonwhite residential segregation are two rather separate processes, although there may be a certain interpenetration of each by the other. Specifically, we would hold that rather macroscopic forces encourage and constrain selective suburbanization. The effects of these forces, we feel, can be discerned adequately in their major outlines by using data for the total population. A partition of the population by race, then, yields information on the interaction of racial segregation and selective suburbanization, but this interaction seems to be quite complex and is deserving of detailed analysis in its own right.

Table 9.   Scoring of dummy variables for regions

	Variable		
Region	1 (Not Deep South)	2 (North & West)	3 (North)
Northeast-North Central	1	1	1
West	1	1	0
Middle South	1	0	0
Deep South	0	0	0

Structural and Intermediate Variables

The list of our "structural" variables, then, is as follows: region 1, region 2, region 3, age, and logarithm of population size. "Intermediate" variables are the manufacturing ratio; percentage of sound housing, with all plumbing; and percentage of the area's population living in the central city. To this list we have added the percentage of the labor force using public transportation to get to work. (This variable seemed in keeping with the other intermediate ones in that it indicates something of the relative costs involved for high-status persons in abandoning the central city for the suburbs.) The first two intermediate variables, then, indicate the relative *desirability* of fleeing the central city, whereas the latter two indicate the relative *possibility* of doing so. Table 10 presents the regression of each intermediate variable on each of the structural ones.

Table 10.   Regression of intermediate variables on all structural ones

Structural Variables and Coefficients	Intermediate Variables			
	Manufacturing Ratio	Per Cent Housing Sound	Per Cent Using Public Transportation	Per Cent of Population in Central City
Betas				
Region 1	-.161	.387[a]	-.302[a]	.197[b]
Region 2	-.126	.247[b]	-.054	-.270[b]
Region 3	.736[a]	-.035	.119	.013
Age	.133	-.535[b]	.657[a]	.005
Size	-.053	.479[b]	.081	-.499[a]
R^2	.407	.412	.563	.259

[b]Significantly different from zero at the .05 level
[a]Significantly different from zero at the .01 level

From the last row of this table we see that about 40% of the variance in the manufacturing ratio can be explained by the structural variables, about 41% for the percentage of sound dwelling units, 56% for the percentage of central city residents using public transit, and about 26% for the percentage of the area's population living in the central city.

On inspecting the beta coefficients we find that size has a minimal linear impact on the manufacturing ratio.[34] Location in the northeastern and north central region, of course, has the highest partial regression. In subsequent analysis we shall drop the size variable in the equation to yield the manufacturing ratio. We shall retain all other variables, although it is not clearly necessary to keep three: region 1, region 2, and age.

In predicting the percentage of sound dwelling units the importance of the distinction between the Deep South and the Middle South is shown by the large beta value for region 1. The importance of further separation of the latter area from the rest of the country is shown by the coefficient for region 2. Separating the combined northeastern and north central region from this latter "residual" area yields little additional information, as shown by the low beta value for region 3. We shall drop this latter distinction in further analysis of this variable. Age has a large negative partial effect on the percentage of sound housing, and size has a large positive one. The former relationship seems to reflect the aging of the housing stock concomitant with the aging of the city. We interpret the effect of size as being indicative of higher land values in the center of large cities; other things being equal, these higher values make for more rapid replacement of depreciated units by new ones in order to yield more appropriate returns.

As expected, the age of the city has a strong and positive association with the percentage of population using public transportation. Separation of the remainder of the country from the Deep South produces a significant regression coefficient for region 1, but further separation of the remainder of the country yields little additional information; hence regional variables 2 and 3 are dropped from further analysis. Size also shows little impact in this equation and is also dropped.

Size, however, has a strong partial association with the percentage of the population in the central city. The Middle South is rather different from the Deep South, as shown by the beta value for region 1, and is also rather different from the remainder of the country, as shown by the value for

[34] Previous research indicates that the relationship between population size and concentration in manufacturing is curvilinear. See Duncan et al., *Metropolis and Region*. Because the addition of terms in a polynomial considerably increases the complexity of the path model toward which we are working, we have left the exploration of this avenue for future research.

region 2. Separation of this remainder into the West versus the northeastern and north central region, however, has little utility and is dropped in further analysis.

The parameters for equations recomputed for the modifications suggested above are listed in Table 11. This table shows almost no change in the values of R^2 for each equation, and the values of the remaining regression coefficients have undergone little change.

There are two ways of investigating the adequacy with which the parameters in Table 11 represent the relationships among all of these variables.

Table 11.   Parameters for regression equations for intermediate variables on selected structural variables

Structural Variables and Coefficients	Intermediate Variables			
	Manufacturing Ratio	Per Cent Housing Sound	Per Cent Using Public Transportation	Per Cent Population in Central City
Region 1				
Beta	−.169	.385	−.281	.196
S of Beta	.098	.099	.054	.110
Region 2				
Beta	−.130	.225	.000	−.260
S of Beta	.120	.099		.109
Region 3				
Beta	.757	.000	.000	.000
S of Beta	.096	--		
Age				
Beta	.088	−.553	.740	.000
S of Beta	.067	.098	.054	
Size				
Beta	.000	.493	.000	−.495
S of Beta	--	.097		.070
R^2	.406	.412	.558	.259

The first way involves examining how well the equations yield the correlations between intermediate variables and the structural ones not involved directly in the equation to predict the intermediate variables themselves. The second way involves investigating how well the equations yield the intercorrelations among the intermediate variables. The pertinent observed correlations and those estimated from the equations are presented in Table 12. We shall return to these differences presently. For the moment we may simply observe that they are small enough for us to judge the equations to comprise an adequate representation of the relationships among the variables.

Table 12. Observed correlations and those calculated from the equation in Table 10

Correlations	Observed Correlation (1)	Estimated From Equation (2)	Difference (2-1) (3)
Between Structural and Intermediate Variables			
Region 3 and:			
Per cent sound housing	.204	.239	.033
Per cent using public transit	.137	.097	.040
Per cent in central city	-.095	-.103	.008
Region 2 and:			
Per cent using public transit	-.077	-.082	.005
Age and:			
Per cent in central city	-.383	-.388	.005
Size and:			
Manufacturing ratio	.051	.069	-.018
Per cent using public transit	.540	.527	.013
Among Intermediate Variables			
Manufacturing ratio and:			
Per cent sound housing	.029	.027	.002
Per cent using public transit	.159	.169	-.010
Per cent in central city	-.034	-.081	.047
Per cent sound housing and:			
Per cent using public transit	-.147	-.200	.051
Per cent in central city	.010	-.084	.094
Per cent using public transit and:			
Per cent in central city	-.336	-.267	-.069

Intermediate and Dependent Variables

Our next task is to investigate the relationships between the intermediate variables and indices of selective suburbanization. In this analysis we focus on three of the six previously presented indices: the education, occupation, and income ratios.

Table 13 presents the multiple regression parameters for each of these ratios vis à vis the intermediate variables. Coefficients of determination show that more than 40% of the variance in each index is explained by the intermediate variables. The manufacturing ratio has a rather more impressive impact on the occupation and education ratios than it does on the income ratio, whereas the impact of the percentage of sound housing is reversed. The latter finding is consistent with the notion that the suburbanizing effect of poor-quality central city housing is more selective for income, whereas the effect of a central city concentration in manufacturing is more selective for education and occupational status. Perhaps the manufacturing ratio indexes more than merely the degree to which central city residential location is generally "unattractive." It may also measure the

Table 13.   Parameters for the regression of intermediate variables on three indices of selective suburbanization

| | Indices of Selective Suburbanization | | |
Intermediate Variables and Coefficient	Education Ratio	Occupation Ratio	Income Ratio
Manufacturing ratio			
Beta	.323	.293	.186
S of Beta	.063	.061	.062
Per cent sound housing			
Beta	-.093	-.158	-.298
S of Beta	.063	.061	.062
Per cent using public transit			
Beta	.272	.295	.308
S of Beta	.067	.066	.067
Per cent in central city			
Beta	-.344	-.353	-.298
S of Beta	.066	.064	.065
R^2	.410	.439	.416

city's relative attractiveness in terms of minimizing the distance from workplace to residence for the occupation and education groups primarily employed in manufacturing jobs. The effects of the remaining two variables seem to be rather even over the three indices of selective suburbanization and need not be discussed in detail.

When we inquire into the degree to which the intermediate variables account for the correlations among indices, we do not do very well. The observed and implied correlations are presented in Table 14. Observed correlations among the indices are quite high. Only about 10% of the variance of the education and occupation ratios is unique to each variable, and about 90% is common to both. Equations to yield this high correlation must necessarily be quite highly predictive of their dependent variables. How are we to understand these large differences between observed and implied correlations? On the one hand, they tell us little that we could not have inferred from the coefficients of determination in Table 13. On the other hand, insofar as the three ratio indices can be taken as three measures of

Table 14.   Observed correlations among indices of selective suburbanization and those implied by the model

| | Type of Coefficient | | |
Correlation Between	Observed	Implied	Difference
Education and Occupation	.952	.413	.539
Education and Income	.840	.420	.420
Occupation and Income	.861	.432	.429

the same phenomenon (a position with which we do not entirely hold), their intercorrelations may be regarded as being indicative of measurement error. However, these very high observed correlations suggest that we must take seriously much of the variance unexplained by the equations in Table 14; we are simply not able to attribute it to some process operating like measurement error.

The Two-Stage Model as a Whole

Our model is clearly a failure as some kind of "complete" explanation of selective suburbanization. But does it provide an adequate representation of the ways in which structural variables affect this process? To answer this question we need only compute the correlations between structural variables and indices that are implied by our two-stage model and compare them with the observed correlations (see Table 14).

Table 15 suggests that our model provides fairly good estimates of the observed correlations and is not greatly at odds with the data. Moreover, some patterns that emerge suggest further work. First, our model under-estimates the zero-order effect of size on the occupation and income ratios. Second, our model misrepresents the actual effect of location in the Deep South on the education and income ratios, as well as the effect of any southern location on the latter. (Perhaps these estimation errors are at-

Table 15.   Observed correlations among structural variables and those implied by the model

	Observed Correlation (1)	Implied Correlation (2)	Difference
Occupation ratio and:			
Region 1	−.021	−.047	.026
Region 2	.008	.043	.035
Region 3	.183	.201	.018
Age	.505	.437	.068
Size	.425	.322	.103
Education ratio and:			
Region 1	.089	−.005	.094
Region 2	.097	.083	.014
Region 3	.240	.232	.008
Age	.535	.423	.112
Size	.444	.318	.026
Income ratio and:			
Region 1	−.048	−.147	.099
Region 2	−.176	−.066	.110
Region 3	.038	.100	.062
Age	.427	.404	.023
Size	.340	.277	.063

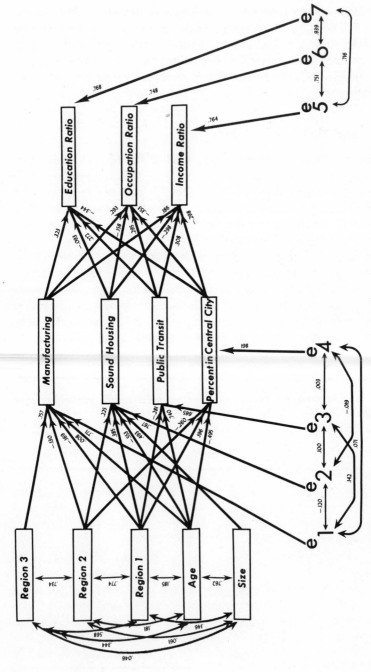

Figure 1 Path diagram for the two-stage model of selective suburbanization.

tributable to the aforementioned interaction of racial segregation with segregation by socioeconomic status.) Finally, the effect of age on the education and occupation ratios is underestimated. The latter finding seems to be consistent with our previous interpretation of selective suburbanization as an evolutionary process, and its exploration is probably better left to longitudinal analysis.

A path diagram is a convenient way of summarizing a causally ordered model of the kind we have presented.[35] Figure 1 portrays our model with all of the inadequacies discussed above. In this diagram the effect of *size* on selective suburbanization is shown to operate through the quality of the housing stock in the central city and through the extensiveness of the city's boundaries. The *age* of the city operates through its effect on housing quality and the character of the public transit system. Although the *regional* variables operate through all intermediate variables, and the most effective regional typology varies from one intermediate variable to another, the most impressive effect is that of location in the Northeast on the manufacturing ratio, the focus of our attention throughout this chapter.

CONCLUSIONS

What can we conclude from this analysis? First, the functions of a city— at least as indicated by the manufacturing ratio—do make a noteworthy difference in the residential distribution of social classes. The manufacturing ratio has been especially useful in disentangling the relationships between region of location and selective suburbanization.

Second, for the present problem, the detailed Forstall economic typology is not as efficient a predictor as the simple manufacturing ratio. For our purposes nothing is gained by using the more complex classification system. (Other classificatory schemes, of course, might yield quite different results.)

Third, our attempts to account for the apparent relationship between city function and selective suburbanization have led us to a promising two-stage model of the latter process, but a great deal remains to be learned concerning the details of this "evolution."

Fourth, as frequently happens, we are dealing with an intrinsically longitudinal problem—the spatial sifting and sorting of social classes over time —with purely cross-sectional data. Further research on this topic would ideally be posed as a set of historical questions with appropriate data indexing the residential *re*-distribution of social classes in relation to the city's ever-changing structure and functions.

[35] Otis Dudley Duncan, "Path Analysis: Sociological Examples," *American Journal of Sociology,* Vol. 72 (July 1966), pp. 1–16.

CHAPTER 5

Urban Typologies and Political Outputs

TERRY N. CLARK

University of Chicago

One of the classic debates in the history of science turns around the proper role of typologies in the development of theory. Although in principle the very existence of a reasoned typology ought to imply a set of interrelated propositions and the associated conditions under which they hold—that is, a theory—not a few observers have been convinced that in practice typological construction often distracts attention from the formulation of more explicit, more powerful, and more precise propositions.

Concern for such issues as the relationships between typologies and propositions has also been more acute in the social sciences and parts of the biological sciences than in the physical sciences. Correspondingly the social scientist has often been more concerned with the explicit consideration of alternative paths to theory construction than his colleagues in the physical sciences—with the result that social scientists may take pride in their refinement in rather philosophical issues, even while lamenting the relative underdevelopment of their systematic theories.[1]

Thus there may well be more than one social scientist who asks, "Why devote a volume largely to typologies?" And of these, some percentage will reply without going much further than the title that such a volume is not needed. More tolerant pessimists might allow that a typological volume could be of some service, but that it nevertheless would represent a fundamental misallocation of scarce resources. The more vociferous defendants

[1] See the discussions in studies by working social scientists, such as Hans L. Zetterberg, *On Theory and Verification in Sociology* (Totawa, N.J.: The Bedminster Press, 1963) and earlier editions; Arthur L. Stinchcombe, *Constructing Social Theories* (New York: Harcourt, Brace & World, 1968), Chapters 1 and 2; Robert Dubin, *Theory Building* (New York: Free Press, 1969).

152

of typologies generally hold that not only do typologies necessarily imply propositions but that, by isolating crucial distinctions between hitherto amorphous phenomena, a good typology will facilitate the creation of further propositions. The last position is most often propounded by the creators of typologies, who often counter the accusations of the antitypologists with the simple suggestion that if typologies have not advanced work in a field, this must imply that the minds of subsequent workers in the field have not been sufficiently fertile.

Without filling in the full details of a Socratic dialogue—the social science journals abound in them—we may suggest that the rejoinder to the last argument is often that many typological categories must either be deleted or reorganized before they can become fully serviceable as building blocks for new propositions. This reshuffling, however, does not imply that typologizing is unnecessary; the variables to be included in new propositions may well have been isolated in an earlier, even if superseded, typological framework.

These general arguments in various guises have been reiterated in several subfields of the social sciences, and they frequently have been found near the center of discussion in studies of urban places, cities, central cities, manufacturing centers, communities, suburbs, standard metropolitan areas (SMAs), metropolises, standard metropolitan statistical areas (SMSAs), conurbations, and megalopolises—this meager sampling of terms amply documents the subject of debate. Variation in definition of each of these terms is also enormous; more than a decade ago an inventory merely of uses of the term "community" disclosed over 100 distinctive preferences.[2] One review emphasizing classifications of urban places based on economic specialization apologized for not elaborating many other typologies of typologies but was extensive enough to affirm that "very little has been done to relate the functional categories to other characteristics of cities" and to conclude that "until there has been substantially more effort to relate the functional classifications to something else, we find ourselves in agreement with Duncan and his collaborators who concluded that 'there is little need for just another functional classification of cities, however ingenious its methodology.' "[3] But this same volume, so critical of typologies, went on to devote its primary attention to elaborating still another, more method-

---

[2] See the review of terminological debates about the concept of community in Terry N. Clark, Ed., *Community Structure and Decision-Making: Comparative Analyses* (San Francisco: Chandler, 1968), Chapter 4, and in Robert J. Havighurst and Anton J. Jansen, "Community Research, a Trend Report and Bibliography," *Current Sociology*, Vol. XV, No. 2 (1967), pp. 5–27.

[3] Jeffrey K. Hadden and Edgar F. Borgatta, *American Cities: Their Social Characteristics* (Chicago: Rand McNally and Co., 1965), pp. 17–18.

ologically ingenious, typology. It is also perhaps significant that factor analysis was the statistical tool employed.

Given the importance of particular statistical procedures to discussions of these matters, we deal with certain methodological and statistical issues in the next section. We propose a slightly different perspective on factor-analysis techniques from those prevalent in past research, suggesting a more important role for them in the development of propositional theory. We then examine materials dealing with community structure and decision-making patterns in a national sample of 51 American communities, in order to compare the results of nearly orthogonal variates with discrete variables in various causal systems.

METHODOLOGICAL AND STATISTICAL ISSUES

Factor-analysis techniques were applied to the census tracts of cities and to entire cities almost as early as the development of the techniques themselves, but studies of this sort have mushroomed since the advent of high-speed computers and associated standardized programs.[4] It is notable, however, that investigations that do little more than replicate earlier studies —that is, essentially attempting to fit a typology to a somewhat different set of data—far outnumber studies that have gone beyond this level of analysis. On the other hand, in the elaboration of more complex models researchers have not made frequent use of factor analysis despite the many evident advantages. The folklore of social science abounds with statements characterizing factor analysis as, for example, a "sledgehammer approach"[5] or damning it with faint praise: "factor analysis is certainly appropriate for some situations, but because of its logical defects it is hard to see how it can be fruitfully used in the development of social and psychological theory."[6]

---

[4] See the reviews of research in Carl-Gunnar Janson, "Some Problems of Ecological Factor Analysis," in Mattei Dogan and Stein Rokkan, Eds., *Quantitative Ecological Analysis in the Social Sciences* (Cambridge, Mass.: M.I.T. Press, 1969), pp. 301–342; Janet L. Abu-Lughod, "Testing the Theory of Social Area Analysis: The Ecology of Cairo, Egypt," *American Sociological Review*, Vol. 34 No. 2 (April 1969) pp. 198–211; Philip H. Rees, "Residential Patterns in American Cities" (dissertation proposal, Department of Geography, University of Chicago, May 1969); Charles M. Bonjean, "The Community as Research Site and Object of Inquiry," in Charles M. Bonjean, Terry N. Clark, and Robert L. Lineberry, Eds., *Community Politics* (New York: Free Press, 1971).

[5] Dogan and Rokkan, *Quantitative Ecological Analysis*, p. 300.

[6] James S. Coleman, *Introduction to Mathematical Sociology* (New York: Free Press of Glencoe, 1964), p. 21.

There is no doubt some justification for this criticism, because many uninspired studies have done no more than apply factor analysis and factor analysis alone to a set of data and baptize ambiguous factors with precise titles, exemplifying with admirable clarity what Whitehead referred to as the fallacy of misplaced concreteness.

Perhaps the sources of some of the difficulties and misunderstandings are the occasionally inflated claims made for factor analysis by its devotees— claims that, when obviously unrealized, have incited overly critical reactions from other users and observers. Then too, as recently as a decade ago, the time involved in simply processing the data for any procedure as computationally demanding as factor analysis was considerable. And, with such a sizable investment in a particular procedure, it is understandable that if meager results emerged, disappointment might be great.

The times and technology, however, have changed, radically. Contemporary computer technology has made numerous sophisticated variations of factor analysis, not to mention other procedures, both simple and inexpensive. Correspondingly it is also far simpler to use a wide range of statistical techniques with minimal computational problems. The more exacting demands are now made not on the techniques but on the researcher himself, who no longer can hope to base an entire career on a profound understanding of the computational routines of one or two statistical procedures. Most social scientists will have to diversify their statistical repertoire considerably if they are not to become hopelessly antiquated in the years ahead. And factor-analysis techniques, *in conjunction with other statistical procedures,* are likely to be used more widely as their strengths and limitations become more generally recognized.[7]

If there is in the social sciences any single statistical approach that currently warrants application of the term "fad," it is some variation of "causal analysis."[8] Although a number of statistical procedures are amenable to

[7] The application of factor-analysis techniques is probed in detail in a forthcoming volume by Duncan MacRae and in Rudolph Rummel's *Applied Factor Analysis* (Evanston, Ill.: Northwestern University Press, 1970). I am grateful to both of them for making their materials available while still in draft form.

   Brian J. L. Berry's article, "An Inductive Approach to the Regionalization of Economic Development," in Norton Ginsburg, Ed., *Essays on Geography and Economic Development* (Chicago: University of Chicago Press, 1960), pp. 78–107, is a striking early analysis combining canonical variates with regression, discriminant function analysis, and other procedures.

[8] The causal interpretation of regression argued by Herman Wold in *Demand Analysis* (New York: John Wiley & Sons, Inc., 1953) was influential in economics. The essays collected by Herbert Simon in *Models of Man* (New York: John Wiley & Sons, Inc., 1957), Part I, were important for sociologists and psychologists, as was the study by

causal interpretation, it is variations of regression analysis that have most often provided the foundation for more elaborate developments. There has been extensive analysis of the purely statistical aspects of regression models, and many observers have advocated their more general application. Certain critics of such models, however, have pointed to the sometimes egregious disparities between the statistical assumptions on which the use of models is predicated and the actual state of much social science data.[9] Given the classical model

$$y = X\beta + e$$

where y is a vector of observations on the regressand, X is the matrix of observations on the regressors, β is the vector of coefficients, and e is the vector of residuals, least squares regression leads to estimates of the regression coefficients as

$$b = (X'X)^{-1}X'y$$

where b is the vector of regression coefficients.[10]

As interdependence among the elements of X increases, the correlation matrix $(X'X)$ approaches singularity, and the x-elements of the inverse matrix $(X'X)^{-1}$, following the dramatic statistical expression, explode. This is the problem that the Norwegian econometrician Ragnar Frisch baptized multicollinearity.[11] Perfect linear dependence of the elements of X implies singularity of $(X'X)$ and an indeterminate set of estimates for b. Complete linear dependence is not common, but, as it is approached, the estimates of β become increasingly unreliable, as shown by larger standard errors. And when influenced by measurement error (which the classical

Hubert M. Blalock, Jr., *Causal Inferences in Nonexperimental Research* (Chapel Hill, N.C.: University of North Carolina Press, 1961), which was also read by political scientists. Articles by Blalock in numerous social science journals have diffused these basic ideas, as have articles by Otis Dudley Duncan, especially "Path Analysis: Sociological Examples," *American Journal of Sociology*, Vol. 72 (July 1966), pp. 1–16, drawing heavily on the work of Sewall Wright. The works of Raymond Boudon, including *L'analyse mathématique des faits sociaux* (Paris: Plan, 1967), and V. Capecchi, in *Quality and Quantity*, have been influential on the Continent.

9 For example, Donald J. Bogue, S. Frank Camerelli, Leo A. Goodman, and that connoisseur of the fourfold table, Paul F. Lazarsfeld. In this chapter we do not attempt to deal with criticisms of scaling of data, qualitative variables, and other issues still being debated.

10 For standard presentations see Arthur S. Goldberger, *Econometric Theory* (New York: John Wiley & Sons, Inc., 1964), Chapter 4, and J. Johnston, *Econometric Methods* (New York: McGraw-Hill Book Co., Inc., 1963), Chapter 2 and *passim*.

11 See Ragnar Frisch, *Statistical Confluence Analysis by Means of Complete Regression Systems* (Oslo: University Economics Institute, 1934).

regression model assumes not to be the case), they are subject to considerable variation. With a limited number of cases in a sample, small measurement errors are translated into sizable variations in the value of the regression coefficients.

The other horn of the dilemma, of course, is the assumption of independence among the elements of e. If an effort is made to minimize intercorrelations in the $(X'X)$ matrix by holding the number of x terms in the model to a bare minimum, complete independence among the elements of e becomes increasingly implausible. And substantively oriented critics point out that the ceteris paribus assumptions on which many theoretical models are based are thereby increasingly unjustified.

One reaction is to throw up one's hands and return to the womb of the fourfold table. But such infantile regression completely bypasses the fundamental issues of multivariate analysis.

One of the most frequently recommended solutions in econometrics literature is to collect additional data concerning the variables most strongly affected by multicollinearity, and, on the basis of "side conditions" imposed on the parameters by such outside data, to replace the set of affected variables by a smaller number of less interdependent variables and continue with "conditional regression analysis."[12] The classical example of this type of procedure in econometrics involves estimating strongly autocorrelated variables in time series from cross-sectional data.[13] Other information, such as the limits on the range of a variable, may also be available from earlier research and can be incorporated into the estimates of coefficients in a probabilistic manner.[14] In many cases, however, additional data simply are not readily available, or their relevance to the problem at hand may be no more than tenuous. The researcher may then estimate the relationships. However, if he is reluctant to estimate definite relationships among assumed parameters from unsure data or theory, he is left only with misery.

Another possible solution is then to orthogonalize some or all of the vari-

---

[12] See Herman Wold with Lars Jureen, *Demand Analysis* (New York: John Wiley & Sons, Inc., 1953), pp. 46–48; Johnston, *Econometric Methods*, p. 207; H. Theil, *Economic Forecasts and Policy* (2d ed.; Amsterdam: North-Holland Publishing Co., 1965), pp. 217, 355–357; Donald E. Farrar and Robert R. Clauber, "Multicollinearity in Regression Analysis: The Problem Revisited," *Review of Economics and Statistics,* Vol. 49 (February 1967), pp. 92–107; E. Malinvaud, *Statistical Methods of Econometrics* (Chicago: Rand McNally and Co., 1966), pp. 187–195 and *passim*.

[13] Guy H. Orcutt et al., *Microanalysis of Socioeconomic Systems: A Simulation Study* (New York: Harper, 1961); Robert Ferber and P. J. Verdoorn, *Research Methods in Economics and Business* (New York: Macmillan Co., 1962), pp. 380–395.

[14] Henri Theil, "On the Use of Incomplete Prior Information in Regression Analysis," *Journal of the American Statistical Association,* Vol. 58 (June 1963), pp. 401–414.

ables in X. This procedure was employed by Stone as early as 1945[15] and suggested in 1957 by Kendall in his widely used text,[16] but it has attracted no more than a handful of followers.[17] The essential problem with this solution is that although orthogonalization is a delightful way of meeting the basic assumptions of the regression model, the substantive meaning of the orthogonal variates may or may not be transparent.

Close to the problem of interdependent elements of the X matrix, of course, lies the actual selection of elements to be included in X. The most direct solution to multicollinearity is simple deletion of highly intercorrelated variables. Although judicious deletion and simplicity in a model are always desirable, there are few systematic criteria that can be applied to indicate the "appropriateness" of any particular model. We need more precise specification of the specification problem.[18]

This juncture between statistical techniques, substantive theory, and empirical methods remains, to a most unfortunate degree, an intellectual no man's land. The literature bearing on such problems is fragmentary and superficial; the relative advantages of alternative solutions have been insufficiently explored. One purpose of this chapter is to provide an examination of the comparative advantages of different types of causal model.

THE 51 COMMUNITIES STUDY

We have raised these methodological issues in order to understand better the causes and consequences of community decision-making patterns. A volume and a series of earlier papers elaborated the theoretical back-

[15] J. R. N. Stone, "The Analysis of Market Demand," *Journal of the Royal Statistical Society,* Vol. 108 (1945), pp. 286–382.

[16] M. G. Kendall, *A Course in Multivariate Analysis* (New York: Hafner, 1957), pp. 70–75. See also M. G. Kendall and Alan Stuart, *The Advanced Theory of Statistics* (London: Charles Griffin; New York: Hafner, 1947, 1966), Vol. 2, *passim*; Vol. 3, pp. 496–500. These authors take up orthogonal polynomials and trace the discussion back to a paper by R. A. Fisher in 1921.

[17] See, however, Douglas P. Ewy, "Dimensions of Social Conflict in Latin America," in Louis H. Masotti and Don R. Bowen, *Riots and Rebellion* (Beverly Hills, Calif.: Sage Publications, 1968), pp. 301–336; Kevin R. Cox, "Voting in the London Suburbs: A Factor Analysis and a Causal Model," in Dogan and Rokkan, Eds., *Quantitative Ecological Analysis,* pp. 343–370; and Bernard Lander, Edgar F. Borgatta, Roland Chilton, and Robert A. Gordon, "Communications," *American Sociological Review,* Vol. 33, No. 4 (August 1968), pp. 594–620.

[18] I am grateful to the University of Chicago econometricians Zvi Griliches, Henri Theil, and Lester Telser for their suggestive remarks and access to several unpublished studies bearing on the specification problem.

ground out of which the current empirical analysis emerges, and hence we limit our presentation to the essentials bearing most directly on the data at hand.[19] Our general strategy has been to test a series of *general formulations* and *propositions* relating community-structure characteristics to decision-making patterns and to such decisional outputs of communities as urban renewal and governmental budget expenditures. One of our most important general formulations is the following:

> The greater the horizontal and vertical differentiation in a social system, the greater the differentiation between potential elites, the more decentralized the decision-making structure, which without the establishment of integrative mechanisms leads to less coordination between sectors and a lower level of outputs.[20]

Numerous middle-level propositions deriving from this general formulation have been tested and supported to varying degrees by the available evidence.[21] Although some analysis has been completed on data from 18 New England communities,[22] from the published results of 166 case studies of decision-making in American communities,[23] and from 18 communities in Yugoslavia and 17 more in France,[24] most empirical investigation to date has been based on a national sample of 51 American communities. The communities range from 50,000 to 750,000 in population and are dis-

[19] See especially Clark, *Community Structure and Decision-Making,* Chapters 1–5.
[20] Ibid., p. 92.
[21] Terry N. Clark, "Community Structure, Decision-Making, Budget Expenditures, and Urban Renewal in 51 American Communities," *American Sociological Review,* Vol. 33, No. 4 (August 1968), pp. 576–593, and "A Comparative Study of Community Structures and Leadership," paper presented at the annual meeting of the American Political Science Association, New York, August 1969.
[22] Ruth Moser, "Correlates of Decision-Making in Eighteen New England Communities" (unpublished Master's essay, Department of Sociology, University of Chicago, 1968).
[23] Terry N. Clark, William Kornblum, Harold Bloom, and Susan Tobias, "Discipline, Method, Community Structure, and Decision-Making: The Role and Limitations of the Sociology of Knowledge," *The American Sociologist,* Vol. 3, No. 3 (August 1968), pp. 214–217. A critique of this approach, and of this article, is Nelson W. Polsby, " 'Pluralism' in the Study of Community Power, or *Erklärung* before *Verklärung* in *Wissensoziologie*," *The American Sociologist,* Vol. 4, No. 2 (May 1969), pp. 118–122.
[24] Terry N. Clark, Peter Jambrek, Janez Jerovsek, and William Kornblum, *Community Decision-Making in Yugoslavia* (Ljubljana: Urbanisticni Institut, 1967); "International Conference on Community Decision Making," *Urban Research News,* Vol. 3, No. 4 (December 23, 1968), pp. 1 and 2; Charles Roig, Christian Mingasson, and Pierre Kukawka, "Social Structure and Local Power Structure in Urban Areas, Analysis of 17 French Townships," *The New Atlantis,* Vol. 1, No. 2 (Winter 1970), pp. 65–84.

tributed in 22 different states; the largest cities in the country are excluded, but such cities as San Francisco, Boston, and New Orleans are included, as are smaller independent cities and metropolitan suburbs. The sample thus presents a considerable range of most of the some 400 variables available for each—drawn from such published sources as the U.S. Census, federal urban renewal and public health reports, and *The Municipal Year Book,* as well as interviews with 11 key informants in each community conducted by a field representative of the National Opinion Research Center at the University of Chicago.

Details concerning the field research and interview schedules have been reported elsewhere and will be passed over rapidly here.[25] The most important result of the interviews for purposes of the present analysis was an *index of decentralization of decision-making.* The index was constructed from the results of what we termed the "ersatz decisional method." Four issue areas were studied: mayoral elections, urban renewal, antipoverty programs, and air-pollution control. For each issue area a series of questions was posed, inquiring essentially:

1. Who initiated action on the issue?
2. Who supported this action?
3. Who opposed this action?
4. What was the nature of the bargaining process; who negotiated with whom?
5. What was the outcome? Whose views tended to prevail?

The 20-cell matrix based on cross-classifying the issue areas by the decisional stages was used to construct the index of decentralization. It incorporated two concepts: *participation,* the number of persons involved in decision-making; and *overlap,* the extent to which actors in one issue were the same in other issue areas, as follows: the number of actors named by

[25] Clark, "51 American Communities," also contains detailed references to data sources for the discrete variables, discussion of index construction, and references to the earlier literature that are almost totally absent from this chapter. The interested reader might well examine it as he reads this chapter. The quantitative findings reported earlier are not exactly the same as those presented here, for though the non-transformed data were close to normal, certain transformations were used in the present analysis to approximate normality more closely, log transformations having been applied to the following variables: civil voluntary organizations (V), general budget expenditures (Z_2) and urban renewal expenditures (Z_1). In each case 0.01 was added to make the variable positive before applying the transformation. Transformations were also applied to the factors as follows: log transformations to factors 5 and 12; square transformations to factors 8 and 13. In each case 4.00 was added to make the variable positive before applying the transformations. The figures for variance explained are corrected for the number of degrees of freedom.

our informants as participating in each issue area was summed, but actors were counted only once even if they were named more than once within a single issue area or in different issue areas; this figure was divided by the number of issue areas present in the community, because in some communities one of the four was not present. The minimum score thus obtained was 3.25, the maximum 9.38, and the mean 6.79.

Our central concern was then to explain variations in centralization across communities. Having elaborated some 38 propositions prior to the empirical research, we were led to the selection of certain variables. We inspected the correlation matrix including the index of decentralization and our other variables, and isolated variables that showed a high zero-order correlation even if they were not related to one of our earlier propositions. The next stages of the process, however, were by no means highly systematized, although in their essentials they resembled those followed by many empirical researchers in the social sciences: too many variables had been isolated, and it was necessary to select a smaller number to be included in the final model or series of models. With only 51 cases, the dangers of bias in the coefficients increase rapidly with the number of variables in a model, but centralization of decision-making is still affected by a large number of variables: we confronted the basic dilemma outlined in the last section. We completed a series of factor and regression analyses on different sets of variables and developed a final set of equations including variables that were either theoretically important but empirically weak, empirically important but theoretically weak, or, in a few cases, both theoretically and empirically important. "Theoretically important" in this context refers to the earlier body of propositions.

Six variables—*population size, percentage of the population with incomes under $3000, percentage of manufacturing establishments in the community with more than 20 employees, economic diversification* (adapted from Nelson's ratings), *median number of years of school completed by community residents,* and *members of the Roman Catholic Church per capita*—explained 39% of the variance in *civic voluntary organization activity* (League of Women Voters' membership per capita). Adding League membership per capita to the model, we explained 45% of the variance in an *index of reform government* based on the number of reform characteristics present: professional city manager, nonpartisan elections, at-large electoral constituencies. With the reform-government index added to the model, 46% of the variance in the *index of decentralization* was explained. With the index of decentralization added to the model, 37% of the federal and local urban renewal expenditure per capita and 60% of the total community governmental budget expenditures per capita were explained. The results were presented by using both path analysis and a system of regression equations.[26]

From the standpoint of the total amount of variance explained, as well as the testing of several interesting propositions, the results were satisfactory, even gratifying. But because of some of the issues touched on in the last section, it seemed useful to replicate the study by using variations of the same basic models.

FACTOR SCORES VERSUS INDIVIDUAL VARIABLES

It was possible to examine changes in the models using a different set of variables by replacing the discrete variables with factor scores for each of our 51 communities derived from the factor analysis of American communities completed by Berry.[27] The score on each of Berry's factors was punched for each of the 51 communities. Although the 14 factors were orthogonal for all American communities with more than 10,000 inhabitants, they were slightly intercorrelated for our 51 communities (see Table 1). We expected that comparison of the results from the two procedures should be interesting from a number of standpoints:

1. The factor scores supply a check on the extent to which the variables most useful in explaining variations in each of the dependent variables were in fact included in the models based on discrete variables. With over 400 discrete variables as candidates for inclusion in a model, systematic comparison of alternatives proves to be extremely useful. A priori one would expect the factor scores to explain more variance in each of the dependent variables than most sets of discrete variables since they emerged from a more systematic procedure for including elements of the large matrix of socioeconomic variables than almost any nonorthogonal and non-exhaustive selection of elements from the matrix. (Nevertheless, we must recall that Berry started with only 97 variables for each community, thus excluding, for example, our religious variables, government-structure characteristics, and, naturally, the information about decision-making patterns.)

2. Use of the nearly orthogonal factor scores as variables in a causal model considerably alleviates the problem of multicollinearity. With a

---

[26] The path diagrams were not published in Clark, "51 American Communities." They may be obtained by writing to the author at the Department of Sociology, University of Chicago, Chicago, Illinois 60637, or by consulting an expanded and revised edition of the article in Bonjean, Clark, and Lineberry, Eds., *Community Politics.*

[27] See Chapter 1 in this volume.

Table 1. Zero-order correlation matrix

Variable Name	F₁	F₂	F₃	F₄	F₅	F₆	F₇	F₈	F₉	F₁₀	F₁₁	F₁₂	F₁₃	F₁₄	V	W	Y	Z₁	Z₂	X₁	X₂	X₃	X₄	X₅
Size F_1																								
Status F_2	-.322																							
Life Cycle F_3	.107	-.205																						
Nonwhite population F_4	.241	.028	-.158																					
Recent Population Growth F_5	-.238	.226	-.181	.236																				
College Towns F_6	-.315	-.073	.139	.132	-.250																			
Foreign Stock Population F_7	-.322	-.096	-.390	-.290	-.057	-.140																		
Recent Employment Expansion F_8	-.379	.278	.328	-.143	.172	-.115	-.139																	
Manufacturing Towns F_9	-.191	.346	.149	.086	.134	-.044	.088	-.048																
Females in Labor Force F_{10}	.314	-.334	.076	.248	.156	.169	-.208	-.096	.078															
Service Centers F_{11}	.208	.210	-.101	-.094	-.295	-.098	-.288	.087	-.466	.128														
Military Installations F_{12}	-.014	-.372	-.126	-.014	-.063	-.122	.050	.093	-.221	-.228	.085													
Mining Towns F_{13}	-.009	.037	-.040	-.105	-.129	-.163	.317	-.366	.012	-.153	.032	-.161												
Elderly Working Males F_{14}	.168	.555	.012	.105	-.226	.151	-.194	.010	.066	.025	.137	-.095	-.150											
Civic Voluntary Organization V	-.290	.447	-.310	.072	.018	.043	.089	.083	-.066	-.249	.041	.253	-.059	-.058										
Reformist Government W	-.132	-.196	-.080	.043	.446	-.092	.389	.336	-.125	-.066	.113	.127	-.317	-.141	.196									
Decentralized Decision-making Structure Y	.211	-.308	-.131	.001	-.230	.057	.324	-.190	.069	.051	-.055	-.310	.061	.165	-.246	-.548								
Urban Renewal Expenditures Z_1	.132	-.065	-.372	.072	-.401	.029	.539	-.272	-.109	.030	-.006	-.053	.230	.282	-.072	-.391	.277							
Population Size Z_2	-.086	-.393	.095	-.003	-.140	.300	.321	-.079	-.303	-.237	.014	-.066	.247	-.127	-.045	-.004	.216	.489						
General Budget Expenditures X_1	.550	.560	-.206	-.202	-.110	.270	.009	-.108	.230	-.107	-.020	-.137	-.153	.278	-.490	-.199	.384	.390	.330					
Community Poverty X_2	.345	-.169	.393	.501	.111	.124	-.313	-.069	.309	-.107	-.355	-.091	-.000	.022	-.300	.077	-.031	.178	.007	.276				
Industrial Activity X_3	.100	.393	-.026	-.112	-.630	.293	-.094	-.061	.230	-.134	-.019	-.212	-.202	.031	.069	-.031	-.008	.199	-.103	-.104	-.141			
Economic Diversification X_4	.481	.170	.112	-.009	-.109	.039	-.263	.352	.076	-.154	-.171	-.171	-.223	.316	-.244	.143	.347	.021	-.007	-.516	-.334	-.154		
Highly Educated Population X_5	-.186	.809	-.036	-.009	.336	.046	-.328	.352	.076	-.154	-.019	.270	-.445	.093	.456	.625	-.332	-.358	-.166	-.238	-.339	-.339	.027	
Catholic Population X_6	-.205	-.057	-.201	-.501	-.407	-.023	.776	-.203	.057	-.220	-.155	.189	.362	-.128	.084	-.425	.254	.393	.573	.037	.441	.204	-.236	-.322

limited number of cases, more variables can be included in a model without the corresponding bias in coefficients that normally results from the use of discrete variables. If the variables are completely orthogonal, they can be added to, or deleted from, a model without seriously affecting the coefficients of the remaining variables.

3. The use of the factor scores provides an opportunity to replicate the earlier models insofar as factors correspond to the discrete variables used previously. Results that consistently emerge from one type of analysis to the next are more firmly supported than those in any single analysis.

4. The new models might disclose new variables that were not included in earlier analyses. Even if future analyses were based on discrete variables rather than factor scores, one or more individual variables could be selected to represent the most interesting aspects of the newly isolated variables.

5. It is possible to evaluate the potential importance of including in a model variables that were not part of the matrix (in this case of 97 socioeconomic variables) but were originally used to complete the factors. We can thus obtain a general picture for assessing the importance of different categories of variables (e.g., socioeconomic versus governmental characteristics).

These considerations do not imply of course that factor analysis should be used to replace discrete variables in general, but they do imply that the elaboration of models with various combinations of individual variables and factor scores is a strategy that might profitably be pursued. Even if one decides against using any factor scores in eventual causal models, experimenting with them at an earlier stage provides a useful basis of comparison for further work. Factor scores are like aerial photographs, which do not always provide the necessary detail for fine analysis but nevertheless afford a useful typology of the landscape.

COMPARISON OF EMPIRICAL FINDINGS

In this section we examine and compare in turn the models based on discrete variables and on factor scores used to explain each of the five dependent variables at each stage of the system: membership in civic voluntary organizations, reform-government characteristics, decentralization of decision-making, urban renewal expenditures, and general budget expenditures. There is a table and a figure for each of the dependent variables, summarizing the results for each of the two types of models. Each table includes zero-order correlations and path coefficients (standardized regression coefficients), relating each of the independent variables in the two systems to the dependent variable.[28] The tables also contain the regression equations in which both discrete variables and factor scores as independent variables were used for the same dependent variable; the unstandardized regression coefficients and standard errors are reported for each variable. Complete path-analysis diagrams are not presented, although all the numerical elements are summarized in tabular form, including the path coefficients of the residual-error terms.

The figures include only the independent variables from the two models that were significant at the 5% level, based on the F ratios.[29] Variables connected with broken lines were those of significance in the model that used exclusively discrete variables, whereas those connected with solid lines were significant in the model consisting principally of the factor scores. Variables connected with both solid and broken lines were significant in both models. Zero-order correlations are indicated by a bowed double-headed arrow. A plus sign over a line indicates a positive contribution in the direction indicated; a negative sign, the opposite. A brief glance at the figures thus indicates the most important variables in each of the two models; the more detailed results are available in the tables.

In order to preserve consistency and to include all the elements necessary for a complete path analysis, the same basic sets of independent variables were used for each of the dependent variables in each model, even if some of the independent variables were not always statistically significant. The weak relationships are in some cases as interesting as the strong ones, especially when the zero-order correlations for the same variables are quite different. In a first stage all of the 14 factors isolated by Berry were included in the successive models. In a second stage 6 of the 14 factors that were not significant at the 5% level of probability in at least one of the regressions were deleted. The eight remaining factors provide the core elements for the factor models that follow. (Factor 1, size, was retained because of its importance in zero-order relationships and in other analyses, although it was just below significance in the regressions.)

[28] Path coefficients are discussed, among other places, in Duncan, "Path Analysis," and in Boudon, *L'analyse mathématique des faits sociaux*.

[29] Recent reviews of the debates about the use of significance tests are contained in Denton E. Morrison and Ramon E. Henkel, "Significance Tests Reconsidered," and Robert F. Winch and Donald T. Campbell, "Proof? No. Evidence? Yes. The Significance of Tests of Significance," *The American Sociologist,* Vol. 4, No. 2 (May 1969), pp. 131–139 and 140–143.

Activities in Civic Voluntary Organizations

This variable, operationalized as the number of members in the League of Women Voters per capita in the community,[30] was explained by the same type of variable in both the discrete-variable and the factor-score models. As shown in Figure 1 and Table 2, the median educational level

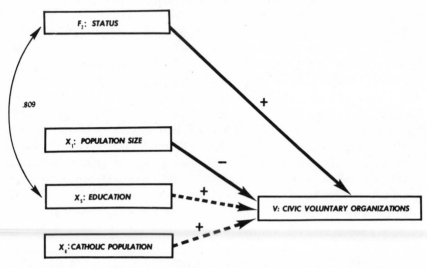

Figure 1   Causes of activities in civic voluntary organizations.

of the community as a discrete variable, and factor 2, status, were by far the most important single variables in each model (median education and status correlated .809). There was a moderately strong negative zero-order relationship between population size and civic activities in each model, but in both cases it was diminished when other variables were introduced.

Reform Government

Some interesting differences emerged between the two models in explaining the presence of what are generally referred to as reform-government characteristics: professional city manager, nonpartisanship, and at-large

[30] See the rationale for this procedure, and the discussion of the League of Women Voters, in Frederick M. Wirt, Ed., *Future Directions in Community Power Research: A Colloquium* (Berkeley, Calif.: Institute of Governmental Studies, University of California, Berkeley, 1971).

Table 2. Correlations and path coefficients with civic voluntary activity (V) as the dependent variable

Independent Variable	Zero-order Correlation	Path Coefficient
X_5: Highly Educated Population	.456	.6007
X_1: Population Size	-.490	-.3828
X_6: Catholic Population	.084	.3323
X_3: Industrial Activity	.069	.1893
X_2: Community Poverty	-.300	.1881
X_4: Economic Diversification	-.244	-.0174
Residual	....	.741

R = .671; Variance explained = 45%

$$V = -1.2541 - .0000 X_1 + .0225 X_2$$
$$\quad\ (1.8500)\ (.0000)\quad (.0196)$$

$$+ .0199 X_3 - .0278 X_4 + .4379 X_5$$
$$\quad\ (.0132)\quad (.2231)\quad (.1165)$$

$$+ .0176 X_6$$
$$\quad\ (.0081)$$

Independent Variable	Zero-order Correlation	Path Coefficient
F_1: Size	-.290	-.2040
F_2: Status	.555	.5092
F_3: Life Cycle	-.310	-.2257
F_5: Recent Population Growth	.018	-.1079
F_6: College Towns	.043	.1904
F_7: Foreign Stock Population	.089	-.0620
F_{12}: Military Installations	.253	.1636
F_{13}: Mining Towns	-.059	.1828

R = .666; Variance explained = 35%

$$V = 3.7424 - .1389 F_1 + .6262 F_2$$
$$\quad\ (1.2921)\ (.0962)\quad (.1734)$$

$$- .1848 F_3 - .3678 F_5 + .723 F_6$$
$$\quad\ (.1100)\quad (.4353)\quad (.1163)$$

$$- .0587 F_7 + .8808 F_{12} + .0304 F_{13}$$
$$\quad\ (.1382)\quad (.6587)\quad (.0224)$$

elections (see Figure 2 and Table 3). Education was the only significant variable in the discrete-variable model, where it showed both zero-order and path coefficients over .60 When factor scores were used instead, the total variance explained was 37 instead of 45%, but the significance of any individual variable was not as clear as it was in the discrete-variable model.

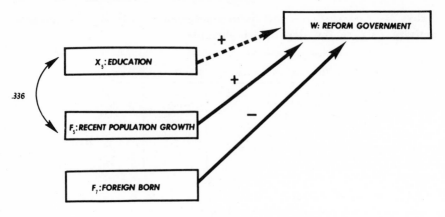

Figure 2   Causes of reform government.

The two most important factors were factor 5, log recent population growth (positively), and factor 7, foreign-born population (negatively). Surprisingly, factor 2, status, even though it showed a zero-order relationship of .809 with the discrete variable education and of .447 with reform government, was not significant in the regression model. We know from more detailed analysis that these variables indicate different aspects of the new, middle-size cities disproportionately concentrated in the western part of the United States, but the use of factors instead of discrete variables does not seem to add much clarification to the relationships here.

The Decision-making Structure

In the discrete-variable model there was a sizable positive zero-order correlation between decentralization and population size, but it disappeared when other variables were introduced. Most important were measures of structural differentiation in two different institutional areas: diversification in the economic sector and reform-government characteristics in the political sector (see Figure 3). In both cases the more differentiated institutional structures led to more decentralized patterns of decision-making.

As shown in Table 4, the total amount of variance explained in the discrete-variable model (46%) was roughly similar in the factor-score model (42%), but the differences between the two were illuminating. The zero-order relationship between the size factor and decentralization was not as strong as that between the discrete variable of population size and decentralization, and the zero-order relationship was not attenuated in the causal model; on the contrary, it was slightly increased.

Table 3. Correlations and path coefficients with index of reform government (W) as the dependent variable

Independent Variable	Zero-order Correlation	Path Coefficient
X_5: Highly Educated Population	.625	.6962
X_2: Community Poverty	.077	.2910
X_1: Population Size	-.199	-.2288
V : Civic Voluntary Activity	.196	-.1162
X_4: Economic Diversification	.143	.1051
X_3: Industrial Activity	-.332	-.0504
X_6: Catholic Population	-.425	-.0189
Residual	....	.694

$R = .721$; Variance explained = 45%

$$W = -6.0794 - .0000 X_1 + .0515 X_2$$
$$(2.5964) \quad (.0000) \quad (.0278)$$

$$-.0078 X_3 - .2477 X_4 + .7495 X_5$$
$$(.0189) \quad (.3116) \quad (.1869)$$

$$-.0015 X_6 - .1715 V$$
$$(.0119) \quad (.2105)$$

Independent Variable	Zero-order Correlation	Path Coefficient
F_1: Size	-.132	-.0960
F_2: Status	.447	.2425
F_3: Life Cycle	-.080	-.1112
F_5: Recent Population Growth	.446	.3251
F_7: Foreign Stock Population	-.389	-.4129
F_{12}: Military Installations	.127	.0939
F_{13}: Mining Towns	-.317	-.0439
V : Civic Voluntary Activity	.196	.0029
F_6: College Towns deleted by regression		

$R = .680$; Variance explained = 37%

$$W = -1.1471 - .0966 F_1 + .4404 F_2$$
$$(2.034290) \quad (.1369) \quad (.2872)$$

$$-.1344 F_3 + 1.6368 F_5 - .5778 F_7$$
$$(.1639) \quad (.6265) \quad (.2007)$$

$$+.7469 F_{12} - .0108 F_{13} + .0043 V$$
$$(.9535) \quad (.0322) \quad (.2183)$$

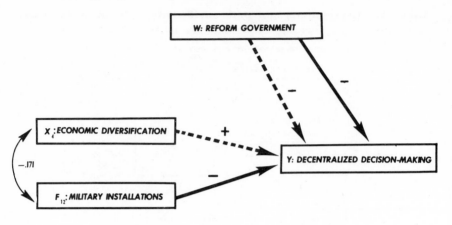

Figure 3   Causes of decentralized decision-making.

The only factor significantly related to decentralization in the causal model was factor 12, military installations, which led to more centralized patterns of decision-making. Observers of radical political persuasion will no doubt interpret this finding as firm evidence of the maliciousness of the military–industrial complex and of the extent to which its tentacles reach into the hearts of small, innocent communities throughout the land.

Alternatively, the finding might be subsumed under several more general ideas. Communities specialized in military activities might be seen as the converse of economically diversified communities, in which case concentration in military activities would be simply one form of economic specialization. Despite the useful measures of specialization in different types of economic activity which emerged from the factor analysis, no one factor was close to what has traditionally been referred to as economic diversification. Indeed the absence of this variable may account for the higher path coefficient from the size factor to decentralization than was the case in the discrete-variable model. Without any measure of economic diversification in the factor-score model, the coefficient for military installations might well be higher, one might think, than it would be if such a measure had been included. But the difference would still probably not be especially great, as the zero-order correlation between economic diversification (adapted from Nelson) and the military-installation factor was only —.171.

Following a second alternative interpretation, one might imagine militarily specialized communities as being small and thus not endowed with many alternative potential elites. However, the correlation of size with the military-installation factor was only —.137.

Table 4. Correlations and path coefficients with decentralized decision-making structure (Y) as the dependent variable

Independent Variable	Zero-order Correlation	Path Coefficient
W : Index of Reform Government	−.548	−.5862
X_4: Economic Diversification	.347	.4521
X_3: Industrial Activity	−.008	−.1882
X_2: Community Poverty	−.031	−.1830
X_5: Highly Educated Population	−.332	−.0733
X_6: Catholic Population	.254	.0452
X_1: Population Size	.384	.0383
V : Civic Voluntary Activity	−.246	−.0146
Residual	....	.680

R = .735; Variance explained = 46%

$$Y = 10.2803 + .0000 \ X_1 - .0385 \ X_2$$
$$(3.2469) \quad (.0000) \quad (.0340)$$

$$- .0347 \ X_3 + 1.2657 \ X_4 - .0938 \ X_5$$
$$(.0223) \quad (.3696) \quad (.2580)$$

$$+ .0042 \ X_6 - .0255 \ V \ -.6964 \ W$$
$$(.0140) \quad (.2498) \quad (.1796)$$

Independent Variable	Zero-order Correlation	Path Coefficient
F_1: Size	.211	.2576
F_2: Status	−.196	.2082
F_3: Life Cycle	−.131	−.1651
F_5: Recent Population Growth	−.230	−.0790
F_6: College Towns	.057	−.0741
F_7: Foreign Stock Population	.324	.2551
F_{12}:Military Installations	−.310	−.3185
F_{13}:Mining Towns	.061	−.1820
V : Civic Voluntary Activity	−.246	−.1934
W : Reform Government	−.548	−.4725

R = .725; Variance explained = 42%

$$Y = \ 14.2825 + .3078 \ F_1 + .4493 \ F_2 - .2373 \ F_3$$
$$(2.3555) \quad (.1643) \quad (.3382) \quad (.1899)$$

$$- .4728 \ F_5 - .1177 \ F_6 + .4241 \ F_7$$
$$(.7829) \quad (.1978) \quad (.2512)$$

$$- 3.0095 \ F_{12} - .0532 \ F_{13} - .3394 \ V$$
$$(1.1229) \quad (.0379) \quad (.2559)$$

$$- .5614 \ W$$
$$(.1763)$$

A third possible interpretation is that the military communities were disproportionately located in authoritarian southern towns; but the correlation between a dummy variable for the southern region of the United States and the military factor was —.235.

Finally, when the regression for the discrete-variable model shown in Table 4 and Figure 3 was rerun with the military factor 12 included, factor 12 was more than statistically significant ($F = 5.15$). Perhaps the military is a pernicious influence on democracy!

But if the presence of military installations leads to moderately more centralized patterns of decision-making, the effects of reform government are far stronger: zero-order correlations and path coefficients of roughly —.5 were found in both the discrete-variable and the factor-score models. Reform government considerably decreases participation in community decision-making; in both models reform government was the strongest of any variable leading toward centralization.

Urban Renewal

The pictures presented by the two models for the explanation of urban renewal (per capita expenditures) were perhaps complementary but in any case somewhat different (see Figure 4). Neither model was particu-

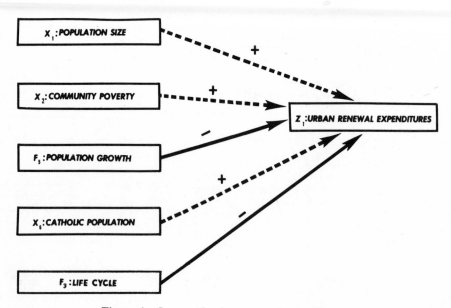

Figure 4 Causes of urban renewal expenditures.

Table 5. Correlations and path coefficients with urban renewal expenditures (Z_1) as the dependent variable

Independent Variable	Zero-order Correlation	Path Coefficient
X_6: Catholic Population	.393	.4628
X_2: Community Poverty	.178	.4796
X_1: Population Size	.390	.4057
X_3: Industrial Activity	.199	.1881
X_4: Economic Diversity	.021	-.1960
V : Civic Voluntary Activity	-.072	.1442
X_5: Highly Educated Population	-.358	.1774
W : Index of Reform Government	-.391	-.1421
Y : Decentralized DMS	.277	.1049
Residual	....	.730

R = .685; Variance explained = 37%

$$Z_1 = - 10.6485 + .0000 X_1 = .0900 X_2$$
$$(3.5063) \quad (.0000) \quad (.0335)$$

$$+ .0309 X_3 - .4900 X_4 + .2026 X_5$$
$$(.0223) \quad (.4056) \quad (.2507)$$

$$+ .0386 X_6 + .2259 V - .1508 W$$
$$(.0136) \quad (.2424) \quad (.2031)$$

$$+ .0936 Y$$
$$(.1497)$$

Independent Variable	Zero-order Correlation	Path Coefficient
F_1: Size	.132	-.0354
F_2: Status	-.308	-.1671
F_3: Life Cycle	-.219	-.3161
F_5: Recent Population Growth	-.401	-.3020
F_6: College Towns	.270	.2638
F_7: Foreign Stock Population	.321	.1344
F_{12}: Military Installations	-.053	-.0047
F_{13}: Mining Towns	.230	.0819
V: Civic Voluntary Activity	-.072	-.0795
W: Reform Government	-.391	-.0887
Y: Decentralized DMS	.277	.0080

R = .643; Variance explained = 26%

$$Z_1 = - .5448 - .0378 F_1 - .3219 F_2 - .4053 F_3$$
$$(3.2845) \quad (.1725) \quad (.3478) \quad (.1949)$$

$$- 1.6129 F_5 + .3739 F_6 + .1995 F_7$$
$$(.7916) \quad (.1999) \quad (.2617)$$

$$- .0399 F_{12} + .0214 F_{13} - .1246 V$$
$$(1.2275) \quad (.0391) \quad (.2631)$$

$$- .0941 W + .0071 Y$$
$$(.1987) \quad (.1591)$$

larly robust: the discrete-variable model explained 37%, and the factor-score model 26%, of the variance in urban renewal (see Table 5). The three significant discrete variables were population size, community poverty (percentage of families with incomes below $3000), and the percentage of the population that was Roman Catholic. All were positively related to urban renewal expenditures. In the factor-score model the only two significant factors (both negatively related to urban renewal) were factor 3, stage in life cycle (generally the new suburbs with young couples), and factor 5, population growth (the more rapidly growing communities). The two models thus complement one another to the extent that they indicate the variables leading to higher urban renewal expenditures on the one hand and to lower expenditures on the other.

A recent study of urban renewal in 582 American communities by Alford and Aiken suggested that the age of a community is a major determinant of the size of its urban renewal expenditures.[31] We therefore added the year in which each of the communities reached 10,000 in population to the discrete-variable model and found, as had they, that it was reasonably important. The size of the Roman Catholic population remained the strongest single variable, but the age of the community was second most important—and it displaced poverty and population size, which were not statistically significant when community age was included. The interpretation of Alford and Aiken, however, that the age and the size of a community—their two most important explanatory variables—are indicators of the number of centers of influence in a community seems to be highly questionable, as our measure of centralization of decision-making was not even statistically significant in either the factor-score or the discrete-variable versions of this regression. Furthermore, as we pointed out, population size also was not significant in our basic discrete-variable model with community age added. Community age is not a particularly satisfying variable from an analytical standpoint; it would seem to act as a surrogate for other unmeasured variables that may well be more important: the existence of a stable political machine, widespread dilapidated housing, or eastern urban progressiveness are three possibilities. The probing of these particular relations, however, must be left to the future.

Governmental Budget Expenditures

The discrete-variable model also seemed to be more satisfactory than the factor-score model for explaining governmental budget expenditures

[31] Robert R. Alford and Michael Aiken, "Community Structure and Mobilization: The Case of Urban Renewal" (unpublished paper, Department of Sociology, University of Wisconsin, not dated).

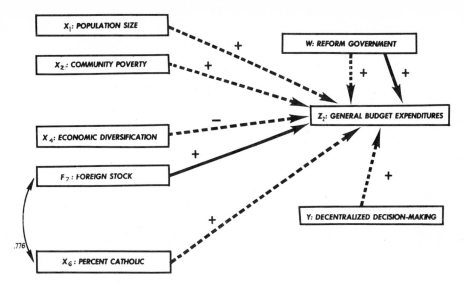

Figure 5   Causes of general budget expenditures.

per capita (see Figure 5 and Table 6). The discrete-variable model explained 60% of the variance, whereas the factor-score model explained somewhat less: just 41%. Moreover, the salience of particular explanatory variables was considerably greater for the discrete-variable model: six different variables were statistically significant in the discrete-variable model, whereas only two were significant in the factor-score one. The only significant factor was factor 7, foreign stock, which was positively related to budget expenditures. The other significant variable was the index of reform government.

We might point out once again what should be apparent from these findings: the analysis of governmental expenditures without the inclusion of governmental variables and other variables of a noneconomic sort not traditionally included in the extensive literature on community public finance[32] represents an unfortunately constricting outlook. Although it is fully evident that a large number of different models may be created to explain the same amount of variance in the same dependent variable, without testing the importance of additional, noneconomic, variables along with the traditional economic ones used in most of the earlier literature, the results will continue to support a misconceived sort of economic determinism.

[32] See Bonjean, Clark, and Lineberry, Eds., *Community Politics.*

Table 6. Correlations and path coefficients with general budget expenditures (Z_2) as the dependent variable

Independent Variable	Zero-order Correlation	Path Coefficient
X_6: Catholic Population	.573	.8080
W : Index of Reform Government	-.004	.5768
X_1: Population Size	.330	.3948
X_4: Economic Diversification	-.007	-.3199
X_2: Community Poverty	.007	.3500
Y : Decentralized DMS	.216	.3209
V : Civic Voluntary Activity	-.045	.0659
X_3: Industrial Activity	-.103	-.0298
X_5: Highly Educated Population	-.166	.0211
Residual	....	.582

$R = .813$; Variance explained = 60%

$$Z_2 = 2.3989 + .0000\ X_1 + .0232\ X_2$$
$$ (.9910)\quad (.0000)\quad\ (.0095)$$

$$- .0017\ X_3 - .2830\ X_4 + .0085\ X_5$$
$$(.0063)\qquad (.1146)\qquad (.0709)$$

$$+ .0238\ X_6 + .0365\ V + .2166\ W$$
$$(.0038)\qquad (.0685)\quad\ (.0574)$$

$$+ .1014\ Y$$
$$(.0423)$$

Independent Variable	Zero-order Correlation	Path Coefficient
F_1: Size	-.086	-.0541
F_2: Status	-.065	-.0073
F_3: Life Cycle	-.372	-.2134
F_5: Recent Population Growth	-.140	-.2646
F_6: College Towns	.029	.1814
F_7: Foreign Stock Population	.539	.5342
F_{12}: Military Installations	.066	.1132
F_{13}: Mining Towns	.247	.2221
V : Civic Voluntary Activity	-.045	-.2420
W : Reform Government	-.004	.5370
Y : Decentralized DMS	.216	.2107

$R = .729$; Variance explained = 41%

$$Z_2 = 4.3793 - .0204\ F_1 - .0050\ F_2$$
$$ (1.0387)\ (.0545)\qquad (.1100)$$

$$- .0969\ F_3 - .5002\ F_5 + .0910\ F_6$$
$$(.0616)\qquad (.2503)\qquad (.0632)$$

$$+ .2806\ F_7 + .3379\ F_{12} + .0205\ F_{13}$$
$$(.0828)\qquad (.3882)\qquad (.0124)$$

$$- .1342\ V + .2016\ W + .0666\ Y$$
$$(.0832)\quad\ (.0628)\quad\ (.0503)$$

CONCLUSIONS

We conclude with a brief comparison of the relative advantages of discrete variables and nearly orthogonal factor scores in the construction of causal models. The most widespread criticism of factor analysis—its tendency to yield ambiguous results—was substantiated in a few cases in our analysis. This shortcoming, however, which we might term *factor ambiguity,* is generally leveled at the absence of distinctive factors with a small number of patently interrelated individual variables having high loadings. When factors are used in regression-type models, the advantage of near orthogonality thus must be weighed against the frequent ambiguities of interpretation. Factor ambiguity may be compounded in causal analysis, however, when a discrete variable that might have been important in explaining a particular variable is not significant in combination with other variables in a single factor.

This second difficulty might be labeled *model muddling.* The most salient examples of model muddling occurred in the factor-score models of the causes of urban renewal and governmental budget expenditures. A number of discrete variables were important in explaining differences among communities in their levels of urban renewal and governmental expenditures. In the factor-score models, however, even though the total variance explained by the factors in the two expenditure variables was not much smaller than that for a smaller number of discrete variables, few of the factors were significant either statistically or substantively. Obviously the models were muddled.

Nonetheless these two disadvantages must be weighed against the advantages, which number at least four. First, we could include a larger number of factors as independent variables in each model with less multicollinearity than was possible with the discrete-variable model. In an analysis in which only a limited number of cases is available—certainly true in this instance—but in which for theoretical reasons it seems advisable to include a large number of independent variables—again the case here—orthogonal variates are decidedly an advantage.

The second advantage follows directly from the first: the larger the number of independent variables in a model, ceteris paribus, the larger the probability that one of them will be significant. If there is at least a minimal exploratory element involved in one's empirical work—and how often is there not?—then this advantage must be taken into account. The factor-score models disclosed the importance of several variables that had not been previously isolated. The most striking example was the importance of a concentration of military installations in a community for its decision-making structure: communities with sizable military installations have more centralized patterns of decision-making. Moreover, the relationship did not appear to be a mere artifact of economic specialization, population size, or regional location.

The third advantage of factor scores is that they provide a convenient means of replicating relationships. And when replication is especially needed—because of high multicollinearity, a small number of cases, or for other reasons—orthogonal variates are especially useful. Because of factor ambiguity, there may not be a direct correspondence between a theoretically interesting discrete variable and every factor, but with close correspondence, positive replication with a different mix of variables augments the importance of consistent results. A number of findings from the discrete-variable analysis were replicated reasonably directly in the factor-score analysis. The importance of high-status community members for active civic voluntary associations was consistent. Reform-government structures were strongly associated with more centralized patterns of community decision-making in both analyses. They also consistently led to higher budget expenditures.

Finally, the use of orthogonal variates deriving from some type of factor analysis permits observations about the overall importance of broad classes of variables. Perhaps the most consistent picture of this sort that emerged was the continuing importance of nonsocioeconomic variables in the explanation of governmental outputs. Socioeconomic characteristics play a fundamental role, but the form of government and the pattern of decision-making remain independently important factors in explaining the forms and the quantities of political outputs.

Although we conclude by listing the advantages of nearly orthogonal variates for causal modeling, clearly these remarks should in no way be seen as suggesting their general substitution for discrete variables. At every stage in this chapter we have included a model composed completely of discrete variables, and if an adjacent model composed primarily of nearly orthogonal variates also has been displayed, it is not to argue for the unmitigated use of nearly orthogonal variates. In this particular case the factor-score models would seem to be most useful as intermediate rather than final, steps in the analysis. There are advantages to both precise distortion and model muddling; used together, the two can be mutually complementary.

PART THREE

Alternative Modes of Classification and Types of Cities

... Canadian and American urban dimensions

... City classification by oblique-factor analysis of time-series data

... Dimensions and classification of British towns
on the basis of new data

... A comparative typology of urban government images

CHAPTER 6

Canadian and American Urban Dimensions[1]

D. MICHAEL RAY

State University of New York at Buffalo

ROBERT A. MURDIE

York University

The preceding chapters indicate the variety of studies, published in the urban literature, in which multivariate statistical analysis was used to examine the underlying structure of urban centers and to classify these centers into relatively uniform types.[2] In the main these studies have focused on identifying the basic structural dimensions of a regional or national system of cities, with little attempt to compare the dimensions resulting from different analyses. A notable exception to this generalization is a recent paper by Hodge,[3] which Berry has extended in Chapter 1.

The lack of comparative studies, particularly between national territories,

[1] The analysis of the socioeconomic characteristics of Canadian cities reported in this chapter was carried out at the University of Waterloo during the spring and summer of 1968.

[2] Qazi Ahmad, *Indian Cities: Characteristics and Correlates,* University of Chicago, Department of Geography Research Paper No. 102 (1965). J. K. Hadden and E. F. Borgatta, *American Cities: Their Social Characteristics* (Chicago: Rand McNally and Co., 1965). T. Bunting and A. M. Baker, *Structural Characteristics of the Ontario–Quebec Urban System,* Research Report No. 3, Component Study No. 3, Urban Development Study (Toronto: Centre for Urban and Community Studies, University of Toronto, 1968). Gerald Hodge, "Urban Structure and Regional Development," Regional Science Association *Papers,* Vol. 21 (1968), pp. 101–123. Leslie J. King, "Cross-Sectional Analysis of Canadian Urban Dimensions, 1951 and 1961," *Canadian Geographer,* Vol. 10 (1966), pp. 205–224. C. A. Moser and Wolf Scott, *British Towns: A Statistical Study of Their Social and Economic Differences* (Edinburgh and London: Oliver and Boyd, 1961).

[3] Hodge, "Urban Structure and Regional Development."

is understandable. Census data are seldom comparable. The numbers and types of variables provided for cities of different size classes, the census definition of a city or metropolitan area, the census year, and the quality of census data all vary from country to country.

To make matters worse, analyses of regional and national systems of cities are usually undertaken with slightly different purposes in mind in different countries. These purposes are in turn reflected by the mix of variables and the relative size of cities contained within each study. For example, Hodge was interested in identifying structural dimensions related to the development of all incorporated urban centers, regardless of population size, in a particular region, with the specific aim of using them as explanatory variables for predicting the growth or decline of urban centers. Berry has attempted to identify the basic structural dimensions of an urban system by using as wide a range of variables as possible for cities of 10,000 or more inhabitants in 1960 as an empirical foundation for the development of urban and regional development theory.[4] The purposes of Moser and Scott's analysis of British urban centers[5] and of Ahmad's study of Indian cities[6] are similar to those of Berry's study. Yet Moser and Scott included only cities whose populations exceeded 50,000 in 1951, whereas Ahmad used a different mix of variables for cities with more than 100,000 inhabitants in 1961.

Since different variables have been included in the various studies, it is impossible to establish a precise quantitative evaluation of the similarities between resulting factor structures.[7] Instead comparisons must be made on the basis of identifying the dimensions that appear to summarize common relationships in different analyses. This is the approach used by Hodge.[8]

Studies that attempt to identify common factor structures in different analyses are searching for *factorial invariance*. To date attempts at measuring factorial invariance in urban analysis have been undertaken more successfully by investigators working at the intracity, rather than the intercity, level.[9] This situation is not surprising, for in spite of problems in data

[4] Brian J. L. Berry, Chapter 1 of this volume.

[5] Moser and Scott, *British Towns.*

[6] Ahmad, *Indian Cities.*

[7] Precise quantitative evaluation implies the use of a correlation coefficient or coefficient of congruence to measure the degree of association between two sets of factor loadings.

[8] Hodge, "Urban Structure and Regional Development," p. 109.

[9] See Robert A. Murdie, *Factorial Ecology of Metropolitan Toronto, 1951–1961: An Essay on the Social Geography of the City,* University of Chicago, Department of

comparability, at the intracity level of analysis there is a set of well-defined hypotheses concerning variations in the socioeconomic structure of individual cities and an outline of the conditions necessary to produce a particular factor structure.[10]

Usually at least three common factors emerge from studies of individual cities in most industrialized nations: the well-known social area dimensions of economic, family, and ethnic status.[11] There is now some evidence that these dimensions may also be common to studies of national city systems that incorporate into their analyses a wide range of census characteristics.[12] Hodge has shown that, in addition, economic (employment) and cultural (ethnic) characteristics are statistically independent at the intercity, as well as the intracity, level of analysis, and Berry confirms this in Chapter 1. Nevertheless no well-defined hypotheses have yet been formulated concerning the basic structural dimensions of urban centers in the aggregate.

A useful beginning for comparing the basic structural dimensions of two or more systems of cities more formally is analysis of Canadian and American urban centers. The similarity between these two countries reduces the problem of identifying the common dimensions of urban structure. Both are advanced economically and have over three-quarters of their populations living in urban places. The two countries are adjacent, and a continual flow of people, goods, and ideas passes across their common border. In each a significant minority group must be taken into consideration in any study of urban differentiation. In both countries a comprehensive series of census characteristics are available for urban centers of 10,000 or more inhabitants for the same general period. A complete American census was undertaken in 1960, and a complete Canadian one in 1961. Moreover, several studies have independently examined the structural dimensions of Canadian and American cities at about the same point in time, and their results are now available. One of these is Berry's study. Another is a recent analysis of Canadian urban dimensions, the results of which are discussed in the next section of this chapter and compared with those obtained by Berry.

Geography Research Paper No. 116 (1969). Frank L. Sweetser, "Factor Structure as Ecological Structure in Helsinki and Boston," *Acta Sociologica,* Vol. 8 (1965), pp. 205–225.

[10] Brian J. L. Berry and Philip H. Rees, "The Factorial Ecology of Calcutta," *The American Journal of Sociology,* Vol. 74 (1969), pp. 463–469.

[11] Eshref Shevky and Wendell Bell, *Social Area Analysis* (Stanford, Calif.: Stanford University Press, 1955).

[12] Berry, Chapter 1 of this volume; Hadden and Borgatta, *American Cities.*

SOCIOECONOMIC DIMENSIONS OF CANADIAN CITIES, 1961: A NEW PERSPECTIVE

Since the results of a multivariate analysis reflect the data selected and the observation units used, it is appropriate to turn first to a discussion of the variables, the observation units, and the analytics that were employed.

Variables

The data can be conveniently divided into three groups: (a) the economic variables, (b) the cultural variables, and (c) the spatial locators. Both the economic and the cultural variables were drawn from the 1961 Canadian census. The data were analyzed twice, first with a complete set of 95 variables and next with a reduced set of 84 variables after nine of the spatial locators and two others were deleted because of statistical redundancy. A list of the variables used in the analysis is provided in Appendix A.

The economic variables include measures of income level and distribution. Income level and distribution were measured in this study by average family income and by the proportion of families whose incomes were under (a) under $4000, (b) $4000 to $6000, and (c) $6000 to $10,000. Testing showed that the proportions of families with incomes below $1000 or $2000 and over $10,000 are too few and the income levels of single persons too erratic to serve as reliable economic indicators. The median value of owner-occupied single detached houses was included to supplement the income measures.

The level and distribution of income are affected directly by the occupation structure and employment level, and indirectly by the population age composition, dependency ratio, and education level. These characteristics themselves, however, are affected by migration and population-growth rates, which reflect income and economic opportunities. Measures of all of these characteristics were therefore included in the economic data set.

Twenty-three occupation categories were included in an effort to identify cities whose labor forces rely heavily on primary activities like farming, logging, fishing, and mining, as well as on secondary and tertiary functions like manufacturing, transportation, and trade. Labor-force participation rates were measured by the male labor force in each city as a percentage of all males 15 years old and older, and by the male-to-female labor-force ratio.

The growth of cities was measured as the index of population growth in 1921–1941 and 1941–1961; by the proportion of dwellings constructed in 1920–1945, 1946–1959, and 1959–1961; and by the proportion of the total number of immigrants who entered Canada in 1921–1940, 1941–1950, and 1951–1960.

Thirty-two cultural variables were included in the analysis because of the cultural diversity of Canadian cities. These cultural variables measure inherited population characteristics (Canadian region or foreign country of birth, mother tongue, and religion) rather than achieved characteristics like education and income.

The final set of variables, the spatial locators, was included to test for association between cultural and economic characteristics and distances from major Canadian cities. Three of these variables were used in the final analysis.

Observation Units

Data were gathered for the 174 cities in Canada with populations of 10,000 and over in 1961. All cities within the metropolitan areas defined by the Canadian census were aggregated to their respective metropolitan units, reducing the number of observation units to 113; for example, it appeared to be more meaningful to treat the cities on Montreal Island as a single Montreal metropolitan center than as separate centers. These aggregations for the metropolitan centers do not equal the aggregations published by the Census of Canada, which include urban areas with fewer than 10,000 inhabitants and rural populations living within metropolitan areas. The procedure used in this study for obtaining metropolitan-area aggregates was adopted for computational convenience, but the differences with the census metropolitan aggregates are unlikely to alter the results of the statistical analyses. For reference purposes the 113 urban centers used in the analysis are listed in Appendix B.

The Analytics

The statistical technique was factor analysis. Since this tool is well known in urban classification literature, no statistical formulas or details of methodology are included here.[13]

Use of a principal-axis factor model revealed that 70% of the variation among the cities described by the 84 variables can be expressed by just

[13] An excellent overview of the factor-analysis technique is provided by R. J. Rummel in "Understanding Factor Analysis," *The Journal of Conflict Resolution,* Vol. 11 (1968), pp. 444–480.

eight factors, summarized in Table 1. The names given to the factors are based on the variables most highly correlated with them. Two sets of factors can be distinguished; cultural (factors 1, 2, and 5) and space economy (factors 3, 4, 6, 7, and 8), although most factors include some variables from both sets of original characteristics.

The Dimensions of Cultural Variation[14]

Factor 1 identifies the *English–French and Ontario–Quebec contrasts* in mother tongue, religion, place of birth, family size, age structure, and education level. Table 2 lists the factor loadings, or correlations, for the 18 variables most closely associated with factor 1. The table shows a .941 correlation between factor 1 and the percentage of the population whose mother tongue is English and a —.908 correlation between the percentage

Table 1.   Summary of factors

Rank	Name	Eigenvalues	Per Cent of Total Variance	No. of Variables with Highest Loading on Factor
Dimensions of Cultural Variation				
1	English-French Contrasts	12.47	15.4	18
2	The Prairie-type City	8.47	10.5	12
5	The B.C.-type City	6.54	8.1	10
Dimensions of the Space Economy				
3	Mining-service Town Contrasts	7.59	9.4	14
4	Postwar Growth Centers	6.91	8.6	11
6	Primary Manufacturing and Special Functions	5.11	6.3	7
7	Ethno-metropolitan Centers	4.99	6.2	5
8	Center-periphery Contrasts	4.89	6.0	7
TOTALS		56.97	70.5	84

[14] For a qualitative interpretation of the cultural diversity within Canadian regions which corresponds closely with the results from our analysis, see Andrew H. Clark, "Geographical Diversity and the Personality of Canada," in Murray McCaskell, Ed., *Land and Livelihood: Geographical Essays in Honour of George Jobberns* (Christchurch: New Zealand Geographical Society Miscellaneous Series No. 4, 1962). Reprinted in Robert M. Irving, Ed., *Readings in Canadian Geography* (Toronto: Holt, Rinehart and Winston, 1968), pp. 3–16. The interested reader is also referred to various articles in the centennial publication of the Canadian Association of Geographers. See John Warkentin, Ed., *Canada: A Geographical Interpretation* (Toronto: Methuen, 1968).

Table 2.   Loadings for factor 1, English–French contrasts

No.	Name	Communality On Eight Factors	Loadings Positive	Loadings Negative
3	% Dwellings 1921-1945	0.780	--	-0.488
7	% Primary Ed. 5 yrs.	0.806	--	-0.466
8	% Secondary Ed. 1-2 yrs.	0.659	0.708	--
9	% Secondary Ed. 3-5 yrs.	0.862	0.645	--
12	% Population Age 0-14	0.845	--	-0.500
13	% Population Age 15-19	0.858	--	-0.732
18	Average Family Size	0.789	--	-0.670
49	% Quebec-born	0.890	--	-0.879
50	% Ontario-born	0.777	0.578	--
53	% United Kingdom-born	0.750	0.713	--
60	% Bilingual	0.607	--	-0.700
61	% English Mother Tongue	0.937	0.941	--
62	% French Mother Tongue	0.942	--	-0.908
67	% Dutch Mother Tongue	0.539	0.516	--
70	% Roman Catholic	0.955	--	-0.898
72	% United Church	0.916	0.918	--
73	% Baptist	0.518	0.633	--
75	Population Growth 1921-1941	0.530	--	-0.554

of the population whose mother tongue is French, including the clear bipolar nature of this factor.

The variables with positive loadings indicate that cities in which English is the mother tongue of a high proportion of the population also have a high proportion of immigrants from the United Kingdom and Holland, above-average educational levels, and Protestant affiliation. The detailed computer output also indicates that immigration generally has been directed to English, rather than French, cities, suggesting a greater cultural heterogeneity and faster growth for these cities than for the French ones. The negative loadings in Table 2 suggest that French cities are characterized by larger families, an above average proportion of population with a primary level of education, and relatively slower postwar growth. As expected, the bilingual population is concentrated among the French cities. Cities with high positive and negative scores on this factor are listed in Table 3.

Factor 2, *the Prairie type of city,* is also a cultural factor stressing the importance of the Prairie-type Slavic component in Canadian cities and regionalism. Twelve variables correlate highly with this factor, including East European country of birth and mother tongue, Greek Orthodox religion, proportion of the population born in the Prairies, and, as expected, the relatively high proportion of the labor force employed in farming (Table 4). The importance of German and American immigration to the Prairies is also made apparent by the factor loadings.

The intercorrelation of some of these variables (Table 5) indicates the

Table 3. Cities with high scores on factor 1, English–French contrasts

City	Pop. 1961	Factor Score	% English MT	% French MT	Av. Fam. Size	% Sec. Ed. 1-5 yrs
The English-type City						
St. Thomas	22,469	1.68	93.1	0.4	3.9	58.1
Trenton	13,183	1.35	91.3	3.8	3.9	54.6
Woodstock	20,486	1.35	90.0	0.7	4.0	52.6
The French-type City						
Rimouski	17,739	-1.82	0.9	98.7	5.4	43.7
Rouyn	18,716	-1.82	4.9	90.4	5.1	31.3
Chicoutimi-North	11,229	-1.77	0.6	99.0	5.8	35.3
Alma	13,309	-1.71	0.7	98.8	5.3	34.3
Average for Canadian Cities (Unweighted by City Size)			59.6	30.5	4.4	48.5

Table 4. Loadings for factor 2, the Prairie-type city

No.	Name	Communality on Eight Factors	Factor Loadings Positive	Factor Loadings Negative
38	% Farmers	0.626	--	-0.558
51	% Prairie-born	0.762	--	-0.751
54	% U.S.A.-born	0.703	--	-0.688
55	% German-born	0.734	--	-0.556
58	% East-European-born	0.771	--	-0.782
65	% East-European Mother Tongue	0.705	--	-0.733
66	% German Mother Tongue	0.594	--	-0.712
71	% Greek Orthodox	0.663	--	-0.713
74	% Lutheran	0.599	--	-0.635
77	% Immigrants	0.925	--	-0.609
80	% Immigrants 1941-1950	0.377	0.331	--
83	Distance from Vancouver	0.886	0.739	--

Table 5. Simple correlations for marker variables: Factor 2

Name	% Prairie-born	% Greek Orth.	% Immigrants	% Farmers	Halifax	Toronto
% Prairie-born	1.00	--	--	--	--	--
% Greek Orth.	.560	1.00	--	--	--	--
% Immigrants	.348	.603	1.00	--	--	--
% Farmers	.563	.193	.341	1.00	--	--
Distance from Halifax	.665	.492	.645	.479	1.00	--
Distance from Toronto	.555	.245	.255	.339	.798	1.00

particular importance of immigration to the growth of the Prairie city and emphasizes the relative contribution of immigration to urban growth in Canada; the effect of this variable increases westward across the country with distance from Halifax. Migration theory, particularly the migration-interaction model, would suggest that the relative contribution of immigration, predominantly from Europe, would diminish from east to west. Evidently the greater economic opportunities in western Canada have more than compensated for the greater distances from the ports of entry. Conversely the geographical location of the Atlantic Provinces has not compensated for their lower opportunities in agriculture and industry.

The factor scores and distinguishing characteristics of eight cities with the highest factor scores are shown in Table 6. All are in the Prairies except

Table 6. Cities with high scores on factor 2, the Prairie type of city

The Prairie-type City	Pop. 1961	Factor Score	% Prairie-Born	% Greek Orthodox	% Immigrants	% Farmers
Medicine Hat	24,484	-2.81	68.7	0.4	25.3	5.7
Swift Current	12,186	-2.28	76.3	0.7	17.1	7.1
North Battleford	11,230	-2.16	76.5	3.7	17.4	5.7
Winnipeg	398,636	-2.14	66.6	3.1	25.0	1.0
Edmonton	311,557	-2.10	67.2	5.1	23.8	1.2
Vernon	10,250	-1.92	23.2	3.6	27.0	1.7
Prince Albert	24,168	-1.84	78.5	3.7	15.1	3.4
Saskatoon	95,526	-1.83	73.5	2.6	18.0	2.7
Average for Canadian Cities (Unweighted by city size)			13.3	0.9	13.4	1.3

Vernon, which, like the other cities in the Okanagan Valley, shares the characteristics of the Prairie city. It is noted that the proportion of immigrants in the Prairie cities is much higher than the 13.4% average for all Canadian cities. Immigration has also made an important contribution to the growth of cities in southwestern Ontario. In 1961 some 33% of Toronto's population was foreign-born.[15]

Factor 5, *the British Columbia type of city* is identified by its cultural characteristics and distinct regionalism, notably the percentages of the population born in British Columbia, Scandinavia, and Asia (Table 7). Four occupational variables (percentages of the male labor force employed as fishermen, longshoremen, carpenters, and loggers) are also correlated

[15] Canada, Dominion Bureau of Statistics, *Census of Canada, 1961,* Bulletin CT-15.

Table 7. Loadings for factor 5, British Columbia type of city

No.	Name	Communality On Eight Factors	Loadings Positive	Loadings Negative
39	% Loggers	0.383	--	-0.506
40	% Fishermen	0.416	--	-0.610
43	% Carpenters	0.451	--	-0.529
46	% Longshoremen	0.459	--	-0.579
52	% British Columbia-born	0.718	--	-0.799
57	% Scandinavian-born	0.834	--	-0.785
59	% Asian-born	0.721	--	-0.680
63	% Asian Mother Tongue	0.714	--	-0.714
64	% Scandinavian Mother Tongue	0.485	--	-0.545
84	Distance from Toronto	0.889	--	-0.747

with this type of city. Table 8 clearly indicates a strong relationship between ethnicity and occupational structure, which sets the British Columbia type of city apart from those of the rest of Canada.

Dimensions of the Space Economy

Factor 3, *contrasts between mining and service towns,* identifies cities clearly associated with mining activities on the positive end of the scale and service or distribution centers on the negative end of the scale. Table 9 shows positive correlations between factor 3 and such variables as the percentage of male population, the male-to-female labor-force ratio, the percentage of population engaged in mining, and average family incomes of $4000 to $6000.

In contrast with the mining cities are the service and distribution centers, which are more closely associated with the percentages of the labor force employed as managers, clerks, lawyers, surgeons, professors, and in

Table 8. Cities with high scores on factor 5, British Columbia type of city

The B.C.- Type City	Pop. 1961	Factor Score	% B.C.-born	% Asian MT	% Fishermen	% Loggers
Prince Rupert	11,987	-5.27	51.5	2.2	9.84	1.84
Port Alberni	11,560	-4.36	48.4	2.2	1.05	5.37
Nanaimo	14,135	-2.85	54.6	1.6	2.66	4.31
Vancouver	441,832	-2.72	39.7	3.6	0.78	0.81
Kamloops	10,076	-2.47	49.9	2.3	0.07	1.42
Victoria	54,941	-2.26	38.7	3.6	0.39	0.46
Prince George	13,877	-2.10	47.3	1.3	0.00	2.41
Average for Canadian Cities (Unweighted by city size)			5.2	0.4	0.17	0.65

Table 9. Loadings for factor 3, mining–service town contrasts

No.	Name	Communality On Eight Factors	Loadings Positive	Loadings Negative
1	% Male Population	0.868	0.675	
6	Median Value One-Owner Occupied Dwelling	0.773	--	-0.510
21	% Family Income $4,000-$6,000	0.577	0.618	--
23	Male/Female Labor Force Ratio	0.662	0.578	--
25	% Managers	0.767	--	-0.701
29	% Professors	0.411	--	-0.395
30	% Surgeons	0.494	--	-0.567
31	% Lawyers	0.647	--	-0.642
32	% Clerks	0.672	--	-0.609
33	% Sales Occupations	0.766	--	-0.809
35	% Transport	0.403	--	-0.549
36	% Railroad Operators	0.141	--	-0.202
37	% Road Operators	0.614	--	-0.566
41	% Miners	0.468	0.548	--

sales occupations. These towns are grouped with centers having concentrations of road and railway operators, and transport and communications personnel.

The scores on factor 3 group mining centers like Flin Flon, New Waterford, and Timmins; whereas Riviere-du-Loup, Quebec, Rimouski, and Swift Current exhibit the highest negative scores and typify the service type of center (see Table 10).

Mining centers extend across the resource frontier of the country and are generally small cities. Service-type centers do not exhibit such a strik-

Table 10. Cities with high scores on factor 3, mining–service town contrasts

City	Pop. 1961	Factor Score	% Male Pop.	M/F LF Ratio	% Miners	% Sales
The Mining-type City						
Flin Flon	11,104	2.86	52.6	3.6	27.4	2.9
New Waterford	10,592	2.77	50.6	4.0	54.6	2.8
Timmins	29,270	1.96	51.8	3.5	29.6	4.9
The Service-type City						
Riviere-du-Loup	10,835	-1.88	47.5	2.0	0.1	9.6
Quebec	266,886	-1.62	47.6	2.0	0.1	8.8
Rimouski	17,739	-1.49	47.1	1.8	0.2	8.2
Swift Current	12,186	-1.21	49.9	2.3	0.6	9.8
Average for Canadian Cities (Unweighted by city size)			49.6	2.6	2.8	6.6

Table 11. Loadings for factor 4, postwar growth centers

No.	Name	Communality On Eight Factors	Loadings Positive	Loadings Negative
4	% Dwellings Built 1946-1959	0.787	--	-0.708
5	% Dwellings Built 1959-1961	0.533	--	-0.597
14	% Population Age 20-29	0.720	--	-0.720
15	% Population Age 30-39	0.789	--	-0.770
16	% Population Age 40-54	0.803	0.558	--
17	% Population Age 55-64	0.900	0.591	--
24	% Male Labor Force	0.607	--	-0.657
76	Population Growth 1941-1961	0.680	--	-0.589
78	% Male Immigrants	0.543	--	-0.414
79	% Immigrants 1921-1940	0.594	0.509	--
81	% Immigrants 1951-1961	0.821	--	-0.757

ing pattern since service activities are a part of every city's economic life. The larger centers, as expected, generally have a negative score because service functions increase with city size. In smaller centers a negative score indicates the absence of a specialized function.

Factor 4 identifies *postwar growth centers*. The characteristics most highly associated with this factor are age structure, immigration, population growth, period of construction, and male labor force (Table 11). This city grouping can easily be identified by its recent growth and young population. The fastest growth has taken place in small centers and for highly specific reasons (Table 12). For example, the growth of Sept-Iles reflects

Table 12. Cities with high scores on factor 4, postwar growth centers

City	Pop. 1961	Factor Score	% Immigration 1951-1961	% Dwellings 1946-61	% Age 40-64	% Age 20-39
Postwar Growth						
Sept-Iles	14,196	-4.84	82.7	93.8	12.5	39.4
Oromocto	12,170	-4.03	45.8	96.7	7.6	38.4
Prince George	13,877	-1.89	50.0	76.0	19.9	32.3
Georgetown	10,298	-1.88	65.4	67.9	18.1	31.7
Postwar Stable						
Glace Bay	24,186	2.03	15.8	14.5	23.9	23.1
New Waterford	10,592	1.99	11.8	21.0	21.5	22.7
Amherst	10,788	1.89	26.9	14.1	26.4	22.4
Truro	12,421	1.48	24.9	24.9	26.6	24.2
Average for Canadian Cities (Unweighted by city size)			36.4	42.3	23.1	27.7

Table 13.   Loadings for factor 6, primary manufacturing and special functions

No.	Name	Communality On Eight Factors	Loadings Positive	Loadings Negative
11	% Degree	0.805	0.724	--
19	Average Family Income	0.670	0.529	--
20	% Family Income $0-4,000	0.860	--	-0.549
22	% Family Income $6,000-10,000	0.873	0.564	--
26	% Professional and Technical	0.850	0.805	--
27	% Engineers	0.740	0.800	--
28	% Scientists	0.732	0.782	--

the production and shipment of iron ore; the growth of Oromocto, the location of a Canadian armed forces installation. In contrast with the fast-growth centers are cities like Glace Bay, New Waterford, Amherst, and Truro, which have older populations and lower rates of construction and immigration.

Apart from the specific cities already mentioned, growth has been concentrated in the manufacturing belt and the large city centers. The process of urbanization in both Canada and the United States has increased the growth of large cities to the detriment of the small centers.

Factor 6 identifies the importance of *primary manufacturing and special functions* in certain Canadian cities that have relatively high concentrations of highly skilled workers, many of whom have university training (Table 13).

Table 14 indicates that in most cities scoring highest on factor 6, including Arvida, Noranda, Sarnia, Flin Flon, and Trail, primary manufacturing

Table 14.   Cities with high scores on factor 6, primary manufacturing and special functions

Specialized Manufacturing	Pop. 1961	Factor Score	% Prof-tech.	% Engineers	% Scientists
Arvida	14,460	5.57	20.6	6.54	2.46
Noranda	11,477	2.93	11.2	2.17	1.50
Sarnia	50,976	2.74	14.9	3.97	1.49
Ottawa	362,712	1.98	14.1	1.57	0.80
Flin Flon	11,104	1.90	7.5	1.06	1.18
Fredericton	19,683	1.77	15.2	2.37	0.29
Calgary	261,904	1.66	10.6	1.59	1.47
Trail	11,580	1.52	8.6	1.52	0.41
Average for Canadian Cities (Unweighted by city size)			8.3	0.97	0.26

is the dominant activity. High scores for other cities, such as Ottawa, Fredericton, and Calgary, can be explained by the high proportion of degree holders and professional and technical people employed in civil service and similar institutions in addition to manufacturing. Specialized manufacturing centers are restricted in number and are distributed in proportion to the number of cities in each Canadian region; that is, four in Ontario, three in Quebec, two in the Prairie Provinces, and one in each of British Columbia and the Maritime Provinces.

Factor 7 identifies the *ethnometropolitan* component in the Canadian urban system. The population increase in Canada during the last intercensal period, 1951–1961, was predominantly in the 17 metropolitan areas recognized by the census. Population growth in metropolitan areas during the same period was double that of nonmetropolitan regions, or 44.8 and 20.3%, respectively.[16] This disproportionately high rate of metropolitan growth testifies to the importance of immigration, which in fact accounted for half the total metropolitan growth. A substantial proportion of the immigrants in Ontario and western Canadian metropolitan centers are foreign born, and in Toronto, the foremost center for postwar immigrants, one-third of the population is foreign born (Table 15). The heavy influx of immigrants imparts to Canadian metropolitan centers a cultural distinctiveness that emerges in the analysis as an ethnometropolitan factor (Table 16).

Table 15. Immigrants in Canadian metropolitan areas, 1961

	Total Immigrants	Per Cent of Total Population
St. John's, Nfld.	2,251	2.5
Halifax, N.S.	12,817	7.0
Saint John N.B.	5,368	5.6
Montreal, Que.	321,091	15.2
Quebec, Que.	7,363	2.1
Hamilton, Ont.	110,511	28.0
Kitchener, Ont.	31,617	20.4
London, Ont.	38,311	21.1
Sudbury, Ont.	17,782	16.1
Toronto, Ont.	607,122	33.3
Windsor, Ont.	44,722	23.1
Winnipeg, Man.	113,038	23.7
Calgary, Alta.	68,952	24.7
Edmonton, Alta.	79,036	23.4
Vancouver, B.C.	226,689	28.7
Victoria, B.C.	44,883	29.1

[16] Yoshiko Kasahara, "A Profile of Canada's Metropolitan Centres," *Queen's Quarterly,* Vol. 70 (1963), p. 305.

Table 16.   Loadings for factor 7, ethnometropolitan centers

No.	Name	Communality On Eight Factors	Loadings Positive	Loadings Negative
2	Population Density	0.559	0.689	--
56	% Italian-born	0.645	0.589	--
68	% Italian Mother Tongue	0.623	0.568	--
69	% Yiddish Mother Tongue	0.519	0.624	--
82	Air Flights	0.570	0.668	--

The identification of factor 7 as an ethnometropolitan factor is based as much on cities scoring high on it as on the variables that load on it. Indeed the most sensitive indicators of metropolitanism—the flow of commodities and services among centers, business service receipts, and wholesale sales per capita; and the proportion of the labor force in such activities as finance, insurance, real estate, and business services—were not included in our analysis.

Wolfe has mapped one measure of interurban flows, air passenger travel for 1964.[17] The four air routes on which Canadian carriers transported over 100,000 passengers in 1964 were, in order of importance, Toronto–Montreal, Toronto–New York, Montreal–New York, and Toronto–Ottawa. The map and accompanying data suggest the primary importance of the Toronto–Montreal axis of the Canadian heartland and its links with both the United States heartland, particularly New York and Chicago, and the Canadian hinterland, particularly Vancouver and Winnipeg.

Stone has examined other measures of metropolitanism and prepared a tentative hierarchy of metropolitan centers.[18] Toronto and Montreal are clearly at the top. At the second level, though not necessarily equal to each other, are Vancouver, Calgary, Winnipeg, and London. At the third level Stone includes Edmonton, Saint John, and Windsor. Factor 7 supports this grouping. Averaging the factor scores for each of Stone's three hierarchical levels gives the values 4.44, 0.98, and 0.51. Some cities score high on factor 7, however, merely because a very high proportion of their population speaks Italian as the mother tongue (e.g., Niagara Falls and Sault Ste. Marie—see Table 17).

Factor 8 is primarily a spatial factor stressing the *center–periphery* distribution of Canadian cities. The center, or heartland, is identified by positive correlations with craftsmen, machinists, laborers, and proportion of the population born in Ontario. Peripheral centers are identified by service

[17] Roy I. Wolfe, "Economic Development," in Warkentin, Ed., *Canada,* p. 214.
[18] Leroy O. Stone, *Urban Development in Canada* (Ottawa: Dominion Bureau of Statistics, 1967), p. 196.

Table 17. Cities with high scores on factor 7, ethnometropolitan centers

Metropolitan Centers	Pop. 1961	Factor Score	Pop. Density	Air Flights	% Yiddish MT	% Italian MT
Toronto	1,780,922	5.43	17,102.9	498	1.44	9.3
Montreal	1,907,910	3.45	8,085.7	516	1.72	4.4
Winnipeg	398,636	2.31	6,107.4	140	2.19	1.0
Niagara Falls	22,351	2.16	8,011.1	0	0.13	15.8
Windsor	132,456	1.61	7,805.3	52	0.53	5.6
Ottawa	362,712	1.47	6,719.3	144	0.36	1.8
Sault Ste. Marie	43,088	1.45	5,559.7	11	0.10	13.5
Timmins	29,270	1.42	8,315.3	6	0.23	5.3
Vancouver	441,832	1.28	8,253.9	188	0.326	2.3
Average for Canadian Cities (Unweighted by city size)			4,002.8	20.0	0.15	1.6

occupations and high concentrations of the population born in the Maritime and Prairie Provinces (Table 18). The original correlation matrix indicates a positive relationship between such characteristics and distance from Toronto. This factor corresponds closely with the results from Maxwell's functional classification of Canadian cities.[19] Maxwell found that the dominant function of all but two of Canada's heartland cities was manufacturing, whereas just over one-third of the peripheral cities had manufacturing as the dominant activity.

Table 19 clearly shows the center–periphery pattern. Cities with high positive scores—Port Colborne, Oshawa, Sault Ste. Marie, and Welland—

Table 18. Loadings for factor 8, center–periphery contrasts

No.	Name	Communality On Eight Factors	Loadings Positive	Loadings Negative
10	% University Ed. 1-4 yrs.	0.597	--	-0.431
34	% Services	0.625	--	-0.491
42	% Craftsmen	0.730	0.810	--
44	% Paper Operators	0.343	0.340	--
45	% Machinists	0.670	0.697	--
47	% Laborers	0.447	0.472	--
48	% Maritime-born	0.684	--	-0.551
50	% Ontario-born	0.777	0.552	--
51	% Prairie-born	0.762	--	-0.339

[19] J. W. Maxwell, "The Functional Structure of Canadian Cities: A Classification of Cities," *Geographical Bulletin,* Vol. 7 (1965), pp. 79–104.

Table 19.   Cities with high scores on factor 8, center–periphery contrasts

City	Pop. 1961	Factor Score	% Maritime-born	% Ontario-born	% Prairie-born	% Craftsmen
			Center			
Port Colborne	14,886	1.92	2.2	65.4	1.9	45.9
Oshawa	62,415	1.73	4.0	68.8	2.3	50.9
Sault Ste. Marie	43,088	1.63	1.7	69.8	1.8	41.4
Welland	36,079	1.61	2.2	62.2	2.5	49.0
			Periphery			
Oromocto	12,170	-4.28	58.8	16.1	7.5	1.3
New Waterford	10,592	-2.26	94.2	0.6	0.1	16.2
Fredericton	19,683	-2.11	85.5	3.2	1.3	19.5
Halifax	139,477	-1.98	82.1	5.5	1.8	20.9
Average for Canadian Cities (Unweighted by city size)			12.6	28.3	13.3	33.0

have high concentrations of craftsmen and Ontario-born population and a relatively small proportion of persons born in the Prairie and Maritime Provinces. The four most "peripheral" cities—Oromocto, New Waterford, Fredericton, and Halifax—are in the Atlantic Provinces, the region with the lowest average family incomes in Canada and the greatest regional development problems.

The center–periphery scores show a gradation from southern Ontario, where most of the cities with central characteristics are found, eastward to the Atlantic Provinces and westward to the Prairie Provinces. Cities in British Columbia that are farthest removed from the center do not conform to the center–periphery pattern. The British Columbia pattern suggests instead that these cities are not peripheral to southern Ontario but are part of an independent system, which may be centered on Vancouver.

COMPARISON OF CANADIAN AND AMERICAN URBAN DIMENSIONS

Comparison of Canadian Factorial Studies

The results of the factor analysis of Canadian cities are briefly compared with other factorial studies of Canadian cities in Table 20. All these studies

Table 20. Comparison of Canadian factorial studies

	King	Bunting-Baker	Hodge (Eastern Ontario)	Ray-Murdie
Number of Cities	106	73	80	113
Selection of Cities	All legal cities over 10,000 in 1951 in Canada	All cities and metropolitan areas over 10,000 in 1961 in Ontario and Quebec	All incorporated cities, towns and villages in Eastern Ontario	All cities over 10,000 in Canada. Cities in CMA's aggregated into single observation units
Number of Variables	54	71	32	84
Type of Variables:				
Economic	24	27	16 .	35
Housing and physical stock	11	18	3	3
Demographic	7	9	5	11
Cultural	3	11	5	32
Locational	9	6	3	3
Data Source	1961 Census Questionnaire	1961 Census	1961 Census Questionnaire	1961 Census
General Factors	Quebec-Prairie; English-French; Central City; Suburban Area; Center-Periphery; Urban Depression	Obsolescent Center; Cultural-Linguistic; Metropolitan; Commercial; Peripheral; Educational-Occupational; Fast Growth; Public Administration; Defence	Physical Development; French-English; Population Age; Industrial-Commercial; Population Size; Education Level; Compact Development	English-French; Prairie-type; Mining-Service; Postwar Growth; B.C.-type; Primary Manufacturing; Ethno-Metropolitan; Center-Periphery

Sources:

1. Leslie J. King, "Cross-Sectional Analysis of Canadian Urban Dimensions, 1951 and 1961," Canadian Geographer, Vol. 10 (1966), pp. 205-224.

2. T. Bunting and A.M. Baker, Structural Characteristics of the Ontario-Quebec Urban System, Research Report No. 3, Component Study No. 3, Urban Development Study (Toronto: Centre for Urban and Community Studies, University of Toronto, 1968).

3. Gerald Hodge, The Identification of Growth Poles in Eastern Ontario (Toronto: Ontario Department of Economics and Development, 1966).

Note: 1. We have assigned shortened names to the factors in King's study based on his interpretation of the factors and the factor loadings given in his paper.

198

are concerned with identifying the contemporary structural components of urban systems. King's study, like ours, is also concerned with the broad spatial patterns of the dimensions, and in ultimately relating these patterns to urban growth and regional development theory.[20] In contrast, the Bunting–Baker[21] and Hodge[22] studies are concerned with the policy implications for urban and regional development and, in the case of Hodge, with the survival of the small urban center.

All the Canadian factorial studies listed in Table 20 use 1961 census and supplementary data on economic, housing and physical stock, demographic, cultural, and locational characteristics. The biggest differences in variable selection among the studies are in the number of cultural and housing and physical stock variables.

Two groups of factors, cultural and space economy, emerge in these studies. The cultural factors underline the strong regionalism in Canadian cities. Four of Canada's five regions emerge as culturally distinct: Ontario and Quebec cities are distinguished by the cultural differences of the two founding nations; the Prairie city by its relatively large Slavic component; and the British Columbia city by the relative concentration of Asian and Scandinavian immigrants. Only two factor analyses fail to identify the importance of cultural differences in Canada, and both of these are restricted to analyses of individual provinces in Canada's Atlantic region.[23]

The cultural differences among Canadian cities are most clearly identified in our own study because of the emphasis given to cultural characteristics. Even in our study, however, the cities of the Atlantic Provinces fail to emerge as a culturally distinct group. Cultural differences in Canada reflect the origin and period of arrival of immigrants. Immigration has clearly continued to play an important role in urban and regional growth in Canada in the twentieth century. Before World War II the number of immigrants tended to increase with distance from the Atlantic Provinces, but immigrants arriving after World War II have tended to concentrate in the Canadian heartland. The failure of the cities of the Atlantic Provinces to emerge as a culturally distinct group reflects their relative failure to attract immigrants.

These studies also reveal a common set of space-economy factors that

[20] King, "Canadian Urban Dimensions."

[21] Bunting and Baker, *Ontario–Quebec Urban System.*

[22] Hodge, "Urban Structure and Regional Development." See also Gerald Hodge, *The Identification of Growth Poles in Eastern Ontario* (Toronto: Ontario Department of Economics and Development, 1966).

[23] The studies by Gerald Hodge of urban centers in Prince Edward Island and Nova Scotia.

identify the preeminence of the metropolitan centers, particularly Montreal and Toronto; the wide variation in rates of population growth; and center–periphery contrasts. In our study, particularly, centers of slow postwar growth are located primarily in the Atlantic Provinces and are distinguished by an older age structure of the population and older housing stock. The slow postwar growth is statistically distinct from, and more important than, center–periphery contrasts. All studies except that of Hodge identify the center, or heartland, as the Canadian manufacturing belt extending across southern Ontario and Quebec from Windsor to Quebec City. Bunting and Baker identify the remainder of their study area, northern Ontario and Quebec, as the periphery. In our study the cities of the Atlantic and Prairie Provinces are included in the periphery; King also includes the British Columbia cities. Although all these studies underline the center–periphery contrasts in urbanization in Canada, particularly in the occupational structure of the labor force, it is uncertain whether British Columbia cities are better regarded as peripheral-type cities or as forming a separate urban system.

Different functional types of city are identified by the authors according to the regions studied and the variables selected. It is not possible to identify, therefore, a common classification of cities according to function.

Additional differences between the factors identified in these studies arise from differences in the definition of urban units. In particular King's study, which treats all legal cities within metropolitan areas as separate observation units, yields factors distinguishing central- and suburban-type cities.

Canadian and American Urban Dimensions

Only two comprehensive factorial studies of American cities have been published. Hadden and Borgatta[24] examined 644 cities with populations of 25,000 and over, and Berry[25] analyzed 1762 cities with populations of 10,000 and over. Given the differences in city sizes and the variables considered in the two studies, their factor structures are surprisingly similar (Table 21).

These factor structures also show some important similarities with the Canadian studies reviewed. American and Canadian urban systems both contain cultural dimensions that depict internal ethnic differences and identify concentrations of foreign-born population.

24 Hadden and Borgatta, *American Cities.*
25 Berry, Chapter 1 in this volume.

Table 21. Comparison of American factorial studies

	Hadden and Borgatta	Berry
Number of Cities	644	1,762
Selection of Cities	All cities 25,000 and over in 1960. Legal city observation units.	All cities 10,000 and over in 1960. Legal city observation units.
Number of Variables	65	97
Type of Variables:		
Economic	33	56
Housing and Physical Stock	16	12
Demographic	9	17
Cultural	3	12
Locational	4	0
Data Source	U.S. Census, 1960	U.S. Census, 1960
Factors	Socioeconomic Status Air Conditioning Nonwhite Age Composition Educational Center Residential Mobility Population Density Foreign-born Concentration Total Population Wholesale Concentration Retail Concentration Manufacturing Concentration Durable Manufacturing Communication Public Administration	Size Socioeconomic Status Stage in Family Cycle Nonwhite Foreign-born Recent Population Growth Recent Growth in Employment Female Participation in the Labor Force Elderly Working Males Manufacturing Mining College Military Service

Sources:
1. J.K. Hadden and E.F. Borgatta, American Cities: Their Social Characteristics (Chicago: Rand McNally and Co., 1965).
2. Brian J.L. Berry, in Chapter 1.

In Canada internal ethnic differences are primarily associated with the English–French contrasts of the heartland. In the United States the internal ethnic differences are identified as Negro concentrations primarily associated with southern cities, although some northern cities (e.g., Centerville, Illinois, 56% of whose population is nonwhite) belong in this category also. In Canada the French minority group has enjoyed the economic opportunities conferred geographically by location in the heartland and historically by precedence in settlement; its concern has been mainly with language rights. In the United States the Negro minority group, whose economic opportunities have been reduced by a long history of slavery and concentration in the periphery, has been concerned with economic equality.

In the factor analyses of American cities data on the country of birth of the foreign-born population is not available and concentrations of foreign-born population group on a single factor. The foreign-born population is a much less important element in the United States than it is in Canada, comprising only 5.4% of the population versus 15.6% in Canada.[26] In Canada the foreign-born population forms distinctive elements in the Prairie and British Columbia cities, in the metropolitan centers, and in some of the smaller Ontario cities.

Space-Economy Dimensions

Three general space-economy dimensions can be identified in United States and Canadian cities. These factors are size, socioeconomic status, and life cycle. Of these three, the first is the most directly comparable between the two countries, although Canada's higher immigration rates give the size factor in Canada important ethnic associations. Differences in the other two space-economy factors between the two countries reflect differences in the use of observation units. Socioeconomic status and life-cycle factors in the United States studies identify intrametropolitan differences associated with high income and with newer suburban areas. King's study identifies directly comparable factors in Canada, distinguishing intrametropolitan differences primarily in Toronto and Montreal. Our study, which aggregates legal cities in metropolitan areas, identifies socioeconomic status and life-cycle factors, but they are associated with primary manufacturing and specialized functions and with English–French contrasts, respectively.

A center–periphery factor has been identified in all the Canadian studies except those of Hodge, who was concerned with a number of small areas. This factor identifies the manufacturing belt in the Canadian heartland and the associated heartland–hinterland differences in occupational structure. Center–periphery differences are apparently less regular in the United States, and, though a manufacturing factor is identified in both studies of American cities, it is not simply a Manufacturing Belt and center–periphery factor.

Highly specific factors—such as manufacturing, mining, education, defense, recreation, and service—emerge in the various factorial studies of

Canadian and American studies. No important functional differences can be discerned between the two urban systems.

CONCLUSIONS

Some of the differences observed reflect the sensitivity of factor analysis to the way in which observation units and variables are defined and selected. Factor analysis is particularly sensitive to the inclusion of characteristics describing urban functions with a highly sporadic distribution, such as military, educational, tourism and recreation, and mining. Therefore the differences in the number of factors identifying such specific functions in the American and Canadian studies cannot be regarded as important. Some differences between the results of the studies reviewed reflect the way in which the observation units are defined. Important intrametropolitan variations are identified in the studies that use the legal definition of a city and treat metropolitan areas as a number of separate observation units.

Despite the differences in the urban characteristics examined and the definitions of urban places used, some important similarities are apparent in the American and Canadian urban systems. All studies of the two systems reveal distinct cultural and space-economy factors emphasizing the independence of cultural and economic characteristics. In both systems the cultural factors focus on internal ethnic differences and on the cultural and demographic impact of immigration on urban growth.

Three general space-economy factors are common to American and Canadian urban systems: a size or metropolitan factor, socioeconomic status, and life cycle. In Canada the metropolitan and life-cycle factors have significant cultural ingredients. The distinction between these general space-economy factors and the specific function factors emphasizes that there is no simple or direct relationship in either country between dominant urban function and size, economic status, or age composition.

A more complete picture of the similarities and differences between the two urban systems might be obtained by including both urban systems in a single factor analysis with a common set of variables. Comparison of these systems at different time periods, and of urban systems for countries at different levels of economic development, should make possible an evaluation of the conditions necessary for the emergence of various cultural and space-economy differences. Factorial studies of urban systems have demonstrated the value of this technique in identifying and describing the fundamental patterns of variation in urban structure. They also exhibit an encouraging degree of factor invariance. However, the studies reviewed have confined themselves largely to examination of the factor structure. Greater attention to the spatial patterns displayed by each factor and the way in which these spatial patterns change through time and are related to other characteristics is needed before factorial studies can contribute to the theory of urban growth and regional development.

APPENDIX A   List of Transgenerated Variables

Population - general characteristics: Census Bulletin 1202
1.   % MALE POP   % male population
2.   POP DENSITY   population density
3.   % DWELS 1921-45   % dwellings built 1921-1945
4.   % DWELS 1946-59   % dwellings built 1946-1959
5.   % DWELS 1959-61   % dwellings built 1959-1961
6.   MEDIAN VALUE   median value one-owner occupied dwellings

Educational achievement of population over 5 years old not now attending
school: Census Bulletin 1210
7.   % PRIM 5   % with 5 years primary education
8.   % SEC 1-2   % with 1-2 years secondary education
9.   % SEC 3-5   % with 3-5 years secondary education
10. % UNI 1-4   % with 1-4 years university education
11. % DEGREE   % with university degree

Per cent of population in given age groups: Census Bulletin 1202
12. % AGE 0-14   0-14 years
13. % AGE 15-19   15-19 years
14. % AGE 20-29   20-29 years
15. % AGE 30-39   30-39 years
16. % AGE 40-54   40-54 years
17. % AGE 55-64   55-64 years

Incomes - per cent of families with stated incomes: Census Bulletin 413
18. AV FAM SIZE   average family size
19. AV FAM INCOME   average family income
20. % FAM INC 0-4 TH   % of families with income 0-4,000 dollars
21. % FAM INC 4-6 TH   % of families with income 4,000-6,000 dollars
22. % FAM INC 6-10 TH   % of families with income 6,000-10,000
                                                                  dollars

Labor force characteristics
23. M/F LF RATIO   male/female labor force ratio
24. % MALE LF   male labor force as a percentage of males
                                    over 15 years of age

Occupations - per cent of male labor force in indicated occupations:
Bulletin 316
25. % MANAGERS   managerial occupations
26. % PROF TECH   professional and technical
27. % ENGINEERS   professional engineers
28. % SCIENTISTs   physical scientists
29. % PROFESSORS   professors and college principals
30. % SURGEONS   physicians and surgeons
31. % LAWYERS   law professionals
32. % CLERICS   clerical occupations
33. % SALES   sales occupations
34. % SERVICES   service and recreation
35. % TRANSPORT   transport and communication
36. % RAIL OPS   railroad operators
37. % ROAD OPS   road operators
38. % FARMERS   farmers and farm workers

39. % LOGGERS   loggers and related workers
40. % FISHERMEN   fishermen
41. % MINERS   miners and quarrymen
42. % CRAFTSMEN   craftsmen, production process, and
                                    related workers
43. % CARPENTERs   carpenters, cabinet workers
44. % PAPER   papermakers and still operators
45. % MACHINISTS   machinists and plumbers
46. % LONGSHOREMEN   longshoremen and stevedores
47. % LABORERS   laborers not previously counted

APPENDIX A   List of Transgenerated Variables

Population by birth as a per cent of total population: Bulletin 1207

48.	% MARITIME BORN	Newfoundland, P.E.I., Nova Scotia, and New Brunswick
49.	% QUEBEC BORN	Quebec
50.	% ONTARIO BORN	Ontario
51.	% PRAIRIE BORN	Manitoba, Saskatchewan, and Alberta
52.	% BC BORN	British Columbia
53.	% UK BORN	United Kingdom
54.	% USA BORN	United States
55.	% GERMAN BORN	Germany
56.	% ITALIAN BORN	Italy
57.	% SCAND BORN	Scandinavia
58.	% EAST-EUR BORN	Eastern Europe
59.	% ASIAN BORN	Asia

Population by official language and mother tongue as a per cent of total population: Bulletin 1209

60.	% BILINGUAL	speaking both English and French
61.	% ENGLISH MOTHER T.	English mother tongue
62.	% FRENCH MOTHER T.	French mother tongue
63.	% ASIAN MOTHER T.	Asian mother tongue
64.	% SCAND MOTHER T.	Scandinavian mother tongue
65.	% E-EUR MOTHER T.	East European mother tongue
66.	% GERMAN MOTHER T.	German mother tongue
67.	% DUTCH MOTHER T.	Dutch mother tongue
68.	% ITALIAN MOTHER T.	Italian mother tongue
69.	% YIDDISH MOTHER T.	Yiddish mother tongue

Population by religious affiliation as a per cent of total population: Bulletin 2206

70.	% ROM CATH	Roman Catholic
71.	% GREEK ORTH	Greek Orthodox
72.	% UNITED CH	United Church and related denominations
73.	% BAPTIST	Baptist
74.	% LUTHERAN	Lutheran

Population growth

75.	POP GROWTH 1921-41	population growth index 1921-41
76.	POP GROWTH 1941-61	population growth index 1941-61

$$200 \ X \ \frac{\text{pop year 2 - pop year 1}}{\text{pop year 2 - pop year 1}}$$

Immigration statistics: Bulletin 1209

77.	% IMMIGRANTS	% Population classified as immigrants
78.	% MALE IMMIGRANTS	% male immigrants
79.	% IMM 1921-40	% immigrants landed 1921-40
80.	% IMM 1941-50	% immigrants landed 1941-50
81.	% IMM 1951-61	% immigrants landed 1951-61

Transportation

82.	AIR FLIGHTS	number of air flights per day on weekdays

Spatial locators

83.	VANCOUVER	distance from Vancouver
84.	TORONTO	distance from Toronto

Note:

1. For detailed census definitions see the 1961 Census of Canada Bulletins referred to above.

APPENDIX B   List of Cities

Sequence Number	City Name	Province Number	Population 1961
1	Alma	4	13,309
2	Amherst	2	10,788
3	Arvida	4	14,460
4	Asbestos	4	11,083
5	Barrie	5	21,169
6	Belleville	5	30,655
7	Brampton	5	18,467
8	Brandon	6	28,166
9	Brantford	5	55,201
10	Brockville	5	17,744
11	Calgary	8	261,904
	Forest Lawn		
12	Cap-de-la-Madeleine	4	26,925
13	Charlottetown	1	18,318
14	Chatham	5	29,826
15	Chicoutimi	4	31,657
16	Chicoutimi-North	4	11,229
17	Cobourg	5	10,646
18	Corner Brook	0	25,185
19	Cornwall	5	43,689
20	Dawson Creek	9	10,946
21	Drummondville	4	27,909
22	Edmonton	8	311,557
	Jasper Place		
23	Edmundston	3	12,791
24	Flin Flon	6	11,104
25	Fort William	5	45,214
26	Fredericton	3	19,683
27	Georgetown	5	10,298
28	Glace Bay	2	24,186
29	Granby	4	31,463
30	Grand'Mere	4	15,806
31	Guelph	5	39,838
32	Halifax	2	139,477
	Dartmouth		
33	Hamilton	5	333,911
	Burlington		
	Dundas		
34	Joliette	4	18,088
35	Jonquiere	4	28,588
36	Kamloops	9	10,076
37	Kelowna	9	13,188
38	Kanogami	4	11,816
39	Kenora	5	10,904
40	Kingston	5	53,526
41	Kitchener	5	135,258
	Waterloo		
	Galt		
	Preston		
42	La Tuque	4	13,023
43	Lethbridge	8	35,454
44	Lindsay	5	11,399

APPENDIX B List of Cities

45	London	5	169,569
46	Magog	4	13,139
47	Medicine Hat	8	24,484
48	Moncton	3	43,840
49	Montreal	4	1,907,910
	Beaconsfield		
	Cote St. Luc		
	Dorval		
	Lachine		
	La Salle		
	Montreal North		
	Mount Royal		
	Outremont		
	Pierrefonds		
	Pointe-aux-Trembles		
	Pointe-Claire		
	Riviere des Prairies		
	St. Laurent		
	St. Michel		
	Verdun		
	Westmount		
	Chomedey		
	Duvernay		
	Laval-des-Rapides		
	Pont-Viau		
	St.-Vincent de Paul		
	Jacques-Cartier		
	Lafleche		
	Longueuil		
	St. Hubert		
	St. Lambert		
	St. Jerome-Terre-bonne County		
	Ste. Therese		
50	Moose Jaw	7	33,206
51	Nanaimo	9	14,135
52	New Waterford	2	10,592
53	Niagara Falls	5	22,351
54	Noranda	4	11,477
55	North Battleford	7	11,230
56	North Bay	5	23,781
57	Orillia	5	15,345
58	Oromocto	3	12,170
59	Oshawa	5	62,415
60	Ottawa	5	362,712
	Eastview		
	Hull		
	Gatineau		
61	Owen Sound	5	17,421
62	Pembroke	5	16,791
63	Penticton	9	13,859
64	Peterborough	5	47,185
65	Portage la Prairie	6	12,388
66	Port Alberni	9	11,560
67	Port Arthur	5	45,276
68	Port Colborne	5	14,886
69	Prince Albert	7	24,168
70	Prince George	9	13,877

APPENDIX B   List of Cities

71	Prince Rupert	9	11,987
72	Quebec	4	266,866
	Charlesbourg		
	Gifford		
	Ste. Foy		
	Sillery		
	Lauzon		
	Levis		
73	Red Deer	8	19,612
74	Regina	7	112,141
75	Rimouski	4	17,739
76	Riviere-du-Loup	4	10,835
77	Rouyn	4	18,716
78	St. Catharines	5	84,472
79	St. Hyacinthe	4	22,354
80	St. Jean	4	26,988
81	St. John's	0	63,633
82	St. Thomas	5	22,469
83	St. John	3	69,001
84	Sarnia	5	50,976
85	Saskatoon	7	95,526
86	Sault Ste. Marie	5	43,088
87	Sept-Iles	4	14,196
88	Shawinigan	4	32,169
89	Shawinigan South	4	12,683
90	Sherbrooke	4	66,554
91	Sorel	4	17,147
92	Stratford	5	20,467
93	Sudbury	5	80,120
94	Swift Current	7	12,186
95	Sydney	2	33,617
96	Thetford Mines	4	21,618
97	Timmins	5	29,270
98	Toronto	5	780,922
	Forest Hill		
	Leaside		
	Longbranch		
	New Toronto		
	Mimico		
	Richmond Hill		
	Oakville		
99	Trail	9	11,580
100	Trenton	5	13,183
101	Trois-Rivieres	4	53,477
102	Truro	2	12,421
103	Val-d'or	4	10,983
104	Valleyfield	4	27,297
105	Vancouver	9	441,832
	New Westminster		
	North Vancouver		
106	Vernon	9	10,250
107	Victoria	9	54,941
108	Victoriaville	4	18,720
109	Welland	5	36,079
110	Whitby	5	14,685
111	Windsor	5	132,456

APPENDIX B   List of Cities

112	Winnipeg	6	398,636
	East Kildonan		
	St. Boniface		
	St. James		
	Transcona		
	West Kildonan		
113	Woodstock	5	20,486

Notes:

1. City names which are indented and not numbered refer to cities of which 10,000 and over in 1961 within Census Metropolitan Areas which were aggregated to their respective central cities.

2. Province number codes are as follows:

0	Newfoundland
1	Prince Edward Island
2	Nova Scotia
3	New Brunswick
4	Quebec
5	Ontario
6	Manitoba
7	Saskatchewan
8	Alberta
9	British Columbia

CHAPTER 7

City Classification by Oblique-Factor Analysis of Time-Series Data

LESLIE J. KING

McMaster University

DOUGLAS JEFFREY

University of New South Wales

It is clear that factor analysis differs from the traditional research designs of the physical sciences in that it is a multivariate approach in which the interaction of several variables is considered simultaneously. It does not necessarily follow, however, that a factor-analysis study permits no inferences to be made about causality. As Cattell points out, "factor analysis can yield evidence on causes to the same extent as any other experimental design and analysis, namely, to the extent that it incorporates known time sequences between the variables."[1]

Unfortunately the published analytic studies of urban structure and related city classifications have tended largely to ignore the important time dimension.[2] Attention has been focused, rather, on the analysis of cross-sectional data for a large number of variables with the aim of describing the complex interrelationships in terms of a limited number of underlying

---

[1] R. B. Cattell, "Factor Analysis: An Introduction to Essentials. II. The Role of Factor Analysis in Research," *Biometrics,* Vol. 21, No. 2 (1965), p. 432.

[2] See, for example, C. A. Moser and W. Scott, *British Towns: A Statistical Study of Their Social and Economic Differences* (London: Oliver and Boyd, 1961); J. K. Hadden and E. F. Borgatta, *American Cities: Their Social Characteristics* (Chicago: Rand McNally and Co., 1965), Q. Ahmad, *Indian Cities: Characteristics and Correlates* (Research Paper No. 102, Department of Geography, University of Chicago, 1965).

factors. There is little, however, that can be inferred from such cross-sectional studies as to the nature of causal influences operating within the system. It is the purpose of this chapter to present an alternative approach to city classification—an approach that is based on time-series data and an oblique-factor-analysis model, and allows certain of these causal inferences to be discussed.

Specifically the chapter focuses on one index of urban economic activity, the bimonthly levels of unemployment over a period of slightly more than 4 years, for a set of some 71 metropolitan areas in the eastern United States. An oblique factor analysis is performed with the aim of (a) classifying the cities in terms of their cyclical responses to short-term economic impulses and (b) providing insights into the ways in which cyclical impulses are transmitted through a system of cities.

In an earlier paper it was hypothesized that unemployment series recorded in urban areas reflect not only causative factors associated with trends and oscillations in the national economy but also spatial factors that affect particular segments of the urban system.[3] For a set of 30 cities in the Midwest a bifactor analysis was used in testing the specific hypothesis that each time series contained three distinct components corresponding respectively to (a) factors operating throughout the whole region, (b) factors common to distinct subregional groups of cities, and (c) factors unique to particular cities. It was found that the data supported the hypothesis.

Certain weaknesses, however, were inherent in the analysis. First, the general factor proved difficult to interpret in that the study was based on only a limited sample of cities, and it could not be determined whether the general factor was related to causative factors operating throughout the entire national urban system or to factors confined merely to the region studied. Second, it had to be assumed that the group factors that were identified were uncorrelated; that is, the spatial factors producing distinct regional components of unemployment were assumed to be unrelated to other spatial factors operating elsewhere in the system. Clearly this is unrealistic, for some degree of correlation should be expected between the economic forces affecting different segments of the urban system. By using an oblique-factor-analysis model both these weaknesses can be circumvented. Only group factors are obtained, and correlation between these factors is permitted.

---

[3] D. Jeffrey, E. Casetti, and L. J. King, "Economic Fluctuations in a Multiregional Setting: A Bi-Factor Analytic Approach" (mimeograph, Department of Geography, Ohio State University, 1968).

FACTOR ANALYSIS AS A CLASSIFICATION PROCEDURE

One of the major uses of factor analysis has been in the development of classificatory schemes. This line of investigation is particularly well developed in the taxonomy literature.[4] In collapsing a set of variables into a smaller number of hypothetical factors one is, in a sense, identifying a series of group types. But, as Cattell and Coulter point out, if the aim is solely a classification of variables according to their degree of similarity, then factor analysis is not an optimum classificatory technique.[5] Cluster search methods based on the correlation matrix or on the output of some prior factor analysis would be preferable. On the other hand, if one is interested in developing, through classification, an understanding of both the structure of a system and the basic causal influences within the system, then factor analysis is essential.

The forms of factor analysis most commonly employed in classificatory procedures have been the centroid and principal-axis methods in which the interrelationships among variables are described in terms of an arbitrary orthogonal system. In most scientific fields, however, the important factors are more likely to be oblique. That is to say, in any given system the basic underlying influences will demonstrate some degree of mutual correlation.

Hence, if the factors obtained in an analysis are to correspond to general factors explanatory of the observed correlations among variables, then, following the principles of simple structure, they must be rotated to whatever degree of obliqueness is indicated. The principle of simple structure requires that any one factor influence only a few of the variables and affect the others little or not at all; that is, it should load on the smallest number of variables. Rotation to simple structure yields a solution that maximizes the likelihood of factors acting causally on variables, and not the reverse situation. Cattell has discussed this point in detail.[6]

---

[4] D. W. Goodale, "Objective Methods for the Classification of Vegetation, III. An Essay in the Use of Factor Analysis," *Australian Journal of Botany*, Vol. 2 (1954), p. 306; F. J. Rohlf and R. R. Sokal, "The Description of Taxonomic Relationships by Factor Analysis," *Systematic Zoology*, Vol. 11 (1962), pp. 1–16; R. R. Sokal and P. H. A. Sneath, *Principles of Numerical Taxonomy* (San Francisco: W. H. Freeman, 1963), pp. 194–198; P. H. A. Sneath, "Annotated Bibliography on Recent Advances in Numerical Taxonomy, with Special Reference to Botanical Systematics," *The Classification Society Bulletin*, Vol. 1, No. 4 (1968), pp. 49–56.

[5] R. B. Cattell and M. A. Coulter, "Principles of Behavioural Taxonomy and the Mathematical Basis of the Taxonome Computer Program," *British Journal of Mathematical and Statistical Psychology*, Vol. 19 (1966), pp. 237–269.

[6] R. B. Cattell, "Factor Analysis," pp. 432 and 433.

A GROUPING OF CITIES IN TERMS OF CYCLICAL RESPONSE

Empirical studies of short-term cyclical fluctuations at the city level are limited by the fact that ideal data for such studies do not exist. Nor is there any real consensus of opinion as to what constitutes ideal data for such studies. In this chapter the problem is somewhat alleviated by the fact that the purpose is to analyze the *relative* reaction of urban economies to short-term economic impulses rather than the absolute levels of economic activity over time. The study does require data on a local level for relatively short intervals.

In view of these requirements it was decided to use unemployment data as an index of cyclical response.[7] The only published data on total unemployment rates over time for urban areas are provided by the Bureau of Employment Security in its publication *Area Labor Market Trends*. The unemployment rates are given on a bimonthly basis for all major labor market areas, which generally coincide with the standard metropolitan statistical areas (SMSAs). This study is concerned with 71 such areas located east of the Mississippi (Figure 1).[8] The time period involved is from May 1960 to September 1964, covering the 1961 recession and the subsequent recovery period.

The unemployment series recorded in each of the 71 urban areas reflect the impact of short-term economic impulses on the urban system. All urban areas demonstrate in their unemployment trends over time a basic similarity that corresponds to trends and oscillations in the national economy. In addition, regional economic forces, affecting only segments of the urban system, will result in groups of cities displaying a close correspondence in the detailed form of their unemployment series. By way of an oblique factor analysis these groups of cities with a high degree of cyclical interaction will be identified.

The method employed here to obtain an oblique "simple structure" solution is the direct oblimin approach of Jennrich and Harman.[9] This method has replaced the indirect and somewhat awkward procedure of the

---

[7] Since only relative changes are to be emphasized, the possible problems associated with the use of unemployment rates as a measure of the level of local economic activity may be disregarded.

[8] The SMSAs chosen are those for which directly comparable data were readily available. The areas in New England were excluded, for example, because of the organization of data by townships rather than by counties.

[9] The authors are indebted to Dr. H. H. Harman for providing the direct oblimin program.

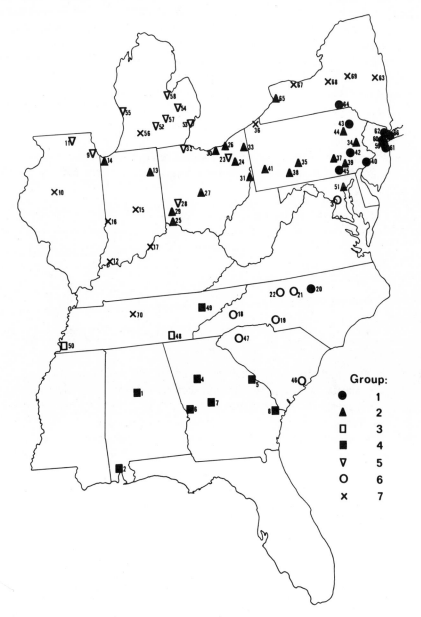

Figure 1 Grouping of cities on first-order factors (the identifying numbers for the cities are listed in Table 2).

215

standard oblimin factor analysis.[10] Instead of working with reference factors that are bi-orthogonal to the primary factors, the direct oblimin solution employs the Jennrich and Sampson criterion for the direct determination of primary factors exhibiting the principles of simple structure.[11]

The direct oblimin program requires as input the factor matrix of an orthogonal factor analysis. This analysis was performed on the city unemployment series data matrix in which the rows were the 25 bimonthly periods and the columns were the 71 cities. Seven significant factors were obtained, accounting for 94% of the total variance.[12] The matrix of loadings on these seven factors was then subjected to the direct oblimin rotation, producing a new set of correlated factors.

The matrix of correlations among these seven oblique factors is presented in Table 1. The oblique-factor solution consists of a factor-pattern matrix

Table 1.   Correlations between factors

Factor	1	2	3	4	5	6	7
1	1.00						
2	.26	1.00					
3	.24	.40	1.00				
4	- .09	- .42	- .31	1.00			
5	.27	.43	.36	- .50	1.00		
6	.43	.43	.38	- .38	.48	1.00	
7	- .35	- .56	- .35	.33	- .41	- .42	1.00

(Table 2), which gives the loadings of factors on variables, and a factor-structure matrix, which gives the correlations between variables and factors.[13] In general the factor structure is useful in estimating factors, but it does not facilitate the grouping of variables, in this case the cities, for, if the factors are correlated, all elements of the factor structure will tend to be different from zero. On the other hand, the factor-pattern matrix, with few high values and many near-zero values, does facilitate classification by minimizing the possibility of two or more factors having approximately equal loadings on any given variable.

By assigning each city in Table 2 to the factor with the highest loading, the 71 cities were classified into seven groups (Figure 1, Table 3). As is

[10] The standard oblimin method is discussed by H. H. Harman in *Modern Factor Analysis* (Chicago: University of Chicago Press, 2nd ed., 1967), pp. 324–334.

[11] R. I. Jennrich and P. F. Sampson, "Rotation for Simple Loadings," *Psychometrika*, Vol. 31 (1966), pp. 313–323.

[12] Only factors with eigenvalues greater than unity were considered.

[13] In the orthogonal case both these matrices fuse into the same factor matrix.

evident from Figure 1, the grouping has a very definite spatial manifestation; for example, factor 1 loads highest on the megalopolis cities (except Baltimore and Washington, D.C.). The cities assigned to factor 2 include the major steel centers of Pennsylvania, Ohio, and Indiana. Factor 4 picks out a group of southern cities focused on Atlanta, and factor 5 groups Dayton, Akron, and Toledo with the Michigan cities.[14] Factor 6 defines a group of cities in North and South Carolina plus Washington, D.C. Only factors 3 and 7 failed to define any distinct regional groups. Factor 3 loaded high on only two cities, Chattanooga and Memphis, and whether or not these are part of a second southern group of cities centered on the lower Mississippi Valley cannot be determined from the present study. Factor 7 defines a group of medium-size light industrial centers within the Manufacturing Belt—a group split into two parts by the intervening steel centers of Ohio.

IMPLICATIONS OF THE GROUPING

How can the groupings we obtained be interpreted in the light of current theory on interregional transmission of business cycles? Two major lines of inquiry have been adopted in the study of regional business cycles: the industrial-mix and export-base approaches.

The industrial-mix approach assumes that a region's industries will exhibit the same trends and oscillations as their national counterparts.[15] In this way a national cycle is transmitted to a region via its component industries, and the region's cyclical response is related directly to its industrial mix. In other words, regions with similar industrial structures should have similar cyclical fluctuations regardless of their relative locations.

The second line of inquiry, the export-base approach, attempts to incorporate explicitly the element of space.[16] Again, the local cycle is

---

[14] Chicago is also grouped with the Michigan cities (though the loading is only —.34). This is probably a reflection of the fact that none of the cities of northern Illinois, Wisconsin, and Iowa was included in the study.

[15] Studies employing the industrial-mix logic, either explicitly or implicitly, include the following: G. H. Borts, *Regional Cycles of Manufacturing Employment in the United States, 1914–1953* (New York: National Bureau of Economic Research, 1960); P. Neff and A. Weifenbach, *Business Cycles in Selected Industrial Areas* (Berkeley: University of California Press, 1949); R. M. Williams, "The Timing and Amplitude of Regional Business Cycles," *Proceedings of the 25th Annual Conference, Pacific Coast Economic Association* (1950), pp. 40–52.

[16] See R. Vining, "Location of Industry and Regional Patterns of Business Cycle Behavior," *Econometrica,* Vol. 14 (1946), pp. 37–68, and "The Region as a Concept in Business Cycle Analysis," *Econometrica,* Vol. 14 (1946), pp. 201–218.

Table 2. Factor-pattern matrix

	1	2	3	4	5	6	7
1. Birmingham	.09	-.49	-.15	.52	-.15	-.03	-.10
2. Mobile	.09	.02	-.24	.48	-.22	-.33	+.08
3. Washington	.03	-.14	-.35	-.15	-.04	-.49	.31
4. Atlanta	.08	-.20	-.09	.57	-.27	-.15	.05
5. Augusta	.16	-.34	.04	.35	-.24	-.29	.05
6. Columbus, Ga.	-.11	-.16	-.29	.60	-.26	.06	-.12
7. Macon	.29	-.09	-.33	.38	-.07	-.31	.15
8. Savannah	.02	-.04	-.08	.47	-.33	-.34	.05
9. Chicago	-.20	-.07	-.18	.12	-.33	-.24	.13
10. Peoria	.06	-.31	-.32	.04	-.18	-.05	.40
11. Rockford	-.03	-.26	-.18	.21	-.35	-.10	.19
12. Evansville	.00	-.17	-.20	.40	-.16	.05	.42
13. Fort Wayne	.01	-.57	-.04	.31	-.08	.03	.24
14. Gary	.03	-.74	-.19	.09	-.16	-.01	-.03
15. Indianapolis	.00	-.17	-.21	.30	-.17	-.18	.33
16. Terre Haute	-.12	-.12	-.29	.20	-.16	.02	.49
17. Louisville	-.01	-.15	-.16	.38	.03	-.14	.39
18. Asheville	.06	-.17	-.16	.18	-.19	-.30	.28
19. Charlotte	-.16	-.17	-.30	.23	.08	-.46	.04
20. Durham	-.94	.21	-.08	-.04	-.16	.08	-.09
21. Greensboro	.03	.00	-.05	.36	-.31	-.39	.26
22. Winston-Salem	-.29	.23	-.28	.25	-.27	-.38	-.24
23. Akron	.01	-.24	-.08·	.09	-.36	-.22	.31
24. Canton	-.01	-.52	-.16	.11	-.26	-.13	.11
25. Cincinnati	-.16	-.31	-.05	.07	-.30	-.28	.16
26. Cleveland	.03	-.41	-.04	.05	-.34	-.17	.17
27. Columbus	-.04	-.42	.00	-.07	-.17	-.21	.40
28. Dayton	-.08	-.26	-.20	.10	-.42	-.03	.27
29. Hamilton	-.11	-.57	-.21	-.17	-.19	-.20	.08
30. Lorain	.03	-.47	.18	.23	-.17	-.05	.43
31. Steubenville	.01	-.92	.01	-.11	.04	-.14	.04
32. Toledo	.01	.07	-.26	.27	-.28	-.24	.12
33. Youngstown	.00	-.89	-.03	.13	-.14	.09	-.07
34. Allentown	-.20	-.54	-.12	-.07	-.06	-.27	.16
35. Altoona	-.01	-.72	-.05	.05	-.01	-.06	.15
36. Erie	-.11·	-.29	-.11	.16	-.19	-.09	.40
37. Harrisburg	.01	-.31	-.29	.17	.06	-.06	.31
38. Johnstown	.07	-.33	-.24	-.31	-.21	-.07	-.04
39. Lancaster	-.09	-.30	.01	.08	-.07	-.19	.22
40. Philadelphia	-.49	-.23	-.19	-.23	-.12	-.30	.11
41. Pittsburgh	.01	-.64	-.27	-.20	-.04	-.03	.06
42. Reading	-.35	-.30	.08	.15	-.26	-.33	.01
43. Scranton	-.35	-.28	-.34	.08	-.01	-.13	.19
44. Wilkes-Barre	-.18	-.43	-.02	.41	.11	-.21	.19
45. York	-.46	-.28	-.37	.25	.02	.05	.11
46. Charleston	.12	-.03	-.30	.41	-.14	-.46	-.07
47. Greenville	.01	.05	-.02	-.07	-.27	-.87	-.10
48. Chattanooga	-.23	-.10	-.83	-.02	.12	-.11	-.05
49. Knoxville	.00	-.02	-.12	.38	-.32	-.15	.30
50. Memphis	-.12	-.30	-.37	´.06	-.12	-.02	.25
51. Baltimore	.00	-.38	-.11	.22	-.08	.01	.38
52. Battle Creek	-.02	-.02	-.26	-.23	.29	-.29	-.23
53. Detroit	.04	-.03	-.14	.35	-.54	-.13	.09
54. Flint	-.07	-.02	.15	.00	-.99	-.02	-.06
55. Grand Rapids	-.32	-.02	-.06	.31	-.37	-.12	.14

Table 2, cont.

	1	2	3	4	5	6	7
56. Kalamazoo	-.22	-.18	-.24	.01	-.27	.03	.45
57. Lansing	-.02	-.03	-.01	-.07	-.92	-.10	.04
58. Saginaw	-.11	-.15	-.07	.14	-.74	-.04	-.02
59. Jersey City	-.47	-.26	.34	.06	.01	-.43	.22
60. Newark	-.46	-.12	-.06	-.06	-.02	-.30	.38
61. New Brunswick	-.40	-.16	-.22	-.17	-.11	-.28	.25
62. Paterson	-.43	.03	.25	.22	.04	-.36	.39
63. Albany	-.22	-.14	-.01	.22	-.15	-.14	.46
64. Binghamton	-.48	-.23	-.35	-.02	.08	-.17	.06
65. Buffalo	-.12	-.29	-.23	.08	-.21	-.22	.11
66. New York	-.62	-.19	.02	.07	.19	-.52	-.05
67. Rochester	-.33	-.06	-.27	.24	-.11	.01	.39
68. Syracuse	-.19	-.10	-.20	.10	-.18	-.07	.40
69. Utica-Rome	-.48	-.28	.14	-.15	-.11	-.02	.48
70. Nashville	-.33	.04	-.16	.24	.01	-.25	.41
71. Newport	-.25	-.27	.20	.57	-.26	.03	.11

Contributions
Direct & Joint:
to Total
Variance (%)

	1	2	3	4	5	6	7
	6.8	12.0	8.2	7.6	8.7	6.6	6.9
1		1.0	0.5	0.1	0.7	2.2	1.8
2			2.1	3.0	3.1	2.7	5.1
3				1.4	1.7	0.9	1.6
4					3.7	2.0	2.0
5						2.8	2.4
6							2.2

Notes: Data for Lorain, Ohio, include Elyria.
Data for Allentown, Pennsylvania, include Bethlehem and Easton.
Data for Paterson, New Jersey, include Clifton and Passaic.
Data for Youngstown, Ohio, cover the Youngstown–Warren area.

envisaged as a reaction to national impulses, but whereas the industrial-mix logic imputes the national cycle pattern to each of the region's component industries, the export-base logic imputes to all local industries the cyclical pattern of the region's export industries. The region is seen as organized around its "exports," which provide the flows whereby it is connected with a larger interdependent system of regions. If the lead of Vining is followed and this export-base logic is allied with central place notions, it might be hypothesized that there exist regional systems of cities each of which is characterized by a particular type of cyclical pattern as a response to fluctuations in demand for the region's "exports"—fluctuations that are transmitted through the regional system via "nonbasic" linkages.[17]

The groups of cities identified in Figure 1 might form the outline of such a regional structuring of the urban system. The fact that a definite regional

[17] R. Vining, "The Region as an Economic Entity and Certain Variations To Be Observed in the Study of Systems of Regions," *Papers and Proceedings, American Economic Association,* Vol. 39 (1949), pp. 89–104.

220

Table 3. Classification of cities according to loadings on seven factors

			Group			
1	2	3	4	5	6	7
Philadelphia	Fort Wayne	Chattanooga	Birmingham	Chicago	Washington	Peoria
Reading	Gary	Memphis	Mobile	Rockford	Asheville	Evansville
Scranton	Canton		Atlanta	Akron	Charlotte	Indianapolis
York	Cincinnati		Augusta	Dayton	Winston-Salem	Terre Haute
Jersey City	Cleveland		Columbus, Ga.	Detroit	Charleston	Louisville
Newark	Columbus		Macon	Flint	Greensboro	Erie
New Brunswick	Hamilton		Savannah	Grand Rapids	Greenville	Kalamazoo
Paterson	Lorain		Knoxville	Lansing		Albany
Binghamton	Steubenville			Saginaw		Rochester
New York	Youngstown			Battle Creek		Syracuse
Durham	Altoona			Toledo		Utica-Rome
	Allentown					Nashville
	Harrisburg					
	Lancaster					
	Johnstown					
	Pittsburgh					
	Wilkes-Barre					
	Baltimore					
	Buffalo					

**Notes: Lorain, Ohio, includes Elyria.
Allentown, Pennsylvania, includes Bethlehem and Easton.**

grouping of cities is obtained is an indication that relative location is an important factor in determining the nature and extent of economic impulses affecting an urban economy.

On the other hand, certain groupings can only be interpreted in the light of industrial mix and interindustry linkages. Dayton and Akron are both grouped with the automobile centers of Michigan. An explanation must be sought in the fact that Dayton specializes in the production of machine tools and electrical accessories for the automobile industry, and Akron, in the production of rubber components for the industry. The grouping of Baltimore with the steel centers of Ohio and Pennsylvania also requires an industrial-mix interpretation. In this respect, however, it is interesting to note that Birmingham, whose industrial mix is similar to those of the steel centers, has its highest loading on factor 4 and is grouped with other southern cities of dissimilar industrial mix.

A HIGHER ORDER CLASSIFICATION

One of the consequences of obtaining an oblique-factor solution is the possibility of further analyzing the correlations between factors in order to derive "higher order" factor systems. If R_1 is the correlation matrix for the first-order factors, a further oblique-factor analysis can be performed on this matrix to yield second-order factors.[18] Such an analysis was performed on Table 1, and two significant second-order factors were obtained.[19] The second-order factor pattern is presented in Table 4. In order to calculate

Table 4. Second-order-factor pattern

		First-order Factors						
		1	2	3	4	5	6	7
Second-order Factors	1	.12	.74	.60	−.85	.77	.58	−.61
	2	−.87	−.07	−.10	−.40	.04	−.37	.29

[18] The process can be repeated to obtain any ith order of factors. The earlier reduced correlation matrix (R_{i-1}) can always be restored from the factor-pattern matrix V_i and the correlation matrix R_i as follows:

$$R_{i-1} = V_i R_i V_i^T.$$

[19] An eigenvalue greater than unity in the original orthogonal factor analysis was the measure of "significance" employed.

Table 5. Loadings of second-order factors on variables and grouping of variables (cities)

	Factor 1	Factor 2
Group 1:		
Birmingham	-.94	-.25
Mobile	-.91	-.12
Washington	-.64	.10
Atlanta	-.97	-.22
Augusta	-.88	-.14
Columbus, Ga.	-.89	-.17
Macon	-.91	-.16
Savannah	-.90	-.09
Chicago	-.81	.30
Peoria	-.86	.10
Rockford	-.92	.05
Evansville	-.93	-.05
Fort Wayne	-.90	-.04
Gary	-.84	-.01
Indianapolis	-.73	-.08
Terre Haute	-.85	.18
Louisville	-.94	-.07
Ashville	-.92	.11
Charlotte	-.75	.27
Greensboro	-.90	.01
Winston-Salem	-.54	.31
Akron	-.89	.13
Canton	-.91	.08
Cincinnati	-.82	.26
Cleveland	-.91	.08
Columbus	-.75	.27
Dayton	-.90	.13
Hamilton	-.73	.31
Loraine	-.85	.03
Steubenville	-.66	.15
Toledo	-.87	.04
Youngstown	-.80	-.05
Allentown	-.75	.38
Altoona	-.74	.10
Erie	-.87	.20
Harrisburg	-.85	.09
Johnstown	-.93	-.12
Lancaster	-.78	.28
Pittsburgh	-.88	.01
Reading	-.74	.37
Scranton	-.72	.42
Wilkes-Barre	-.85	.15
York	-.72	.36
Charleston	-.86	-.09
Greenville	-.55	.30
Chattanooga	-.52	.32
Knoxville	-.91	-.01
Memphis	-.75	.21
Baltimore	-.81	.04
Battle Creek	-.88	.06
Detroit	-.94	-.10
Flint	-.66	.01
Grand Rapids	-.78	.23

Table 5, cont.

	Factor 1	Factor 2
Group 1:		
Kalamazoo	-.76	.32
Lansing	-.75	.07
Saginaw	-.85	-.04
Albany	-.80	.29
Buffalo	-.87	.21
Rochester	-.76	.32
Syracuse	-.80	.24
Newport	-.84	.00
Nashville	-.69	.41
Group 2:		
Philadelphia	-.48	.69
Jersey City	-.47	.59
Newark	-.54	.65
New Brunswick	-.55	.61
Paterson	-.48	.54
Binghamton	-.49	.55
New York	-.43	.65
Utica-Rome	-.44	.62
Durham	.25	.78

Notes: Data for Lorain, Ohio, include Elyria.
Data for Allentown, Pennsylvania, include Bethlehem and Easton.
Data for Paterson, New Jersey, include Clifton and Passaic.
Data for Youngstown, Ohio, cover the Youngstown–Warren area.

the loadings of these factors directly on variables (rather than on the first-order factors) the following matrix formula given by Cattell was used:[20]

$$V_{on} = (V_1)(V_2)(V_3) \cdots (V_n) = \prod_{i=1}^{n} V_i$$

where V_1 through V_n are the successive common-factor pattern matrices and V_{on} is the matrix of loadings of the nth-order factors on the variables. The loadings on the original variables and the second-order classification are presented in Table 5. The second-order factors, though not necessarily of greater importance than the first-order ones, do represent a higher level of aggregation, indicative of more pervasive causal influences in the system. Since the two factors were not highly correlated ($r = -.24$), the twofold classification possibly is indicative of basic differences in the type of short-term economic forces affecting megalopolis, as opposed to nonmegalopolis, cities.

[20] R. B. Cattell, "Higher Order Structures: Reticular-vs.-Hierarchical Formulae for Their Interpretation," in P. Broadhurst and C. Banks, Eds., *Studies in Honour of Sir Cyril Burt* (London: University of London Press, 1964).

CONCLUSIONS

The conclusions to be drawn from this study, based as it is on only a limited sample of cities and restricted to a time series encompassing but one national business cycle, must be regarded as merely tentative ones. Nevertheless, the study has contributed on two levels:

1. It has been shown that an oblique-factor analysis of time-series data permits the identification (at different levels of generalization) of basic causal influences operating within a system. The factor analysis of time-series data is not unknown in certain areas of physical science research,[21] but the use of oblique-factor analysis in this context is certainly not well developed. The possibility of using more than one time series in an extension of the present analysis might be handled within the framework of three-mode factor analysis.[22]

2. The identification of regional groups of cities introduces a new dimension to business-cycle analysis—the spatial dimension. The fact that definite groups of cities could be identified in terms of their cyclical response suggests that their cycles are influenced by distinct subnational forces. That cities show a marked tendency to be grouped spatially points to the importance of space in conditioning and setting restraints on the transmission of these cyclical forces through an urban system.

---

[21] For example, J. E. Kutzbach, "Empirical Eigenvectors of Sea-Level Pressure, Surface Temperature and Precipitation Complexes over North America," *Journal of Applied Meteorology*, Vol. 6, No. 5 (1967), pp. 791–802.

[22] L. R. Tucker, "Implications of Factor Analysis of Three-Way Matrices for Measurement of Change," in C. W. Harris, Ed., *Problems in Measuring Change* (Madison: University of Wisconsin Press, 1963), pp. 122–137.

CHAPTER 8

Dimensions and Classification of British Towns on the Basis of New Data

SEYMOUR SACKS
ROBERT FIRESTINE

Syracuse University

This chapter provides a comparative analysis of an additional important aspect of the typology of cities: the amount and nature of their land use. The analysis is based on the comprehensive data available for British towns with more than 50,000 inhabitants in 1966. Although they do not lead directly to a complete typology, the results present a systematic analysis of a class of characteristics that are often overlooked when typologies are based on a variety of often unsystematically gathered data. Furthermore, the classification in Britain is almost exhaustive with respect to land uses— an exceptional advantage in comparison with other nations, where certain land uses are difficult to ascertain. The findings both update and modify in a substantive fashion the pioneering work of Moser and Scott.[1]

Most earlier studies dealt with the residents of the city rather than the city itself. Thus the question emerges as to whether a metropolitan area can be depicted with equal accuracy by either residential or nonresidential measures. This should be the case for Davis' "truebounded city," wherein "the political and demographic-ecological boundaries correspond."[2] Although this definition of conformity of demographic and nondemographic areas does not, and perhaps cannot, completely satisfy all the criteria of residen-

---

[1] C. A. Moser and Wolf Scott, *British Towns: A Statistical Study of Their Social and Economic Differences* (London: Oliver and Boyd, 1961).

[2] Kingsley Davis, *The World's Metropolitan Areas* (Berkeley: International Urban Research, Institute for International Studies, University of California, 1959), p. 7.

tial–nonresidential urban measurement, it appears to be a good working approximation.

The socioeconomic city may also be "overbounded"; that is, contain large areas of nonurban land use. Although this is clearly a problem in the United States, it is less so in England; but it does arise there in connection with jurisdictions that are not integrally related to their surrounding metropolitan areas. The concept of the "underbounded" area is more applicable to England and Wales. Certain jurisdictions may be excluded from *any* metropolitan area when they appear to interact functionally with more than one such area; rather than being included in more than one area, they are excluded entirely. Middlesex and Somerset counties in New Jersey are American analogies to this situation. In the case of cities this phenomenon is even more pronounced, since the boundaries of political units may well impose an artificial separation between the residential (demographic) and nonresidential (nondemographic) characteristics of the area. Although it has been noted by many observers, this conceptual deficiency has not deterred the drawing of conclusions almost exclusively from demographic considerations.[3]

In an attempt to bridge this gap this chapter relates urban land use within the political jurisdiction to both the demographic and nondemographic characteristics of the jurisdictions under consideration. Although this exercise is confined to the singular national area of England and Wales, we show that its approach is equally relevant for intercountry comparisons.

CONCEPTS OF DENSITY AND THE FRAMEWORK FOR ANALYSIS

Urbanism involves the intensity of land use. This can be measured most easily by *physical density:* the number of dwellings, shops, offices, schools, etc., per unit of area. This apparently straightforward measure of either residential or nonresidential land use nevertheless presents distinct problems for both types. In the former there are important differences between apartment houses and detached houses. Even greater difficulties occur in the case of nonresidential uses (offices, shops, industrial, etc.) because the individual *size* of each establishment obviously greatly affects the impact of that form of land use on its urban habitat. Square footage per unit of land use would be of great assistance in constructing a better measure of physical

[3] See especially the articles by Eric Lampard, Leo F. Schnore, and Philip Hauser in Hauser and Schnore, *The Study of Urbanization* (New York: John Wiley & Sons, Inc., 1966).

density, but such data are not even unreadily available on a comparable basis between areas. Again, although some efforts are presently under way toward the collection of such data, the results appear not by political jurisdictions but by geographic locations within a metropolitan or other area.

An alternative measure of density and urbanism that circumvents many of the above problems is *value density:* the simple valuation of a given type of land use per unit of area. This statistic generally provides greater comparability within and across political boundaries than does physical density —for both residential and nonresidential uses. It also provides a measure of spatially determined "economic" rents. Value density, the measure used in this chapter, thus makes possible a typology of urbanism for any particular area to which other, nondensity, characteristics can then be applied. *Total* value densities (as opposed to *residential* densities, either in physical or in value terms) show a continuous gradient toward the central place within a metropolitan area. Furthermore, where this central place is both a *census-taking* and a governmental *decision-making* unit, total value densities will show its true urban character unambiguously. Thus it will be with the small City of London, which is at the heart of London, the World City. A problem is that there are often differences in value without comparable differences in the physical utilization of the area, but this in turn tells us something about the area itself via the theory of rent.

This analysis of urbanism in England and Wales is specifically designed as a 1966 counterpart to the study conducted by Moser and Scott for 1951.[4] The rules Moser and Scott established for the inclusion of units of the analysis are followed here, but they are applied to a system that has undergone some fundamental political reorganization since 1959. In particular the analysis is based on units of local government, or "local authority areas," as they are called in England and Wales. (This structure differs from that of Scotland and Northern Ireland.) There is no consideration of the counties, which would have permitted a direct comparison with the United States (though English counties are slightly larger than American ones). In conformity with Moser and Scott, the local jurisdictions being considered are county boroughs, municipal boroughs (noncounty boroughs), and urban districts. All rural districts are therefore excluded, regardless of their nature, size, or other characteristics, although some are more "urban," in any respect, than their *officially* "urban" counterparts.

Special rules are applied to the London area, again in conformity with the Moser and Scott practice. During the period from 1959 to 1966 the London area was reorganized politically. The inner area, which was formerly

---

[4] Moser and Scott, *British Towns.*

designated as the London County Council, was consolidated from the 28 metropolitan boroughs and the City of London into 12 larger Inner London boroughs plus the City of London and is now called the Inner London Education Authority (ILEA). A large number of outlying jurisdictions were also consolidated into 20 outer boroughs, which with the ILEA make up the Greater London Council. In both the Inner and Outer London areas, the consolidations combined and, in some cases, abolished numerous political jurisdictions, thereby impeding comparisons with previous studies.

This chapter thus does not analyze urban England per se, for jurisdictions that could be so classified are excluded on the basis of either definition ("urban" versus "rural") or size (those with less than 50,000 inhabitants in 1966 were not considered). The focus of this effort, like that of Moser and Scott, is an analysis of individual political units, although some attempt is made to examine the national aggregate as well.

The current sample contains 172 areas, as contrasted with 152 areas in the Moser and Scott study. These 172 jurisdictions had a population of over 26.4 million in 1966. The difference between the Moser and Scott 23.0 million and the 1966 numbers reflects both definitional changes and population growth, although the Inner London area and many of the central cities have actually declined in population during the period 1950–1966.

The various aspects of this study examine the 172 "towns" in their entirety and also in the following structural groups:

1. Central cities (48 towns).[5]
2. Noncentral cities (124 towns).
3. London metropolitan area (49 towns).
4. Non–London area (123 towns).
5. Central cities ILEA (47 towns).
6. Noncentral cities less London area (76 towns).

Our categories differ somewhat from those of Moser and Scott, whose grouping criteria are less straightforward because they reflect classifications after factor analysis.

LAND-USE CLASSIFICATION

Rateable Values

Clarifying the basic definition of urbanism used in this chapter requires a statement as to the exact meaning of the "rateable values." The English

[5] The classification of central cities is taken from Davis, *The World's Metropolitan Areas,* pp. 58–60 and 106–110. Second cities are excluded.

system of local government has depended for many centuries on a system of rates (local property taxes) based on the *rental* value of property. The basic principle of rating is that each ratepayer should contribute toward the cost of local services according to the rental value of the property (or "hereditament") he *occupies*. This is fundamentally different from the American system of property taxation wherein the tax is paid by the *owner* of the land. In Britain, for example, the individual who occupies rented property pays the rate (tax) on that property, *not* the landowner. The higher the rent any property will attract, the higher its rateable value. Unoccupied property is not rated and hence not taxed. Since 1950, when it was removed from local assessors, responsibility for rate assessment has been the task of the valuation officers of the Board of Inland Revenue. This provides much more uniform assessment and classification of the rolls than is true of the decentralized system existing in the United States.

The rates are designed to be paid by everyone who occupies land, though exemptions ("deratings") in former years had resulted in apparently considerable inequities and in subsequent revisions of the exemption regulations. Agricultural properties have been derated since the 1920s. Industrial properties that were also derated at the time have seen their deratings eroded and are currently rated on the same basis as other properties.[6]

Property Classification

The current property classification more closely resembles a true land-use classification scheme than did the previous arrangements:[7]

Rateable values. The values are those included in the valuation lists as of April 1, 1966.

Domestic. Includes houses, maisonettes, flats, etc., but not agricultural dwellings and separately assessed single caravan (trailer) sites. Rateable values of the excluded hereditaments amount to about 1.60% of the total of all domestic rateable values.

Shops. Includes shops assessed with living accommodation, banks in shopping areas, and cafés.

Offices. Includes banks in office areas.

Other commercial. Includes public houses; hotels and boarding houses; restaurants; holiday camps and caravan fields (trailer parks); warehouses, stores, and workshops; commercial garages, petrol-filling stations, car

[6] A detailed history of rating and valuation of properties in Great Britain may be found in J. M. Drummond, *The Finance of Local Government* (London: Allen and Unwin, Ltd., 1962), Chapter II.

[7] Ministry of Housing and Local Government and Welsh Office, *Rates and Rateable Values, 1966–67, Part II* (London: Her Majesty's Stationery Office, 1966), p. 1.

parks; lock-up garages separately assessed; advertising stations and signs; markets.

Industrial. Refers to factories, mills, and other premises of a similar character but excludes mineral-producing hereditaments, and coal, water, power, and transport undertakings.

Crown. Comprises National Health Hospitals and Crown-occupied property of all types, including properties provided and maintained by local authorities for purposes connected with the administration of justice, police functions, and other Crown purposes.

Other. Covers the balance of rating classifications, including places of entertainment, education and culture, power and transport, and the like.

The land-use classification is thus much more comprehensive than that of the United States in its real-property list, although it does not include any personal property.

LAND-USE PATTERNS

For England and Wales as a whole, rateable values equalled £ 59 per acre. For the sample urban areas the figure was £ 699. The weighted and unweighted averages are listed below:

Area	Weighted Average		Unweighted Average	
	Total	Less ILEA	Mean	Standard Deviation
All England and Wales	£ 59	£ 50	[8]	[8]
Urban sample	699	549	£585	(439)
Central cities	1099	626	680	(595)
Noncentral cities	499	499	548	(357)
London area	1018	633	800	(680)
Urban sample, less London area	5507	507	499	(298)
Rest of nation (Nonsample)	45	45	[8]	[8]

The sample urban areas thus have a value of £ 699 per acre, and the value for the rest of the nation is £ 45 per acre. This is due to the fact that

[8] Data not available.

with less than 10% of the land area they have over 66% of the total value. The effect of the Inner London Education Authority is shown above. The rateable values of Inner London are generally at least twice those of the nation as a whole, although they do not differ too much from those of some of the London area jurisdictions. Although these figures provide norms for further evaluation, the use of weighted averages allows a certain number of the larger communities to affect the average value. Thus the unweighted average will be utilized throughout the remainder of this analysis, and it should be borne in mind that the average value will be affected accordingly.

In a sense all domestic properties can be considered as representing the demographic (i.e., residential) land-use characteristics, and all remaining types are considered to encompass nondemographic uses. As shown below, 47% of the nation's rateable valuation comprises "demographic" uses, with the remainder being classified as nondemographically oriented land uses.

| | Percentage of Total Valuation[9] | | | Percentage of National Totals in Urban Sample | |
| | | | | Rate-ables By Value | Rate-ables By Number |
Category	National Total	Urban Sample	Unsampled Remainder		
Domestic	47.0	43.3	53.0	60.8	55.1
Shops	9.6	11.1	6.6	76.1	60.1
Offices	5.7	8.2	0.8	95.2	77.7
Other commercial	9.1	7.9	5.5	73.6	53.4
Industrial	14.3	14.6	14.1	66.6	65.1
Crown	3.9	3.7	4.3	62.0	[10]
Other	12.3	10.0	16.5	54.0	[10]
Total	100.0	100.0	100.0	Mean = 66.3	[10]

The spatial nature of urbanization may be evaluated in terms of the intensity of different land uses as well as the aggregate density. The London Metropolitan Area provides one of the clearest illustrations of this, due to the availability of information on the individual local authorities making up both the Greater London Council (London's "metropolitan government") and the outer metropolitan area.

[9] Columns may not add to indicated totals due to rounding.
[10] Data not available.

Inner London, with an average value density of £4438 per acre, is made up of a variety of areas, ranging from Greenwich, with a valuation density of £828 per acre, to the City of London, with a valuation density of £68,264 per acre. Lewisham has a density of £1426 and Westminster, £19,542. What is clearly evident is that the density of population is related in a complex fashion to the amount of urbanization and that in the highest value land areas there is a tradeoff between residential and nonresidential uses which cannot be easily determined. The emergent pattern, however, clearly conforms to the a priori notions that urbanization measures interactions and that the largest number of interactions per unit of area take place in the City of London. Conversely interactions in the Borough of Greenwich are reduced in number not only by the low population density but also by the absence of nonresidential land uses.

The regularity of the land-use pattern is shown as one goes further out. Of course, there are some exceptions due to favorable locations and earlier developments, but the pattern clearly shows that as one goes out from the urban core, the value densities fall very rapidly to levels that approximate those of the rest of England.

Only slightly less dramatic contrasts emerge from maps of the other conurbations, emphasizing the pertinent objections to the English concept of conurbation, which often encompasses a multiplicity of central cities.

When the measure of urbanism is applied to the various groupings of British towns, there emerges a pattern, not only in the measure of urbanization but also in terms of the various land uses. The method used attempts to minimize the effect of individual jurisdictions, such as the Inner London Education Authority; nonetheless, where any such large area still departs sufficiently from the norm, the effect is a major one.

This effect is also made evident by a comparison of the weighted and unweighted averages. The unweighted average of rateable values for all 172 towns is £585 per acre, as contrasted with the £699 weighted average for the same area. The difference is accounted for, not only by London, but by the other major conurbation centers as well. The level of valuation per acre is higher in the central cities (£680) than it is in the noncentral towns (using Kingsley Davis' 1955 definitions), where it is £548. As expected, it is also evident (although the data are not presented) that the lowest levels of urbanization occur in the noncentral city areas outside the London area. The more detailed picture of values by conurbation demonstrates this most clearly.

The differences in urbanization are only in part a function of the variations in population densities, for the population densities show modest differences between the town groups as classified in the study. The density for all towns averaged 12.45 persons per acre, with the central cities averaging 14.61 persons per acre and the outside central cities 11.61 persons per acre. In the London area the density is 13.22, although in the Inner London area itself it is 39.90, and there is little difference in density between the London area (13.22 persons per acre) and the non–London area (12.14 persons per acre).

The factors that "account" for these differences lie in the mix and special distribution of property densities. As shown in Table 1, though 51.8% of the property holdings in the full urban sample are utilized for domestic purposes, there are major differences between groups in the proportions devoted to the various land uses. As would be expected, central cities have a higher proportion devoted to nonresidential uses (58.1% as compared to 49.0% in the noncentral city area), with no real difference between the London and the non–London portions of the nation.

Further decomposition of the data indicates, however, that these differ-

Table 1.   Measures of urbanization

	All Towns n=172	Control Cities n=48	Non-control Cities n=124	London Area n=49	Non-London Area n=123	Inner London (ILEA) Exhibit	Central Cities Less London n=47	Noncentral Cities Less Non-London Area n=76
	Composition of the Tax Rolls by Value, 1966 (unweighted averages)							
Domestic 1(£-£100)	31.3%	31.6%	31.2%	23.0%	36.5%	9.5%	34.6%	38.7%
Domestic 2(£101-£200)	14.0	7.9	17.0	21.8	9.2	12.0	7.1	10.4
Domestic 3(over £200)	2.7	2.2	2.9	4.2	1.8	9.4	1.0	1.9
Total Domestic	48.2%	41.9%	51.1%	49.1%	47.4%	31.0%	42.7%	51.0%
Shops	11.3	13.2	10.4	10.3	11.8	8.7	13.1	10.3
Offices	3.4	6.3	2.0	5.3	2.4	25.0	4.0	1.3
Other Commercial	7.2	8.5	6.6	7.0	7.4	10.7	8.3	6.4
Industry	16.6	14.0	17.7	17.4	16.0	7.0	16.1	17.5
Crown	2.7	3.4	2.6	3.3	2.4	7.1	2.8	2.3
Other	10.8	11.9	10.2	9.0	12.0	7.8	12.5	11.5
Total Nonresidential	51.8%	58.1%	49.0%	50.9%	52.6%	69.0%	57.3%	49.0%
Total Value Per Acre	£585.	£680.	£548.	£800.	£499.	£4438.	£600	£437

Source: Ministry of Housing and Local Government and Welsh Office, Rates and Rateable Values in England and Wales, 1966-1967, Part II, London Her Majesty's Stationery Office, 1966.

ential land-use patterns are not uniformly distributed among the various types of nonresidential land use. For example, shops account for a slightly higher proportion of property values in the central cities than in the other town groups. In surprising contrast to this (at first blush, at least) shops play a relatively smaller proportional role in London than elsewhere, but this may doubtless be explained by the distorting effect of office uses on data for that metropolitan area. As one would anticipate, a great preponderance of office usage is a unique feature of Inner London, although it is also characteristic of the London area as a whole, especially when compared with the "less urban" town groups. The highest valued land uses in the nation are associated with office usage—a fact that will be brought out later.

The "other commercial" land-use category shows only moderate differences between the central and noncentral city groups, and there is virtually no difference between the London area and the rest of the nation.

Perhaps the most interesting finding is the absence of any major differences between the proportions in industrial land uses. If there is any surprise here, it is that the proportion of land value in industrial use is slightly lower in the central cities than it is in the outside areas. Generally, however, the proportions are very much as expected, with the special cases so far out of line that they are clearly evident.

In the case of Crown (i.e., governmental) property little difference is to be found among the various town groups. The national-capital, public-office nature of London is confirmed by its highest proportion of Crown values, thereby reinforcing the private-office figures. The category of all "other" land uses also exhibits a slightly higher proportion in the central city group, but the difference is quite nominal.

The urban dimensions of land uses become most apparent when they are analyzed spatially, but they also have meaning when they are placed in their more ordinary per capita terms—that is, relative to their residential populations.

On a spatial basis it is possible to distinguish between the number of occupiers—domestic, shops, offices, etc.—and the value of these establishments. Both these measures are important, for the nonhomogeneity of land use effects a nonlinear relationship between value and number. Therefore there exists a functional circularity between the higher land rents in the more centrally located areas and the concomitantly greater intensity of land use in those areas.

In addition, land uses take on additional meaning when they are specified in terms of the number of persons served per dwelling unit or per establishment, as shown in Table 2. Strictly speaking, such data should, of course, be modified to the extent that nonresidents are serviced or employed

Table 2.   Characteristics of British towns, socioeconomic groupings (unweighted average)

	All Towns n=172	Control Cities n=48	Non-control Cities n=124	London Area n=49	Non-London Area n=123	Inner London (ILEA) Exhibit	Central Cities Less London n=47	Noncentral Cities Less Non-London Area n=76
Per cent:								
Professional	4.5% (2.4)	3.3% (1.3)	4.9% (2.6)	6.2% (2.5)	3.9% (2.1)	4.5%	3.3% (1.4)	4.3% (2.4)
Managerial	10.4 (4.5)	8.0 (2.1)	11.3 (4.9)	12.9 (4.6)	9.3 (4.1)	9.2	8.0 (2.1)	10.2 (4.7)
Skilled	38.9 (5.7)	41.1 (4.0)	38.0 (6.1)	35.3 (5.3)	40.3 (5.3)	33.8	41.2 (3.9)	39.7 (6.0)
Nonmanual	18.1 (4.6)	16.0 (3.1)	18.9 (4.9)	22.0 (3.7)	16.5 (4.0)	22.0	16.0 (3.0)	16.9 (4.5)
Semiskilled	16.4 (4.3)	18.3 (3.4)	15.7 (4.4)	14.1 (3.3)	17.3 (4.3)	15.9	18.4 (3.4)	16.7 (4.6)
Unskilled	8.8 (3.4)	10.6 (2.7)	8.1 (3.4)	6.6 (2.6)	9.7 (3.3)	10.8	10.6 (2.7)	9.1 (3.5)
Armed forces, other	2.9 (2.5)	2.5 (2.0)	3.0 (2.7)	2.9 (1.5)	2.8 (2.8)	3.8	2.5 (2.0)	3.1 (3.2)
Socioeconomic Class I	14.9 (6.7)	11.4 (3.0)	16.3 (7.2)	19.1 (6.9)	13.2 (5.8)	13.7	16.2 (7.1)	14.4 (6.8)

Values in parentheses are standard errors.

Source: General Register Office, Sample Census 1966, England and Wales, County Report, London, Her Majesty's Stationery Office, 1967.

by these establishments, for the urban town is only in the rarest of cases "truebounded." However, information for such an undertaking could not be included in the present study.

The number of residents per housing unit shows very little variation among the various town groups, the entire urban sample, of the nation as a whole. Throughout the statistic is approximately 3.19 persons per dwelling unit. Apart from the effect of transients, this measure accurately reflects the residential characteristics of the area. In contrast, both the residents and the nonresidents of a given jurisdiction are serviced by the nonresidential (nondemographic) land uses, thus complicating the formulation of a per capita measure of the intensity of nonresidential land use.

Several fascinating patterns emerge, generally confirming in quantitative terms a number of previously held a priori assumptions. The number of persons per shop is smaller in the central city areas, 62, with 56 in Inner London, than it is in the outlying areas, 74. The differences are on the average quite small.

Offices present the greatest central city to noncentral city differentials, however, with 212 persons per office in the central cities and 344 in the noncentral city areas. Since offices in Inner London service the whole of England as well as the extensive London area, it is no surprise to find that there is one office for every 81 persons in this most urbanized portion of England. However, it is the real core of the London conurbation that provides the most sensational statistic of all, where the diminutive City of London exhibits an astounding 2.34 offices for each of its 4500 residents. This is explicable, of course, in terms of the limited area and the exceedingly high density of office land use in the core of the British commercial and financial empire. Westminster, which contains the other great concentration of offices in Britain, is far larger in area than is the "City."

On the other hand, the number of "other commercial" establishments is practically invariant to the resident population in all groupings, and London itself fits very well with the national pattern. There are 30 persons for each such establishment, with a slightly higher figure for the central cities, 31, than for the noncentral city areas, 30.

Regarding the industrial pattern, the analysis shows a smaller population per industrial establishment in the central cities than in the outside central city areas, 452 versus 517, respectively. However, as will be shown later, this is due to the large number of small establishments in the central city areas and in a number of the smaller Lancashire and Yorkshire communities.

The actual number of establishments is but one indication of their relative importance. They may also be large or small, as in the case of the industrial establishments just mentioned. Size may be expressed in terms of property valuations, which are related either to the areas involved or to their resident populations. As such, it is likely that valuation density (property values per unit of area) stands as the best available measure of land-use intensity and of urbanization characteristics.

In examining valuation densities the resident, or domestic, land uses are to be distinguished at the outset. In this analysis, though there are only slight differentials between central and noncentral cities, there is a major difference (see Table 3) between the London area, £393 per acre, and the non–London area, £237 per acre. This contrast cannot be wholly explained by variations in population densities because, as shown in Table 4, they do not differ to any extent.

Shops show clearly greater valuation densities in the central cities than outside and substantially higher values in the London area than in the non–London area. Only a part of this difference may be accounted for by the impact of Inner London.

Weighted and even the unweighted valuation densities for offices are

Table 3.   Characteristics of British towns, per capita valuations (unweighted averages)

	All Towns n=172	Control Cities n=48	Non-control Cities n=124	London Area n=49	Non-London Area n=123	Inner London (ILEA) Exhibit	Central Cities Less London n=47	Noncentral Cities Less Non-London Area n=76
Per Capita Valuations:								
Shops	£5.04 (2.44)	£5.83 (2.33)	£4.74 (2.42)	£5.85 (2.70)	£4.72 (2.26)	£12.74	£5.68 (2.12)	£4.12 (2.14)
Offices	1.20 (2.25)	1.87 (3.92)	.95 (.97)	2.12 (3.95)	.84 (.71)	27.79	1.32 (.88)	.55 (.35)
Commercial	3.16 (2.33)	3.58 (1.82)	2.99 (2.50)	3.70 (3.33)	2.94 (1.78)	11.82	3.42 (1.37)	2.65 (1.94)
Industry	7.70 (7.15)	7.29 (7.67)	7.87 (6.97)	10.06 (6.84)	6.77 (7.08)	17.81	7.29 (7.75)	6.46 (6.67)
Crown	1.21 (1.16)	1.30 (1.19)	1.17 (1.16)	1.74 (1.46)	.99 (.95)	7.93	1.18 (.69)	.88 (1.06)
Other	5.02 (1.34)	5.48 (1.29)	4.84 (1.31)	5.38 (1.64)	4.87 (1.17)	8.65	5.43 (1.22)	4.54 (1.01)
Domestic (All)	22.47 (8.14)	19.20 (6.14)	23.63 (8.44)	29.31 (6.51)	19.58 (7.07)	34.44	18.88 (5.78)	20.28 (7.76)
Total	45.49 (14.11)	44.89 (14.49)	45.72 (14.01)	57.12 (14.08)	40.85 (11.20)	112.27	43.60 (10.80)	39.23 (11.17)
Exhibit:								
Domestic Less Than £100	14.79 (2.58)	14.82 (1.91)	14.78 (2.81)	14.19 (3.49)	15.03 (2.10)	10.60	14.91 (1.83)	15.10 (2.25)
Domestic £101 To £200	6.45 (7.08)	3.63 (4.95)	7.54 (7.48)	12.60 (7.14)	4.00 (5.38)	13.40	3.42 (4.79)	4.36 (5.72)
Domestic more Than £200	1.22 2.71	.75 (1.97)	1.40 (2.94)	2.51 (3.30)	.71 (2.25)	10.44	.55 (1.39)	.82 (2.67)

Values in parentheses are standard errors.

Source: General Register Office, Sample Census 1966, England and Wales, County Report, London, Her Majesty's Stationery Office, 1967.
The Institute of Municipal Treasures and Accountants, Return of Rates and Rates Levied per Head of Population (England and Wales), 1967-1968, London, The Institute of Municipal Treasurers and Accountants, June, 1967.
Ministry of Housing and Local Government and Welsh Office, Rates and Rateable Values in England and Wales, 1966-1967, Part II, London, Her Majesty's Stationery Office, 1966.

completely dominated by the presence of London, the distorting effect of which is clearly evident even though it is only one observation in 48. Even when the values for Inner London are excluded from the analysis, the central cities (and, perhaps more accurately, the central business districts) still strongly reflect relatively higher valuation densities than do the outlying areas. The higher valued land use is also reflected in the "other commercial" category, but, as expected, the difference is not as striking as in the case of offices.

Rather surprising is the absence of valuation-density differentials for

Table 4. Characteristics of British towns, measures of urbanization: number per acre (unweighted averages)

	All Towns n=172	Control Cities n=48	Non-control Cities n=124	London Area n=49	Non-London Area n=123	Inner London (ILEA) Exhibit	Central Cities Less London n=47	Noncentral Cities Less Non-London Area n=76
Shops	.18 (.11)	.24 (.12)	.16 (.10)	.17 (.14)	.19 (.10)	.71	.23 (.10)	.16 (.10)
Offices	.04 (.05)	.08 (.08)	.03 (.02)	.04 (.07)	.04 (.04)	.49	.07 (.05)	.03 (.02)
Commercial	.40 (.21)	.46 (.22)	.38 (.20)	.45 (.25)	.38 (.19)	1.21	.44 (.19)	.35 (.18)
Industry	.03 (.02)	.03 (.03)	.02 (.02)	.03 (.03)	.03 (.02)	.13	.03 (.02)	.02 (.02)
Domestic (All)	4.50 (1.85)	4.54 (1.74)	3.65 (1.84)	4.03 (2.24)	3.85 (1.68)	11.15	4.40 (1.46)	3.51 (1.72)
Persons	12.45 (6.10)	14.57 (5.91)	11.61 (5.99)	13.22 (7.63)	12.12 (5.36)	39.90	14.03 (4.63)	10.94 (5.47)
Domestic Less Than £100	3.19 (1.67)	4.06 (1.53)	2.86 (1.61)	2.52 (1.53)	3.45 (1.66)	11.15	4.02 (1.52)	3.11 (1.66)
Domestic £101 to £200	.65 (.88)	.44 (.70)	.74 (.99)	1.38 (1.17)	.36 (.50)	5.93	.36 (.45)	.36 (.53)
Domestic More Than £200	.06 (.16)	.05 (.17)	.06 (.16)	.12 (.19)	.03 (.14)	4.09	.03 (.06)	.04 (.17)

Values in parentheses are standard errors.

Source: General Register Office, Sample Census 1966, England and Wales, County Report, London, Her Majesty's Stationery Office, 1967.
    The Institute of Municipal Treasurers and Accountants, Return of Rates and Rates Levied per Head of Population, (England and Wales), 1967-1968, London, The Institute of Municipal Treasurers and Accountants, June, 1967.
    Ministry of Housing and Local Government and Welsh Office, Rates and Rateable Values in England and Wales, 1966-1967, Part II, London, Her Majesty's Stationery Office, 1966.

industrial properties in the central cities as compared to the noncentral cities. Exclusion of London, however, does reduce the figures for central cities to below those of the noncentral city areas.

The emerging picture is generally reinforced when analyzed on a per capita basis. The data abstract from the question of population densities and population size. The per capita statistics focus on some special problems such as the income nature of the area and the nondemographic nature of the community. Thus, on the average, the domestic values in the central cities are lower than those in the noncentral cities, £19.05 and £23.63, respectively.

In addition, there exist considerable variations in per capita and per unit area valuations among jurisdictions in all areas. These differentials, in fact, provide proxies, especially as they reflect the different classes of domestic properties, for the income characteristics—proxies that are superior to the

Table 5. Characteristics of British towns, measures of urbanization: value per acre (unweighted averages)

	All Towns n=172	Control Cities n=48	Non-control Cities n=124	London Area n=49	Non-London Area n=123	Inner London (ILEA) Exhibit	Central Cities Less London n=47	Noncentral Cities Less Non-London Area n=76
Shops	£66 (54)	£90 (73)	£57 (42)	£83 (79)	£59 (39)	£508	£81 (34)	£46 (32)
Offices	20 (85)	43 (158)	11 (15)	42 (157)	12 (15)	1109	20 (20)	6 (5)
Commercial	42 (50)	58 (67)	36 (40)	56 (82)	37 (27)	474	49 (28)	29 (24)
Industry	97 (95)	95 (58)	97 (106)	139 (132)	80 (69)	312	90 (48)	73 (79)
Crown	16 (27)	23 (44)	14 (15)	26 (45)	12 (14)	316	16 (10)	10 (15)
Other	63 (40)	81 (48)	56 (34)	72 (56)	60 (31)	345	76 (28)	50 (28)
Domestic (All)	282 (187)	286 (190)	281 (187)	393 (253)	239 (131)	1374	263 (104)	224 (144)
Total	585 (439)	680 (595)	548 (357)	800 (680)	499 (248)	4438	600 (220)	437 (246)
Exhibit:								
Domestic Less Than £100	184 (91)	215 (81)	172 (92)	183 (107)	184 (84)	1374	210 (76)	167 (84)
Domestic £101 to £200	83 (114)	56 (91)	93 (120)	174 (151)	46 (68)	422	45 (59)	47 (73)
Domestic More Than £200	16 (49)	15 (61)	16 (42)	34 (65)	9 (37)	534	7 (16)	10 (45)

Values in parentheses are standard errors.

Source: General Register Office, Sample Census 1966, England and Wales, County Report, London, Her Majesty's Stationery Office, 1967.

The Institute of Municipal Treasurers and Accountants, Return of Rates and Rates Levied per Head of Population, (England and Wales), 1967-1968, London, The Institute of Municipal Treasurers and Accountants, June, 1967.

Ministry of Housing and Local Government and Welsh Office, Rates and Rateable Values in England and Wales, 1966-1967, Part II, London, Her Majesty's Stationery Office, 1966.

socioeconomic and occupational groups ordinarily used and reported in Table 5.

These and other relevant characteristics are reported in Tables 2 through 6. The detailed use of the standard deviations would make it possible to classify cities in great detail. A more extended analysis of the individual towns based on their group and national standard deviations and averages is currently in process. In the more detailed analysis this will be done for each of the 172 towns.

Table 6. Characteristics of British towns, persons per rateable unit in 1966 (unweighted averages)

	All Towns n=172	Control Cities n=48	Non-control Cities n=124	London Area n=49	Non-London Area n=123	Inner London (ILEA) Exhibit	Central Cities Less London n=47	Noncentral Cities Less Non-London Area n=76
Persons								
Per shop	71	62	74	82	66	56	62	69
	(20)	(14)	(21)	(20)	(18)		(14)	(20)
Per Office	296	212	349	309	291	82	220	363
	(223)	(100)	(303)	(367)	(154)		(94)	(177)
Per Commercial	30	31	30	28	31	33	31	31
	(12)	(10)	(12)	(14)	(10)		(10)	(11)
Per Industry	497	452	517	533	484	303	457	503
	(223)	(234)	(335)	(301)	(302)		(240)	(346)
Per Domestic Hereditament	3.19	3.19	3.18	3.28	3.15	3.44	3.19	3.13
	(.27)	(.27)	(.27)	(.17)	(.29)		(.27)	(.30)

Values in parentheses are standard errors.

Source: General Register Office, Sample Census 1966, England and Wales, County Report, London, Her Majesty's Stationery Office, 1967.
The Institute of Municipal Treasurers and Accountants, Return of Rates and Rates Levied per Head of Population (England and Wales), 1967-1968, London, The Institute of Municipal Treasurers and Accountants, June 1967.
Ministry of Housing and Local Government and Welsh Office, Rates and Rateable Values in England and Wales, 1966-1967, Part II, London, Her Majesty's Stationery Office, 1966.

RELATIONSHIPS OF LAND USES

The analysis up to this point has not dealt with the specific relationships of individual land uses to other specific land uses. Up to this time each land use, though obviously related to other land uses, has been viewed independently. In this section the individual land uses are viewed in relation to the others as well as to the overall urban characteristics of the area. The analysis is in terms of both physical numbers of units and valuation characteristics.

The measures have all been indicated earlier, although they appear here in their raw form. Table 7 relates the number of rateables per acre for each land-use class to all other classes in a simple correlation matrix. Total domestic units are divided into three classes: those of less than £100 rateable value, those between £100 and £200 rateable values, and those whose rateable values exceed £200. These are standard classes for assessing residential properties in England and Wales.

Other classes of property are also considered in detail. In addition, socio-

Table 7. Correlations among land uses, number and value per acre (all towns, $n = 172$)

Number of Units	Dom 1	Dom 2	Dom 3	Shops	Offices	Other Commercial	Industrial	Socioeconomic Class I
Domestic 1	1.0000	-.0999	-.1280	.8005	.5114	.5883	.6780	-.5066
Domestic 2		1.0000	.7132	.3527	.2527	.3399	.2199	.4525
Domestic 3			1.0000	.2905	.3744	.2857	.1943	.3629
Shops				1.0000	.6875	.7166	.7928	-.2671
Offices					1.0000	.4802	.5818	-.1574
Other Commercial						1.0000	.6502	-.1961
Industrial							1.0000	-.3060
Socioeconomic Class								1.0000

Value of Units	Dom 1	Dom 2	Dom 3	Shops	Offices	Other Commercial	Industrial	Socioeconomic Class I
Domestic 1	1.000	.1595	.0536	.6024	.2706	.4881	.5406	-.3372
Domestic 2		1.0000	.7095	.5527	.3708	.5021	.3084	.4616
Domestic 3			1.0000	.5534	.6545	.5420	.1340	.3179
Shops				1.0000	.7125	.8000	.4231	-.0665
Offices					1.0000	.7644	.2291	-.0013
Other Commercial						1.0000	.4556	-.0538
Industrial							1.0000	.2795
Socioeconomic Class I								1.0000

Correlations of Values of Units Per Acre
with Numbers of Units Per Acre by Class of Property

Domestic (total)	.7839
Domestic 1	.8960
Domestic 2	.9964
Domestic 3	.9873
Shops	.7317
Offices	.7801
Other Commercial	.5807
Industrial	.5919

See text for definitions of categories

economic class as measured by class I of the British census, the proportion of professionals and managers of the total number of males employed and retired, is also included. Finally each of these characteristics is measured against the general measure of urbanization, total property valuation per acre.

The problem initially is to determine the existence of relationships between land uses. The basic hypothesis is to disprove the contention that there is no relationship between the pairs of land-use values. The hypothesis will be rejected at an .01 level ($r \geq \pm .2540$).

The first result indicates that the number of units of low-value rateable housing per acre is unrelated to other housing characteristics per acre. The signs are negative, but not significantly so. Low rateable housing is significantly correlated with the high density of shops per acre ($r = .8005$). It is also closely related to other land uses, measured in terms of establishments per acre of offices, and other commercial and industrial uses, the categories for which such data are available. There is a correlation between the two higher housing categories, but, perhaps surprisingly, not between the lower and either of the higher. Nonetheless the relationships of these higher housing categories to other land uses are far weaker than was true with the lowest housing category, although in some cases they were statistically significant.

The relationships among the nonresidential categories are significant but again in no way unique. The highest association is between the number of shops per acre and the number of industrial plants per acre, where $r = .7928$. The lowest is between the number of offices per acre and the number of commercial establishments: $r = .4806$.

In terms of the social class index (i.e., class I, the percentage employed in professional and managerial occupations), the results show the expected diversity. Low-value housing per acre is inversely related to the index as $r = -.5006$, whereas the two higher valued classes are positively related: $r = .4525$ and $r = .3629$. These relationships, although statistically significant, are much lower than expected. In part this is due to the definitions involved. The relationships—in terms of numbers—abstract from differences in the size of the enterprises involved.

By looking at the relationships in value terms (i.e., values per acre), it is possible in part to distinguish the effect of size from a simple tally count. In some cases this leads to fundamental changes, whereas in others it makes no difference. Insofar as the lowest housing unit is concerned, a distinct shift emerges when one considers its relationships to values rather than to numbers. First, the high correlation of the lowest housing category to the number of establishments is reduced when considered in terms of values per acre. Although it is still significant, the "value" correlation of .4539 is much lower than the correlation with "number," $r = .8002$. Second, although while the number of shops is not highly related to either of the two higher housing classes, the value of shops per acre is closely related to the value of housing. Furthermore, office valuation densities are most closely related to the highest housing-value classification. Commercial establishments show almost the same patterns relative to the housing distributions.

No really high correlations appear within the matrix of nonresidential relationships. This seems to be true whether their relationships are measured in number or in value terms. Perhaps most surprising is the fact that, for industrial uses, the relationships to all other uses are lower when valuation densities are used than they are when physical (numerical) densities, are used, but these relationships are enhanced for shops, offices, and other commercial establishments. The presumption is that there are a number of separate land-use (i.e., city class) groupings: those associated with the domestic 1 category; those associated with the domestic 2 and 3 categories; those associated with shops, offices, and other commercial activities; and those associated with industrial land uses.

The very last step of the analysis is designed to determine the combined and separate contributions of the different physical land uses (i.e., residences per acre, shops per acre, etc.) on the level of urbanization, as measured by the value densities. The simple correlations for the 172 towns are shown below for each class of land use and urbanization.

Type of Land use	Correlation of Number per Acre And Value Density		
	Simple r	Simple r^2	Value of Standardized Regression Coefficient[11]
Domestic 1	.4509	.2033	+.4118
Domestic 2	.6895	.4754	+.5748
Domestic 3	.6119	.3744	+.1517
Shops	.7298	.5326	+.2884
Offices	.7164	.5132	+.3644
Other Commercial	.6238	.3891	+.0446
Industrial	.6477	.4195	+.2005

Although each of these variables is clearly significant, none is unique by definition, for the highest coefficient of simple correlation is that of shops, where the r is .7298, with an r^2 only slightly in excess of .5.

The analysis of the joint importance of the classes of land uses indicates that they are additive but only to an extent. Furthermore, when account is taken of other variables, the individual importance of the several variables reveals wide variations from that observed in the simple case. In the case of one variable there is a change in sign, from an expected positive relationship to a significant, and, to the writers, an unexpected negative relationship.

First, the joint importance of variables was determined in two stages. The first stage involved the inclusion of the residential (demographic)

[11] Drawn from multiple regression including all of these variables in the all-town sample (n = 172).

uses—namely, domestic categories 1, 2, and 3—to "explain" the variations in valuations per acre. The multiple correlation of all residential land uses ($R = .8929$) "accounts for" 79.9% of the variations in valuations per acre. The introduction of the nonresidential uses increases the R to .9392, and the coefficient of multiple determination, R^2, to .8820.

Second, the several independent variables fall into three classes: first are those that are significantly associated with the valuation densities; second are those that are unrelated; and, finally, in the case of shops, there is a negative relationship. What is surprising is that the observed simple correlations were all of the same order of magnitude, but the picture is fundamentally altered if these situations are taken into account. The standardized regression coefficients, in their order of importance, are as follows for the total value per acre:

Domestic 2	$+.5748$
Domestic 1	$+.4118$
Offices	$+.3644$
Shops	$-.2884$
Industries	$+.2005$
Domestic 3	$+.1517$
Other commercial	$+.0446$

All the values are significant with the exception of the "other commercial" category, which appears to be purely passive when other land uses are included in explaining variations in valuation per acre. The domestic land uses, though of prime importance, must be related to other land uses —particularly offices and industries. Of particular interest is the fact that the number of shops per acre is inversely related to the level of urbanization after all the other land uses are taken into account.

Similar analyses were carried out for each of the groupings of towns. Although some of the results showed slight differences, the basic pattern of relationships between land uses and total value densities were approximately the same throughout.

CONCLUSIONS

The analysis of British towns provides a unique opportunity to apply statistical techniques to comparative urban analysis. The comparability of data and definitions is the key to the problems of such an analysis. Because of the specific nature of the data available, it is possible to deal with British towns not only in such combinations as individual metropolitan areas, central cities, noncentral cities, the London area, and the rest of the nation but also by using other classifications for which there is some a priori basis. This "grouping" method is also conducive to comparison of British towns with towns in other nations for which similar information is available, such as the United States, Canada, and West Germany.

The purpose of this chapter was to analyze not only the existence of urbanization but also differences in the levels and nature of urbanization. Value densities (rateable values per acre) served as the principal measure of urbanization. Unlike population densities, this measure yields a knowledge of the nondemographic as well as the demographic nature of the area. Special analysis of the Inner London Education Authority area indicated that the method holds in detail as well as in the aggregate. The most highly urbanized subjurisdiction in the nation is the City of London, and there is a downward gradient from that high point. Similar analyses of the other conurbations indicated similar situations, even where the population density figures were ambiguous.

A major distinction has been made here between the residential and the nonresidential uses of urban land. Presented in terms of unweighted town group averages, certain nonresidential land uses appear to be functions of the residential pattern, whereas others were discovered to be independent. The data on numbers of units in each type of land use and valuation density proved to be especially interesting when examined spatially, with the valuation density arising as a most revealing measure of urbanization characteristics.

The last part of the paper was devoted to the interrelationships among land uses. The analysis confirmed many of the patterns that scholars and students had previously observed. Moreover, these results go beyond those of previous studies, for they provide the basis for determining operationally useful parameter values relating land uses in physical and value terms by political unit.

The results of this analysis readily suggest that factor analysis or other types of multivariate analysis, when applied to the land-use and associated data of British towns, would add considerably to our knowledge of those characteristics that generally have been considered to be necessary in establishing more meaningful and powerful classifications of cities. Furthermore, these classifications do not have to wait for census years updating, for they are available in a continuous annual series. An enhanced perspective is inserted into the analysis when it moves away from data based primarily on the residential characteristics to one that places the latter characteristics in their land-use environment. The "industrial suburb" may be an enclave (although there are surprisingly few in England and Wales), or it may be industrial both in its land use and residential character, or it may be one in which industrial workers reside. The information on industrial land use, both in value and in number, is superior to the ambiguous information on occupational character which is used as a proxy measuring the "industrial nature" of a community. In addition, the housing-value information provides an excellent proxy for income.

Finally the analysis of land use permits the establishment of criteria for classifying cities—criteria that are superior to those developed for the United States because of their contemporaneity, comparability, and comprehensiveness. They offer measures appropriate not only to cross-sectional analysis but to time-series analysis. The availability of such data may provide the basis for a better understanding of cities in the United States, Canada, Great Britain, and elsewhere. And it is toward that end that the classification of cities assumes meaning.

CHAPTER 9

A Comparative Typology of Urban Government Images

CHARLES R. ADRIAN

University of California at Riverside

While collecting data for our study of four Michigan cities in the 50,000 to 80,000 population range in the late 1950s we became aware of an implicit notion that seemed to be in the minds of community leaders of what they considered to be the proper tasks of local government.[1] In an effort to give a more effective, better organized, and more theoretical framework to our reported findings, we developed a fourfold typology of urban government images. Because of financial and perhaps to some extent methodological problems, we were not able to test empirically whether these images were actually held by community leaders, not to mention ordinary voters in the communities. The purpose of this chapter is to suggest measures that might appropriately identify each of these community types, assuming that they exist, and thereby to suggest yet other parameters in developing city classifications of practical utility.

TYPES OF GOVERNMENT IMAGE

The typology of government images we hypothesized is as follows:

1. Promoting economic growth, or "boosterism."
2. Providing for or securing life's amenities, or "amenities."

[1] Oliver P. Williams and Charles R. Adrian, *Four Cities* (Philadelphia: University of Pennsylvania Press, 1963).

3. Maintaining nothing but traditional local government services, or "caretaker" government.

4. Arbitrating among conflicting interests—the "arbiter," or "brokerage," function.

Economic Growth

The type 1, or "boosterism," government image has as its object the growth of both population and wealth in the community. Commenting at the time, we noted:

Born of speculative hopes, nurtured by the recall of frontier competition for survival, augmented by the American pride in bigness, the idea that the good "thriving" community is one that continues to grow has [long] been political thinking. It is essentially an economic conception and still remains a widely held assumption in urban [government theory] drawing an analogy between municipal and business corporations. Just as the firm must grow to prosper, so must the city increase in population, industry, and total wealth. But the parallel is not simply an analogy, for according to this view the ultimate vocation of government is to serve the producer.

Although this image is endorsed most vigorously by those specific economic interests which have a stake in growth, its appeal is much broader. The drama of a growing city infects the inhabitants with a certain pride and gives them a feeling of being a part of progress: an essential ingredient of our national aspirations. The flocking of people to "our" city is something like the coming of the immigrants to our national shores. It is a tangible demonstration of the superiority of our way of life in that others have voluntarily chosen to join us. Growth also symbolizes opportunity, not only economically, but also socially and culturally. Large cities have more to offer in this respect than smaller ones.

Certain groups have such concrete stakes in growth that they are likely to be the active promoters of this image, while others in the city may have only tacit consent. The merchant, the supplier, the banker, the editor, and the city bureaucrat see each new citizen as a potential customer, taxpayer, or contributor to the enlargement of their enterprise, and they form the first rank of civic boosters.[2]

Amenities

The type 2, or "amenities," government is not at all concerned with the growth of the community. Perhaps it would be more accurate to say that it is opposed to community growth except along existing lines, with the prevailing life style carefully preserved. It is oriented toward the use of

[2] Williams and Adrian, *Four Cities,* pp. 23 and 24.

wealth rather than its production, and toward the wants of a community that is able to pay its own tax assessments rather than toward one that is concerned primarily with the passing of the tax burden on to other sources of wealth besides that of the home owner. As we noted in our study:

> Most communities recognize the demand for amenities in some fashion, but only an occasional community makes this the dominant objective of collective political action. Many cities have their noise- and smoke-abatement ordinances, but the idea of creating a quiet and peaceful environment for the home is hardly the central purpose of government.
>
> The policies designed to provide amenities are expressed by accent on the home environment rather than on the working environment—the citizen as consumer rather than producer. The demands of the residential environment are safety, slowness of traffic, quiet, beauty, convenience, and restfulness. The rights of pedestrians and children take precedence over the claims of commerce. Growth, far from being attractive, is often objectionable. That growth which is permitted must be controlled and directed, both in terms of the type of people who will be admitted and the nature of physical changes. It is essentially a design for a community with a homogeneous population, for civic amenities are usually an expression of a common style of living. Furthermore, because amenities are costly, the population must have an above average income. All expenditures for welfare are unwanted diversions of resources. Those asking for public welfare assistance are seeking necessities which other citizens provide for themselves privately. Consequently, this image finds expression chiefly in the middle- and upper-income residential suburb.[3]

Caretaker Government

Type 3, maintaining traditional services, or "caretaker" government, is primarily a concern of the small town or the middle-size city that is relatively isolated from industrial America and is therefore growing relatively slowly, if at all. As we noted:

> "Freedom" and "self-reliance of the individual" are the values stressed by this view. Private decisions regarding the allocation of personal resources are lauded over governmental allocations through taxation. Tax increases are never justified except to maintain the traditional nature of the community. This substitution of individual for public decisions emphasizes a pluralistic conception of the "good." The analogy to laissez-faire economics is unmistakable. The caretaker image is associated with the policy of opposition to zoning, planning, and other regulation of the use of real property. These sentiments are peculiarly common to the traditional small town.

[3] Williams and Adrian, *Four Cities,* pp. 25 and 26.

Among the individuals most apt to be attracted by this view, especially in its extreme form, are retired middle-class persons, who are home owners living on a very modest fixed income. Squeezed by inflation and rising taxes, it is not surprising if they fail to see the need for innovation, especially when it means to them an absolute reduction in living standards. The marginal home owners, the persons who can just barely afford the home they are buying, whatever its price, are also likely to find the caretaker image attractive. They must justify a low-tax policy.[4]

The Arbiter

Image 4, the arbiter function, has long been associated with the larger cities of the nation and reflects, in particular, the heterogeneous urban community with a large percentage of first and second generation migrants. As we noted:

Emphasis is placed upon the process rather than the substance of governmental action. Although the possibility of a "community good" may be formally recognized, actually all such claims are reduced to the level of interests. The view is realistic in the popular sense in that it assumes "what's good for someone always hurts someone else." Given this assumption, government must provide a continuous arbitration system under which public policy is never regarded as being in final equilibrium. The formal structure of government must not be subordinated to a specific substantive purpose; rather the structure must be such that most interests may be at least considered by the decision makers.

That the proper role of government is to serve as an arbiter is held most logically by interest groups that fall short of complete political control, including, especially, the more self-conscious minorities. The numerical or psychic majority does not have to settle for a process, but can act directly in terms of substantive conceptions of the community good. The minority can only hope for success.

The most conspicuous interests that self-consciously espouse an arbiter function for government are neighborhood and welfare-oriented groups. Ethnic blocs reaching for a higher rung on the political ladder, and home owners and businessmen with stakes in a particular neighborhood, especially one threatened by undesired changes, make claims for special representation. The psychological minorities—persons low on a social economic scale—also stress the need for personal access.[5]

The Utility of the Images

Can these types of government images be operationalized for empirical study? This question was not investigated by us in our work on the four

[4] Williams and Adrian, *Four Cities,* pp. 27 and 28.
[5] Williams and Adrian, *Four Cities,* pp. 28 and 29.

cities. The answer is still not available, although the findings of Hahn in analyzing the data presented by the Kerner Commission are encouraging.[6] Hahn found that cities that most readily responded to civic disorders were those that were most politicized and most centralized—that is, cities that operated under the strong-mayor system. His findings also indicate that communities in which all or most councilmen were elected at large presumably chose representatives that were "community regarding"[7] and hence willing to act to prevent the recurrence of a riot or other disturbance after one had occurred, whereas communities that elected councilmen by wards apparently had representatives who were parochial in their orientation and hence had representatives who reflected their constituents' opposition to making concessions to minorities concentrated in a relatively few wards. Different images of the function of municipal government appear to be at work in these reactions to stress, and the differences were related to scalable community characteristics.

Other types than those we developed are conceivable. We do not argue that they are the only ones possible. For example, an image of the company town in a mining or lumbering area might be developed. It is possible that there is a type (at least for leaders) based on power for its own sake. Or one might conceive of a radical image calling for the use of the municipality as an instrument for widespread social reorganization. Such an image is not necessarily a blending of types 1 and 2. It is, however, not likely to dominate the decision-making process in any American city. We believe that the vast majority of contemporary American cities and villages can be subsumed under one of our four types, at least during the middle decades of the twentieth century.

After we had finished preparing the typology and had completed the field research on our four cities, we felt that we had a conceptually useful model but were concerned about the paucity of data. We concluded the discussion of the typology with the following comment:

If we had some measure of value preferences in all American cities, our scale would expand revealing differences more precisely in a comparative fashion. There probably are prototype cities which subordinate most policy to a single standard. The company towns, the upper-middle-class suburbs, and the

[6] Harlan D. Hahn, "Civic Responses to Riots: A Reconsideration of the Kerner Commission Data," *Public Opinion Quarterly,* forthcoming. See also Robert R. Alford, "The Comparative Study of Urban Elites," in Leo F. Schnore and Henry Fagin, Eds., *Urban Research and Policy Planning* (Beverly Hills, Calif.: Sage Publications, Inc., 1968).

[7] James Q. Wilson and Edward C. Banfield, "Public-regardingness as a Value Premise in Voting Behavior," *American Political Science Review,* Vol. 58 (1964), pp. 876–887.

isolated village provide examples where policy is dominated by producer interests, consumer interests, or status quo interests. Inclusion of such varied places would give greater polarity to a scale.[8]

The typology, though impressionistic, is empirically derived. It does not scale unidimensionally, for example, because the first three types are concerned primarily with the content of policy, whereas the brokerage function deals with the policy-making *process*. Furthermore, none of the cities we investigated fitted perfectly into any one of the four types. Indeed even in ranking cities by type we were operating under a handicap. We were not able to check the fit of each city to type by attitudes of either leaders or voters. We could only deduce the apparent image held by a dominant proportion of the decision-makers on the basis of the implications found in the actual performances of the city governments, or, in contemporary vocabulary, by the policy outputs.

Because the types were empirically, rather than logically, derived, they are not mutually exclusive categories but represent only the dominant tendencies in a particular city or even only in an office or group. (It is possible that the manager, the councilmen, and the business leaders all hold different images.) Similarly each type does not possess a reciprocal, as would be the case if they were logically derived. The classifications represent merely a dominant tendency, and the tendency cannot in all likelihood be measured in any absolute sense. The classification of a city must be viewed as a tendency *relative* to the tendencies in other cities of other types.

Some Weaknesses

The typology has some weaknesses. For one thing, it is possibly too expensive to do the necessary work to operationalize it, and such less-expensive-to-derive variables as a city's location or size may be equally effective predictors of public policy. The typology, furthermore, may well be both time and culture bound. Whether it would apply to medieval European cities is doubtful, as is the question of whether it would be useful in looking at the contemporary cities of Africa, Asia, or even of Europe. It is also likely that the typology would be useful mainly in cities of under 100,000 population, for it seems likely that cities larger than that would, for the most part, fall under the brokerage category because in such cities the interests and goals of various groups are likely to be so complex as to make government essentially a bargaining and compromising agency. Even

[8] Williams and Adrian, *Four Cities,* p. 36.

so, the larger cities can probably be scaled in relative terms; that is, if we control for size, tendencies toward domination by one of the substantive categories may still appear. Furthermore, it might be useful to use the typology for analyzing certain aspects of large-city government through the classification of neighborhoods, using such agencies as local school districts or civic associations, or by analysis according to type of office (manager, planning director, police chief, councilman). The typology might also be of assistance in analyzing the characteristics of different wards within a large city by applying the typology to the images of city councilmen or to their votes which indicate public policy preferences. The typology, in other words, would still seem to be useful, even though it is limited by time, culture, and size considerations.

Our findings, resulting from empirical research, led me to believe that it would be possible to classify many American cities according to our four types without interviewing either leaders or a sample survey of voters. Certain data that are either easily available or of a sort that could be gathered, at little cost, or through the development of indices, should be useful in identifying the dominant type in a given city or identifying the fact that the city is not committed to any single one of the types.

SCALES FOR AN INDEX

Further research should indicate the possibility of an index being developed from the items indicated in Table 1. Whether or not this index should involve a weighting of all items listed cannot be determined without further inquiry. Weighting may not be possible without a great deal of subjective judgment and may not be necessary in any case since differences in the importance of each scale tend to become less important as the number of scales increases.

In order to move toward a meaningful index, derived from the summed scales, the rankings on the scales are established so that the lowest ranking will always, where possible, occur for either the "booster" or the "amenities" type. Usually these two will be ranked 1 or 2, whereas "caretaker" and "arbiter" types were 3 or 4. If this pattern were followed for all 22 items, of course, we would derive only two types rather than four. This is not the case, however, since certain items sharply distinguish the two types in each of the groupings. Distinctions between the "booster" and "amenities" images, for example, are expected to be made in items 7, 10, 11, 12, 13, 15, 16, 17, and 21. Distinctions between the "caretaker" and "arbiter" types should be made through items 2, 7, 14, 19, 20, 22, and 23.

Table 1. Rank-order scales of community types, expected rankings

	Booster	Amenities	Caretaker	Arbiter
1. Recentness of current city charter (1 = most recent)	1.5	1.5	4	3
2. Average population of cities (1 = lowest)	3	2	1	4
3. Strength of local political party organization (1 = weakest)	2	1	3	4
4. Percentage of cities with nonpartisan elections (1 = highest)	2	1	4	3
5. Percentage of cities with at-large councilman elections (1 = highest)	2	1	3	4
6. Percentage of councilmen in business and industry (1 = highest)	1	2.5	2.5	4
7. Percentage of council votes nonunanimous (1 = lowest)	3	1	2	4
8. Percentage of cities under council-manager plan (1 = highest)	2	1	4	3
9. Percentage of budget expenditures devoted to professional planning activities (1 = highest)	2	1	4	3
10. Percentage of land area zoned commercial or industrial (1 = lowest)	4	1	2	3
11. Tax provisions favoring new business and industry (1 = lowest)	4	1	2	3
12. Business and industry assessment as percentage of tax base (1 = lowest)	4	1	2	3
13. Homogeneity of income (1 = highest)	4	1	2	3
14. Homogeneity of educational level (1 = highest)	4	1	2	3
15. Percentage of press release column inches devoted to attracting industry (1 = highest)	1	4	3	2
16. Percentage of press release column inches devoted to city as a pleasant place to live (1 = highest)	4	1	2	3
17. Percentage of budget expenditures and budget messages devoted to consumer services (1 = highest)	4	1	2	3
18. Percentage of municipal employees under merit system (1 = highest)	2	1	4	3
19. Percentage of population as ethnic or racial minorities (1 = lowest)	3	1	2	4
20. Percentage of eligible voter turnout, municipal elections (1 = lowest)	3	1	2	4
21. Size of police force as percentage of municipal employees (1 = lowest)	3	2	1	4
22. Per capita budget expenditures in proportion to other cities of similar size (1 = lowest)	2.5	2.5	1	4

General Community Characteristics

The expected rankings in Table 1 are derived as follows: item 1 assumes, and this can be empirically tested, that "booster" and "amenities" cities have adopted their present charters more recently than have the "care-taker" or the "arbiter" types, both of which tend to operate under more traditional structures and to be less concerned about formal rules and lines of authority. Item 2 is one of the few scales on which neither the "booster" nor the "amenities" type can be given the lowest ranking. Cities with "care-taker" governments tend to be small, usually isolated communities, whereas those with the "arbiter" function are among the largest cities. The other two types fall in between.

The third item concerns itself with the strength of the local political party organization. The assumption here, borne out by some existing research,[9] is that in cities that have undergone major "reform" reorganizations, the political party structure has been weakened and the probability is that local elections are on a nonpartisan ballot. Big cities using the "booster" or the "amenities" image, having been through a period of reformation and having newer charters, are also more likely to have elections on a nonpartisan basis, since the trend is in that direction and the more recently reorganized cities are more likely to have such elections. The reversal of the rank ordering of the "caretaker" and the "arbiter" types between items 3 and 4 is a result of the fact that the former is even less likely than the latter to have been reorganized or to have home-rule charters, or otherwise to have undergone fundamental structural changes in recent decades, and are therefore likely to have the traditional partisan elections. (This, however, is only an assumption. The degree to which the variables are interrelated will have to be determined statistically.)

Councils and Councilmen

The series of items dealing with councils and councilmen reflect both recent charter changes (versus the absence of changes in other cities) and other factors that may affect the makeup of the council. Item 5 is based on the fact that at-large elections for councilmen were advocated by the reformers of the twentieth century. In addition, advocates of both the "boosterism" and the "amenities" type of government image have generally

---

[9] Eugene C. Lee, *The Politics of Nonpartisanship* (Berkeley: University of California Press, 1960); Richard S. Childs, *Civic Victories* (New York: Harper and Row, Publishers, 1952).

favored a charter in which "community-regarding"[10] councilmen are to be preferred over those with pronounced parochial views. This is even more the case, presumably, in cities emphasizing amenities.

One would expect that persons owning businesses or deriving their incomes from business and industry would tend to be dominant in cities emphasizing boosterism. The "amenities" type of city has almost no industry and little business, but it tends to be inhabited by businessmen. In the "caretaker" type of city there is almost no industry, but the main-street merchants tend to be the most prestigious persons in town and hence to be members of the council.

Item 7 is based on the assumption that value consensus within a community differs according to the image held of the ideal community. The inhabitants of municipalities devoted to the "amenities" image are most likely to share values, education levels, and life styles,[11] and hence to be the most homogeneous and least likely to have policy differences that are sufficient to produce divided votes on the council. The "caretaker" type of community is only slightly less likely to show this pattern, for it is also in large measure socially and economically homogeneous. On the other hand, cities promoting economic growth usually have at least some councilmen who do not support this approach and will occasionally refuse to go along with the majority of the council in the formal vote.[12] A community committed to view the city as arbiter is the most likely to have divided views as to the most desirable approach and hence most likely to have nonunanimous votes on formal council decisions. In addition, cities that have been reorganized through reform-movement activities are likely to have small councils, as are the generally smaller communities operating under the "caretaker" image, whereas "arbiter" cities are likely to have larger councils. According to small-group theory, the larger the voting body, the more likely nonunanimous votes.[13] (An "intervening variable" problem arises here: Do unanimous votes stem from policy consensus or from size of council or, in what proportion, from both?)

The council-manager plan is a product of twentieth century reform movements.[14] It is also the plan most commonly found in middle-class and upper-middle-class cities, whatever their dominant ideological approach.[15]

[10] Wilson and Banfield, "Public-regardingness."

[11] Williams and Adrian, *Four Cities,* pp. 25–27 and Chapter 10.

[12] Williams and Adrian, *Four Cities,* Chapter 9.

[13] Charles R. Adrian and Charles Press, "Decision Costs in Coalition Formation," *American Political Science Review,* Vol. 62 (1968), pp. 556–563.

[14] Childs, *Civic Victories.*

[15] See the current issue of *The Municipal Year Book* (Chicago: International City Management Association, annually) for data on forms of government.

As we would expect, a suburban community of businessmen is likely to be the most common community using the council-manager plan, whereas older communities, concerned about tax levels and devoted to Jacksonian principles, should be the least likely to have this form of government.

Tax and Land-Use Measures

Item 9 is designed to reflect the generally high commitment that "boosterism" and "amenities" cities have to the use of professional planning in order to secure their goals. On the other hand, in cities with "caretaker" governments planning activities are characteristically at a very low level if present at all, and "arbiter" communities have generally seen land-use policies as a matter of negotiation rather than the subject of synoptic planning. The results of planning are a different matter, however, and in item 10 we find a sharp difference between the "boosterism" and "amenities" types concerning the amount of land zoned for commercial or industrial use.

The same type of distinction is made in item 11 concerning the tax structure as it is designed to aid or hinder business and industry. This indicator may be a bit difficult to use because of the fact that tax concessions of this sort are not legally possible in some states and, where possible, are often controlled by state, rather than local, regulations. The actual concessions may be made not on the basis of a tax break, but through deliberate underassessment, and this is difficult and time consuming to document.

Item 12, however, is easier. Business and industry should provide a relatively small percentage of the total tax base in "amenities" cities and a high percentage in "boosterism" cities, excepting for newly founded ones, which have not yet had any success in attracting what they want. (This exception, however, should wash out in the large number of cases involved if we were to measure all American cities.) Business and industry should offer relatively low percentages also in "caretaker" cities, which customarily have few businesses and often no industry.

Homogeneity Factors

Items 13 and 14 are designed to measure life-style characteristics as they relate to municipal images. "Boosterism" and "arbiter" cities tend to have heterogeneous populations and hence highly similar patterns of personal income. "Amenities" cities characteristically have middle- to upper-middle-class inhabitants with high incomes. "Caretaker" cities are also homogeneous, but their inhabitants characteristically belong to the lower middle and working classes and have low incomes.

Content Analysis

Some work could be done with content analysis of the outputs from city hall. The percentage (or column inches) of press releases from the office of mayor or manager (or chamber of commerce) devoted to attracting industry should provide some sharp differences between the "boosterism" and the "amenities" types. The same should be true of the percentage of budget expenditures or budget messages devoted to consumer services. This percentage would be highest in amenities-oriented cities and second highest (as a percentage but not in absolute terms) in "caretaker" cities.

Although not included as an index, a content analysis of campaign speeches or of talks to service clubs by mayors and councilmen might also be revealing. "Boosterism" cities should show up highest in discussions of the need to attract industry for the sake of providing jobs and strengthening the tax base. The quality and quantity of consumer services should be emphasized in "amenities" cities. Economy should be the main pitch in "caretaker" cities, whereas those with an "arbiter" image should center on the art of compromise, cooperation, and the allocation of city services to all segments of the population.

Other Measures

Persons influenced by the efficiency and economy movement and middle-class values generally tend to favor the merit system of personnel administration, whereas cities with a large working-class population or cities in which reform has not been a major activity are likely to be more heavily oriented toward a patronage system of personnel administration. Once again "boosterism" and "amenities" cities are distinguished here from the "caretaker" and "arbiter" types. "Caretaker" governments tend to be dominated by persons beholden to the traditional jack-of-all-trades orientation of the small towner rather than to the professional-specialist orientation of the upper-middle class. "Arbiter" cities have traditionally found patronage, when assigned to various wards or to various ethnic and racial groups, to be an effective aid in coalition building.

The percentage of the population of a city that belongs to identifiable ethnic or racial minorities would be highest in "arbiter" cities for many reasons, including the fact that these are the larger cities, often the core cities rather than the suburbs, and their government structures are built around long-time needs for arbitration among competing and potentially conflicting groups. "Boosterism" cities, with their goal of attracting industry, will also attract working-class minority groups. On the other hand, "caretaker" cities tend to be small communities, often outside the mainstream of contemporary urban developments, and ethnically homogeneous. Homogeneity is also the characteristic of cities with the amenities orientation. Their middle-class and upper-middle-class residents either have backgrounds that have never been viewed as self-conscious minorities or have shed their minority identification.

Voter-turnout patterns, item 20, follow the same configuration as that relative to the percentage of minorities in the community. In general, the more homogeneous the population of a community, the lower the voter turnout in municipal elections.[16]

Hence in "amenities" communities—even in upper-middle-class cities, whose people ordinarily turn out for elections with alacrity—municipal voting is likely to be low, simply because public policy is consensual in character. There is little to fight about, and, since the population shares an essentially common life style, one councilman or mayor can be assumed to perform in about the same way as any other. "Caretaker" communities show generally the same pattern, and political bickering is over trivial matters.[17] "Boosterism" cities, however, are more likely to have campaign issues—for example, over questions of the type, amount, and location of industry—and hence to have a relatively high turnout at municipal elections. In "arbiter" cities there are tensions and rivalries between and among groups, and under the ward system, which provides for more of a grassroots political structure, voter turnout is likely to be relatively high. Indeed in a few of these cities the turnout for a mayoralty election will occasionally exceed that for a presidential election.

The size of the police force as a percentage of total municipal employees is a reflection both of the concentration of wealth in a community and of the level of conflict. Both of these tend to be higher in "boosterism" and "arbiter" cities than in the other two types. In "caretaker" cities, which have little crime, social conflict, and wealth concentration, the police force may be essentially a token one, and probably few members, if any, are professionals. "Amenities" cities want more policemen to protect the valuable homes of the residents, to preserve calm and decorum, and particularly to control and slow down traffic movement. But even a wealthy

[16] Williams and Adrian, *Four Cities,* Chapter 4.
[17] A. J. Vidich and Joseph Bensman, *Small Town in Mass Society* (Princeton, N.J.: Princeton University Press, 1958).

community with an amenities orientation will have a relatively low assessed valuation in relation to cities with heavy industry.

In looking at per capita expenditures by communities it is necessary to control for size, since the cost of performing a number of municipal functions increases disproportionately with the population.[18] After so controlling, we would find that "caretaker" cities, with their tax consciousness and emphasis on economy, would rank lowest. The "boosterism" and "amenities" types would be virtually tied for second place—this measure would not help to distinguish them—because both of these types expend considerable effort toward achieving their rather definite policy goals. With control for size, "arbiter" cities should have the highest per capita budget expenditures, if for no other reason than that they have traditionally intermixed personnel administration with welfare activities. To put it another way, "arbiter" cities are likely to have the highest number of municipal employees per 1000 inhabitants.

CONSTRUCTING AN INDEX

The process by which the typology could be operationalized is one that would proceed somewhat as follows:

1. The identification of a number of communities each closely fitting an idealized version of each image. This could be done (a) by applying the analysis to cities which have been investigated by competent social scientists and on which a detailed written report is available or (b) by having a panel of specialists from various parts of the nation identify and list communities appropriate for each type, this to be verified through further investigation in the communities themselves. The verification could be carried out either through an examination of actual policy performances over several years or by surveying leader attitudes toward policy. Because the latter method was not used in *Four Cities,* it might be confusing to introduce it at this time, but it might be worthwhile if it would actually reduce the subjectivity of the approach.

The approach through existing literature may be the simpler one and may well be quite feasible, since there is a large bibliography of studies on community power structure or decision-making.[19] Excepting where the time span between the different communities that were studied is too great

[18] Louis H. Masotti and Don R. Bowen, "Communities and Budgets: The Sociology of Municipal Expenditures," *Urban Affairs Quarterly,* Vol. 1 (1965), pp. 39–58.
[19] Charles Press, *Main Street Politics* (East Lansing, Mich.: Institute for Community Development, 1962) and many other bibliographical summaries.

or where certain necessary data are missing and can no longer be retrieved, this approach might be very satisfactory. One might say, for example, that Middletown is a "booster" city[20] and Park Forest one built around amenities.[21] Certainly Springdale, the small community in a mass society, has a "caretaker" type of government,[22] whereas Chicago is run on the arbiter principle.[23]

2. The scales will have to be related to the selected communities in order to determine the closeness of fit. At this stage the expected rankings may have to be modified if the results in the prototype cities consistently vary from what are listed as the expected results. If any important changes are made, it will be necessary to investigate to determine why the empirical findings differed from those theoretically expected.

3. The scales that demonstrate a poor fit with the empirical findings will have to be rejected, particularly if little significant difference is found among the various types or if the results are inconsistent within the same type of city. It may be possible that for a rough approximation of type only a few scales will need to be developed for a given community, and it may be possible to rework these into a uniform scalar pattern so that the numerical summation of the scale rankings will make it possible to identify the type of a community simply from its total index number. Alternatively factor analysis may be used and may reveal clusters of variables that identify a particular type and also help to identify the degree of "purity" of each city or the degree to which it represents a mixture of ideal types. One would expect the type receiving the score of 1 to load high on the factor and the type receiving a score of 4 to have a high negative loading. Factor analysis may not tell us much about types receiving scores 2 or 3, but these are not of much theoretical interest in any case. High positive or negative factor loadings should be discoverable for the isolation of each type.

4. Cities can next be classified as desired by applying the appropriate scales or factors.

5. The image-identification process will have to be replicated every few years in order to determine whether the typed images are still valid and to gain insights into the possibility of new images emerging. If such

[20] Robert S. Lynd and Helen M. Lynd, *Middletown* (New York: Harcourt, Brace & Co., 1929).

[21] William H. Whyte, Jr., *The Organization Man* (New York: Simon & Shuster, 1956).

[22] Vidich and Bensman, *Small Town*.

[23] Martin Meyerson and Edward C. Banfield, *Politics, Planning and the Public Interest* (New York: Free Press of Glencoe, 1955).

replications are conducted over a sufficient number of years or decades, it will be possible to gain good insights into whether the types are time-bound within the American culture and to what degree.

6. This entire procedure should, finally, be attempted in other nations to help determine the degree to which the typology is culture-bound. It may be that some of the types, at least, are not culture-bound. Alternatively studies in other cultures may indicate that these types, with certain modifications, can become broad, universal images of man's concept of the proper function of the city in civilization.

The purpose of classification is, above all, to permit prediction. If it is possible to develop a typology that classifies cities in a relatively simple and consistent pattern, we shall be able to learn more than we now know about both cities and man.

PART FOUR

Strengths and Weaknesses of Alternative Classificatory Procedures

... Problems of classifying subareas within cities

... Critical evaluation of the principles of city classification

CHAPTER 10

Problems of Classifying Subareas within Cities

PHILIP H. REES

Leeds University

Most of the chapters in this volume are concerned with the sorting into classes of a set of individuals, or operational taxonomic units (OTU is the abbreviation used in classification theory to refer to the object being classified), called cities—or with exploring the characteristics of cities that vary significantly from one class to another. This chapter is an exception, being concerned with reviewing critically the attempts that have been made to classify areas *within* the city. We justify its presence very simply by saying that it merits inclusion because it *is* concerned with classification and with cities, and because various attempts at city classification have included both central cities and their suburbs as OTUs and have hence implicitly dealt with intrametropolitan as well as intermetropolitan differences and similarities.

The OTU in city classification is an entity called the city. This entity has been defined very differently by the various branches of social science —each has, in effect, adopted a subsystem definition for what is a complex of interdependent subsystems. The city has been defined legally (as an incorporated entity) by applying a density threshold and contiguity constraint (the urbanized area concept of the U.S. Bureau of Census), through the use of a journey-to-work definition along with a minimum size and criterion of metropolitan character [the Census' standard metropolitan statistical area (SMSA) concept], and through the use of a fixed-distance radius (Friedmann's urban field concept[1]), to mention but a few examples.

---

[1] John R. P. Friedmann and John Miller, "The Urban Field," *Journal of the American Institute of Planners,* Vol. 31 (1965), pp. 312–319. Of course the fixed-distance radius in the paper was merely illustrative of the magnitude that the authors felt a city's daily influence field would reach in the short-term future.

However, the definition of the individual used in the classification of cities is simple compared with the definition of such an individual in within-city classification. The definition will depend on what aspect of the urban system is being considered. In the case of the classificatory studies we devote most attention to here, the household, located at a particular position in the city, would be the logical individual to be classified. However, data at the household level are rarely available, and the areal units for which data are conveniently provided by the census authorities must be adopted as OTUs, for practical and operational reasons, by the worker interested in within-city classification. In the United States city blocks are sometimes used as OTUs (if labor and money resources are available), but more often census tracts are employed. The problem of census-tract homogeneity is occasionally considered, and the degree of homogeneity is tested for. In general it is assumed, rather than demonstrated, that the spatial patterning of the social phenomena being studied has a "frequency" greater than the areal mesh of the census-tract units. Finer elements of spatial variance are essentially filtered out in studies that use census tracts.

In this chapter we examine the ways in which researchers have attempted to classify areal units within the city into a set of classes, with particular concentration on attempts to classify the residential areas within the city.[2] These classifications have been a response to a need felt in social science (and a need that occurs at the embryonic stage in most disciplines) to break down the large and complex modern city into parts that can be conceived of as a totality and studied as a system. Although this need is acknowledged, the utility of such within-city classifications still requires justification, and in order to assess whether within-city classifications have been of utility we must estimate the following:

1. How well they have adhered to the principles of classification.
2. How well they have fitted the purposes of their designers.
3. How useful they have been as inputs to further research.
4. How productive of insight into the processes that have produced or are creating the structure of the city they have been.

BASIC DEFINITIONS AND PROCEDURES IN CLASSIFICATION

In two very useful papers David Grigg has summarized the principles and procedures of classification.[3] The exposition here leans heavily on his efforts.

---

[2] Neglecting, unfortunately, the classification of the other sorts of land use—industrial, commercial, recreational, public, etc.—for want of space.

[3] David B. Grigg, "The Logic of Regional Systems," *Annals of the Association of*

The following steps are involved in carrying through a sound classification:

1. The *purpose* of the classification must be thought out explicitly (and preferably explicitly stated).

2. The *individual,* or *OTU,* involved in the classification must be defined. The *universe,* or *population,* of individuals to be classified must be delimited.

3. The *differentiating characteristics,* or *criteria,* on which the classification is to be based must be selected. These differentiating characteristics should be properties of the OTUs and not other characteristics held to have causal influence on the OTU. The selection of differentiating characteristics is usually based on theory or prior understanding, though certain multivariate methods (factor analysis, multidimensional scaling) enable the researcher to determine the criteria he will use in part by empirical means. There are three types of properties of the individual that may be used:[4]

a. *Structural* properties: those involving only the OTU itself.

b. *Relational* properties: at least one other object other than the OTU in question is involved.

c. *Dynamic* properties: those involving properties of the first or second type at two or more time periods.

Most classifications concern themselves with the first type of property, though some notable within-city classifications have been based on relational properties.[5]

4. The *method of classification* to be used must be chosen. The principal choice is between methods that adopt the procedure of *logical division* and methods that use *grouping, or clustering,* procedures. Logical

American Geographers, Vol. 55 (1965), pp. 465–491, and "Regions, Models and Classes," in Richard J. Chorley and Peter Haggett, Eds., *Models in Geography* (London: Methuen and Co., Ltd., 1967), pp. 461–509.

[4] An excellent exposition of the use of these three properties of OTUs to construct a comprehensive picture of a regional system is given in several papers by Brian J. L. Berry. See in particular Brian J. L. Berry, "Interdependency of Flows and Spatial Structure: A General Field Theory Formulation," in Brian J. L. Berry et al., *Essays on Commodity Flows and the Spatial Structure of the Indian Economy* (Department of Geography Research Paper No. 111; Chicago: University of Chicago, 1966), pp. 189–255, and "A Synthesis of Formal and Functional Regions Using a General Field Theory of Spatial Behavior," in Brian J. L. Berry and Duane F. Marble, Eds., *Spatial Analysis: A Reader in Statistical Geography* (Englewood Cliffs, N.J.: Prentice-Hall, Inc., 1968), pp. 419–428.

[5] Brian J. L. Berry, *Commercial Structure and Commercial Blight* (Department of Geography, Research Paper No. 85; Chicago: University of Chicago, 1963). See especially "Spatial Arrangements and Areas Served," pp. 61–71, in which the trade areas of the retailing centers of the city of Chicago are delimited.

division may proceed by regular division (dividing the range of the differentiating characteristic into equal intervals) or by selection of division points at break points in the OTU distribution. The division may be hierarchic; that is, different criteria may be adopted at different levels of the process.

Grouping procedures are methods of arranging objects whose likenesses or differences are summarized in a similarity matrix X. The cell x_{ij} of this matrix contains a coefficient that measures the similarity of objects (or OTUs) i and j. The similarity coefficient has a range, one end of which represents complete similarity, the other end complete dissimilarity. The similarity coefficient is the product of a series of operations on the differentiating characteristic(s): it may be the distance between the OTUs in Euclidean space whose dimensions are the differentiating characteristics or it may be the Pearson r coefficient of correlation between the objects defined over the differentiating characteristics, to cite the two most commonly used statistics.

The grouping procedures that have been used in scientific and social science literature to order these similarity matrices have been reviewed by Taylor,[6] who classifies grouping techniques by logical division based on two criteria: *entrance-decision nature* and *threshold-decision character*. By *entrance-decision nature* is meant the number of linkages required between a potential group member and a group for the potential member to be admitted. The linkage is defined by the *threshold decision:* the threshold is the critical value, at any single stage in the grouping, that denotes the level of connection (measured in terms of the similarity coefficient) necessary for potential group entrance. To illustrate these concepts, consider membership in Lloyd's of London, an exclusive group of private insurance underwriters. Candidates for membership must be supported by six existing members and are elected by ballot—that is, at least six linkages, and probably more, are needed for entrance. However, there is also a threshold: candidates are considered for membership only after they have proved to the satisfaction of the committee of Lloyd's that their resources are sufficient to meet any of the liabilities likely to be incurred.

Taylor's classification of grouping methods is reproduced in Table 1. There are very many to choose from, depending on what sort of groups are wanted, and Taylor provides some rules of thumb as to choice depending on the classification's purpose. Very few of these methods have been used in within-city classification. Where explicit procedures of classifica-

6 Peter J. Taylor, "Grouping Analysis in Regional Taxonomy," Department of Geography, University of Newcastle Upon Tyne, Seminar Paper No. 1, 1968.

Table 1. Taylor's typology of grouping techniques

		Threshold Decisions			
		Bonded	Linkage	Hierarchic	Nuclear
Entrance Decisions	Single	Ramifying Linkage Method	Elementary Linkage Analysis	Clustering by Single Linkage	Nuclear Clustering
		Approximate Delimitation Method Primary P Groups	Elementary Hierarchical Linkage Analysis	Hierarchical Clustering Scheme -- (1) Minimal Method	Graph Theory Analysis
	Multiple	Basic Pair P Groups	Nearest Neighbor Linkage Analysis Comprehensive Hierarchical Linkage Analysis	Clustering by average linkage: (1) Weighted Variable Group Method (2) Unweighted Variable Group Method (3) Unweighted Group Method	Nodal Clustering Location-based Nodal Clustering Multidimensional Group Analysis Multiple Linkage Algorithm β Coefficient Method
				Multifactor Regionalization (1) Unconstrained (2) Constrained by Contiguity	
	Complete	Algorithm for Finding "Tight Clusters" in Bonner's Clustering Program II	Rank Order Typal Analysis	Clustering by Complete Linkage Hierarchical Clustering Scheme (2) Maximum Method	

tion have been used, logical divison has been preferred for logistical reasons: division is simple to apply; grouping of any more than a handful of OTUs on an "objective" basis necessitates using a computer, and, even then the number of OTUs that can be handled is limited by the storage available in even the largest of today's computers.

5. The final step involved in classification is *to set the restrictions on the classification.* Taylor identifies two constraints—the *overlapping constraint* and the *contiguity constraint*—to which we might add a third, ap-

plicable only in certain cases and particularly when relational properties are being used as criteria—the *definition of nodes* constraint.

The degree of constraint in the overlapping case is defined by the number k, where $(k - 1)$ is the number of OTUs in overlaps between groups. Constraint by contiguity in effect restricts the linkages that can be searched between any OTU and the rest of the individuals: the constraint is normally based on locational proximity or a common border. Finally, in the case of a relational classification based on nodes, the classification may require the nodes to be fixed a priori.

The nature of these restrictions may be made clearer if we consider how they might apply to a hypothetical city whose residential population we are classifying (Figure 1). If the figure is followed through by the reader, the dependence of the nature of the final classification on the decisions adopted at each stage of the classification procedure will become clear. Each classification uses the same differentiating characteristic, but three different, though related, solutions result: *mapped social groups* (classes mapped), *social areas* (areal classes mapped), and *social regions* (regions mapped). It is important to distinguish between these solutions, as they are often confused in the literature.

We must now consider some of the within-city classifications that have been made in the light of these principles of classification and regionalization.

SINGLE COMMUNITIES

Social science literature abounds with studies of single communities. These communities have been studied by a number of intensive methods, such as participant observation or social survey, and at a number of scales.[7] The largest community capable of being portrayed with accuracy by the participant observer is really only a small town on the scale of world urbanism (e.g., Muncie, Indiana, or Banbury, Oxfordshire); in *city*

---

[7] The classic American community studies have been reviewed by Maurice R. Stein, *The Eclipse of Community: An Interpretation of American Studies* (Princeton, N.J.: Princeton University Press, 1960). More recent studies of local communities are the following: Herbert J. Gans, *The Urban Villagers* (New York: Free Press, 1962) and *The Levittowners* (New York: Pantheon Press, 1967); and Gerald Suttles, *The Social Order of the Slum* (Chicago: University of Chicago Press, 1968). British studies are reviewed in Ronald Frankenberg, *Communities in Britain: Social Life in Town and Country* (Harmondsworth, Middlesex, England: Penguin Books Ltd., 1966).

(1) Definition of Terms

	OTU Not Areally Defined	OTU Areally Defined
No Contiguity Constraint	CLASS	AREAL CLASS
Contiguity Constraint		REGION

(2) Properties of the Terms

Stages in Classification	Terms		
	Class	Areal Class	Region
2. OTU Definition	Individuals or Households	Census Tract Populations	Census Tract Populations
3. Differentiating Characteristic	Socioeconomic Status Scale with Range from 0 to 100 and Median 50		
4. Method of Classification	Division	Division	Division
Classes are A:	OTUs greater than or equal to 50 on the SES scale		
B:	Less than 50 on the SES scale		

5. Classes Mapped

Hypothetical City

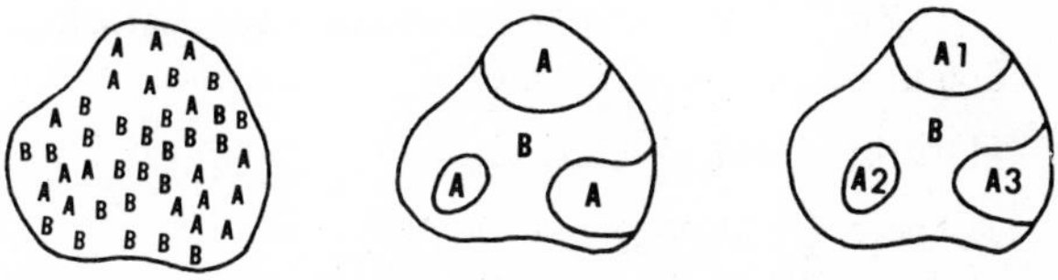

Membership	A. OTUs 1,3, 7,...,n B. OTUs 2,4, 6,...,m	A. Tracts 1, 2,7,8,11, 12,13 B. Tracts 3, 4,5,6,9, 10,14,15	A_1. Tracts 1,2 A_2. Tracts 7,8 A_3. Tracts 11, 12,13 B. Tracts 3,4, 5,6,9,10, 14,15

Figure 1 Classes, areal classes, and regions within the city.

studies the researcher must of necessity limit his canvas to only a part of the wider urban region.

The within-metropolitan community is usually defined on an "ad hoc" basis for the purposes of the particular study: the community is known by a common name by its residents and contains a population having at least some common characteristics, interests, and organizations, engaged in some social intercourse, the nature of which it is the purpose of the investigation to elucidate. This type of single-community delimitation has been characterized as "dichotomous division" by Grigg,[8] in which the area is set apart from the rest of the world.

NATURAL AREAS

The history of the *natural area* concept in the field of human ecology is one that has been repeated many times in social science. Geographers will immediately recognize the parallels between the natural area concept and that of their own *natural region*.[9]

The human ecologists who employed the natural area concept were somewhat vague concerning its definition. Thus Zorbaugh says:

A natural area is a geographical area characterized both by a physical individuality and by the cultural characteristics of the people who live in it.[10]

Hatt, in a critical analysis of the concept, defines it more succinctly:

There are two general emphases in the definition of the concept, natural area. One of these views the natural area as a spatial unit limited by natural boundaries enclosing a homogeneous population with a characteristic moral order. The other emphasizes its biotic and community aspects and describes the natural area as a spatial unit inhabited by a population united on the basis of symbiotic relationships.[11]

The parallels between Hatt's two notions and the geographer's concept of formal and functional regions are remarkable. The natural area was regarded as a concrete object with real existence which the researcher had only to look for to find. Hence it was not important to describe in explicit detail the ways in which these natural areas were delimited. The same "concrete" thinking was associated with the geographer's view of the re-

[8] Grigg, "Regions, Models and Classes," p. 481.
[9] See Grigg, "Regions, Models and Classes," pp. 465–467.
[10] Harvey W. Zorbaugh, "The Natural Areas of the City," in George A. Theodorson, Ed., *Studies in Human Ecology* (Evanston, Ill.: Harper and Row, Publishers, 1961), p. 47.
[11] Paul K. Hatt, "The Concept of Natural Area," in Theodorson, Ed., *Human Ecology*, p. 104.

gion in the same period and still persists among many Soviet geographers.

The purpose of delimiting natural areas was usually made clear: it was to outline the basic territorial units within which the social and economic life of the city residents took place. Residents within a natural area were expected to have a high degree of interaction with one another, though it was recognized that there might be residential areas in which little social interaction or community life took place. The definition of the individual, or OTU, involved in the natural area classification was never very clear, though in practice any convenient areal unit that was available was used. The criteria used in the classification, as is clear from the two definitions quoted above, were many and various: they included marked physical boundaries (which were presumed to have a marked effect on social interaction), housing characteristics (e.g., rental levels), and social characteristics (e.g., ethnicity). How these various criteria were combined and used was not made clear, and neither was the method of classification. Of Chicago's community areas, which were a citywide application of the natural area concept emphasizing in particular people's perceptions of the community in which they lived, the latest edition of the *Local Community Factbook* says:

The boundaries of the 75 community areas were originally drawn up on the basis of several considerations, chief among which were: (1) the settlement, growth and history of the area; (2) local identification with the area; (3) the local trade area; (4) distribution of membership of local institutions; and (5) natural and artificial barriers such as the Chicago River and its branches, railroad lines, local transportation systems, and parks and boulevards.[12]

Little further is said, and it is admitted that today these areas are merely a useful summary device for reporting census and local statistics.

Thus, even if we accept, with Hatt, that the concept of natural area is merely a device used by the researcher to present his data on population patterns in the city, and not a concrete entity, the classification procedure falls short on a number of counts of the model of classification procedure outlined in the first section.

SOCIAL AREAS

The attempt at within-city classification was renewed in California after World War II. There several sociologists were unimpressed with the prin-

[12] Evelyn M. Kitagawa and Karl E. Taeuber, *Local Community Factbook: Chicago Metropolitan Area, 1960* (Chicago: Chicago Community Inventory, University of Chicago, 1963), p. xiii.

ciples of ecological organization enunciated in the universities of the large cities of the Northeastern United States. They turned from a consideration of the way social organization was spatially manifested in the urban region to the way the various areal units of the metropolis, irrespective of geographical location, were positioned in social space. The method of analysis developed by Shevky and Williams,[13] later modified by Shevky and Bell,[14] was called social area analysis.

Social Area Analysis in the Strict Sense

The developmental sequence of social area analysis in its widest sense is set forth in Figure 2. Here we are concerned with the original methodology, of which continuing applications are being made.

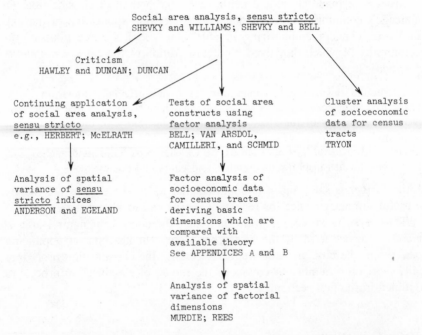

Figure 2 The development of social area analysis. Cluster analysis is Tryon's proposed alternative to factor analysis. (All of the works mentioned in the figure are cited in Appendix B.)

[13] Eshref Shevky and Marianne Williams, *The Social Areas of Los Angeles: Analysis and Typology* (Los Angeles: University of California Press, 1949).
[14] Eshref Shevky and Wendell Bell, *Social Area Analysis: Theory, Illustrative Ap-*

The problem facing Shevky, Williams, and Bell was one that would have delighted earlier urban sociologists. It was how to cope with the flood of information being provided about small areas within selected metropolises by the U.S. Bureau of the Census (the censuses of 1940 and 1950 are the ones in question). The solution was to classify the census tracts of the city into a number of classes that, because of their essentially territorial nature, were called social areas. The explicit procedures of classification that were outlined enabled other workers in other cities to replicate the original analysis—a substantial improvement over the natural area methodology.

The purposes of the classification were set forth in some detail and were as follows:

1. The delineation of socially homogeneous subareas within the city.
2. Comparative studies of the distribution of such areas at two or more points in time.
3. Comparative studies between two or more places in the nature of their social areas.
4. Provision of a framework for the execution of other types of research, particularly a framework for the design and execution of behavioral field studies—that is, as a framework for sampling.

The *individual,* or *OTU,* involved in the classification was defined to be the census tract. Some concern was expressed concerning the homogeneity of census tracts as OTUs, but no explicit test of the homogeneity assumption was made.[15] The *universe,* or *population,* of individuals was defined to be the maximum number of census tracts within the urban regions of the Los Angeles or San Francisco Bay areas for which information was available. These study areas, though not covering the whole of the functional urban area, the active labor and housing markets, covered enough of them to ensure that the larger part of the range of urban populations was included in the studies.

The *differentiating characteristics* used in the classification were defined to be three construct indices built up from a larger number of basic census variables. The methods of index construction were laid out in considerable detail. However, the theoretical justification for the adoption of the three

---

plication and Computational Procedures (Stanford, Calif.: Stanford University Press, 1955).

[15] Though the homogeneity assumption was tested for San Francisco in 1940 in a parallel work: Robert C. Tryon, *Identification of Social Areas by Cluster Analysis: A General Method with an Application to the San Francisco Bay Area* (Berkeley and Los Angeles: University of California Press, 1955), pp. 38–44.

indices was too generalized, vague, and diffuse, and the authors (Shevky and Bell) were soundly berated for it,[16] though the critics failed to supply an alternative rationale for what turned out to be at least in part an empirically sound choice of indices. The three indices (standardized to a 0 to 100 range) were the following:

1. An *index of social rank* (or economic status) made up of one education and one occupation variable.
2. An *index of urbanization* (or family status) made up of the variables fertility, the proportion of women in the labor force, and the proportion of single-family dwellings in the housing stock.
3. An *index of segregation* (or ethnic status) made up of the combined proportions of minority ethnic groups (Negroes, other races, foreign-born whites from Eastern and Southern Europe, foreign-born persons from continents other than Europe).

Each census tract was therefore located in a particular position in a three-dimensional attribute space.

The method of classification adopted was that of logical division. The exact procedure differed somewhat in the two monographs. Shevky and Williams divided the attribute space in which census tracts were located as follows: the social rank index was divided into three parts of equal range (Figure 3, top); the urbanization index was also divided into three parts, not equally but spaced +1 and −1 standard errors about the regression line of urbanization on social rank. This schema resulted in nine classes or social areas. In their 1955 monograph Shevky and Bell revised the method (Figure 3, bottom): the two axes were made orthogonal, and the ranges of both indices were divided into four equal parts, yielding 16 social areas. Use of the index of segregation to divide the 16 areas further into those with a higher than average proportion of minority group members was made optional. Generally the two-dimensional classification has been used in further research, and the third dimension has been dealt with by examining the distribution of ethnic group populations among the social areas.

The revised classification method had the advantage of not being dependent on a unique regression of urbanization on social rank in Los Angeles

16 Otis D. Duncan, Review of Social Area Analysis by Eshref Shevky and Wendell Bell, *American Journal of Sociology,* Vol. 61 (1955), pp. 84–85. Bell replied in the *American Journal of Sociology,* Vol. 61 (1955), pp. 260–262. In a later article Amos H. Hawley and Otis D. Duncan—see "Social Area Analysis: A Critical Appraisal," *Land Economics,* Vol. 33 (1957), pp. 337–345—make the valid point that Shevky and Bell did not answer the fundamental question of why residential areas within cities should differ from one another.

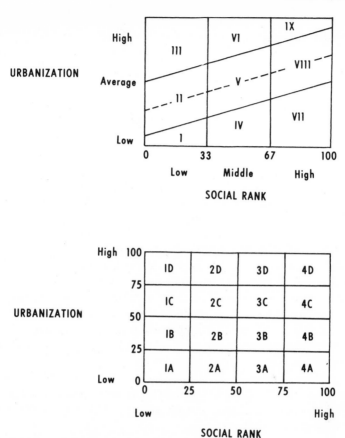

Figure 3 The social area classifications.

in 1940 and of having more classes and therefore greater differentiating power for cities smaller than Los Angeles or San Francisco, assuming those cities had smaller ranges on the social area indices. However, the standardization procedure, based on the absolute range of the indices in Los Angeles in 1940, left much to be desired: one based on a national norm, rather than on one city, would seem to be preferable.

Although the distribution of tracts in social space formed by the indices of social rank and urbanization was presented, and a list of tracts falling in the various social areas was given by Shevky and Bell, the social areas were not mapped (as in Figure 1) and there was little or no comment on their spatial distribution. Before turning to a consideration of some of the other criticisms directed at the social area methodology, the uses to which the social area framework has been put are considered.

Use of the Social Area Framework in Further Research

The social area framework has been used in three types of behavioral study. The social area scores have been used as independent variables in behavioral work;[17] unfortunately ecological correlations as used in such studies are somewhat suspect.[18] The second type of application is in social-survey-type sampling in metropolitan areas: it informs researchers about where certain social strata needed in the sample are likely to be located or where a particular social environment will be found. Finally it is useful in assessing the generality of a particular study in a particular location.

One of the key questions that the social area framework is helpful in answering is whether the individual's or household's characteristics alone are sufficient for the prediction of behavior, or whether it is essential to consider the social environment as well. Reviewing the work on this problem, Bell came to the conclusion that there was "convincing evidence that the social character of local areas within a city as defined by economic, family and ethnic characteristics is an important predictor of individual attitudes and behaviors, subcultural patterns and social organization,"[19] at least for the behavior under study, namely, social intercourse, where at the minimum two actors are required.[20] Thus housewives not in the labor force are far less likely to act in the roles of neighbors in residential areas of high urbanization (apartment areas inhabited by an older population with work-

---

[17] For example, Kenneth Polk, "Juvenile Delinquency and Social Areas," *Social Problems,* Vol. 5 (1957–1958), pp. 214–217.

[18] For an excellent treatment of this topic see Hayward R. Alker, Jr., "A Typology of Ecological Fallacies," in Mattei Dogan and Stein Rokkan, Eds., *Quantitative Ecological Analysis in the Social Sciences* (Cambridge, Mass.: M.I.T. Press, 1969), pp. 69–86.

[19] Particularly his own work [e.g., Wendell Bell, "The Utility of the Shevky Typology for the Design of Urban Sub-Area Field Studies," *Journal of Social Psychology,* Vol. 47 (1958), pp. 71–83] and that of Scott Greer and Ella Kube, "Urbanism and Social Structure: A Los Angeles Study," in Marvin B. Sussman, Ed., *Community Structure and Analysis* (New York: Thomas Y. Crowell, 1959), pp. 93–112. A more recent example involving voting behavior is Kevin R. Cox, "Suburbia and Voting Behavior in the London Metropolitan Area," *Annals of the Association of American Geographers,* Vol. 58 (1968), pp. 111–127.

[20] Wendell Bell, "Social Areas: Typology of Urban Neighborhoods," in *Community Structure and Analysis,* pp. 62–92. Unfortunately neither Bell nor Greer nor Kube made a quantitative estimate of the importance of individual characteristic and social environment influences on neighboring patterns.

ing mothers and fewer children) than in a neighborhood of low urbanization (single-family-dwelling areas inhabited by families in the child-rearing stage).

This link between social environment and behavior is an essential one if we are to consider the possibility that social regions (social areas formed through application of the contiguity constraint—see Figure 1) contain communities, where a local area is considered to be a community (rather than just a collection of residences, service facilities, and workplaces) if it has a sufficient level of communication flow, interaction, community identification, and social integration among its residents.

Further Work on the Dimensions of Variation

Factor Analysis of the Sensu Stricto Variables

Several of the criticisms that were directed at social area analysis have already been mentioned in the course of our discussion. One of the most persistent concerns the validity of the differentiating characteristics—the three construct indices. It was objected that no tests were employed to ascertain whether the particular way in which the variables were used was the valid one. In an effort to provide empirical justification for the way in which the variables were selected to index the constructs, Bell and later Van Arsdol employed factor analysis to discover whether the variation among the census tracts in the component variables making up the indices could in fact be summarized by three dimensions in the way postulated.[21] Bell's analysis with oblique rotation confirmed that the dimensions were as Shevky and Williams had originally postulated, but that they were associated in the two cities studied (Los Angeles and San Francisco) and that economic status and ethnic status, in particular, were moderately associated.

Van Arsdol found that for 6 of the 10 cities he and his co-workers studied the factor structures were in accordance with the social area construct indices, but for 4 cities they deviated from this norm. Thus Shevky's original notions were partly confirmed and partly shown to need modification. But the tests posed a further question: Why employ simply the variables used by Shevky and Bell? Why not include more variables detail-

---

[21] Wendell Bell, "A Comparative Study in the Methodology of Urban Analysis" (unpublished Ph.D. dissertation, Department of Sociology, University of California at Los Angeles, 1952), and "Economic, Family and Ethnic Status: An Empirical Test," *American Sociological Review,* Vol. 20 (1955), pp. 45–52; Maurice Van Arsdol, Santo F. Camilleri, and Calvin F. Schmid, "The Generality of Urban Social Area Indices," American Sociological Review, Vol. 23 (1958), pp. 277–284.

ing the way in which census-tract populations vary according to socio-economic characteristics in the study and use some technique to isolate objectively the fundamental patterns of variation in the data, be they Shevky–Bell patterns or nay. From that rationale has blossomed a very large number of studies concerned with the social dimensions of variation among residential area populations in the metropolis. In the course of time and with the refinement of methods the original classificatory goal was partly lost sight of. However, it will be useful to consider in some fair detail such studies employing factor analysis since they lead in a roundabout fashion to the beginning of an answer to the fundamental question that Shevky and Bell were accused of failing to answer: Why do residential areas within cities differ from one another?

Cluster Analysis of a Wider Set of Variables

Tryon was the first to use a wider set of census variables in order to identify social areas within the city.[22] The OTUs in the classification were census tracts, and the universe was the tracted area of San Francisco Bay. The differentiating characteristics on which the classification was based were the three variable clusters called *family life, assimilation,* and *socio-economic independence.* These variable clusters were the three most independent dimensions that emerged from a cluster analysis of some 33 variables. Tryon explains the methodology of cluster analysis in an appendix to the monograph. Unfortunately the method of matching correlation profiles is not wholly objective; that is, another researcher given the same data might produce a somewhat different set of clusters of variables. Finally, it is not entirely clear why these particular three clusters (from an initial group of seven) were selected. Cluster scores for the tracts are calculated from a linear combination of the variables that go to make up the clusters. Each tract has a two-digit F (family life) score, a two-digit A (assimilation) score, and a two-digit S (socioeconomic independence) score. These correspond closely to Shevky and Bell's urbanization-index, segregation-index, and social-rank scores, respectively.

The tracts are in turn grouped in an object-cluster analysis (a cluster analysis of the OTUs rather than the variables) of a matrix of census tracts and FAS scores. The similarity coefficient used in this grouping analysis is somewhat obscure: it is not clear again whether Euclidean distance between tracts in three-dimensional FAS space or 33-dimensional variable space or whether some average correlation between tracts on their FAS scores is being used. The result of the grouping procedure is a set of eight groups

[22] Tryon, *Identification of Social Areas by Cluster Analysis.*

labeled by their average *FAS* scores (taking only the first digit of each individual score), which Tryon calls *general social areas,* some of which are named.[23]

The essential nonreproducibility of the methods of dimension derivation and OTU grouping adopted by Tryon meant that the approach was not widely adopted.[24] Most subsequent papers have used factor analysis in some form or another rather than factor analysis as a result, though there are undoubtedly several well-described algorithms for extracting clusters from a similarity matrix of variables or OTUs.[25]

Factor Analysis of a Wider Set of Variables

Following the lead of Bell and Van Arsdol, most subsequent researchers have opted for factor analysis rather than Tryon's cluster analysis. In this section we examine the numerous individual city studies that have used factor analysis to search an area-based within-city data matrix for pattern. The question posed is whether similar dimensions of differentiation have emerged in the various factorial ecologies, as such studies are now commonly called. Our ability to compare within-city classifications based on such dimensions as differentiating characteristics will depend on the answer to that question.

In order to be able to review the many and various studies on at least a partially comparable base, standard-format summaries were prepared. The studies for which standard-format summaries were prepared are listed in the column labeled "Factorial Ecology" in Appendix A. A fuller citation of each published work is presented in the bibliography (Appendix B). The sources of data were as follows:

1. Published studies on 15 American and 6 non–American cities.

2. Student projects and term papers associated with the Center for Urban Studies at the University of Chicago (22 American and 1 non–American city).

3. Unpublished papers on two American and two non–American cities.

---

[23] For example, group 1, *FAS* score 768, is called "the exclusives"; group 5, *FAS* score 533, is labeled "the workers"; group 6, *FAS* score 164, is named "the downtowners"; and group 8, *FAS* score 224, is called "the segregated."

[24] An exception is Earle McCannell, "An Application of Urban Typology by Cluster Analysis to the Ecology of Ten Cities" (unpublished Ph.D. dissertation, University of Washington, Seattle, 1957).

[25] Several alternative types are listed in Table 1. Taylor, "Grouping Analysis in Regional Taxonomy," cites references to these methods. Cluster analysis is also discussed in Chapter 7, "Classification Systems," of John W. Harbaugh and Daniel F. Merriam, *Computer Applications in Stratigraphic Analysis* (New York: John Wiley & Sons, Inc., 1968).

Table 2. A sample factorial ecology summary: Toledo, Ohio

1. Identification
   - City: TOLEDO
   - State: Ohio
   - Study Area: Central City
   - Source: T.R. Anderson and L.L. Bean, "The Shevky-Bell Social Areas: Confirmation of Results and Reinterpretation," Social Forces, Vol. 40 (1961), pp. 110-124.

2. Study Parameters

   m = 13
   n = 54
   Model: Multiple group factor analysis
   Data for 1950

3. Study Output

3.1 Simplified Factor Loadings Matrix

Variables				
	I	II	III	IV
Occupation			-1	
Education			-1	
Fertility Ratio	-2	1		
Females in Labor Force	1	-2		
Multifamily Dwelling Units	1			
Negro		-(2)		-1
Residential Mobility	-1		-(2)	
Per Cent Married	-1			
Income	-1		2	
Families	-1			
Owner-occupied	-1			
Double Occupancy	(4)	-1	-2	-3
Crowding	3		-2	-1

3.2 Factor Interpretation

Factor	Name
I	Urbanization
II	Family status
III	Prestige Value of Neighborhood
IV	Segregation

3.3 Factor and Variable Set Matrix

A. Loadings 1 and (1)

Variable Sets	I		II		III		IV		Totals	
1 (SES)	3	42.8	1	14.3	2	28.5	1	14.3	7	100.0
	42.8	23.0	50.0	7.6	100.0	15.4	50.0	7.6	53.9	53.9
2 (LC)	3	75.0	1	25.0					4	100.0
	42.8	23.0	50.0	7.6					30.7	30.7
3 (E)							1	100.0	1	100.0
							50.0	7.6	7.6	7.6
4 (Change)	1	100.0							1	100.0
	14.3	7.6							7.6	7.6
Total	7	53.9	2	15.4	2	15.4	2	15.4	13	100.0
	100.0	53.9	100.0	15.4	100.0	15.4	100.0	15.4	100.0	100.0

B. Loadings 2 and (2)

Variable Sets	I		II		Factors III		IV	Totals	
1 (SES)					3	100.0		3	100.0
					75.0	42.8		42.8	42.8
2 (LC)	1	50 0	1	50.0				2	100.0
	100.0	14.3	50.0	14.3				28.5	28.5
3 (E)			1	100.0				1	100.0
			50.0	14.3				14.3	14.3
4 (Change)					1	100.0		1	100.0
					25.0	14.3		14.3	14.3
Total	1	14.3	2	28.5	4	57.1		7	100.0
	100.0	14.3	100.0	28.5	100.0	57.1		100.0	100.0

4. Spatial Pattern of the Factors

   No information

NOTE: The following abbreviations are used for the variable sets: SES—socioeconomic status; LC—stage in life cycle; E—ethnicity or minority-group status. Set 4 ("change") includes change and mobility variables.

Several other studies were summarized informally. Since the formal summaries were completed in 1968, many more factorial ecologies have been completed or are in progress for American, British, Indian, and Brazilian cities among others, and the conclusions of this review may need revision in the light of the new evidence.

A sample standard-format summary for the city of Toledo, Ohio, is reproduced in Table 2. The first section of the summary identifies the city, the state, the section of the metropolitan area chosen for study, and the original source. The second section provides some key information about the analysis: the number of variables (m); the number of units of observation, or OTUs (n), which in the case of American city studies are usually census tracts; the factor-analysis model; and the year in which the data were gathered. In the first part of the third section of the summary (section 3.1) the matrix of variables and factors whose cell entries are factor loadings has been converted to a simple-structure format in the following manner:

1 : Highest loading of a variable on a factor, loading > .400.
(1): Highest loading of a variable on a factor, loading between .300 and .399.
2 : Second highest loading of a variable on a factor, loading > .400.
(2): Second highest loading of a variable on a factor, loading between .300 and .399.
3 : Third highest loading of a variable on a factor, loading > .400.

(3): Third highest loading of a variable on a factor, loading between .300 and .399.

A positive loading carries no sign.

A negative loading is indicated by a minus.

This reduction to simple structure aids the comparison of the individual city studies.

In section 3.2 of the summary a note is made of the interpretation of the factors that emerged in the analysis by the authors of the paper, and, on occasion, a comment is added if it is felt that this interpretation is unsatisfactory.

Section 3.3 is the crucial aid in interpreting the factor-analysis results. Here the assumption is made that most factorial ecologies are in effect tests of the dimensionality (how many dimensions?), independence (are the constructs independent?), and additivity (do they add up to a parsimonious picture of the patterns in the data?) of the constructs of socioeconomic status, family status, and ethnic status, originally proposed by Shevky and Williams. What is done in the summary is to allocate the variables used in each study to a standard number of sets (see Table 3) based on an evaluation of the social meaning of each variable in American society or in the particular society in which the city is located. Assignment of variables to sets makes possible the conversion of an $m \times r$ factor-loadings matrix, where the m-variables represent a variety of variable mixes and r is the number of factors extracted, to an $s \times r$ matrix, where s is the number of variable sets. This makes possible a standard comparison of studies based on different numbers and mixes of variables. The cell entries in the $s \times r$ matrix are the number of variables of a given set that have their highest loadings on a particular factor. A second matrix containing information about high secondary loadings supplements the first table, and these two tables are the kernel of each factorial ecology summary. Finally the summary is rounded off with a comment on the spatial patterns displayed by the factors.

The problem with comparing individual factorial ecologies is that each one is different in terms of the inputs used. Factorial ecologies will differ in terms of (a) variables, (b) study area, (c) units of observation, (d) time base, and (e) factorial model.

Nothing can be done to make studies more comparable if they use different study areas, time bases, or factorial models, short of attempting a new study. The units of observation (at least for American city studies) are usually comparable, all being census tracts, which do not vary too greatly in total population. Most attention in the preparation of standard-format

Table 3. Classification of variables employed in factorial ecology

1. Socioeconomic Status Variables
   - 1.1 Population Variables (direct indicators of social status)
     - 1.1.1 Education
     - 1.1.2 Occupation
     - 1.1.3 Income
   - 1.2 Housing Variables (indirect indicators of social status)
     - 1.2.1 Quality
     - 1.2.2 Value of Rent
   - 1.3 Household Material Possessions
   - 1.4 Mixed Population and Housing Variables (for instance, the degree of overcrowding)

2. Family Status or Life Cycle Stage Variables
   - 2.1 Population Variables (direct indicators of family status) --the Life Cycle Subset
     - 2.1.1 Age
     - 2.1.2 Family Size
     - 2.1.3 Fertility
     - 2.1.4 Marital Status
   - 2.2 Housing Variables (indirect indicators of family status) --the Urbanization Subset
     - 2.2.1 Type
     - 2.2.2 Age

3. Ethnicity or Minority Group Status Variables
   - 3.1 Racial Group
   - 3.2 Nativity Group
     - 3.2.1 National Group
   - 3.3 Linguistic Group
   - 3.4 Regional (Migrant) Group

4. Change and Mobility Variables
   - 4.1 Mobility
     - 4.1.1 Movement Rates
     - 4.1.2 Movement Classified by Origin or Destination
   - 4.2 Population Change

5. Scale Variables
   - 5.1 Population
   - 5.2 Area
   - 5.3 Population Density (may act as indirect family status indicator)
   - 5.4 Locational Measures (may act as indirect family status indicator e.g., distance from city center)

6. Health, Welfare, and Social Problems
   - 6.1 Mental Health
   - 6.2 Physical Health
   - 6.3 Welfare
   - 6.4 Crime and Delinquency
   - 6.5 School Population Statistics
   (These are usually local government statistics)

7. Other Variables
   A number of other variables such as commuting statistics or land-use measures have been included in factorial ecologies.

summaries was devoted to finding a lowest common denominator in terms of the variables used by converting the factor-loadings matrix to simple structure and by constructing concept set and factor tables. Using the information provided by these steps some attempt is made to assess what sort of dimensions emerged in various American cities.

Almost all the authors of the studies were able to interpret one (and usually only one) of the dimensions that emerged from the factor analysis in terms of the concept of socioeconomic status, even if the study was restricted to a small part of the metropolitan area.[26] Where more than one factor was characterized by many principal loadings of socioeconomic status indicators this was because an overfine breakdown of a distribution had been used, inevitably resulting in the production of more than one dimension.

Most of the studies revealed at least one factor that indexed the segregation of a population group (usually the black population or a group of recent immigrants). Some revealed as many as five. In the case of American cities where an ethnic group or minority group factor was absent there were two possible explanations: the author had neglected to include any minority group indicators or the minority group indicators loaded on the socioeconomic status factor, revealing the intimate association between racial or ethnic status and socioeconomic status. Cities in the Deep South (Birmingham, Miami, and Shreveport) displayed this kind of factor structure. A third explanation, that the minority group was not significantly segregated from the majority population, might apply in terms of white ethnic groups but not to black minorities, which are significantly segregated from the white majority in all of the nation's metropolises.[27]

In fact many of the studies containing racial status factors also reveal some degree of association between socioeconomic status and racial status in the form of some primary and some secondary loadings of social status indicators on the racial status factor.[28] Cities in the North, Border South, and West all exhibit this kind of factor structure. Cities with a factor structure that revealed socioeconomic and racial status to be independent tended to be those with somewhat serious study defects: either too few variables of each type had been included to make the test critical or the study area

---

[26] Such a small portion of the larger metropolitan area was regarded as a poor choice of study area essentially because it was very much an open system with respect to residence choice.

[27] See Karl E. Taeuber and Alma F. Taeuber, *Negroes in Cities* (Chicago: Aldine Press, 1965).

[28] This was first pointed out by Bell in "Economic, Family and Ethnic Status."

was a very restricted portion of the metropolitan area, making the overall conclusions of the study somewhat suspect.

However, it was not possible to determine directly from the pattern of factor loadings the degree to which a minority group was disadvantageously distributed in the social and economic hierarchy because of the ecological, rather than whole population, base of the factor analysis.

Most studies of American cities showed some form of family-status or life-cycle-stage factor. A plurality of studies exhibited one (and one only) factor that contained loadings of both population and housing type and age indicators.[29] However, there were a substantial number of studies in which two factors bearing some connection with the theoretical construct emerged. The nature of the two factors differed somewhat from city to city: some secondary factors identified the small-apartment district of a smaller city, others appeared to isolate the skid-row inhabitants or particularly deprived minorities in the inner city. The dual factor structure appeared to be unrelated to the regional location of the city, but it did show some association with city size.

What of the factors in these factorial ecologies of American cities that were not related to the three concepts originally proposed as bases of urban residential differentiation by Shevky and Bell? Many of the studies picked out factors related to the mobility or stability of residential area populations, to the degree of recent inmigration, to areas of recent population growth. And it has been suggested that a factor indexing the level of population mobility and growth that distinguished areas of the city with high population-growth rates and much inmigration from areas of declining population and lower entry rates might be added to the triad of Shevky and Bell constructs as a fundamental base of differentiation of urban subareas. However, intraurban mobility and urban growth are complex topics worthy of study in their own right, and it might be argued that to introduce dynamic variables into a static context would serve to cloud, rather than to clarify, our view of urban structure.

International Comparisons

At the time of writing, in addition to the 35 or so factorial ecologies of American cities that have been analyzed in the last section, some 20 factorial ecologies of non–American cities are known to the author. Many more are in the course of preparation.

---

[29] This, it is argued, reflects a matching on a metropolitan scale of family needs and preferences on the one hand, and housing types on the other.

The summarizing procedure adopted in the case of American cities was applied experimentally to a handful of the 20 studies (the factorial ecologies in which the author reported the full factor-loadings matrix). This was perhaps a somewhat dangerous procedure in that the classification of variables into variable sets adopted for American cities[30] could not be applied to foreign cities. Authorities and colleagues familiar with the given foreign society were consulted where possible, and variable allocations were made to the same sets.[31] Such allocations and the accompanying summary analysis should be regarded, however, as tentative in the extreme, especially for non-Western cities.

The foreign cities covered by the studies are listed in Appendix A in roughly decreasing order of economic development level,[32] and we discuss them in that order.

Canada.   The two largest Canadian cities, Toronto and Montreal, have been the focus of much scholarly attention. Berry and Murdie, in their study of Toronto for the Toronto Metropolitan Planning Board, employed what is probably the widest range of socioeconomic variables used in a factorial ecology: some 75 measures of occupational, educational, income, family, age, ethnic, and housing characteristics.[33] These were reduced after a nor-

---

[30] This represented the author's best judgment as to the nature of the various socioeconomic indicators in American society *as a whole*. The judgment was not altered to take into account sectional differences in the meaning of given indicators (e.g., proportion Negro) in order that such contrasts stand out in the standard summary format.

[31] For example, whereas in the United States a crude literacy index (ability to read a newspaper) would have little or no power as an index of social class because of almost universal literacy at that level, in India literacy is probably one of the best indicators of social status in a society where large numbers of persons, even in cities, are still illiterate.

[32] The per capita income in 1965 of the countries containing the cities listed in Appendix A was as follows:

United States	$2893	Italy	$833
Sweden	2046	Ghana	245
Canada	1825	Ivory Coast	188
Denmark	1652	Egypt	96
Britain	1451	India	86
Finland	1399		

Source: David Simpson, "The Dimensions of World Poverty," *Scientific American*, Vol. 219 (1968), pp. 27–35.

[33] Brian J. L. Berry and Robert A Murdie, *Socioeconomic Correlates of Housing Condition* (Toronto: Metropolitan Planning Board, 1965). A full version of Murdie's later, more detailed, analysis of Toronto's factorial ecology in 1950 and 1960 is available in Robert A. Murdie, *Factorial Ecology of Metropolitan Toronto, 1951–*

mal varimax rotation of a principal-components factor solution to four principal factors:

Factor I: economic achievement.
Factor II: family structure.
Factor III: household characteristics.
Factor IV: residential stability.

A unitary demographic housing-type and family-structure factor emerged akin to the modal American type of family-status factor. The socioeconomic status set, however, split into two components, the larger loading on the factor I, and the smaller, including many housing-quality indices, on factor III. The economic achievement factor had a predominantly sectoral distribution, the household-characteristics factor a predominantly zonal distribution.

In the Berry and Murdie study the variable "percentage of population of Italian origin" loads most highly on the first factor of economic status; in the later Murdie study it loads both in 1951 and in 1961 on an ethnic status factor. It is not possible to resolve this conflict in results because the Berry and Murdie study employed blocks as units of observation and used only the central city of Toronto as study area, whereas the Murdie study employed census tracts as units of observation and covered the whole of the Toronto metropolitan area. Thus, although a similar mix of variables was employed and the same factoring routine (principal-components analysis with varimax rotation) was applied, there was still a conflict in outcomes.

The moral is this. Only exact comparability of inputs is sufficient for the exact comparison of outputs in a comparative study.

This moral is underlined by similar incongruities between two somewhat similar studies of *Montreal*,[34] making our discourse a "tale of two cities!" Table 4 summarizes the principal results together with the data and analysis specifications of the two studies. The factor structures are very different: whereas in the Greer-Wootten study a simple social rank dimension emerges, in the Cliffe-Phillips, Mercer, and Yeung study socioeconomic status is linked with ethnic status in both economic achievement factors.[35]

1961: An Essay on the Social Geography of the City (Department of Geography, Research Paper No. 116; Chicago: University of Chicago, 1969).

[34] Bryn Greer-Wootten, "Cross-sectional Social Area Analysis: Montreal 1951–61" (unpublished paper, Department of Geography, McGill University, 1968); Geoffrey Cliffe-Phillips, John Mercer, and Yue Man Yeung, "The Factorial Ecology of Montreal, 1961" (termpaper prepared for Urban Studies 371, University of Chicago, 1968).

[35] Though these two conceptual dimensions are not linked in quite the same way in Montreal as in either Southern U.S. or in Western cities. The minority group is an

Table 4. Two factorial studies of the social geography of Montreal

A. Nature of the Factor Structures

Type of Factor	Author and Year of Analysis		
	Greer-Wootten		Cliffe-Phillips, Mercer, and Yeung
	1951	1961	1961
Simple Socioeconomic Status Factor	Factor I: Social Rank	Factor I: Social Rank	
Socioeconomic Status and Ethnic Status Factor			Factor I: Economic Achievement (English-speaking); Factor IV: Economic Achievement (French-speaking)
Simple Ethnic Status Factor	Factor II: Ethnic Differences (English-French)	Factor II: Ethnic Differences (English-French)	Factor III: New Canadians
Unidimensional Family Status Factor			Factor II: Family Structure
Split Family Status Factor	Factor III: Urbanization I Factor IV: Urbanization II	Factor III: Urbanization I Factor IV: Urbanization II	

B. Study Specifications

Specification			
Data Source	Canadian Census	Canadian Census	Canadian Census
Number of Variables	27	27	40
Number of Variables Common to all Three Studies[a]	17	17	17
Unit Areas Used	Census Tracts or Pseudo-tracts	Census Tracts or Pseudo-tracts	Census Tracts
Number of Unit Areas Used	281	281	384
Study Area	Metropolitan Montreal in 1951	Metropolitan Montreal in 1951	Metropolitan Montreal in 1961
Type of Factor Analysis	Image Analysis	Image Analysis	Principal Components Analysis

[a]All the variables are common between the 1951 and 1961 Greer-Wootten analyses except for the definition of low and high wages.

A simple unidimensional factor of family structure emerges in the Cliffe-Phillips, Mercer, and Yeung study; two factors labeled "urbanization" emerge in the Greer-Wootten study, the first somewhat akin to the Cliffe-Phillips, Mercer, and Yeung factor. And, finally, the ethnic status factor picked out English–French differences in the Greer-Wootten case, but in the case of the other study it isolated areas recently settled by European immigrants of neither French nor English origin from the rest of the Montreal population.

These differences between the studies cannot really be ascribed to differences in variable mix since many of the variables are identical, and many more very similar (Table 4). The two 1961 study areas are somewhat different in extent, but this would not seem to be sufficient to cause such radical differences in factor structures.[36]

The major contrast between the studies was in the mode of factor analysis employed. In the principal-components model, used by Cliffe-Phillips, Mercer, and Yeung, the analysis is performed on the original correlation matrix, where in image analysis the matrix being analyzed is the covariance matrix of estimated data rather than the original correlation matrix. The factors and factor scores produced by these methods have rather different properties—sufficiently different, perhaps, to account for the observed differences in factor structures. This suggests that considerable care has to be exercised in choosing the factor model to be used in a comparative analysis.

Europe. The link between North American and European cities has been provided by a series of papers by Sweetser, who compared in a rigorous and very fruitful way the social and factorial ecologies of Helsinki and Boston.[37] An attempt was made to match the variables used in the analysis as closely as possible: for some variables this was not possible,

elite in Montreal, and minority-group status is associated with high socioeconomic status (factor I: British high-trend-low). Factor IV identifies the status differentiation within the French majority community.

[36] Arguing by analogy with the Chicago study of Rees, where the effect of study area was explicitly tested for, the same set of three principal factors emerged, although the weight of link between socioeconomic and racial status varied somewhat.

[37] Frank L. Sweetser, "Factorial Ecology: Helsinki, 1960," *Demography,* Vol. 2 (1965), pp. 372–386, "Factor Structure as Ecological Structure in Helsinki and Boston," *Acta Sociologica,* Vol. 8 (1965), pp. 205–225, "Ecological Factors in Metropolitan Zones and Sectors," in Dogan and Rokkan, Eds., *Quantitative Ecological Analysis.* Frank L. Sweetser and Dorrian Apple Sweetser, "Social Class and Single Family Housing: Helsinki and Boston," in Sylvia Fleis Fava, Ed., *Urbanism in World Perspective: A Reader* (New York: Thomas Y. Crowell, 1968).

but by and large the variable lists are very similar and factors can be compared.[38]

Some three matching factors emerged in both studies: *socioeconomic status, child-centered familism,* and *residential status* (a dimension indexing the degree of population movement.[39] Two factors were peculiar to Helsinki, *career women* and *postgeniture,* and one to Boston, *ethnicity.* The social class dimensions are very similar, with one notable exception: the meaning of the variable "percentage of single-family or detached dwellings" as a social class indicator. In Boston the social class of the suburban single-family-home dwellers is generally higher than that of the inner urban apartment dwellers. The reverse is the case in Helsinki: the detached dwellings in the suburbs (a much lower proportion of the city's housing stock consists of single-family dwellings) are older structures of lower quality built before the corporate limits and municipal services reached the areas in which they stand. Today they represent cheap, low-quality housing occupied predominantly by working-class families.

The distinctive Helsinki dimension "career women" undoubtedly reflects the different meaning of work for women in Finnish society, where half the labor force is female, and 58% of females over 15 work. The division of the familism factor into two parts that the postgeniture factor reflects may be partly a function of the large number of age and family status variables included, but it may also reflect the variable fertility history of postwar Finland.

The two ethnicity dimensions—Irish middle class and Italian/Negro factors—that emerged in the study of Boston have no counterparts in the case of Helsinki, although some five ethnic variables were included in the latter study. The variable diagnostic of the Swedish-speaking population loaded on the socioeconomic status factor with a sign indicating that Swedish-speaking Finns tended to be of fairly high social status. Although this finding, as our discussion of the factorial ecologies of Southern U.S. cities indicated, does not necessarily imply that the Swedish-speaking Finns are not segregated from the Finnish-speaking Finns, Sweetser does not draw attention to any such fact. He concludes that "ethnicity is not a meaningful factor in Helsinki."[40]

An ethnic factor is also absent from Pedersen's study of Copenhagen, because no ethnic variables were included in an analysis of what the author

---

[38] The study areas were metropolitan in scope, and the same mode of factor analysis —multiple group factor analysis—was applied in both cases.

[39] These three factors also emerged in Pedersen's study of Copenhagen and Rees's study of Chicago.

[40] Sweetser, "Factor Structure on Ecological Structure," p. 225.

perceived of as a homogeneous society. However, great care should be exercised in arguing thus from omission of variables or from perceived social homogeneity.

Whereas the studies of Canadian and Finnish cities are fairly amenable to comparison with the studies of American cities we have summarized, the British ones are difficult to compare. No careful linking study, such as Sweetser's study of Helsinki and Boston, has been done. Whereas a substantial effort has been made to maintain comparability among them, British studies differ considerably from American ones in terms of the unit areas used and the exact factor-analysis technique, but not too greatly in terms of variable mix and study area (Table 5).

Herbert, in his studies of Cardiff and Swansea,[41] finds a basic four-factor structure: component 1 is a dimension that distinguishes public housing areas, or, as they are more usually called in Britain, municipal housing areas with a young family population. The author recognizes, however, that the association of family status with the ownership and tenure characteristics of housing is in part a function of the exclusion from the study area of new private housing outside the county borough boundaries, though in part it is a function of the criteria used in selecting municipal housing tenants. The spatial pattern of the factor is that of the municipal housing estates, to be explained not in terms of ecological factors but in terms of the decisions made by the local government authority, subject to the constraints of the land market as expressed in land-acquisition costs.[42]

The second component distinguishes inner-city substandard housing from outer-city standard housing.[43] The third component associates areas of higher social class with higher proportions of immigrant Britons. However, in a city like Cardiff there are very few colored inhabitants (excepting the polyglot and multiracial society of Tiger Bay), and this association is probably spurious. The final component is one of family type and age structure.

---

[41] D. T. Herbert, "Principal Components Analysis and Urban Social Structure: A study of Cardiff and Swansea," in H. Carter and W. K. D. Davies, Eds., *Urban Essays: Studies in the Geography of Wales* (forthcoming), "The Application of Principal Components Analysis to the Studies of Urban Social Structure" (unpublished paper, Department of Geography, University College of Swansea, 1968), and "Principal Components Analysis and British Studies of Urban Social Structure," *Professional Geographer*, Vol. 20 (1968), pp. 280–283.

[42] My impressionistic view is that the public authority today tends to build the same type of housing at given locations in urban physical space as would private developers: apartments in the central regions of the city, semidetached dwellings on the outskirts.

[43] This factor also emerged in the study of Sunderland by Robson. See Brian Robson, *The Social Ecology of Sunderland* (Cambridge: Cambridge University Press, 1969).

Table 5. Key elements in American and British factorial ecologies

Study Specification	American Studies	British Studies
Variables: (1) Common	Measures of Occupation, Education, Housing Quality, Age Structure, Sex Ratio, Family Type, Ethnicity, Mobility Status.	
(2) Unique	Income Measures, Housing Type Measures	Housing Tenure Measures
Unit Areas	Census Tracts, averaging 1,000-2,000 households	Enumeration districts, averaging 250 households
Study Area	Various: Central (Politically defined) City, Urbanized Area or Standard Metropolitan Statistical Area	Central Cities (County Boroughs) except for London, where both Inner London (old London County Council) and Greater London (G.L.C. area or approximate equivalent) have been used
Factor Model	Various: most common is Principal Components Analysis with Normal Varimax Rotation	Principal Components Analysis without Rotation

The dimensions of social class and family status do not emerge as clear-cut and dominant factors in this study nor in other studies of British towns.[44] Dimensions, including housing characteristics, of varying character do emerge, though their social class or family-status associations differ from city to city. Whether these contrasts with American city factor structures are a product of fundamental differences between British and American housing markets and choice mechanisms or at least partly a product of the operational differences in the various analyses cannot be determined without a careful comparative study along the lines pioneered by Sweetser.

Non–Western Cities.   Although it has been used in many studies of the social geography of Western cities, factor analysis has been applied in only two published studies of non–Western cities: Cairo and Calcutta.

---

[44] Other studies include Elizabeth Gittus, "An Experiment in the Definition of Urban Sub-Areas," *Transactions of the Bartlett Society,* Vol. 2 (1964–1965), pp. 109–135, and "The Structure of Urban Areas," *Town Planning Review,* Vol. 35 (1964), pp. 5–20; J. A. Giggs, "Socially Disorganized Areas in Barry: A Multivariate Analysis," in Carter and Davies, Eds., *Urban Essays.*

CAIRO.[45] Only a relatively few variables (13) were available to Abu-Lughod on small-area basis for Cairo, but a principal-axes factor analysis of the 216 × 13 data matrix revealed quite clearly that social status and family status sets collapsed to a single dimension, *style of life,* in which class and family patterns are inextricably linked:

Thus, census tracts with high Factor I scores are characterized by commodious housing accommodations, a highly literate population, low rates of dependency and unemployment, and by the presence of resident domestic servants . . . . At the opposite extreme are the lowest scoring tracts on Factor I, where house overcrowding often reaches astronomical heights, where most residents are illiterate, and where females seldom attend school or work at paid employment outside the home.[46]

The association between class and family patterns (which Abu-Lughod had earlier reported at a nonecological level, confirming that the ecological correlations were not spurious) led the author to outline the conditions necessary for the emergence of separate and independent dimensions of social class and family status.

The second factor extracted in the study, that of *male dominance,* isolated inner Cairo areas of the settlement of primarily unattached males, inmigrants from the rural lands along the Nile. The concentrations of migrant males appear to be characteristic of many non-Western cities: the men go to the city to find work and send money back to their families in the village. Only when established do they send for their families.

The third significant factor to emerge was one of social *disorganization,* high scores on which dimension were associated with the very highest population densities.

CALCUTTA.[47] A complex factor structure emerged from a principal-component analysis of a matrix of some 37 variables and 80 wards. The variables used differed considerably from those used in American studies. The social groups considered to be significant, of course, differed radically, and therefore the variables used to measure their distribution in the city also differed. Occupational statistics were unavailable and hence industry of employment had to serve as a surrogate, and, in addition, several land-

---

[45] Janeṭ Abu-Lughod, "The Ecology of Cairo, Egypt: A Comparative Study Using Factor Analysis" (unpublished Ph.D. dissertation, University of Massachusetts, Amherst, 1966) and "A Critical Test for the Theory of Social Area Analysis: the Factorial Ecology of Cairo, Egypt" (unpublished paper, Department of Sociology, Northwestern University, February 1968).

[46] Abu-Lughod, "Factorial Ecology of Cairo," pp. 24–25.

[47] Brian J. L. Berry and Philip H. Rees, "Factorial Ecology of Calcutta," *American Journal of Sociology,* Vol. 74 (1969), pp. 445–491.

use variables were included in the study in order to assess the influence of land-use mix on the ecology of the city.

Certain of the factors that emerged from the analysis resembled factors common in American studies:

Factor I: a land-use and familism gradient—family status.
Factor II: Muslim concentrations—ethnic status.
Factor III: axiality in literacy—social status.
Factor IV: the substantial residential areas—social status.

There were two social status factors, of which factor III appeared to be more general. Examination of the spatial distribution of "social areas" defined in the social space of factors I and III revealed a pattern that was essentially the inverse of that of Chicago, which had been similarly examined.

Other factors proved peculiar to Calcutta: the non–Bengali and Bengali commercial quarters were picked out by factors V and VI; special land-use distributions were associated with factors VII to X.

It was abundantly clear even from two studies that the factorial ecology of non–Western cities was very different from that of Western cities but capable nevertheless of being examined within the same framework.

Use of Factorial Dimensions in Within-City Classifications

It would be interesting to pursue the nature of the factorial dimensions further and to develop a theory that would explain the emergence of particular dimensions and factor structures in terms of the underlying urban conditions, urban history, and current processes. But that is left to another time and place. Here we examine the ways in which the factorial dimensions have been used as *differentiating characteristics* in within-city classifications.

Most factorial ecologies stop short of applying their dimensional findings to the problem of classifying residential areas within cities. However, there are a small number of studies that do go on to use factor scores as differentiating characteristics. The principal features of these studies are summarized in Table 6.[48]

[48] Chicago: Philip H. Rees, "The Factorial Ecology of Metropolitan Chicago, 1960," in Brian J. L. Berry and Frank E. Horton, Eds., *Geographic Perspectives on Urban Systems* (Englewood Cliffs, N.J.: Prentice-Hall, Inc., 1970).

Calcutta: Berry and Rees, "Factorial Ecology of Calcutta."

Rockford: Gerald F. Pyle, "A Factorial Ecology of Rockford, 1960," *Proceedings of the Illinois State Academy of Sciences* (1970).

Table 6. Within-city classifications based on factor scores as differentiating characteristics

Components of Classification	Chicago	Calcutta	Rockford	Melbourne	Inner London
Purpose	To describe the social geography of the city	To describe the social geography of the city	To describe the social geography of the city	Clearer understanding of residential area differentiation	A typology of London districts
OTU	1. Community Areas and Suburban Municipalities 2. Census Tracts	Wards	Census Tracts	Aggregated collectors' districts	Enumeration districts
Differentiating Characteristics	Factor 1. Socio-economic Status Factor 2. Stage in Life Cycle	Factor 4. Substantial Residential Areas Factor 1. Familism and land-use Gradient	Factor 1. Socio-economic Status Factor 2. Stage in Life Cycle Factor 3. Negro Segregation	Factor 1. Socio-economic Status/Ethnicity Factor 2. Household Composition	First 14 principal component scores
Basis of Selection	Principal Components Analysis	Principal Components Analysis	Principal Components Analysis	Principal Components Analysis (without rotation)	Principal Components Analysis
Method of Classification	1. Division 2. Two factor hierarchical grouping algorithm (neighborhood limited)	1. Division 2. Ten factor hierarchical grouping algorithm (Ward's criterion)	Intuitive Visual Grouping	Williams and Lance hierarchical grouping algorithm, using Squared Euclidean Distance as Similarity Coefficient	Howard's grouping algorithm

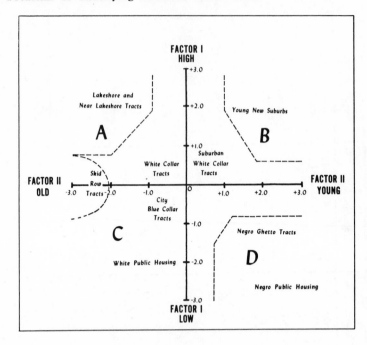

Figure 4 Chicago's social space: factor I (socioeconomic status) versus factor II (stage in life cycle).

The Chicago and Calcutta groupings that are compared in the same paper[49] are based on a species of division (Figures 4 and 5).[50] Two factors were chosen as principal differentiating characteristics: *socioeconomic status* and *stage in life cycle* in the Chicago case and *substantial residential areas* and *familism and land use* in the Calcutta case. Both "social spaces" formed by these factors were divided into four quadrants (*A, B, C, D*), and the spatial distributions of the tracts or wards in these quadrants were

Melbourne: F. Lancaster Jones, "Social Area Analysis: Some Theoretical and Methodological Comments Illustrated with Australian Data," *British Journal of Sociology*, Vol. 14 (1968), pp. 424–444.

Inner London: Peter Norman, "Third Survey of London Life and Labor: A New Typology of London Districts," in Dogan and Rokkan, Eds., *Quantitative Ecological Analysis*, pp. 371–396.

[49] Berry and Rees, "Factorial Ecology of Calcutta," and Nigel Howard, "Least Squares Classification and Principal Component Analysis: A Comparison," in Dogan and Rokkan, Eds., *Quantitative Ecological Analysis*, pp. 397–412.

[50] Source: Berry and Rees, "Factorial Ecology of Calcutta," pp. 486 and 487.

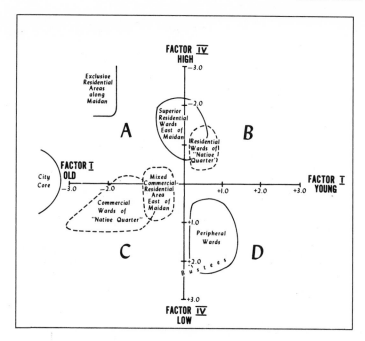

Figure 5 Calcutta's social space: factor IV (substantial residential areas) versus factor II (familism and land use).

compared (Figure 6).[51] In both instances the high-status residential areas front superior amenities (Lake Michigan in Chicago and the Maidan in Calcutta). On the other hand, the geographic pattern of the other three social areas is inverted from one city to the other.

In addition, particular areas of social space are picked out and given labels: "Lakeshore and near Lakeshore tracts" and "skid row tracts" or "exclusive residential areas along maidan" or "city core." The regions of social space are classified according to external correlates of race, housing tenure (Chicago), or location and function (Calcutta), all attributes not included in the original factorial ecology. Similar segments of the social space of the two cities are occupied by somewhat analogous areas, though the dimensions making up the social space have a greater significance in describing the socioeconomic patterning of residences in Chicago than in Calcutta. And yet the method of delimiting the segments, involving different

[51] Source: Berry and Rees, "Factorial Ecology of Calcutta," pp. 486 and 487.

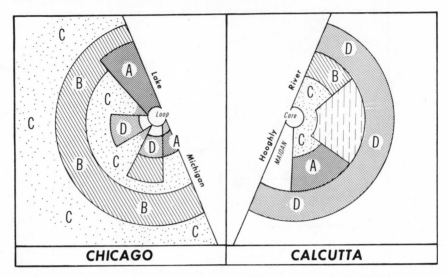

Figure 6 The generalized social areas of Chicago and Calcutta mapped.

external criteria for different segments, is one contrary to the principles of taxonomy.[52] The moral is that one does not need a nutcracker, let alone a sledgehammer, to crack some nuts.

In the case of Chicago the more sophisticated hierarchical grouping analysis proved to be somewhat unsatisfactory. Since only two factors (socioeconomic status and stage in life cycle) were used as differentiating characteristics and OTUs were normally distributed along both dimensions about the mean of 0.0, the result was one large undifferentiated cluster at the center of the social space diagram surrounded by a ring of more dispersed OTUs. In such a case, where natural groupings are not present, division would seem to be preferable to grouping as a classification method,[53] though the addition of more differentiating characteristics might have helped.

This appears to have been the case in the "Third Survey of London Life and Labor."[54] There 14 principal components (output of a principal-com-

---

[52] Grigg, "Regions, Models and Classes," p. 488. Principle 6 of regionalization reads: "When dividing, the division should proceed at every stage and as far as possible throughout the division upon one principle."

[53] As Taylor, "Grouping Analysis in Regional Taxonomy," p. 10.

[54] This is a research project in progress at the Centre for Urban Studies, University College, London, undertaken by Wolf Scott, Nigel Howard, and Peter Norman under the direction of Ruth Glass. A preliminary report is made in Norman, "Third Survey of London Life and Labor."

ponents analysis of 38 socioeconomic and housing variables) were used as differentiating characteristics. The grouping algorithm differs somewhat from that used in the Chicago and Calcutta studies:[55] an initial partition of the OTUs is made (e.g., above and below the mean for the first principal component), and this partition is improved until it is optimal by examining the sum of squared distances over all component scores of any OTU to its group mean and reallocating the OTU if another group mean is shown to be nearer. New means are computed for the new grouping, and the process is continued until a test shows that every element is closer to its own group mean than to the mean of any other group. The algorithm then proceeds from two to three groups by dividing up the group with the largest internal variation, and the procedure continues until a sufficiently large number of groups has been obtained.

For a typology of Inner London's districts the following six groups were chosen:

1. Upper class
2. Bed–sitting room
3. Poor
4. Stable working class
5. Local authority housing
6. Almost suburban

This typology combines both population and housing data, the authors arguing that "stratification of areas cannot be satisfactorily achieved without recognizing that housing conditions and 'transience,' as well as occupation and schooling, play an important differentiating role."[56]

In his preliminary report Norman includes a map of a small portion of inner Northwest London (the Metropolitan Borough of Camden) in which all six types are present and thoroughly intermingled in a relatively small area. This would seem to contrast with the situation in a city like Chicago, in which wide areas are socially homogeneous and the different types of social area are well separated. However, remembering the caution advised in our review of different factorial ecologies, the technical differences between the two studies are such as to make comparisons invalid.

A third classification method of a rather different kind that employs the results of factorial ecology in an indirect way has been applied to the city. In his study of Toronto, Murdie says: "When the dimensions of social

---

[55] This is similar to the one used in the Melbourne study. The Melbourne study is not discussed here because the author uses his grouping analysis for illustrating a methodological point rather than for some substantive purpose.
[56] Norman, "Third Survey of London Life and Labor," p. 391.

space are overlaid on the map of the city . . . the effect should be to isolate areas of social homogeneity in cells defined by the spider's web of the sectorial-zonal lattice."[57]

However, Murdie's "communities" of Metropolitan Toronto[58] are intended for illustrative purposes only, and he does not pursue the analysis further. In a similar analysis of Chicago,[59] the author divided the metropolis into six rings (inner city, outer city, inner suburbs, outer suburbs, industrial satellites, and rural periphery) and five sectors (North Shore, Northwest, West, Southwest, South). The mean factor scores for socioeconomic status and stage in life cycle for the OTUs contained in each cell of the concentric ring-sector design were calculated together with their standard deviations. The rationale behind such a division is as follows: if socioeconomic status is distributed predominantly in a sectoral fashion (rather than in any other fashion or randomly) across the metropolis, and if family status or life-cycle stage is distributed concentrically, then as Murdie notes we should expect to isolate areas of homogeneity in the differentiating characteristics. However, if the spatial patterns of the differentiating characteristics are not as predicted or not as strong, there will be considerable internal variation in the cells of the design (as revealed by many of the Chicago cell standard deviations). Such a spatially based classification, though theoretically and aesthetically pleasing, may not have empirical validity.

Thus it is difficult at this stage in the game to make integrative generalizations about the types of social area (areas of social homogeneity) that are to be found in the modern American city, and we can point to no study of more than one city that shows modern metropolises to contain similar types of residential area. Yet intuitively we can say that the industrial city of the Northern United States contains the following areas:

1. Skid-row district of the aged poor, the male "down and out," and the alcoholic living in rooming houses.

2. Exclusive areas of apartments and townhouses inhabited by single persons or childless couples who are rich.

3. Middle-class apartment areas of the city inhabited by an older population.

4. Working-class apartment areas of the city inhabited by an older population.

[57] Murdie, "Factorial Ecology of Toronto," p. 168.
[58] Murdie, "Factorial Ecology of Toronto," Figure 29, p. 169.
[59] Rees, "Factorial Ecology of Chicago."

5. Exclusive areas of single-family homes and young families in the outer city and suburbs.

6. Middle-class areas of single-family homes and young families in the outer city and suburbs.

7. Working-class areas of single-family homes and young families in the outer city and suburbs.

Superimposed on some of these areas in the inner city, are the following:

8. Enclaves of the foreign stock of various ethnic groups.

9. The black ghetto (a miniature of the whole metropolis in social composition but with a restricted stock of housing).

RELATIONAL AREAS AND COMMUNITIES

After considering the ways in which the city can be divided into social areas or social regions by using structural properties as differentiating characteristics, we turn to a discussion of some of the attempts at using relational properties instead and of the notion of community that has been associated with these attempts.

The purpose of within-city classifications based on relational attributes is to describe how the complexity of urban life and the behavior of city dwellers are organized, or, to use a well-known phrase from the geographic literature, to describe "the areal functional organization" of the city.[60] The OTUs are usually the households of the city or, rather, the small sample of households surveyed in the particular study. The differentiating characteristics used in this sort of within-city classification involve either the flow of goods, money, or information to the household from some external node or the movement of members of the household to some external node or, in some cases, merely the perception by the individual or household of a link between the individual and the node. There may be many nodes in the city (e.g., grocery stores) or just one (the metropolitan government headquarters): each node will have connections to households, and the space occupied by these households will constitute its region of influence. Regions of influence of nodes may overlap, however, and, if an overlapping constraint is imposed on the classification, some classificatory decisions, usually fairly simple, have to be made.

Each household has myriad connections to other places or nodes in

[60] Allen K. Philbrick, "Principles of Areal Functional Organization in Regional Geography," *Economic Geography,* Vol. 33 (1957), pp. 299–336.

the metropolis. How has this complex web of relations been ordered? There is a considerable literature on *journey-to-work trips,* but since the nodes are so many there have been few, if any, attempts to divide the city into journey-to-work regions. The CBDs worksheed overlaps all others, and any attempt to impose a nonoverlapping constraint on the other worksheds in the metropolis would be unworkable. The journey to work is usually considered as an aggregate phenomenon; alternatively attention is restricted to individual establishments[61] or particular industries.[62]

For *shopping trips* there exists a whole elaborate theory of organization and a growing body of empirical literature.[63] Within the metropolis shopping centers can be regarded as nodes, and nodal regions can be defined through customer or household survey. However, the role of retail or service outlets in ribbons or specialized areas cannot be ignored, and a map of the trade areas of the hierarchy of centers tells only part of the story.

School trips are closely ordered by a public bureaucracy, responsive(?) to the needs and desires of households with school-age children. The degree of overlap of catchment areas is smaller than the case of work trips and shopping trips—though if there are competing public and private systems, the overlap is likely to be considerable.

Finally, there are trips for "voluntary" purposes: recreation trips, socializing with neighbors, visiting friends, trips to clubs, to organizational meetings, to political activities. These expressions of *social participation* have been the traditional concern of the sociologist. Considerable work has been done in the field, though little of it has been devoted to the definition of regions of influence or interaction within the city on a spatial frame.[64]

---

[61] John E. Galt, "The Residential Distribution of the Employees of Argonne National Laboratory: Patterns and Implications" (unpublished M.A. dissertation, Department of Geography, University of Chicago, June, 1968).

[62] Beverly Duncan, "Variables in Urban Morphology," in Ernest W. Burgess and Donald J. Bogue, Eds., *Urban Sociology* (Chicago: University of Chicago Press, 1967), pp. 17–30.

[63] Brian J. L. Berry, *The Geography of Market Centers and Retail Distribution* (Englewood Cliffs, N.J.: Prentice-Hall, Inc., 1967).

[64] Thus Form et al., in their discussion of within-city classification approaches, as applied to Lansing, Michigan, report considerable research on the degree of social participation and included in their social survey a question that asked respondents to name the community in which they lived and to describe its boundaries. But they failed to map the answers to that question or to portray spatially their respondents' perceptions of Lansing's community structure. See William H. Form, Joel Smith, Gregory P. Stone, and James Cowhig, "The Comparability of Alternative Approaches to the Delimitation of Urban Sub-areas," *American Sociological Review,* Vol. 19 (1954), pp. 434–440.

However, Greer has provided an overview of what such a regional hierarchy within the metropolis would look like.[65]

"There are three fields," Greer says, "concentric in scope, that constitute the social structure of 'the community of limited liability.' " The hierarchy of social organizational areas is summarized below.

Level	Name	Activities Linking Households to Each Other or to Nodes
A. Central city:		
Lowest	Neighborhood	Neighboring; mutual aid; negotiation over conflicts
Intermediate	Local residential area or community	Community press reading; local voluntary organizations
Highest	The city	Relations with City Hall
B. Suburban area:		
Lowest	Neighborhood	Neighboring; mutual aid; negotiation over conflicts
Intermediate	Local residential area or community = municipality	Community press reading; local voluntary organizations; political activity

Delimitation of neighborhoods in space is probably an impossible task if social interaction is employed as the differentiating characteristic. To quote Greer, "Neighborhoods overlap as do households, and the neighborhood structure of a metropolis resembles St. Augustine's definition of God, an infinite circle whose center is everywhere and whose periphery nowhere." Definition of the community is an easier task in the suburban area of the metropolis, as political units are frequently coterminous with social communities. There remains, however, the problem of allocating the residential areas outside an incorporated municipality to a particular social community since politically the households in many cases have considerable resistance to political integration.

Within the central city the problem of community definition is more difficult. The work of Burgess and later Palmer on dividing the city into a

[65] Scott Greer, "The Social Structure and Political Process of Suburbia, *American Sociological Review,* Vol. 25 (1960), pp. 514–526, and, *The Emerging City: Myth and Reality* (New York: Free Press, 1962), particularly Chapter 4, "The Community of Limited Liability," pp. 107–137.

set of mutually exclusive community areas has already been mentioned in the course of considering the natural area concept. At present an attempt is under way to reevaluate the communities and community boundaries of Chicago.[66] Hunter asked over 800 respondents in the city to name the community in which they lived and to describe its boundaries. The answers were many and varied. In certain parts of the city there was strong consensus on the name and boundaries of the community to which people felt attached; in other areas there were conflicting opinions and considerable overlap of adjacent communities, and in yet other regions of the city there was no feeling of belonging to a local residential community—the attachment was to the neighborhood only. Development of a new exhaustive partition of Chicago into communities (along the lines of the present scheme dating from the earlier work) would be a complex task: core areas might be easily defined, but the peripheries would be much fought over by interested observers and community residents.

THE LINKS BETWEEN WITHIN-CITY AND CITY CLASSIFICATION

Finally, we use certain of the factorial dimensions that emerged in Berry's study (Chapter 1 of this volume) to examine the links between within-city and city classification in a partial way. We look at the similarity of national and metropolitan dimensions, and at the bounds of the social spaces of a handful of national metropolises in national social space.

Examination of the factor-score maps of four of the factors extracted in this national study suggested that a large part of the variation among cities on these factors was a function of the variation among urban places within

National Factor	Metropolitan Factor
Socioeconomic status of community residents	Socioeconomic status
Stage in life cycle of community residents	Stage in life cycle
Nonwhite population of communities	Race and resources
Foreign-born or foreign-stock population	Immigrant and Catholic

[66] Allan Hunter, "Symbolic Communities and Community Change" (Ph.D. dissertation in preparation, Department of Sociology, University of Chicago).

Table 7.   Relations between the national and the metropolitan factor scores for a common set of 66 Chicago suburbs

Regression Equations

$$N_{SES} = 0.69 + 0.91 \; M_{SES} \qquad r^2 = 0.89$$
$$\phantom{N_{SES} = }(0.05) \quad (0.04)$$

$$N_{LC} = 0.49 + 1.16 M_{LC} \qquad r^2 = 0.81$$
$$\phantom{N_{LC} = }(0.06) \quad (0.07)$$

$$N_{NW} = 0.11 - 0.33 \; M_{RR} \qquad r^2 = 0.06$$
$$\phantom{N_{NW} = }(0.11) \quad (0.16)$$

$$N_{FS} = 0.55 + 0.50 \; M_{IC} \qquad r^2 = 0.35$$
$$\phantom{N_{FS} = }(0.07) \quad (0.10)$$

N_{SES} – score on National Socioeconomic Status factor

N_{LC} – score on National Stage in Life Cycle factor

N_{NW} – score on National Nonwhite Population factor

N_{FS} – score on National Population Foreign-born and Foreign Stock factor

M_{SES} – score on Metropolitan Socioeconomic Status factor

M_{LC} – score on Metropolitan Stage in Life Cycle factor

M_{RR} – score on Metropolitan Race and Resources factor

M_{IC} – score on Metropolitan Immigrant and Catholic factor

Figures in parentheses are the standard errors

each metropolis. The Chicago study,[67] which contains factors very similar to those in the national study, enables us to make a fairly tight test of our hypothesis. For some 66 Chicago suburbs of over 10,000 inhabitants there were available both metropolitan and national factor scores for four similarly labeled factors (see table, page 306).

Table 7 reveals that the first two pairs of factors are very closely associated, that the 66 Chicago suburbs rank very similarly in terms of social and family status in both the national and metropolitan studies. The national scores are uniformly higher than the metropolitan ones (the intercepts of the regression equations are positive and the regression coefficients

[67] Rees, "Factorial Ecology of Chicago."

Table 8.   Variables loading on similar factors in the national and in the Chicago studies: socioeconomic status

Variable	Loadings on National Factor II: Socioeconomic Status of Community Residents	Loadings on Chicago Factor I: Socioeconomic Status
Median Income	0.876	0.787
Per cent Incomes Over $10,000	0.897	0.907
Per cent Incomes Below $3,000	-0.747	-0.437[a]
Per cent with High School Education	0.834	0.868
Median School Years	0.805	0.845
Value of Occupied Housing Units	0.676	0.893
Median Rent	0.534	0.559
Per cent Housing Units Sound	0.755	0.453[a]
Per cent Housing Units Owner-occupied	0.413	0.329[a]
Median Rooms Per Housing Unit	0.557	-
Per cent White Collar	0.783	0.915
Unemployment Rate	-0.514	-0.368[a]
Per cent Professional or Managerial	-	0.930
Per cent Craftsmen or Operative	-	-0.874
Per cent Clerical or Sales	-	0.664
Per cent Housing in Two-unit Structures	-	-0.437
Canadian Location Quotient	-	0.434

0.876 - Principal factor loading of a variable
  -   - Indicates variable not present in study
  a   - These variables have their principal loadings on the third factor in the Chicago study, Race and Resources

are not very different from unity), which would seem to indicate that the Chicago metropolis was of higher status and contained a younger, more familial population than American metropolises and urban places in general. The second two pairs of factors were not very closely associated.

The reasons for the close association of social and family status, and the disparity between racial and immigrant status at the national and metropolitan levels are not hard to find. Comparison of the variables that loaded most highly in the national and metropolitan studies respectively reveals (Tables 8 through 11) that the socioeconomic status and stage-in-life-cycle factors are made up in great part of identical or very similar variables in both studies, whereas this is not so in the case of the racial and immigrant status factors, as Table 12 makes clear.

The composition of variables loading most highly on the national study's factor IV (nonwhite population in communities) indicates that this is a dimension that distinguishes not only between communities with high pro-

Table 9. Variables loading on similar factors in the national and in the Chicago studies: stage in life cycle

Variable	Loadings on National Study Factor III: Stage in Life Cycle of Community Residents	Loadings on Chicago Study Factor II: Stage in Life Cycle
Median Age	−0.806	−0.765
Per cent Population Under 18	0.869	0.893
Per cent Population Over 65	−0.838	−0.891
Fertility Rate	0.775	−
Population Per Household	0.906	0.919
Persons Per Dwelling Unit	0.869	−
Per cent Homes Built 1950-60	0.627	0.743
Rate of Growth 1950-60	0.484	−
Per cent Housing Stock Built Before 1940	−	−0.761
Per cent Women in Labor Force	−0.079[a]	−0.717
Per cent Housing Units in One-unit Structures	0.406[b]	0.599
Per cent Housing Units in Three or More Unit Structures	−	−0.598
Per cent Housing Units Owner-occupied	0.892[c]	0.585
Per cent Commuting by Foot	−	−0.453

Key
0.869 - principal factor loading of variable
0.406 - loading other than principal
   −   - indicates variable not present in study

Notes
a - this variable has its principal loading on Factor X: Female
    Participation in the Labor Force
b - this variable has its principal loading on Factor VII: Population
    Foreign-born or Foreign Stock
c - this variable has its principal loading on Factor II: Socio-
    economic Status of Community Residents

portions of nonwhite inhabitants and communities with few nonwhites but also among Negro communities in terms of income and overcrowding in housing with the Negro population being wealthier but more poorly housed in cities with higher than average proportions of Negroes. The metropolitan factor, on the other hand, shows that there is a tendency for residential areas with high proportions of Negroes to be characterized by concentrations of low-income families, underemployed or unemployed workers, and overcrowded housing. The two sets of findings are not necessarily contradictory, but they are clearly different. The immigrant status factors have similarly slightly variant interpretations.

Armed with the finding that the national study essentially replicates the ranking of large suburban communities in one large metropolis on two sig-

Table 10. Variables loading on similar factors in the national and in the Chicago studies: racial status

Variable	Loadings on National Factor IV: Nonwhite Population in Communities	Loadings on Chicago Factor III: Race and Resources
Per cent Population Nonwhite	0.850	-0.743
Per cent Housing Units Nonwhite	0.848	-
Per cent of Nonwhite Housing Units Overcrowded	0.831	-
Nonwhite Housing Units Owned	0.826	-
Median Income, Nonwhite	0.798	-
Per cent Married Couples Without Own Household	0.465	-
Negro Location Quotient	-	-0.750
Native White Location Quotient	-	0.725
Per cent Protestant (White)	-	0.708
Per cent Incomes Under \$3,000	0.394[a]	-0.667
Per cent Laborers	-	-0.645
Per cent Unemployed	0.080[a]	-0.618
Per cent in Service Occupations	-	-0.558
Per cent Housing Units Overcrowded	-	-0.535
German Location Quotient	-	0.526
Per cent Housing Units Sound	-0.355[a]	0.509

Key
0.848 - Principal factor loading of a variable
  - - Indicates variable not present in study

Notes
a - These variables have their principal loadings on Factor II: Socioeconomic Status of Community Residents

nificant dimensions, we made the assumption[68] that it did a similar job in other large metropolises and furthermore provided a means whereby the spread of communities in social space (the two-dimensional space formed by the two factors) in a number of metropolises could be compared. The scores on national factors II and III for suburban communities in the 10 largest American metropolises were plotted graphically. The plots were then converted into two summary figures, covering five metropolises each (Figures 7 and 8).[69] Each labeled line on the figure encloses the distribution of communities of the particular metropolis it refers to. This procedure tends to assign somewhat exaggerated importance to extreme values, but

[68] Somewhat of a leap of faith since the similarity of the national and metropolitan factors really requires justification for every city. However, it is the belief of the author that without such assumptions (to be verified or discarded) there would be little progress in social science.

[69] Only the 10 largest metropolises in the United States (as measured by their functional economic area population given in Berry, Goheen, and Goldstein, "Metropolitan Area Definition") were investigated since only these had sufficiently large suburbs (only places with over 10,000 inhabitants were included in the study) to constitute a valid sample.

Table 11. Variables loading on similar factors in the national and in the Chicago studies: foreign-stock population

Variable	Loadings on National Factor VII: Population Foreign-born or Foreign Stock	Loadings on Chicago Factor IV: Immigrant and Catholic
Per cent Population Foreign-born	0.822	0.655
Per cent Population Foreign Stock	0.755	-
Per cent Population Foreign-born— Mother Tongue not English	0.567	-
Per cent Elementary School Children in Private School	0.480	-
Per cent Housing Units One Unit	-0.483	-0.012[a]
Per cent Using Public Transportation	0.390	-
Foreign Stock Location Quotient	-	0.828
Per cent Native-born of Foreign or Mixed Parents	-	0.857
Per cent Native-born of Native Parents	-	-0.830
Per cent Catholic (White)	-	0.760
Polish Location Quotient	-	0.583
Per cent Commute by Rail	-	-0.390
Czech Location Quotient	-	0.362

Key
0.822 - Principal loading of variable
  -   - Indicates variable not present in study

Notes
a - This variable loads principally on Factor II: Stage in Life Cycle

for the particular metropolises chosen this effect is not considered to be too serious.[70]

The metropolises tend to occupy, particularly the five largest, more of the upper half of the graph (the higher status half) than of the lower, reflecting (a) the fact that the central city scores (indicated on the figures) hide a great internal variability, which, if captured by the inclusion of central city communities in the study, would push the area spanned by each metropolis further into the lower status half, and (b) the tendency for many smaller cities in poorer regions of the United States to occupy this lower portion of national social space.

Each metropolis spans a considerable portion of the space and contains within its bounds a large fraction of the variation in social and economic characteristics of the whole national system of cities. A substantial portion of the space is common to all 10 metropolises. There are differences between the metropolises: metropolitan Los Angeles contains a substantial

[70] Conventionally distributions in two dimensions are summarized by a cross centered on the mean with arms extending one standard deviation outward along each dimension. Two functions could be constructed, however, which would enclose a given proportion of the observations, given normal distributions of observations about the mean on both axis.

Table 12. Similarities of the variable "mixes" of the factors being compared

Type of Variable	Number of Variables			
	Socioeconomic Status Factors	Stage in Life Cycle Factors	Racial Status Factors	Immigrant Status Factors
Variables with principal loadings in both studies	7	5	1	1
Variables with principal loading in national study but with other loading in Chicago study	4	0	0	0
Variables with principal loading in Chicago study but with other loading in national study	0	3	3	0
Variables with principal loading in national study but absent from Chicago study	1	3	5	4
Variables with principal loading in Chicago study but absent from national study	5	3	7	7

proportion of elderly communities; metropolitan Chicago contains a substantial portion of young ones. In comparing the factorial ecologies of some 35 American cities we were essentially assuming that the lengths of the factors being compared were essentially the same. Our examination of the spread of metropolitan communities in a common national space indicates that this assumption is partly correct and partly incorrect. In any study of a whole system of cities it would therefore be wise to determine how much variation between submetropolitan communities can be assigned to a between-metropolises component and how much to a within-metropolis component.

CONCLUSIONS

In this chapter we have examined some of the ways in which social scientists have approached the problem of dividing the internal area of the city into a series of internally homogeneous and externally heterogeneous sets of areal classes or regions. Some effort has been made to assess the

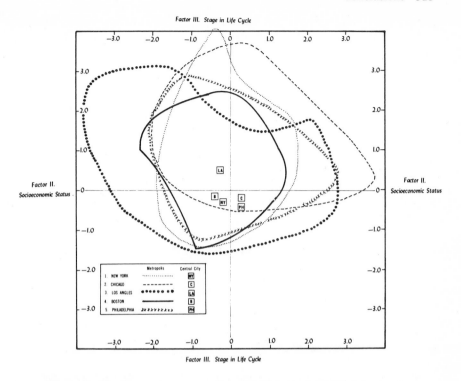

Figure 7 The largest five metropolises (1960) in national "social space."

success of such classifications in light of the principles of classification and regionalization about which there is general agreement.[71]

Early attempts at within-city classification (e.g., natural areas) were shown to be somewhat lacking in rigor. Social area analysis in the strict sense, though operationally simple and therefore attractive, was shown to have a number of drawbacks as a classificatory method. Some of these drawbacks were remedied by the employment of a further range of differentiating characteristics and the use of factor analysis to extract the principal dimensions from the extended variable set. Practitioners of this mode of analysis, which came to be called factorial ecology, tended to rest on their laurels once the principal dimensions had been extracted and did not pursue the analysis to its classificatory end. However, there was much ex-

[71] There is still some debate about the role of location in classification. Should it be included as simply another differentiating characteristic in any taxonomic analysis, or should it be accorded a special status as one of the constraints on an areal classification? For a discussion of these issues, see Peter J. Taylor, "The Location Variable in Taxonomy," *Geographical Analysis,* Vol. 1 (1969), pp. 181–195.

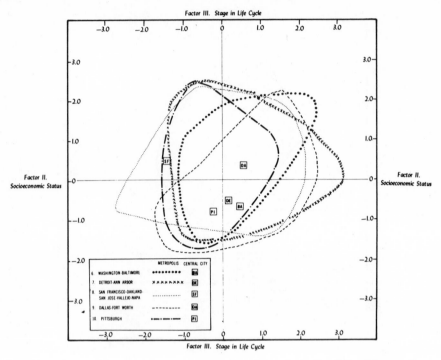

Figure 8 The second largest five metropolises (1960) in national "social space."

plicit concern with the spatial patterns of the principal social dimensions, and in further work (on which there was not space to report in this chapter) a beginning has been made on the development and testing of a theory of urban residential patterning. The transition of a field from purely classificatory analysis to work of a more causative nature marks the start of its adolescent phase.

Within-city classifications based on relational, rather than structural, characteristics were discussed all too briefly: more often than not they are part of a much broader and more involved analysis of a complex system (e.g., trade areas within the city), discussion of which was not possible here. Nothing was said concerning within-city classifications involving dynamic properties because the leap from cross-sectional to longitudinal studies has not been made.

Finally, some of the links were forged between the city and the nation (the United States), and the large American metropolis was shown to contain within its boundaries a major portion of the range of urban communities that characterize the nation as a whole.

APPENDIX A A Consolidated List of Social Area Analyses, Sensu Lato

Country	City[b]	Types of Analysis[a]				
		Social Area Analysis Sensu Stricto	Factor Analysis of Sensu Stricto Variables	Factorial Ecology	Cluster Analysis	Analysis Spatial Variance
United States	Akron		Van Arsdol (1957) Van Arsdol, Camilleri, and Schmid (1958)		McCannell (1957)	Anderson and Egeland (1961)
	Atlanta		Van Arsdol (1957) Van Arsdol, Camilleri, and Schmid (1958)		McCannell (1957)	
	Birmingham		Van Arsdol (1957) Van Arsdol, Camilleri, and Schmid (1958)	CUS (1958)[c]	McCannell (1957)	
	Boston			Sweetser (1961) (1962a), (1962b) (1965a), (1965b) (1968); Sweetser and Sweetser (1968)		
	Buffalo	Imse and Murphy (n.d.)		Salins (1969)		
	Canton			CUS (1969)[c]		

APPENDIX A   A Consolidated List of Social Area Analyses, Sensu Lato

Country	City[b]	Social Area Analysis Sensu Stricto	Factor Analysis of Sensu Stricto Variables	Factorial Ecology	Cluster Analysis	Analysis of Spatial Variance
United States (Continued)	Chicago	McElrath and Barkey (1964)	Kaufman (1961)	Berry and Tennant (1965) Rees (1968) and (forthcoming)		McElrath and Barkey (1964) Rees (1968)
	Cleveland	Moush, Scrivens, and Aresing (1960)		Bershers (1957) and (1959)		
	Columbus			CUS (1968)[c]		
	Dayton					Anderson and Egeland (1961)
	Fort Worth			CUS (1968)[c]		
	Gary			CUS (1968)[c]		
	Homestead			CUS (1968)[c]		
	Honolulu			CUS (1968)[c]		
	Indianapolis			Salins (1969)		Anderson and Egeland (1961)

Types of Analysis[a]

APPENDIX A   A Consolidated List of Social Area Analyses, Sensu Lato

Country	City	Social Area Analysis Sensu Stricto	Factor Analysis of Sensu Stricto Variables	Factorial Ecology	Cluster Analysis	Analysis of Spatial Variance
United States (Continued)	Kansas City		Van Arsdol (1954) Van Arsdol, Camilleri, and Schmid (1958)	Salins (1969)	McCannell (1957)	
	Los Angeles	Shevky and Williams (1949)	Bell (1952) and (1955)			
	Louisville		Van Arsdol (1954) Van Arsdol, Camilleri, and Schmid (1958)	CUS (1968)[c]	McCannell (1957)	
	Miami			CUS (1968)[c]		
	Milwaukee			Goodwin (forthcoming)		
	Minneapolis		Van Arsdol (1954) Van Arsdol, Camilleri, and Schmid (1958)		McCannell (1957)	
	Newark			Janson (1968)		
	New Haven			CUS (1968)[c]		
	New Orleans	Reeks (1953)				

Types of Analysis[a]

317

APPENDIX A   A Consolidated List of Social Area Analyses, Sensu Lato

Country	City	Social Area Analysis Sensu Stricto	Types of Analysis [a]			
			Factor Analysis of Sensu Stricto Variables	Factorial Ecology	Cluster Analysis	Analysis of Spatial Variance
United States (Continued)	New York City (1) Manhattan (2) Northern Bronx County and Westchester County (3) Harlem (4) Yonkers (5) Bronx County	Sullivan (1951)		Carey (1966) Greenburg (1968) CUS (1968)[c] CUS (1968)[c]		
	Omaha			CUS (1958)[c]		
	Portland		Van Arsdol (1957) Van Arsdol, Canilleri, and Schmid (1958)		McCannell (1957)	
	Providence		Van Arsdol (1957) Van Arsdol, Canilleri, and Schmid (1958)	CUS (1968)[c]	McCannell (1957)	
	Richmond			CUS (1968)[c]		
	Rochester		Van Arsdol (1957)		McCannell (1957)	

APPENDIX A A Consolidated List of Social Area Analyses, Sensu Lato

Country	City[b]	Social Area Analysis Sensu Stricto	Factor Analysis of Sensu Stricto Variables	Factorial Ecology	Cluster Analysis	Analysis of Spatial Variance
			Types of Analysis[a]			
United States (Continued)	Rockford			Pyle (forthcoming)		
	Sacramento			CUS (1968)[c]		
	St. Louis	Curtis, Avesing, and Klosek (1957)		CUS (1968)[c]		
	San Diego	Polk (1957) and (1957-58)		CUS (1968)[c]		
	San Francisco	Bell (1952) and (1953) Shevky and Bell (1955)	Bell (1952) and (1955)		Tyron (1955)	
	San Jose			CUS (1968)[c]		
	Seattle			Schmid and Tagashira (1964)		
	Shreveport			CUS (1968)[c]		
	Spokane			Salins (1969)		
	Syracuse			CUS (1968)[c]		Anderson and Egeland (1961)
	Tacoma			CUS (1968)[c]		

APPENDIX A   A Consolidated List of Social Area Analyses, Sensu Lato

Country	City[b]	Types of Analysis[a]				
		Social Area Analysis Sensu Stricto	Factor Analysis of Sensu Stricto Variables	Factorial Ecology	Cluster Analysis	Analysis of Spatial Variance
United States (Continued)	Toledo			Anderson and Bean (1951)		
	Worcester			CUS (1968)[c]		
	Washington, D.C.			Carey, Greenburg and Macomber (1958)		
Canada	Montreal			Greer-Wootten (1968) CUS (1968)[c]		
	Quebec	Gagnon (1960)				
	Toronto			Berry and Murdie (1965); Murdie (1969); Goheen (1970)		Murdie (1969)
	Winnipeg			Baxter (1968) Herbert (forthcoming)		
Britain	Barry			Giggs (forthcoming)		
	Cardiff			Herbert (1968a), (1968b), and (forthcoming)		

APPENDIX A A Consolidated List of Social Area Analyses, Sensu Lato

Country	City[b]	Types of Analysis[a]				
		Social Area Analysis Sensu Stricto	Factor Analysis of Sensu Stricto Variables	Factorial Ecology	Cluster Analysis	Analysis of Spatial Variance
Britain (Continued)	London			Gittus (1964) Cox (1968) and (1969); Norman (1969)		
	Luton			Timms (1965)		
	Merseyside			Gittus (1964) and (1965)		
	Newcastle-under-Lynne	Herbert (1967)				
	Swansea			Herbert (1968a) (1968b), and (forthcoming)		
	Sunderland			Robson (1966), (1967), and (forthcoming)		
Denmark	Copenhagen			Pedersen (1967a) and (1967b)		
Sweden	Stockholm and 15 other large Swedish cities			Janson (forthcoming)		

APPENDIX A A Consolidated List of Social Area Analyses, Sensu Lato

Country	City[b]	Types of Analysis[a]				
		Social Area Analysis Sensu Stricto	Factor Analysis of Sensu Stricto Variables	Factorial Ecology	Cluster Analysis	Analysis of Spatial Variance
Finland	Helsinki			Sweetser (1965a), (1965c), (1966), and (1968); Sweetser and Sweetser (1968)		
Italy	Rome	McElrath (1962)				
Egypt	Cairo			Abu-Lughod (1966) and (1968)		
Ghana	Accra	McElrath (1968) Clignet and Sween (1969)				
Ivory Coast	Abidjan	Clignet and Sween (1969)				
India	Calcutta			Berry and Rees (1969)		
	Hyderabad	Alam (1966)				
	Ahmadabad			Spodek and Berry (1969)		

APPENDIX A   A Consolidated List of Social Area Analyses, Sensu Lato

Country	City[b]	Types of Analysis[a]				
		Social Area Analysis Sensu Stricto	Factor Analysis of Sensu Stricto Variables	Factorial Ecology	Cluster Analysis	Analysis of Spatial Variance
India (Continued)	Bombay			Spodek and Berry (1969)		
	Madras			Spodek and Berry (1969)		
	Poona			Spodek and Berry (1969)		
	Sholapur			Spodek and Berry (1969)		
Brazil	Rio de Janeiro			Pyle and Morris (1969)		
Australia	Brisbane			Timms (forthcoming)		
	Canberra			Jones (1965)		
	Melbourne			Jones (1965)		

NOTES TO APPENDIX A

a. The types of analysis are defined as follows:

1. Social area analysis, _sensu stricto_: the type of analysis proposed by Shevky and outlined in Shevky and Bell (1955). Some _seven_ census variables are used to construct _three_ indices: social rank (economic status), urbanization (family status), and segregation (ethnic status). The terms in parentheses are Bell's, the preceding terms Shevky's.

2. Factor analysis of _sensu stricto_ variables: application of factor analysis to the census variables used by Shevky and Bell.

3. Factorial ecology: factor analysis of a wider set of socioeconomic variables.

4. Cluster analysis: a variant type of factor and grouping analysis proposed by Tryon.

5. Analysis of spatial variance: analysis of the variance of either Shevky-Bell indices or the dimensions of factorial ecology using a two-day design of sectors and concentric rings about the center of the city.

b. Studies are classified under the appropriate SMSA for 1960. For example, there are four studies listed under the N.Y. SMSA. Further consolidated on the basis of SCA's or on the basis of FEA's and CUR's (Berry, Goheen, and Goldstein [1968]).

c. CUS (1968): unpublished paper, Center for Urban Studies, University of Chicago, 1968; written by graduate student in the Urban Studies 371 Class.

d. The full citation of each study is given in Appendix B, A Bibliography of Social Area Analysis, _Sensu Lato_.

APPENDIX B   A Selected Bibliography of Social Area Analysis, Sensu Lato

Social Area Analysis, Sensu Stricto

Alam, Shah Manzoor. 1966. "Social Area Analysis of Metropolitan Hyderabad." Technical Bulletin No. 3, The Hyderabad Metropolitan Research Project (Hyderabad: Osmania University).
Bell, Wendell. 1952. "A Comparative Study in the Methodology of Urban Analysis" (unpublished Ph.D. dissertation, University of California at Los Angeles).
-----. 1953. "The Social Areas of the San Francisco Bay Region." American Sociological Review, Vol. 18, pp. 39-47.
-----. 1959. "Social Areas: Typology of Urban Neighborhoods." Community Structure and Analysis, edited by Marvin B. Sussman (New York: Thomas Y. Crowell Company).
Clignet, Remi and Sween, Joyce. 1969. "Accra and Abidjan: A Comparative Examination of the Theory of the Increase in Scale," Urban Affairs Quarterly, Vol. 4, pp. 297-324.
Curtis, Jack H., Avesing, Frank, and Klosek, Ignatius. 1967. "Urban Parishes as Social Areas," The American Catholic Sociological Review, Vol. 18, pp. 319-325.
Gagnon, Gabriel. 1960. "Les Zones Sociales de l'Agglomeration de Quebec," Recherches Sociographiques, Vol. 1, pp. 255-267.
Greer, Scott. 1960. "Bibliography of Social Area Analysis" (Department of Sociology, Northwestern University).
Herbert, D. T. 1967a. "Social Area Analysis: A British Study," Urban Studies, Vol. 4, pp. 41-60.
-----. 1967b. "The Use of Diagnostic Variables in the Analysis of Urban Structure," Tijdschrift voor Economische en Sociale Geografie, Vol. 48, pp. 5-10.
Imse, Thomas and Murphy, Austin. n.d. "Social Area Analysis." Metropolitan Buffalo Analysis. Buffalo Redevelopment Foundation, Inc.
McElrath, Dennis. 1962. "The Social Areas of Rome: A Comparative Analysis." American Sociological Review, Vol. 27, pp. 376-391.
-----. 1968. "Social Change and Urban Social Differentiation: Accra, Ghana." The New Urbanization. Edited by Scott Greer (New York: St. Martin's Press).
McElrath, Dennis and Barkey, John W. 1964. "Social and Physical Space: Models of Metropolitan Differentiation" (unpublished paper, Department of Sociology, Northwestern University).
Moush, Edward, Scrivens, J., and Avesing, F. 1960. "Social Area Analysis of Cleveland and Metropolitan Area, 1950." Le Play Research, Inc.
Polk, Kenneth. 1957. "The Social Areas of San Diego" (unpublished M.A. dissertation, Northwestern University).
-----. 1957-1958. "Juvenile Delinquency and Social Areas," Social Problems, Vol. 5, pp. 214-217.
Reeks, Olive. 1953. "The Social Areas of New Orleans" (unpublished M.A. dissertation, University of California at Los Angeles).
Shevky, Eshref and Bell, Wendell. 1955. Social Area Analysis: Theory, Illustrative Applications and Computational Procedures (Stanford: Stanford University Press).
Shevky, Eshref and Williams, Marianne. 1949. The Social Area of Los Angeles: Analysis and Typology (Berkeley and Los Angeles: University of California Press).
Sullivan, Terrance. 1961. "The Application of Shevky-Bell Indices to Parish Analysis." American Catholic Sociological Review, Vol 22, No. 2, pp. 168-171.
Udry, J. R. 1964. "Increasing Scale and Spatial Differentiation: New Tests of Two Theories from Shevky and Bell." Social Forces, Vol. 42, pp. 403-413.

APPENDIX B A Selected Bibliography of Social Area Analysis, Sensu Lato

Criticism of and Comment on Social Area Analysis

Bell, Wendell. 1955. "Reply to Duncan's Comments on Social Area Analysis." American Journal of Sociology, Vol. 61, pp. 260-262.
Bell, Wendell and Greer, Scott. 1962. "Social Area Analysis and Its Critics," Pacific Sociological Review, Vol. 5, pp. 3-9.
Bell, Wendell and Moskos, Charles C. Jr. 1964. "A Comment on Udry's Increasing Scale and Spatial Differentiation," Social Forces, Vol. 42, pp. 414-417.
Duncan, Otis Dudley. 1955. Untitled review of Social Area Analysis by Eshref Shevky and Wendell Bell. American Journal of Sociology, Vol. 61, pp. 84-85.
Hawley, Amos and Duncan, Otis Dudley. 1957. "Social Area Analysis: A Critical Appraisal," Land Economics, Vol. 33, pp. 337-345.
Schnore, Leo F. 1962. "Another Comment on Social Area Analysis," Pacific Sociological Review, Vol. 5, pp. 13-16.
Tiebout, Charles M. 1958. "Hawley and Duncan on Social Area Analysis: A Comment," Land Economics, Vol. 34, pp. 182-184.

Behavioral Studies Using a Social Area Framework

Bell, Wendell. 1956. "Social Structure and Participation in Different Types of Formal Associations," Social Forces, Vol. 34, pp. 345-350.
-----. 1957. "Anomie, Social Isolation and the Class Structure," Sociometry, Vol. 20, pp. 105-116.
-----. 1958. "The Utility of the Shevky Typology for the Design of Urban Sub-area Field Studies." Journal of Social Psychology, Vol. 47, pp.71-83.
-----. 1965. "Urban Neighborhoods and Individual Behavior," Problems of Youth, edited by Muzafer Sherif and Carolyn Sherif (Chicago: Aldine Press).
Bell, Wendell and Boat, Marion. 1957. "Urban Neighborhoods and Informal Social Relations," American Journal of Sociology, Vol.62, pp. 391-398.
Bell, Wendell and Force, Maryanne. 1956. "Urban Neighborhood Types and Participation in Formal Associations," American Sociological Review, Vol. 21, pp. 23-33.
Cox, Kevin R. 1968. "Suburbia and Voting Behavior in the London Metropolitan Area," Annals of the Association of American Geographers, Vol. 58, pp. 111-127.
Feldman, Arnold S. and Tilly, Charles. 1960. "The Interaction of Social and Physical Space." American Sociological Review, Vol. 25, pp. 877-883.
Greer, Scott A. 1962. The Emerging City (New York: The Free Press).
Greer, Scott A. and Kube, Ella. 1959. "Urbanism and Social Structure: A Los Angeles Study," Community Science and Analysis, edited by Marvin B. Sussman (New York: Thomas Y. Crowell).
Polk, Kenneth. 1957-1958. "Juvenile Delinquency and Social Areas," Social Problems, Vol. 5, pp. 214-217.

Factor Analyses of Sensu Stricto Variables

Bell, Wendell. 1952. "A Comparative Study in the Methodology of Urban Analysis" (unpublished Ph.D. dissertation, University of California at Los Angeles).
-----. 1955. "Economic, Family and Ethnic Status: An Empirical Test," American Sociological Review, Vol. 20, pp. 45-52.
Kaufman, Walter. 1961. "Social Area Analysis: An Explication of Theory, Methodology and Techniques, with Statistical Tests of Revised Procedures, San Francisco and Chicago, 1950" (unpublished Ph.D. dissertation, Northwestern University).
Van Arsdol, Maurice. 1957. "An Empirical Evaluation of Social Area

APPENDIX B   A Selected Bibliography of Social Area Analysis, Sensu Lato

Analysis in Human Ecology" (unpublished Ph.D. dissertation, University of Washington).

Van Arsdol, Maurice, Camilleri, Santo F., and Schmid, Calvin F. 1958a. "The Generality of Urban Social Area Indices," American Sociological Review, Vol. 23, pp. 277-284.

————. 1958b. "An Application of the Shevky Social Area Indexes to a Model of Urban Society," Social Forces, Vol. 37, pp. 26-32.

————. 1961. "An Investigation of the Utility of Urban Typology," Pacific Sociological Review, Vol. 4, pp. 26-32.

————. 1962. "Further Comments on the Utility of Urban Typology," Pacific Sociological Review, Vol. 5, pp. 9-13.

Van Arsdol, Maurice, Camilleri, Santo F., Schmid, Calvin F., and McCannell, Earle H. 1958. "Methods of Differentiating Urban Social and Demographic Areas," Papers Presented at the Census Tract Conference, Dec. 29, 1958 (Washington, D.C.: U.S. Department of Commerce, 1959, pp. 1-10).

Factorial Ecology

Abu-Lughod, Janet. 1966. "The Ecology of Cairo, Egypt: A Comparative Study Using Factor Analysis" (unpublished Ph.D. dissertation, University of Massachusetts, Amherst).

————. 1968. "A Critical Test for the Theory of Social Area Analysis: the Factorial Ecology of Cairo, Egypt" (unpublished paper, Department of Sociology, Northwestern University).

Anderson, T. R. and Bean, L. L. 1961. "The Shevky-Bell Social Areas: Confirmation of Results and Reinterpretation," Social Forces, Vol. 40, pp. 119-124.

Baxter, Richard. 1968. "The Factorial Ecology of Winnipeg." Paper presented to the Annual Meeting of the Canadian Association of Geographers, Calgary.

Berry, Brian J.L. and Murdie, Robert A. 1965. Socioeconomic Correlates of Housing Condition (Toronto: Metropolitan Planning Board).

Berry, Brian J.L. and Rees, Philip H. 1969. "The Factorial Ecology of Calcutta," American Journal of Sociology, Vol. 74, pp. 445-491.

Berry, Brian J.L. and Tennant, Robert J. 1965. "Socioeconomic Classification of Municipalities in Northeastern Illinois Metropolitan Area," Commercial Structure (Chicago: Northeastern Illinois Metropolitan Area Planning Commission).

Beshers, J. 1957. "Census Tract Data and Social Structure: A Methodological Analysis" (unpublished Ph.D. dissertation, University of North Carolina).

————. 1959. "The Construction of 'Social Area' Indices: an Evaluation of Procedures," Proceedings of the Social Statistics Section (American Statistical Association, Washington, D.C.), pp. 65-70.

Carey, George W. 1966. "The Regional Interpretation of Population and Housing Patterns in Manhattan through Factor Analysis," Geographical Review, Vol. 46, pp. 551-569.

Carey, George W., Macomber, Lenore, and Greenburg, Michael. 1968. "Educational and Demographic Factors in the Urban Geography of Washington, D.C.," Geographical Review, Vol. 48, pp. 515-537.

Cox, Kevin R. 1968. "Suburbia and Voting Behavior in the London Metropolitan Area," Annals of the Association of American Geographers, Vol. 58, pp. 111-127. A revised version of this paper appears as "Voting in the London Suburbs: A Factor Analysis and a Causal Model," Chapter 13, Quantitative Ecological Analysis in the Social Sciences, edited by Mattei Dogan and Stein Rokkan (Cambridge: The M.I.T. Press, 1969), pp. 343-369.

Giggs, J. A. Forthcoming. "Socially Disorganized Areas in Barry: A Multivariate Analysis," Urban Essays: Studies in the Geography of

APPENDIX B A Selected Bibliography of Social Area Analysis, Sensu Lato

Wales, edited by Harold Carter and Wayne K.D. Davies.

Gittus, Elizabeth. 1964. "The Structure of Urban Areas," Town Planning Review, Vol. 35, pp. 5-20.

-----. 1965. "An Experiment in the Definition of Urban Sub-Areas," Transactions of the Bartlett Society, Vol. 2, pp. 109-135.

Goheen, Peter. 1970. The North American Industrial City in the Late Nineteenth Century: the Case of Toronto (Chicago: University of Chicago Press).

Greenburg, Michael. 1968. "An Analysis of Socioeconomic, Housing and Mobility Patterns in Westchester County and in Northern Bronx County through Factor Analysis" (unpublished M.A. dissertation, Faculty of Political Science, Columbia University).

Greer-Wootten, Bryn. 1968. "Cross-sectional Social Area Analysis: Montreal, 1951-1961" (unpublished paper, Department of Geography, McGill University).

Herbert, David T. 1968a. "The Use of Diagnostic Variables in the Analysis of Urban Structure," Tijdschrift Voor Economische en Sociale Geografie, Vol. 58, pp. 5-10.

-----. 1968b. "Principal Components Analysis and British Studies of Urban-Social Structure," Professional Geographer, Vol. 20, pp. 280-283.

-----. Forthcoming. "Principal Components Analysis and Urban Social Structure: A Study of Cardiff and Swansea," Urban Essays: Studies in the Geography of Wales, edited by Harold Carter and Wayne K.D. Davies.

Herbert, David T. and Williams, W. M. 1964. "Some New Techniques for Studying Urban Sub-Divisions," Applied Geography II, Geographica Polonica 3, Warsaw, pp. 93-117.

Janson, Carl-Gunnar. 1968. "The Spatial Structure of Newark, New Jersey; Part I: The Central City," Acta Sociologica, Vol. 11, pp. 144-169.

-----. 1969. "Some Problems of Ecological Factor Analysis," Quantitative Ecological Analysis in the Social Sciences, edited by Mattei Dogan and Stein Rokkan (Cambridge, Mass.: The M.I.T. Press, 1969), pp. 301-341.

Jones, F. Lancaster. 1965. "A Social Profile of Canberra, 1961." Australian and New Zealand Journal of Sociology, Vol. 1, pp. 107-120.

-----. 1968. "Social Area Analysis: Some Theoretical and Methodological Comments Illustrated with Australian Data," British Journal of Sociology, Vol. 14, pp. 424-444.

Murdie, Robert A. 1968. The Factorial Ecology of Metropolitan Toronto, 1951-1961: An Essay on the Social Geography of the City (Department of Geography, Research Paper No. 116; Chicago: University of Chicago.

Norman, Peter. 1969. "Third Survey of London Life and Labor: A New Typology of London Districts," Quantitative Ecological Analysis in the Social Sciences, edited by Mattei Dogan and Stein Rokkan (Cambridge, Mass.: The M.I.T. Press), pp. 371-396.

Pedersen, Poul O. 1967a. Modeller for Befolkningstruktur og Befolkningsudvikling i Stoveryomrader Specielt med Henblik pra Storkobenhavn (Copenhagen: State Urban Planning Institute).

-----. 1967b. "An Empirical Model of Urban Population Structure: A Factor Analytic Study of the Population Structure in Copenhagen," Proceedings of the First Scandinavian-Polish Regional Science Seminar (Warsawa: Polish Scientific Publishers).

Pyle, Gerald F. Forthcoming. "A Factorial Ecology of Rockford, 1960," Proceedings of the Illinois State Academy of Sciences.

Pyle, Gerald F. and Morris, Fred B. 1969. "The Factorial Ecology of Rio de Janeiro" (unpublished paper, Center for Urban Studies, University of Chicago).

Rees, Philip H. 1970. "The Factorial Ecology of Metropolitan Chicago,

APPENDIX B   A Selected Bibliography of Social Area Analysis, Sensu Lato

1960," in Brian J.L. Berry and Frank L. Horton's Geographic Perspectives on Urban Systems (Englewood Cliffs, N.J.: Prentice-Hall, Inc.).

Robson, Brian T. 1966. "Multivariate Analysis of Urban Areas." Institute of British Geographers Study Group in Urban Geography, Proceedings, pp. 1-14.

-----. 1969. The Social Ecology of Sunderland (Cambridge: Cambridge University Press).

Salins, Peter D. 1969. "Household Location Patterns in Selected American Metropolitan Areas" (unpublished Ph.D. dissertation, University of Syracuse).

Schmid, Calvin F. and Tagashira, Kiyoshi. 1964. "Ecological and Demographic Indices: A Methodological Analysis," Demography, Vol. 1, pp. 194-211.

Spodek, Howard and Berry, Brian J.L. 1969. "The Ecological Structure of Indian Cities" (unpublished paper, Center for Urban Studies, University of Chicago).

Sweetser, Frank L. 1961. The Social Ecology of Metropolitan Boston, 1950 (Boston: Massachusetts Department of Mental Health).

-----. 1962a. The Social Ecology of Metropolitan Boston, 1960. (Boston: Massachusetts Department of Mental Health).

-----. 1962b. Patterns of Change in the Social Ecology of Metropolitan Boston, 1950-60 (Boston: Massachusetts Department of Mental Health).

-----. 1965a. "Factor Structure as Ecological Structure in Helsinki and Boston," Acta Sociologica, Vol. 8, pp. 205-225.

-----. 1965b. "Factorial Ecology: Zonal Differentiation in Metropolitan Boston, 1960," Paper presented at the Population Association of America Annual Meeting, Chicago.

-----. 1965c. "Factorial Ecology: Helsinki, 1960," Demography, Vol. 2, pp. 372-386.

-----. 1966. "Ekologisk Differentiering i Helsingfors Ar 1960," Helsinki City Statistical Monthly Review, Vol. 17, pp. 17-18.

-----. 1969. "Ecological Factors in Metropolitan Zones and Sectors," Quantitative Ecological Analysis in the Social Sciences, edited by Mattei Dogan and Stein Rokkan (Cambridge: M.I.T. Press), pp. 413-456.

Sweetser, Frank L. and Sweetser, Dorrian Apple. 1968. "Social Class and Single-Family Housing: Helsinki and Boston," Urbanism in World Perspective: A Reader, edited by Sylvia Fleis Fava (New York: Thomas Y. Crowell Company).

Timms, D.W. G. 1965. "The Spatial Distribution of Social Deviants in Luton, England," Australian and New Zealand Journal of Sociology, Vol. 1, pp. 38-52.

-----. Forthcoming. Social Area Analysis in Brisbane (Brisbane: University of Queensland Press).

Cluster Analysis

McCannell, Earle. 1957. "An Application of Urban Typology by Cluster Analysis to the Ecology of Ten Cities" (unpublished Ph.D. dissertation, University of Washington, Seattle).

Tryon, Robert C. 1939. Cluster Analysis: Correlation Profile and Orthometric Analysis for the Isolation of Unities in Mind and Personality (Ann Arbor: Edwards Brothers Press).

-----. 1955. Identification of Social Areas by Cluster Analysis: A General Method with an Application to the San Francisco Bay Area (Berkeley: University of California Press).

Analysis of the Spatial Variance of Social Area Dimensions

Anderson, Theodore R. and Egeland, Janice A. 1961. "Spatial Aspects of Social Area Analysis," American Sociological Review, Vol. 26, pp. 392-398.

APPENDIX B A Selected Bibliography of Social Area Analysis, Sensu Lato

Berry, Brian J.L. 1965. "The Internal Structure of the City," Law and
Contemporary Problems, Vol. 30, pp. 111-119.

McElrath, Dennis C. and Barkey, John W. 1964. "Social and Physical Space:
Models of Metropolitan Differentiation" (unpublished paper, Department of Sociology, Northwestern University).

Murdie, Robert A. 1968. The Factorial Ecology of Metropolitan Toronto,
1951-1961: An Essay on the Social Geography of the City (Department
of Geography, Research Paper No. 116; Chicago: University of Chicago).

Rees, Philip H. 1970. "The Factorial Ecology of Metropolitan Chicago,
1960" in Brian J.L. Berry and Frank L. Horton's Geographic Perspectives on Urban Systems (Englewood Cliffs, N.J.: Prentice-Hall, Inc.).

Salins, Peter D. 1969. "Household Location Patterns in Selected American
Metropolitan Areas" (unpublished Ph.D. dissertation, University of
Syracuse).

CHAPTER 11

Critical Evaluation of the Principles
of City Classification

ROBERT R. ALFORD

New York University

This chapter evaluates some assumptions underlying factor analyses of city characteristics and assesses their utility in creating city classifications. It takes as its starting point Berry's chapter in this volume (chapter 1), which is typical of most of the literature. First, the principles and assumptions underlying the factor analyses of cities are critically analyzed. Second, the empirical relationships of six selected variables with some other variables are presented. The chapter ends with some suggestions of a wider range of characteristics that should be taken into account in city classification, not only for studies within the United States but also for cross-national studies.

We assume (a) that the goal of both the social scientist and the policymaker is ultimately to discover the causes and consequences of observed characteristics of cities, not simply to find correlates, and (b) that generalizations about correlations contain causal theories, implicit or explicit. Correlations or clusters of associated characteristics related to some postulated underlying common "factor" are regarded by the social scientist as having some causal significance, rather than being accidentally or spuriously related to each other, even if the specific causal processes are difficult to discover. Similarly we assume that the policymaker is not interested in aggregations of causally unrelated data, no matter how closely correlated, but that he wants to discover critical developmental or causal sequences of events and processes, particularly those that he has some chance to influence.

THE ASSUMPTIONS OF FACTOR ANALYSIS

Factor analyses of cities suffer from a number of arbitrary research decisions. These arbitrary decisions concern (a) the unit of analysis, (b) the particular cases selected, (c) the attributes or variables chosen for inclusion, and (d) the factor names that are assigned. As a consequence causes and effects cannot be distinguished, and it is extremely difficult to know what the resulting data summaries mean, for either scientific or policymaking purposes.

The meaning of the "city" as the unit of analysis can be questioned, except as a convenient unit for the collection of data. Even though the proportion of the labor force in manufacturing may be the same in two cities —one in a highly industrialized country and the other in a basically agrarian society—the meaning of these particular statistics may be highly dependent on national contexts. The same point is true within a single country for regions that differ in their histories, economic development, and political traditions. We tend to assume that nations and cities are entities that can be regarded as homogeneous for the purpose of collecting and interpreting statistical data.

Cities are not fixed entities. The problem with using data based on a population within given city boundaries at a given point in time is that these are subject to change, and this change is related to factors outside the range of variables usually included in the factor analyses. Failure to annex, for example, is related to a low level of "professionalism" in city government, as Dye has shown, for cities with city managers are more likely to annex surrounding territory than cities without city managers.[1] Thus many of the basic city characteristics that are measured and form the basis of city classifications are themselves "dependent variables," not merely independent ones. Such complex interrelated causes and consequences are to be expected, but they call into question the implicit assumption of the factor analysts that they are dealing with a fair sample of those city characteristics which are somehow "basic," or "underlying," and which form the basis for deriving city types that predict other characteristics, such as public policies.

There is no explicit rationale for the selection of the particular "population" of the cities included—those with over 10,000 inhabitants in the case of Berry's study. Why is size used as a sampling frame? Why choose only American cities? Why deal with the entire United States, rather than

[1] Thomas R. Dye, "Urban Political Integration: Conditions Associated with Annexation in American Cities," *Midwest Journal of Political Science,* Vol. 8 (1964), p. 445.

a region? These initial selection procedures are justifiable on the grounds of convenience, the availability of data, and as a starting point for analysis, but they involve theoretical assumptions and consequences that are not made explicit.

The purpose for which a classification of cities is devised should determine not only the selection of a unit of analysis and the particular set of those units but also the choice of data that are collected and summarized about those units. Berry makes the same point at the beginning of Chapter 1, but he fails to consider its relevance to the selection of the 97 primary variables included in his factor analysis. In fact no criteria for the inclusion of those 97 primary variables are presented. The result is that the factor structure that is produced necessarily reflects the nature of the input data, which refer primarily to the characteristics of the population, labor force, economic base, income, and a variety of demographic indicators.

It is impossible to assess whether or not the high correlations that produce identifiable factors are the result of both causes and consequences being included in the data matrix. Low education can be regarded as a cause of unemployment (Berry's factor 2). Population growth, or lack thereof, influences the age structure of a city (Berry's factor 3). Heavy outmigration causes a high vacancy rate (Berry's factor 5). Each of these pairs of items loads on the same factor. These causal interpretations may or may not be accurate, but the point is that there is nothing in the factor analysis that allows one causal interpretation to be chosen over another. In fact it could be argued that the factor analysis prevents *any* causal inferences, because it artificially lumps some variables under one factor and others under another factor in a manner that exaggerates their independence and makes it difficult to analyze their relationships.

The arbitrary inclusion of some measures and not others actually determines the contours of the factor structure. For example, in their study of British towns Moser and Scott did not include many variables closely related to population size, and therefore they did not find a factor that they labeled "size."[2] They note as a "finding" that few of their characteristics were correlated with population size, which is true, except that it is an artifact of the decision not to include variables correlated with size in the first place. Berry finds a size factor, because he includes a number of labor-force characteristics highly correlated with size, as well as the size of the city counted twice, 5 years apart. Given the arbitrariness of the selection

---

[2] See C. A. Moser and Wolf Scott, *British Towns* (Edinburgh and London: Oliver and Boyd, 1961).

of variables, the factor structure is determined by the selection of certain variables and not others.

Furthermore, there is no consistency from study to study in the variables included. Even if the initial selection were entirely arbitrary, one could begin to compare the patterns if the same type of selection rules were followed in different studies. The array picked by Moser and Scott, however, is, as already indicated, quite different from that picked by Berry. Moser and Scott included voting turnout and Labor party voting, which Berry did not, and they excluded a number of size-related characteristics. Certain data are easier to obtain and code than others, but this is not an adequate justification, particularly when no attempt is made to assess the consequences of the selection.

These points about the arbitrary selection of variables for inclusion are highly important and cannot simply be answered by saying that "We have to start somewhere, and we might as well start with the conveniently available measures." For one thing, the data that are conveniently available may be seriously biased because of the interests of the groups that influenced the original gathering of the data. Political influences on the content of the U.S. census are well known; the best example is the exclusion of religious questions. But the interests of political leaders in avoiding controversy and the ability of corporate and academic interests to influence government agencies to collect certain kinds of data and not others may produce available data that are seriously biased and hence make difficult the study of certain problems.

Once the units of analysis are defined and data on them are gathered and summarized, they must be interpreted. The factor analyses almost always label the clusters of variables that are isolated by the statistical procedure by the name of the variable or variables most closely associated with that factor ("size," "social class," "nonwhite composition," and so forth). But then the analysis usually stops, with the presentation of a list of the units of analysis by their "loading" on the factor. No attempt is made to assess any further the meaning of the data or the consequences of the initial research decisions to select the unit of analysis. At most the factor-analysis procedure is repeated for subsets of data—cities within different regions, central cities and suburbs, large and small cities—but, aside from noting differences and similarities in the factor structure, nothing more is said.

This procedure is unsatisfactory for both scientific and policy concerns. No problems are defined, for either scholarly or public purposes. Data can be analyzed from many points of view, and there is no single classification of cities that will serve all purposes. Factor analyses purport to isolate independent factors: the underlying dimensions of cities that are *not* correlated with each other. The other side of the coin, however, would seem to be just as important: what are the aspects that *are* correlated with each other?

On the one hand, the factor analysts assume that all data can be treated as if they refer to phenomena operating at the same "level"—the city as a whole—and therefore implicitly assume that the city as a single entity is a meaningful whole, in some sense that is left unspecified. On the other hand, the factor analyses isolate *independent* dimensions of that single entity, which implicitly assumes that the single entity contains major subsystems that have causal independence.

Their findings, in other words, create the presumption that the causes and consequences of the factors, once they are found and labeled "population size," "socioeconomic status," "nonwhite population," "manufacturing level," and so forth, are independent of each other. The two sets of implicit assumptions seem to be a bit contradictory. A single system about which data can legitimately be gathered is postulated at the beginning of the investigation, but several independent subsystems are discovered at the time of interpreting the data. At the very least, the various assumptions should be confronted with some explicit set of data-based inferences and interpretations. It is possible, for example, that neither the causes nor the consequences of the observed correlations are associated with the city as a territorial aggregate of persons. If we are concerned with estimating causal processes, we must be concerned with the relevance of the unit of analysis, the sample of units, the variables measured, and the interpretation of the data. The factor analyses of cities have seldom been concerned with the theoretical criteria for making any of these critical research decisions.

These comments are not intended to call into question the usefulness of factor analysis as a device for reducing a complex and large body of data about some phenomenon or unit of analysis to a smaller number of independent dimensions that form the main empirical indices of independent variables for subsequent analyses. This procedure, however, cannot serve as both the beginning and the end of analysis, starting with unquestioned arrays of input characteristics and ending with unexamined labels for the output factors. Nor, in all fairness, did Berry intend Chapter 1 to be so.

USES OF CITY CLASSIFICATIONS BY POLICYMAKERS AND SOCIAL SCIENTISTS

The uses of city classifications by policymakers and social scientists are influenced by several characteristics of the statistical procedures of factor analysis: the inclusion of socioeconomic, but not political, variables; the assumption that the city as a single entity is the unit of analysis; and the assumption that the resulting factors constitute an adequate array of independent variables for further analysis. These assumptions and procedures may reduce the usefulness of the resulting classifications, especially for the policymaker. These points are expanded in this section.

Although we cannot here suggest the full range of additional possibilities, a few questions of potential interest to policymakers as well as social scientists can be offered and illustrated with empirical data:

1. What is the city's *political culture:* its party allegiances, its voting turnout, the norms and values of leaders and voters? What characteristics of a city seem to be conducive to the formation and change of a political culture? What leeways and constraints on the actions of local leadership are created by the historical commitments of the city to certain ways of making decisions?

2. What is its *political structure:* form of government, degree of partisanship, size of the city bureaucracy, the powers of the city and of agencies within it?

3. What are the actual *policies* of the city toward the performance of essential services, annexation, the innovation of new services, obtaining federal aid, the establishment of bureaucratic agencies of government? How much relationship is there between policies in one area and in another regarding the scope of activity, the professionalization of the staff, and the level of commitment?

4. What are the characteristics of the city's *political and socioeconomic environment:* the political complexion of the surrounding cities or suburbs, of the state in which it is located, or of its region? The amount of influence that the city can have over its own fate may be heavily determined by how much potential power it can exert in affecting practices and policies in the metropolitan area or in the state.

5. What are the relationships of the political culture, the policies, and the environment of the city to the basic socioeconomic dimensions isolated by factor analysis?

These additional dimensions of cities are mentioned for two reasons: (a) to suggest that typologies should take into account a far broader range of characteristics than they have so far and (b) to suggest specific political dimensions that may have at least as much relevance to urban policymakers as the economic and demographic characteristics forming the basic data used so far.

Since there is no acknowledged differentiation between independent and dependent variables in the initial choice of variables for a factor analysis, there is no reason for either including or excluding *any* city characteristic and, in particular, no reason for restricting the data to population, demographic, and socioeconomic characteristics. If factor analysis is seen as a statistical procedure for reducing a complex set of interrelated variables to a set of underlying dimensions, then ideally the widest range of characteristics should be included in the initial set. There is no logical reason for excluding public policies, political structure, or features of the political, economic, and social environment of the city, unless the presumption is made that population and economic characteristics are causally prior to political and environmental factors, and that the former types of variables constitute an adequate sample of all possible independent variables. Plausible theoretical arguments could be constructed on behalf of a wide variety of variables as being causally important, and in attempting to arrive at basic classifications of cities it seems crucial to avoid loading the empirical dice in favor of any particular theory. The variables chosen for inclusion in a factor analysis are chosen either because they fit into a logical theory about the causes and consequences of city development and character or else more or less randomly on the basis of data availability. In the former instance it becomes important to see how the isolated dimensions or factors are associated with widely different types of characteristics. In the latter case it is important to consider all possible empirical variables.

One assumption that is usually implicit in most city classifications is that the "city" as a single entity is the unit of analysis. This assumption must, at the very least, be regarded as empirically problematic. A city can be regarded as an aggregate of individuals, groups, organizations, and institutions—an aggregate that is extremely loosely integrated, perhaps to the point where predictions about the behavior of one "part" of the city are not at all easy to make from knowledge of another part. Whether or not the zoning board of appeals tends to approve side-yard variances may not be predictable from knowledge of the number of poor families in the city. Whether the mayor has veto powers over council actions may not be predictable from knowledge of the scope of activity of the city planning commission. These points may seem to be obvious, but their implications are far from self-evident in considering the principles of city classification, particularly from the policymakers' point of view. To put the point abstractly, classifications of cities based on data and comparisons drawn from the "micro" characteristics of the city—the behavior of the zoning board, the behavior of the mayor—are as legitimate as those based on "macro" characteristics—such as the number of poor families and the rate of city growth. The purpose of the investigation must dictate the phenomena being compared, and the empirical data taken into account must be determined by the theoretical criteria and expectations of the causes and consequences of the phenomena. This "subsystem" problem is important to both the social scientist and the policymaker. The degree of autonomous causation among the developments occurring in one geographic segment of the city (or one organization, one government agency, one social group, one neighborhood) influences whether or not the city can be regarded for purposes of classification as a single entity, to be described by a single set of characteristics, or as an aggregate of diverse parts.

The urban policymaker ordinarily wants to know about the causes and consequences of city characteristics about which he can or cannot *do* something—not abstract correlations which may explain much of the economic, political, and social variations among cities, but about which no conceivable coalition of administrative or political leadership could do anything. This point has a number of implications for the construction and uses of city classifications. If the basic factors that consistently turn up in the factor analyses—size, metropolitan location, economic base, ethnic and religious composition, regional and state location (the characteristics that account for most of the variations among cities)—are for all practical purposes unchangeable, at least by local policymakers, then the policymakers have little use for them except insofar as they now know about important factors that they *cannot* change. Typologies that are to be useful to the policymaker must "hold constant" those basic characteristics that he must regard as permanent or given—"parameters" or external conditions. In other words, what will be useful to him will be studies of regular patterns of interrelationships *within* major city types (however ultimately arrived at): small and large, industrial and nonindustrial, racially and ethnically homogeneous or heterogeneous, suburbs and central cities, old and physically dilapidated versus new cities.

Despite these critical comments on the character of the factor analyses of cities, if we accept their limitation to population and labor-force data, it is still possible to regard the underlying dimensions uncovered by those procedures as important variables—even if not necessarily the ultimately desirable classification—and to use them for further analysis, by studying the relationship of these key dimensions to quite different city characteristics. In the remainder of this chapter we present some data linking the socioeconomic dimensions of cities uncovered by factor analyses with certain dimensions of the political environment, political structure, and political cultures of American cities. Our concern here is basically methodological and evaluative, not substantive.

SOCIOECONOMIC CHARACTERISTICS OF CITIES

Most factor analyses stop short after isolating the underlying factors that statistically account for the most variance in the data, and after the factors have been named, almost always according to the items that are correlated most highly with the factors. This procedure, however, leaves aside a central question: What do the results mean? What does the factor name tell us in addition to the meaning inherent in the empirical content of the principal items? This question logically follows the prior question concerning the scope of the data to be included in the statistical analysis, but neglect of this question is related to neglect of the first, since both have to do with theoretical issues surrounding the selection of data and their interpretation.

We cannot here offer an alternative theoretical framework that could lead to a different classification system. As a compromise, let us take as given the data and the major factors that have emerged from existing studies and consider their implications. For purposes of illustration we use six items identified with six principal factors in the factor analysis by Berry in Chapter 1. Table 1 shows the intercorrelations of these items, together with the number of the factor to which they are most closely related, and the correlation of the item with the factor. In three of the cases the items are those loading most highly on the factor (size, median income, and nonwhite population), in two cases second highest (foreign stock, labor force in manufacturing), and in one case fifth (migration). Data were chosen in order to allow maximum comparability with other data available to the author.

The major purpose of factor analysis is to discover the *independent* underlying dimensions that account for a given set of correlations of observed characteristics. As Berry puts it, "the redundancies of overlapping variables have been eliminated by factor analysis." Table 1 shows that in fact some of the principal items (not the factors) are fairly closely related to each other. The indicator of migration is correlated .53 with an indicator of manufacturing. Heavily nonwhite cities are less likely to have a high proportion of persons with foreign parentage than cities with few nonwhites (.49), and so forth. Some correlations are indeed low or nonexistent; for example, large cities are not more likely than small ones to have a high proportion of the labor force engaged in manufacturing.

The results of factor analysis are thus "factors" that can only be used as independent variables—postulated causes—at least in relation to any of the items composing the original matrix, because by definition the factors

Table 1. Intercorrelations of selected principal items loading on six different factors—675 American cities with over 25,000 inhabitants in 1960

Factor	Item	Correlations with the Factor	Size	Median Income	Non-white	Foreign Stock	Migrant	Manu-facturing
1	Population size	.97	--	-.12	.33	.02	-.16	-.06
2	Median income of families	.88		--	-.48	.40	.07	.21
4	Per cent of population that is non-white (natural logarithm)	.85			--	-.49	-.02	-.28
7	Per cent of native population of foreign or mixed parentage (foreign stock)	.76				--	-.34	.38
5	Per cent of persons five years old and over who were migrants from one country to another between 1955 and 1960	.57					--	-.53
9	Per cent of the labor force engaged in manufacturing	.67						--

Note: these variables are selected from among those items loading most highly on the factor analysis by Brian Berry included in this volume.

are independent and uncorrelated with each other. But if we want to study the causes or consequences of some of the phenomena indicated by the original items—city growth, migration of ethnic groups or nonwhites, city wealth and average social status—we would have to regard some of the variables as potential causes or consequences of others. A correlation of .61 between the proportion of families with incomes below $3000 and the proportion of nonwhites may very well have some causal meaning.

For this reason we have not used the factors themselves in the illustrative data, because the procedures of factor analysis make it difficult to construct causal theories.

The objection might be raised that Table 1 is based on data different from those appearing in Berry's factor analysis. This is true. He isolated the factors from which we drew the six illustrative items from data on the 1762 urban places with populations of over 10,000 in 1960. Table 1 is based on 675 cities with more than 25,000 inhabitants in 1960. It is possible, though not likely, that the correlations displayed in Table 1 would change sharply if Berry's original data were used to examine these same correlations. That possibility, however, raises in another context the original question of the theoretical reasons for including data on some cities and not others. What is the rationale for selecting urban places with more than 10,000 inhabitants instead of cities whose population exceeds 25,000? What criteria and assumptions are involved in such choices? Suppose we find that the factor structure is quite different for large versus small cities, northern versus southern cities, or high-status versus low-status cities. How could we interpret the results? By itself the data-reduction process of factor analysis gives us few clues.

If population size and growth are fundamental factors conditioning many others, then adding over 1000 small cities and towns to the analysis might weight certain types of characteristics more than others and almost certainly alter the factor structure. But what then does the factor structure mean? Berry is aware of this problem, as is evident in his remark that "parallel analyses at the intermetropolitan and intrametropolitan levels" found that the "principal dimensions of intermetropolitan and intrametropolitan differentiation appear to be the same: size, socioeconomic status, stage in life cycle, recent growth behavior, etc." But, once again, why was this particular control variable (metropolitan status) chosen? Why was it assumed that this particular dimension of cities might upset the emergence of common underlying factors? Why not compare sets of cities differing in size, regional location, or age instead? No criteria for making these decisions about basic initial classifications of the data are given, but the statistical results are then taken as if their interpretations are self-evident and obvious.

In order to show the effect of region on the correlations (the basic data from which the factor analysis is done), the cities are simply divided into North and South. Table 2 presents the intercorrelations of six principal variables loading on each of six of the factors isolated by Berry's factor analysis, separately for the North and the South. Aside from substantive interpretations, the point that first has to be made is that the correlations are highly unstable for the two populations of cities. Out of the 15 intercorrelations, five are significantly altered in magnitude (by at least .21), and two of these actually have different signs in the two regions.

In the North larger cities are the slightly poorer ones; there is no relationship in the South. In the North ethnic cities have high migration; in the South ethnic cities have low migration. In the North ethnic cities are more

Table 2. Intercorrelations of principal variables on six factors—cities within northern and southern regions

Variable	Size	Income	Variable Manufacturing	Migrant	Nonwhite	Foreign Stock
Population size	--	-16 (.02)	-03 (-11)	-17 (-19)	.41 (.20)	.05 (.06)
Median income		--	-06 (.30)	.20 (.25)	-25 (-49)	.15 (.09)
Manufacturing			--	-52 (-41)	-10 (-08)	.29 (-26)
Migrant				--	-12 (-26)	-37 (.13)
Nonwhite					--	-18 (-54)
Foreign stock						--

The first correlation is that for 484 northern cities, the second (in parentheses below the first) is for 191 southern cities in 16 states:

Alabama
Arkansas
Florida
Georgia
Kansas
Kentucky
Louisiana
Mississippi
Missouri
North Carolina
Oklahoma
South Carolina
Tennessee
Texas
Virginia
West Virginia

likely to be manufacturing cities; in the South the reverse is true. The other 12 correlations remain the same in direction, but some shift in magnitude. The nonwhite composition of a northern city is much less closely related (negatively) to its ethnic composition than it is in a southern city. Probably these shifts are partly due to the lower proportion of persons of foreign parentage in the South.

These results indicate that the particular population of the cities that are chosen will affect the basic pattern of factors that are isolated. For example, it seems likely from the correlation of —.54 between nonwhite and foreign-stock composition in the South that they would load together in a factor analysis performed on data from southern cities alone. Southern cities with many nonwhites have few persons of foreign parentage. This is not surprising, since we know from other studies something about the settlement patterns of southern versus northern cities. But what can we then make of factors as "underlying dimensions" if many different patterns are discoverable for many different sets of cities? Dimensions of what?

The major point is that some theoretical justification for the selection of the set of cities about which data are to be gathered must be presented. That theoretical justification must be derived from knowledge of empirical relationships, obviously, but the data do not speak for themselves. It seems likely from these data that the factor structure will differ considerably from region to region even when only population and labor-force data are included.

POLITICAL CHARACTERISTICS OF CITIES

Table 3 displays the intercorrelations of a series of characteristics of political structure, voting turnout, and party complexion of American cities. None of these is included in any of the standard factor analyses of city characteristics, nor are they discussed from the point of view of their relevance to city typologies. Yet from the point of view of developing theories of the causes and consequences of city growth and character, surely these attributes have some significance on a priori grounds.

The table shows some significant relationships. The "reform government" cluster shows up clearly. The correlation coefficients between the four different characteristics usually associated with reformism—city-manager government, nonpartisan and at-large elections, and small city councils —range from .26 to .62 in the expected direction. However, the fact that the correlations are not extremely high shows that historically parallel and related developments are not necessarily closely associated in a statistical or empirical sense with cross-sectional data.

Democratic cities (assuming that county voting is a fair estimate of city voting patterns) are less likely to have a city manager and have more city employees per capita. Cities with a high voting turnout tend to be non-reformed and more Democratic.

If a parallel matrix for northern and southern cities is examined (the data are not given here in detail for lack of space), some interesting similarities and differences appear. The "reform government" cluster appears to be about the same in both regions, but four of the six correlations are weaker in the South than they are in the North. The relationship of non-

Table 3. Intercorrelations of characteristics of political structure, voting turnout, and party voting—American cities of over 25,000 population in 1960

Characteristic	Characteristic							
	Employees	Manager	Non-partisan	At Large	Size of Council	Demo. Vote	Regis. Vote	Adult Vote
Number of full-time city employees per 1,000 population	--	-18	.01	-07	.27	.20	.22	.18
Presence of city-manager government		--	.38	.35	-29	-20	-41	-45
Presence of nonpartisan elections			--	.28	-26	.03	-37	-36
Per cent of city council elected at large				--	-62	-06	-27	-29
Size of city council					--	.10	.29	.33
Per cent of county presidential vote for Democratic Party, 1960						--	.25	.25
Per cent of registrants voting in last local election 1961-62							--	.81
Per cent of adults voting in last local election, 1961-62								--

Data on political structure are taken from the 1963 Municipal Year book. City employee and Democratic voting data are from the 1962 County and City Data Book, published by the U.S. Bureau of the Census. Voting turnout data are from a survey conducted by the International City Management Association in 1962. See Robert R. Alford and Eugene C. Lee, "Voting Turnout in American Cities," American Political Science Review, 62 (September, 1968), pp. 796-813, for a more detailed description and discussion of these data.

partisanship with the city-manager form of government and with at-large elections stays the same in both regions; all other correlations are smaller in the South.

Almost all of the correlations of the size of the local government labor force with other political characteristics either reverse or dwindle to nothing in the South. In the North cities with many local government employees per capita are mayor–council, ward-based, large-council, Democratic, high-voter-turnout cities. None of these relationships persists in the South. Voting turnout is more weakly related to other aspects of political structure in the South than it is in the North, perhaps because efforts to suppress black political activity override any other factors influencing political participation.

The general point, again, is that the historical meaning of a particular characteristic, such as the size and powers of the local government, and the reasons for Democratic allegiances and high or low voting turnout, will affect its relationships with many other characteristics. Interpretations of the results must consider the nature of this historical and environmental context.

Table 4 shows the relationships between the variables chosen to represent six of the chief socioeconomic factors isolated by factor analysis and eight political characteristics of American cities. Generally the correlations are relatively low, and we can assume that these items would load on different factors and hence be regarded as independent dimensions of American cities.

Table 4. Intercorrelations of socioeconomic and political characteristics of 675 American cities of over 25,000 population in 1960

Political Characteristics	Socioeconomic Characteristics					
	Size	Median Income	Manufacturing	Migrant	Nonwhite	Foreign Stock
City employees	.24	-.28	.04	-.27	.19	.20
City-manager form	-.11	.09	-.26	.37	.00	-.20
Nonpartisan elections	-.04	.03	-.19	.27	-.11	-.11
At-large elections	-.02	-.03	-.18	.14	.12	-.15
Size of city council	.28	.03	.22	-.24	-.05	.22
Democratic vote	.12	-.04	.21	-.32	.01	.34
Registrants voting	.08	-.03	.15	-.34	-.01	.37
Adults voting	.05	.17	.33	-.45	-.19	.53

See previous Tables 1 and 3 for details on these measures

Almost all of the political characteristics are most closely related to the level of migration and ethnicity of cities. Cities in which higher proportions of the population are of foreign stock and those that are losing population are more likely to have many city employees per capita, "nonreform" governmental structures, higher Democratic voting, and higher voter turnout. These relationships probably reflect the "historical factors" related to patterns of migration, settlement, and the stages of economic development reached in different regions at the time that governmental structures were being adopted or when political party commitments and participation levels were being established. The cities of the Northeast are at one end of this scale, those in the Far West at the other.

It is interesting to note that the size of a city is related to the size of the city government's labor force and the size of the city council, even when the city's population size is normalized by a logarithmic transformation, and when the government labor force is computed per capita. Larger cities generate a larger local government at a rate far greater than is proportional to their growth. This fact has numerous implications for planning, the development of professional staffs, and the differentiation of functions within local governments as they grow.

Manufacturing cities tend to have nonreform governments, with large councils, Democratic allegiances, and high voting turnout. This is consistent with the picture given by the migration and ethnic characteristics.

Median income is related only to the size of the government labor force. Higher status cities have fewer city employees per capita. No other political characteristic of the city is related to median income. The size of the nonwhite population is not related to any political characteristic of American cities, considering the nation as a whole.

When the same relationships of socioeconomic to political characteristics are separately analyzed within the North and the South, 8 of the 48 correlations reverse direction, and 9 additional ones change in magnitude by at least .20. However, there is no emergence of a new pattern that would suggest that a fundamentally different factor structure for political characteristics might exist in the two regions. Further research is clearly needed on the regional differentiation of American cities.

We turn now to selected indicators of policy outputs. Table 5 presents the interrelationships of six different policy outputs in American cities—their participation in four different federal programs (poverty, urban renewal, housing, and Model Cities) and two local programs, one public, one private: the Community Chest and fluoridation.[3] The table suggests

---

[3] For analyses of three of these federal programs from the point of view of how they

several points important for our discussion here. First, it would be possible to construct a factor analysis including public policies parallel to those dealing with the socioeconomic and demographic characteristics of cities. This table makes clear that (a) there are interrelationships between different areas of policy and (b) that there seem to be distinctively different dimensions, although what these are cannot be discerned from this table. But participation in a variety of federal programs seems to be linked together. Cities that built many public housing units under the Housing Act of 1949 were also likely to get more money for the "War on Poverty" and to apply for the Model Cities program. On the other hand, the level of contributions to the Community Chest and whether or not the city decided to fluoridate its water are not related to participation in any of the federal programs.

More generally these data indicate that if these policy outputs comprise any kind of sample, cities are not centralized decision-making systems in the sense that one decision is highly predictable from another. On the other hand, the decisions are not completely unrelated to each other. Even though we can assume that different individuals were involved, in different periods of time, with different incentives for participating in the various federal programs, we can still predict the likelihood of participation in one federal program from knowledge of participation in another.

The implications for developing principles of urban classification are that policy outputs should not simply be considered separately but included as part of the basic data on the basis of which cities are classified. Since a number of the basic socioeconomic characteristics might change sharply as policy decisions are made (e.g., to annex a large suburb, to develop a mass transit system, to raise taxes on private homes as compared to apartments, to change housing segregation policies) there seems every reason to include possible causes of those socioeconomic and demographic changes in the basic data from which city classifications are derived. (The same argument holds for features of the city's environment, to be taken up later.)

Table 6 presents the correlations between the six policy outputs and six selected socioeconomic variables isolated by factor analysis. Although none of the relationships is particularly strong, greater policy outputs are asso-

represent innovations in city programs see the following articles by Michael Aiken and the author: "Community Structure and Innovation: The Case of Urban Renewal," *American Sociological Review,* August 1970; "Community Structure and Innovation: The Case of Public Housing," *American Political Science Review,* September 1970; and "Community Structure and the War on Poverty: Theoretical and Methodological Considerations," in Mattei Dogan, Ed., *Studies in Political Ecology* (Paris, 1970).

Table 5. Intercorrelations of various policy outputs of American cities of over 25,000 population in 1960

Policy Output	Policy Output						
	Poverty	Urban Renewal	Housing	Model Cities	Community Chest	Fluori-dation	Number of Cases
Number of dollars per capita for "War on Poverty" programs as of June 30, 1966 (natural logarithm)[a]	--	.43	.30	.41	.08	.07	(675)
Number of dollars per capita reserved for urban renewal projects since 1949 (natural logarithm)[b]		--	.43	.47	.13	.02	(601)
Number of low-rent housing units per 100,000 population under the Housing Act of 1949[c]			--	.22	.10	.02	(636)
Presence of application for a Model Cities program (either first or second round, 1966-67)[d]				--	.16	-.05	(675)
Amount raised for the 1965 Community Chest as a per cent of the "effective buying income" of the city[e]					--	.22	(468)
Presence of any type of adoption of fluoridation[f]						--	(490)

[a]Data taken from Office of Economic Opportunity, Poverty Program Information as of June 30, 1966, Washington, D.C., 1966. The raw data are transformed to a natural logarithm because of the skewing of the data. [b]Data from Department of Housing and Urban Development, Urban Renewal Director, June 30, 1966, Washington, D.C., 1966. [c]Data from Report S-11A, Consolidated Development Director, Statistics Branch, Housing Assistance Administration, Department of Housing and Urban Development, Washington, D.C., June 30, 1967. [d]Data from Deck 62: "First Model Cities Grant Recipients' Names," Journal of Housing 24 (November, 1967), pp. 547-549, and The Model Cities Administration, Department of Housing and Urban Development. [e]Data from "Effective Buying Income" as computed from National Community Chest, 1966. [f]We are indebted to Robert L. Crain, Elihu Katz, and Donald Rosenthal for release of the fluoridation data, which are analyzed in their book, The Politics of Community Conflict: The Fluoridation Decision (Indianapolis: Bobbs-Merrill, 1969).

Table 6. Intercorrelations of policy outputs and selected principal socioeconomic variables—675 American cities with over 25,000 inhabitants

Policy Outputs	Socioeconomic Characteristics					
	Size	Median Income	Manu-facturing	Migrant	Non-white	Foreign Stock
Dollars for "War on Poverty"	.37	-.39	-.16	-.08	.35	-.02
Dollars for urban renewal	.33	-.30	.00	-.24	.40	.03
Community Chest contributions	.18	-.12	.36	-.39	.09	-.04
Adoption of fluoridation	.04	-.04	.06	.00	.06	-.11
Housing units constructed	.12	-.46	-.09	-.18	.47	-.20
Model Cities application	.53	-.20	-.03	-.18	.30	.07

See Tables 1 and 5 for a description of the variables in detail.

ciated fairly consistently with size, median income, migration, and color composition. Larger, poorer cities with more nonwhites and lower migration levels have more poverty and urban renewal dollars, applied more frequently for Model Cities programs, and gave more to the Community Chest. Fluoridation is not associated with any of these socioeconomic characteristics of cities. The only reversals occur with respect to the manufacturing variable, but they are slight. None of the socioeconomic variables is distinctly associated with most of the policy outputs. Racial composition was most closely associated with urban renewal and public housing, median income with poverty program participation, migration with Community Chest contributions, the size of the city with Model Cities applications.

When cities are subclassified as northern and southern and the same correlation matrix is examined, the same general pattern appears, although some striking regional deviations from the national pattern occur. In the South higher income, less ethnic cities give more to the Community Chest (.16 and —.30); northern highly ethnic cities give more (—.30); income makes no difference. Racial composition is more closely related to the city's obtaining "War on Poverty" funds in the North than in the South (.43 versus .19). The income level of the city is more closely related to both poverty and urban renewal funds in the North (—.48 and —.38) than it is in the South ($-.18$ and $-.12$). It is beyond our ability to speculate here on the meaning of these relationships, but, at least with respect to these policies, there are no substantial differences between the North and the South. Few of these correlations of policy outputs with socioeconomic characteristics of cities reach the level of intercorrelation of the federal programs with each other, shown in Table 5. These two findings suggest that socioeconomic factors (at least at the city level) are not strongly determinative of policy outputs. Policymaking processes may possibly be regarded as encompassing a subsystem of causal factors with a significant degree of autonomy.

Although these particular policy outputs are not a sample of all possible outputs, the findings suggest two implications for city classification: (a) policy ouputs should be regarded as data equivalent to socioeconomic characteristics for the purposes of arriving at basic city types, since in many cases socioeconomic characteristics are the direct consequence of public policies and vice versa, and (b) types should be constructed to take account of the degree of autonomy of subsystems within the city. The correlations displayed in Tables 3 and 5 would seem to justify at least an initial assumption that there is a "political" cluster of characteristics of American cities which is potentially independent of socioeconomic characteristics. To what extent are the policies of cities associated with socioeconomic, rather than political, structural characteristics? We cannot answer that question in detail here, but research already cited by the author and Michael Aiken shows that policy outputs are in fact more closely correlated with the age, size, wealth, and social heterogeneity of a city than with any feature of its local government (see Chapter 5 in this volume for a somewhat different conclusion).

THE SOCIOECONOMIC AND POLITICAL ENVIRONMENTS OF CITIES

The apparent properties of the city itself may be properties of the state or region in which it is located—from the point of view of the causes and consequences of those properties. Properties of the environment should be brought directly into the basic data set that provides the raw materials for classificatory typologies, and not merely analyzed in relation to a typology based solely on the socioeconomic characteristics of the city itself.

In order to illustrate an alternative procedure, a number of characteristics of the state or urbanized area in which a city is located have been converted into characteristics of the city for statistical purposes. Some of these characteristics are exactly the same for both units of analysis—for example, median income or the size of the nonwhite population. Others, however, are "global" properties of the state—for example, the degree of centralization of the state legislature—by which we mean that they are not derived from adding up characteristics of the population but rather are characteristics of institutions whose essential boundaries are those of the state. For the purposes of computing correlation coefficients each state figure has been regarded as an attribute of all the cities located in that state. Such variables can be treated exactly as any others for the purposes of statistical analysis.

These characteristics of states and urbanized areas have just as much logical and theoretical reason for being included in a primary data set describing cities and used as the basis for classifications as the population and labor-force data usually selected. In fact, from the point of view of using these data for assessing the causes and consequences of various city characteristics, and the range of freedom that urban policymakers have, they may be even more important than other data. The major forces influencing city population size and growth—the location of major industries (and therefore the composition of the labor force) and the migration to the city of nonwhites and various ethnic groups—may not be (and probably are not) under the control of any likely actions of leaders and officials of that city, but are statewide, regional, or even national in their origins and operations. If this is the case, we must ask: What really is the meaning of the "factors" isolated by the technique of factor analysis? In what sense are they "factors" in any fundamental sense of the word? And, once again, what is the meaning of the "city" as the basic unit of analysis?

In our present analysis state characteristics are regarded for analytic purposes as properties of each city within a given state. This has both the advantage and the disadvantage of "weighting" a given state's characteristic by the aggregate characteristics by the number of cities in that state. Our assumption is that the more cities within a state, the more impact their characteristics will have on the state, and therefore we are allowing the aggregate characteristics of the cities to influence the resulting correlations.

Table 7 shows the correlation of the six principal socioeconomic characteristics already considered for both a city and the state within which it is located. In effect the correlations tell us how well we can predict the characteristics of a city if we know only the overall totals for that same characteristic for its state. As Table 7 shows, the ethnicity of the city is fairly well determined by that of its state; the correlation is .83. But we do not know anything at all about a city's population size by knowing its state's population. Larger cities are not necessarily located in larger states.

Table 7. Intercorrelations of six principal variables for state and city by region—American cities with over 25,000 inhabitants in 1960

Variable	All Cities	North	South
Population size	.01	.02	.09
Median income	.57	.32	.42
Manufacturing	.68	.64	.48
Migrant	.58	.59	.48
Nonwhite	.60	.34	.59
Foreign stock	.83	.72	.55

See Table 1 for a full description of each variable. Each figure in the above table represents the correlation of each city's value on a variable with the value of its state on the same variable.

It seems plausible to infer that the ethnic character of a city, in a causal and explanatory sense, derives from historical processes of settlement and migration—processes that had little to do with the features of the city itself but rather were related to factors attracting populations with a certain ethnic stamp—factors that were at least statewide in scope if not regional in character.

Such a correlation may help us to understand the causal or explanatory forces behind the development of populations with certain characteristics, but it does not tell us anything about their consequences. From the point of view of the city as an ongoing entity, its ethnicity is an established fact, regardless of its origins. Correlations of city and state characteristics of migration, manufacturing, nonwhite population, and wealth are somewhat lower than that of ethnicity, ranging from .58 to .69. But even here the origins of city characteristics—even the main ones singled out by factor analysis—seem to be at least statewide and not local in character if we can assume that these correlations reflect the consequences of historical patterns of establishment of an economic base, the fortunes of its population, and subsequent migrations. These correlations raise the whole problem of the appropriateness of different units of analysis, and what the questions of analytic and explanatory concern really are. Decisions about the choice of data and the analytic techniques will differ, depending on whether we are trying to explain the characteristics of cities as they are, showing the historical processes of settlement, economic growth and decline, and their role in the regional and national economy, or trying to develop a framework of description within which the urban policymaker can make decisions in the light of the best information about the consequences of his actions.

Table 7 also shows the city–state correlations within the North and the South separately. A high correlation for all cities that is reduced by a regional control indicates that the characteristic is an attribute of the region more than of a state or city. Low correlations within either the nation as a whole or within regions indicates that the characteristic is an attribute of the city alone—population size is the best illustration in this table—since the population of a city cannot be predicted from knowledge of the population of the state. In at least one case, racial composition, the city–state correlation is significantly lower in the North than it is in the South, indicating that one can predict the city's racial composition more accurately from state information in the South than in the North. Again, the substantive point is obvious, but its methodological implications may not be. Whether or not a city's attributes are really those of its state or its region may be important from the point of view of developing causal theories about the causes of growth, development, and also for purposes of policymaking.

Again, our major concern is not to assess the substantive meaning of the data, but rather to consider what a wider range of city characteristics tells us about principles of city classification. If a "micro" characteristic of a city—that is, a property that relates not to the city as a whole, in any global sense, but rather to some subgroup within it—can be regarded as legitimately included in a factor analysis, why should we not consider characteristics "outside" the city, such as the level of wealth or manufacturing in the state in which it is located? The number of persons enrolled in college, for example, is intrinsically related to the "city" only in the sense that the counting unit is the territory of the political unit at the time of the census, and these boundaries are subject to frequent change, with considerable consequences for all population figures. If this is true, and if we are concerned with causes and effects, then the characteristics of the political system that determine the boundaries within which data are collected should be part of the basic inquiry.

Another type of environmental property is the political environment within which cities must function. Our example is the degree of centralization or coordination of decision-making within the state legislature. If most significant decisions within a state legislature are made by negotiations of legislative leaders with the governor or in a policy committee representing both houses and both parties, the decision-making system of the state could be regarded as being more centralized and coordinated than one in which most decisions are made on the floor of a house or in regular committee meetings. Such a characteristic of the state can be regarded as a meaningful property of each city within the state—and one that may have critical consequences for the range of constraints on policymakers within any given city or for those within the state who wish to influence urban decisions. As such, it might be the type of characteristic that should be taken into account in constructing typologies of cities, at least if factors that have *causal significance* for internal processes in a city are of prime importance for the classification.

Other things being equal, we would expect that the decisions within a city that require more state cooperation would be more affected by the type of decision-making system existing in a state than those requiring less cooperation. Whether or not greater coordination and centralization within the state legislature would alter the quantity and quality of urban policy outputs could be argued both ways, depending on what assumptions one would want to make.

Table 8 presents the relationship of the level of centralization or coordination of decision-making in a state with the level of policy outputs in the six different areas already discussed. It shows that in the two cases requiring state cooperation—urban renewal and public housing—the more centralized and coordinated states contain cities that obtained more urban renewal funds and built more housing units. The two federal programs that did not require as much state cooperation—the "War on Poverty" and the Model Cities program—and the two completely local programs—fluoridation and Community Chest contributions—were not related or were more weakly related to the character of the state decision-making system. What this finding may indicate is that cities whose political and administrative leaders are more desirous of obtaining federal funds are able to create more coordination in the state legislature or are able to exploit an existing political system for their benefit. These factors may influence a city's growth and economic character. The stronger association of state legislative centralization with urban renewal and housing in the South than in the North also shows the importance of the political environment of a city for its internal functioning.

Because of lack of space, we do not discuss other environmental effects. But again, the point is that classifications of cities should be based on a much wider range of types of data than those usually included. If we accept as the initial premise the assumption that we are not distinguishing between independent and dependent variables—causes and effects—there is no reason arbitrarily to restrict the types of data included. These data strongly suggest that the characteristics of the political environment of cities should be considered.

Table 8. Correlates of the degree of centralization of the state legislature with urban policy outputs[a]

	Correlations with Legislative Centralization[b]		
	All Cities	North	South
URBAN POLICY OUTPUTS REQUIRING A HIGH DEGREE OF STATE COOPERATION			
Number of dollars per capita reserved for urban renewal projects since 1949 (natural logarithm)	.22	.15	.40
Number of low-rent housing units per 100,000 population constructed under the Housing Act of 1949	.21	.23	.41
URBAN POLICY OUTPUTS REQUIRING A LOW DEGREE OF STATE COOPERATION			
Number of dollars per capita for "War on Poverty" programs as of June 30, 1966 (natural logarithm)	−.02	−.04	.05
Presence of application for a Model Cities program in either the first or the second round (1966-67)	.06	.04	.08
Presence of any type of adoption of fluoridation	.00	−.06	.12
Amount raised for the 1965 Community Chest as a per cent of the "effective buying income" of the city	.11	.04	.20

[a]see Table 5 above for details on the other policy outputs

[b]Data on the centralization of state legislatures were drawn from Dwayne L. Francis, Legislative Issues in the Fifty States (Chicago: Rand McNally, 1967), Table V-1, pp. 74-75. Each legislator was asked where in his state's legislature he would say the most significant decisions were made. A centralization index ranging from 0 to 1 was then computed to rank the states. If the answer was that most significant decisions were made "in the governor's office" or "in policy committee," a score of 1 was assigned. "In party caucus" was given a score of .50, and "in regular committee meetings" or "on the floor" responses a score of 0. The scores were totaled for each state and then divided by the number of respondents in that state.

CONCLUSIONS

The purpose of city classification *for the policymaker* is to provide some clues as to the possible consequences of different decisions. If the universe of cities about which data are gathered has an unknown relationship to the particular city about which he is concerned, then it is difficult for the policy-maker to discover the relevance of the data to his decision-making problem. The purpose of city classification for the *social scientist* is to provide some meaningful bases for understanding the causal processes that have produced the observed patterns of relationships. If the selection of data is arbitrary, if the number and categories of cities selected are arbitrary, and if the interpretation of the data is confined to labeling the factors, then we may have a parsimonious description of a particular data set, but we are only at the beginning of our analysis, not at the end.

The policymaker in a city may well conclude that abstract classifications of characteristics of cities and their correlations have little to tell him about his concrete tasks and opportunities, and he may be right. Particular historical circumstances—the people who happen to be in office, considerations of timing and strategy unique to a situation—are often the important factors that the decision-maker must take into account. Moreover, the range of freedom of action that the decision-maker has is severely limited by previous budgetary and organizational commitments. Under these conditions, which are ordinarily present, regular patterns or interrelationships of city characteristics that *any* typology presents will not be of help to him. Decision-making studies have discovered that it is extraordinarily difficult to gain all the information about consequences or costs and benefits that must be taken into account in a single decision. Similarly studies of budgeting have found that federal, state, and local budgets remain much the same from year to year, and that the freedom of maneuver to reallocate or increase budgetary items is highly limited for any conceivable coalition of power groups or leaders. The policymaker is thus faced with a combination of contingencies and constraints that makes his concerns quite different from those of the academic social scientist.

Let us assume that the major factors discovered by the various factor-analysis studies—size, metropolitan location, economic base, wealth, etc.—are not subject to change by any short-run decisions of policymakers in American cities, although they may very well change in time as a result of decisions influencing the taxes on business, the levels of amenities available to residents, the adequacy of transportation services, and the like. These long-range consequences, however, though undoubtedly kept in mind by policymakers as they go about their business, are apparently not taken into account in any immediate sense for three reasons. First, information is not available on the probability of any given consequence. Second, there are more immediate pressures based on the short-run consequences for the affected social and political groups. Third, the long-range consequences are subject to so much change in the future that the policymaker should not rationally take them heavily into consideration in the immediate situation.

If these assumptions are correct, the policymaker and the academic social scientist may have quite different needs for city classifications. If the policymaker had a considerably increased amount of control over major consequences, the regularities and patterns discovered by the social scientist might become much more random, much less predictable; that is, if the leaders of a city could quickly and easily alter the size, economic base, and wealth of a city, the stable underlying characteristics discovered by almost all the factor analyses of American cities would be much less stable and not at all "underlying." Instead, political and administrative features of city government and private or public leadership would assume much greater importance. If these political and administrative features were subject to considerable shifting from election to election and from one incumbent manager to another, there would be even more instability in city characteristics. Fortunately (and here the social scientist speaks), city characteristics are not that unstable. The range of freedom is not great, at least within the context of American politics in the present period.

Finally, let us repeat our two major conclusions about the principles of city classification:

1. *A far broader range of data should be included* in the materials on which city classifications are built, because the main data used in the factor-analysis studies concern relatively stable and unchanging characteristics, at least from the point of view of the immediate decision of policymakers. If American governments—federal, state, or local—had greater powers to affect decisions on industrial location, wage rates, city growth and size, the above generalization concerning stability would not hold. The economic and demographic data usually included refer mainly to what might be regarded as the long-run causes and consequences of city growth and development, but they do not include data on the intervening processes of administrative, political, and governmental decisions. There is no reason why such processes could not be subjected to similar classification.

2. For the purposes of the policymaker, *knowledge of variations within major types of cities* (however arrived at) may be more useful than a restatement of the major parameters already discovered. After the gross effects of size, economic base, political environment, etc., have been taken account of or controlled, what accounts for the remaining variation in those

characteristics? Are they factors about which policymakers can do something? This question leads to the suggestion that there be *two* stages in the development of city classifications, one in which all measurable characteristics are correlated, to see what underlying factors account for them, and another in which correlations between city characteristics are studied within subsets of cities classified by major type: large industrial central cities, small, suburbs, etc. If political and environmental data were included in the basic data, the list of potential "control variables" would be much longer.

Consideration of the principles and criteria underlying classifications of cities is important for yet another reason: providing guidance to the agencies gathering data on cities. This is an important problem not only for American policymakers and social scientists but also for non–Americans. The kinds of data collected will be critically influenced by the great variations in the autonomy of local governments, the degree to which the market is allowed to influence the decisions of families and industries to locate in a certain place, and many other features of the national environment. It is thus important for the principles and criteria guiding data collection to be as broadly and uniformly defined as possible. The United Nations has recently become concerned with the development of criteria for cross-national data collection on cities, and a recent discussion by Rabinovitz has made it clear that definitions based primarily on American experience will be excessively narrow.[4]

The categories for data collection on a cross-national basis proposed by Rabinovitz indicate the wider range of characteristics that should be built into the basic array of variables on the basis of which cities are classified. She summarizes the types of data suggested under the following headings: elections, formal government structure, political party structure, group structure, bureaucratic structure, intergovernmental relations, urban government outputs, communications, conflict, cooperation and stability, leadership, environment, social structure, and economic structure. Such a broader data base would be necessary for city classifications that are theoretically adequate for both cross-national and regional studies of urban growth and character.[5]

[4] A paper prepared for the United Nations Conference on Cross-National Urban Data Collection, November 28, 1969, makes this point clear. See Francine F. Rabinovitz, "Data Resources for Cross-National Urban Research on Administration and Politics: A Proposal," *Social Science Information*, June 1970, and the report of the conference also included there.

[5] For an attempt by the present author to develop an "accounting scheme" of theoretical variables for comparative studies of urban policymaking see "Explanatory Variables in the Comparative Study of Urban Administration and Politics," in Robert T. Daland, Ed., *Comparative Urban Research: The Administration and Politics of Cities* (Beverly Hills, Calif.: Sage Publications, 1969), pp. 272–324.

PART FIVE

Overview

. . . Classification as part of urban management

CHAPTER 12

Classification as Part of Urban Management

DAVID S. ARNOLD

International City Management Association

In 1943 an article entitled "A Functional Classification of Cities in the United States" appeared in the *Geographical Review*. This article by Chauncy D. Harris of the University of Chicago is generally credited with being the pioneering American effort to classify cities systematically on the basis of economic activity. Earlier classification efforts had been made with simple demographic indicators, but Harris' effort was much more thorough in methodology and coverage.

The work attracted the attention of the editors of *The Municipal Year Book,* published since 1934 by the International City Management Association; as a result the "Economic Classification of Cities," based largely on Harris' work, appeared in *The Municipal Year Book* for 1945. With some modifications, the classification has appeared several times since in *The Municipal Year Book,* most recently in the 1967 edition.

The functional classification (often termed "economic" since it gave much weight to employment) has been cited often by city managers, city planners, and other local government officials in explaining how their cities are similar to, or different from, other cities, in explaining or defending budget proposals before the city council, and for other purposes.

As this volume so abundantly shows, however, classification is now considered more as a process to be adapted to relatively specific purposes in different regions of the country and in different portions of metropolitan areas. Although it would be pretentious to call it a decision-making tool, the classification of cities does provide an analytical framework within which data and methodologies can be conceptualized and applied.

The Harris classification with subsequent modifications on the basis of additional census data and changes in economic development patterns has

361

served well over the last quarter century. It has been a base point constantly referred to by geographers, economists, sociologists, political scientists, and other students of urbanism. Its place in the history of urban studies is secure.

The economic emphasis reflected Harris' point of view as a geographer and the widely recognized importance of economic characteristics as descriptions of cities. On the basis of other empirical observations economic classification seemed to coincide with the economic dominance of community life in our nation.

Today this has changed. Economic characteristics are seen to be relatively (if not absolutely) less important and sociological characteristics to be more important. At the same time we now have fewer cities that are highly specialized in given economic activities, and hence the economically oriented approach no longer seems as obvious as it did in the 1940s. In addition, the economic classification as originally constructed did not and could not give attention to factors that have come to the fore in recent years, especially the social indicators of age, ethnic composition, race, education, and income, among others.

Recognition of this need was one of the reasons for convening a small group of scholars by the International City Management Association in June 1965 to explore the possibility of a revision and expansion of the classification concept. This meeting made it clear that at least four developments were affecting classification:

1. The accelerating social problems of cities.
2. Wider ranges of census and other nationally gathered data.
3. Development and refinement of mathematical methodologies, especially multivariate analysis.
4. Advent of the computer to make it possible to apply multivariate analysis to a large group of cities and a large number of variables.

THE URBAN DATA BASE

Classification serves as a framework, rather than as a developer of alternatives or a predictor for management decision-making. Thus, classification can better be understood in the context of today's information explosion, which involves such esoteric terms as heuristic programming, simulation, and systems analysis.

Classification is no more nor less than an attempt to group items (physical objects, biological characteristics, economic and social data, words, etc.) on the basis of similarities or differences as measured by data. It begins with the assembly of information in the form of data.

This country generates enormous quantities of statistics on almost every conceivable subject. The federal government unquestionably is the nation's largest producer of data. It is easy to look at the volumes of information published just for the decennial censuses of population and housing and to conclude that there is more than enough information to satisfy any reasonable person. Of course it does not work out that way. Too often the data are disparate when intended to be complementary, overlapping when intended to be supplementary, incomplete when intended to be comprehensive.

Data receive an astonishing degree of attention from statisticians, sociologists, geographers, political scientists, and representatives of other disciplines and professions. Although neutral in intent—as, for example, when presented in census reports—data often become political weapons in proposing or carrying out governmental programs, in justifying business policies, and in arriving at many kinds of decisions.

Because they often appear in print and have been gathered by well-respected agencies, data often take on a halo of validity that is not claimed by statisticians and other data professionals who are well aware of the fallacies that can be inadvertently built into a conceptual framework and the hazards of data gathering by personal interview, of incomplete and erroneous responses, of clerical errors in coding data for key-punching, and above all of premature analysis and fallacious conclusions.

With all of these environmental and professional constraints, it still must be recognized that the operational users of data are the governmental decision-makers—the city managers and other administrators, urban planners, state and federal executives, and general officers in the Armed Forces. These men, however, rarely are professionals in factor analysis, information systems, data processing, and allied fields.

Too often in looking at data on a local scale and from a local perspective we fail to appreciate how it fits into a larger national framework. It helps, as a starting point, to work deductively—that is to consider a national urban system and work from there down to the local area.

CHANGING NATURE OF CITIES

In an earlier period of American history agriculture was dominant.[1] Arable land with appropriate climate, water, and transportation was the

[1] The following discussion of the underlying national characteristics that affect the national urban data base is taken from Brian J. L. Berry and Elaine Neils, "Location, Size and Shape of Cities as Influenced by Environmental Factors: The Urban Environment Writ Large," in Harvey S. Perloff, Ed., *The Quality of the Urban Environment* (Baltimore: Johns Hopkins Press, 1969), pp. 257–304.

highest form of wealth. As industrialization set in, from the mid-nineteenth century on, mineral resources and hydro power became more important because they provided the basic ingredients for manufacture, the expanding sector of the economy. In the twentieth century, especially since World War II, the service sector has risen to a dominance that could not have been imagined by nineteenth and early twentieth century businessmen.

The evidence is all around us in the forms of hundreds of white-collar employments ranging from writers, economists, graphic artists, computer programmers, systems analysts, journalists, and other professionals offering intellectual and creative skills to the many kinds of service enterprises, such as restaurants, hotels, motels, food-service establishments, and many others. The trend is too well known to need documentation.

The critical point is the need to understand the evolution of the American urban system, the ways in which economic and social growth have taken place, and the new and distinctly different ways in which the city interacts with this environment. Classification is one of the most useful techniques for increasing this understanding.

Historically, the "heartland" of the American Manufacturing Belt, spreading from New York State in a generally westerly direction through Buffalo, Cleveland, Detroit, and on to Chicago, has conditioned regional development elsewhere.[2]

Two more recent developments have modified this pattern of industrial development: amenity resources and the service sector. It has been reflected in the increase in "footloose industries"—aircraft, aerospace and defense, research and development, and other white-collar and technologically oriented industries. The competitive shifts are reflected in the movement of employment to Florida, the Southwest, and the West.

Thus the pattern of urbanization has been not only the well-known migration to the central cities and from the central core to the suburbs but also a profound regional shift caused in part by defense and defense-related industries locating in the South, Southwest, and West.

A new phenomenon has risen out of this urban revolution: the "post-industrial city"—the city in which industries, employees, and their families are seeking out education, cultural attractions, open countryside, and other "amenity resources." The postindustrial city will make a profound difference in this nation, a difference that is going to persist for the forseeable future. Stated another way, although the large central city is not dead, it has lost its position of relative dominance both on a national and a metropolitan scale:

---

[2] Berry and Neils, "Location, Size, and Shape of Cities."

The essence of the large industrial city was concentration and high densities—absence of open space, crowding, increasing problems of environmental pollution, etc. Large industrial cities have also been the principal sources of blue-collar employment, with attendant accumulations of members of the lowest rungs in the status system in deteriorating, crowded, riot-prone slums. New industries and the white-collar middle class characteristically avoid such areas, so that the revolutionary innovations in the post-1950 period implied substantial changes in system form, rather than the system-maintenance of evolutionary sequences.[3]

Stated another way, post-1950 economics shows two major trends: (a) a strong outward pull within metropolitan areas and (b) a movement toward the southern and western portions of our nation. The change has come about because of many complex and interacting factors, including such direct factors as truck transportation, interstate highways, and national defense policies, and such indirect factors as industrial technology, rising educational levels, and rising educational requirements for employment.

The postindustrial city has been influenced by many factors, some well known (defense policies, industrial technology, the interstate highway system, racial migration), others not so well known (shifts in industrial location from source of supply to proximity to markets, rising educational requirements for workers in automated and semiautomated manufacturing and distributive processes, and even the influence on technically oriented industry of educational and research organizations, notably in the Boston, San Francisco Bay, and Southern California areas).

The effects are both positive and negative. In material terms, and on a national scale, we have attained new heights in the standard of living. By other measures—environmental pollution, psychological stress, and waste of resources—the outlook is anything but pleasant. Of major importance in weighing these factors is the role of amenities. As people become better educated, better paid, and more aware of refinements in their surroundings, they will demand more.

The role of amenities in locational choice is of increasing importance today because of generally rising real incomes and improved transportation that is breaking down the closeness of the tie to workplace in all but the lowest income groups. Advantages of site and micro-climate . . . are hence of increasing significance—they are new resources in that with increasing demand they are more valued.[4]

The changing nature of cities also is reflected profoundly in sociological

[3] Berry and Neils, "Location, Size, and Shape of Cities," p. 34.
[4] Berry and Neils, "Location, Size, and Shape of Cities," p. 39.

characteristics. For a number of reasons, including employment, younger and more affluent people usually will avoid the central city as a place of residence. The trends of intercity mobility and outward movement in metropolitan areas are well known and will be further documented by the 1970 Census of Population. In describing a city Berry and Neils point out that the ecology seems to be based on three principal elements:

1. Stage of families in the life cycle which affects housing, automobile transportation, parks and recreational facilities, and other aspects of city life.
2. Socioeconomic status of residents, primarily as reflected in the educational background and income level.
3. Segregation—the irrational element that has been too well documented to require elaboration here.[5]

It has been already stated that city classification has been based largely on economic indicators, but this is somewhat misleading since it depends on the definition of "classification." The decennial census of population has been classifying cities for over 150 years, by population groups, and other simple demographic classifications have been available for a long time.

In the last generation, however, outstanding work has been done in the development of other data that more accurately describe the population by social characteristics. The challenge now, as Berry and Neils point out, is to integrate the social and economic measures for more accurate and descriptive classifications.

It is likely that other aspects of social change are just as important as population growth, migration, and composition, but they are not easily measured. They include one of the most adverse consequences of population mobility—rootlessness—together with alienation of the individual from his family and environment and the adverse psychological aspects of modern tensions, frustrations, and environmental hazards.

In addition to the social conditions, two other considerations will have a profound influence in the future: human development and land use.

Human development has at least three aspects. The first is cultural diversity. An indication is the growth of special-interest magazines and other publications and the declining influence of mass-circulation magazines. Movies, book clubs, and the performing arts also reflect this diversified public interest. As these factors are reflected in measurable aspects of society—housing, employment, transportation, and the like—classification will become increasingly complex.

[5] Berry and Neils, "Location, Size, and Shape of Cities," p. 39.

Second, and probably at a slower pace, some racial and ethnic integration will occur, and will affect life styles.

Finally, education will be increasingly diversified, specialized, and qualitative. In terms of the political dimension, it means the following:

In a technological society of increasing size and complexity, responsibility for urban policy development and implementation will necessarily and increasingly fall into the hands of professionals: highly trained administrative, professional, and technical persons who devote their full time and skill to problems of urban living.[6]

The physical characteristics of cities, especially land use, will be changing much more rapidly in the future. Increased governmental commitment to public transportation, including mass transit; local government control of space, especially land; and higher residential densities—these are signs of changes that will profoundly affect classification as methodologies are enlarged to handle more complex comparative data.

In summation, cities are becoming more fluid, are changing more rapidly, are more interdependent with metropolitan areas and urban regions, are more dependent on a moderate climate and other amenities, and are more dependent on higher education and education-related enterprises. The historic factors of transportation, location, and manufacturing, wholesaling, and retailing are still highly important, but the other factors have come to the fore, so that all must be considered in assessing the position of the city in relation to other cities.

The data have been documented persuasively by the geographers, resource economists, regional scientists, sociologists, demographers, political scientists, and others. The challenge is now for mayors, city managers, city planners, and other urban government administrators to relate their cities to the broader environment in setting objectives, short- and long-range planning, and the delivery of services.

WHAT TO CLASSIFY?

Classification can be done in many ways ranging from obvious classifications (big cities and small cities) to such a level and specialization of detail as to permit few if any classes of more than one city. Some middle ground must be sought in relation to the purposes of the classification (city

---

[6] James M. Banovetz, "The City: Forces of Change," in *Managing the Modern City* (Washington, D.C.: International City Management Association, 1970), Chapter 2.

planning, distribution of federal grants, location of state and interstate highways, etc.).

Classification on the basis of social and economic variables has been discussed briefly above, and it was pointed out that economic indicators were among the earliest data used. Later demographic and other social indicators were added, and now attempts are being made to integrate the two broad sets.

Other kinds of classification that may have value in the future, particularly if reliable data can be developed, include visual elements,[7] physical characteristics,[8] and temporal characteristics.[9] Classification could even cover environmental "insults"—visual, aural, and olfactory characteristics as well as aesthetic inelegancies.

Two other aspects of classification that seem promising for future work are spatial (area and subarea) and governmental analysis.

An example of the former is Rees' "The Factorial Ecology of Metropolitan Chicago, 1960" which showed the following:

> Within the limits of the technology and resources at their command, people choose to minimize, through living apart from those unlike themselves, the possibilities of conflict because of class, generational, racial, religious, or national differences. In other words, that we tend to seek our own kind.[10]

Stating the obvious? Not at all. The factorial ecology demonstrated

---

[7] See Kevin Lynch, "City Design and City Appearance," in *Principles and Practice of Urban Planning* (Washington, D.C.: International City Managers' Association, 1968), Chapter 9, for suggested perceptual criteria that could be developed schematically.

[8] See U.S. Urban Renewal Administration and U.S. Bureau of Public Roads, *Standard Land Use Coding Manual: A Standard System for Identifying and Coding Land Use Activities* (Washington, D.C.: Urban Renewal Administration and the Bureau, 1965). See also Harland Bartholemew, *Land Uses in American Cities* (Cambridge: Harvard University Press, 1955).

[9] See Charles N. Glaab, *The American City: A Documentary History* (Homewood, Ill.: Dorsey Press, 1963).

[10] Master's dissertation, Department of Geography, University of Chicago, 1968. The study provides historical background on earlier factorial ecologies developed in Toronto and elsewhere together with historic information on the concentric ring and other theories of urban development. The study was applied to subareas of the Chicago standard metropolitan statistical area with factor analysis of 57 variables. The major factors were socioeconomic status, stage in life cycle (by family size, number of children, age composition, etc.), and "race and resources." Other factors that emerged in descending order were immigrant and Catholic status, population size and density, Jewish and Russian population, housing built in the 1940s and commutation by car, Irish and Swedish population, population mobility, and other nonwhites and Italians. The first four—socioeconomic status, stage in life cycle, race and resources, and immigrant and Catholic status—accounted for most of the variance and thus were the most descriptive of underlying dimensions.

very well how the multivariate methodology can be used in another setting —within a metropolitan area—an idea that Rees extended in this volume.

A kind of classification that has not been developed but that would be extremely useful to urban administrators would be based on the form of government in relation to such variables as municipal budgets, number of city employees, financial relationships with other local governments, financial relationships with state and federal governments, and service outputs (crime and other police statistics, refuse collection and disposal data, etc.).

Several studies have been made of cities in relation to forms of government and social impact indicators, but these are not classification systems in the sense defined in this volume. They do illustrate, however, the potential for developing classifications that will tie social and economic data much more closely to form of government and city government production or output.[11]

As Alford points out in Chapter 11, almost no attention has been given to political factors that he identifies as political culture (party affiliation, voting turnout, etc.), political structure (form of government, partisan and nonpartisan elections, number of city employees, etc.), city policies, and the political and socioeconomic environment of the city. Alford is correct when he suggests that ". . . specific political dimensions may have at least as much relevance to urban policy-makers as the economic and demographic characteristics forming the basic data used so far."

We are a long way off from a political or governmental dimension of classification that can be used with the degree of confidence that we now attach to economic, demographic, and social measures. Probably the most that can be hoped for at this time is for mayors, city managers, planning directors, and other urban administrators to use city classifications as a reference point for detailed development of objectives and consideration of alternatives (in the sense of systems analysis) within the limitations of the local political environment. This is not a plea for expediency or the art of the possible, but it is rather recognition that capable administrators will make every effort to assess the intangibles as well as quantified data.

USES OF CLASSIFICATIONS

Preceding portions of this chapter have sketched in some of the changes taking place in our society that are profoundly changing the nature of our

---

[11] A good example is Robert R. Alford and Harry M. Scoble, "Political and Socioeconomic Characteristics of American Cities," in *The Municipal Year Book 1965* (Chicago: International City Managers' Association, 1965).

cities and therefore the classification of those cities. In addition reference has been made to the constraints on classification and the difficulties inherent in using classification as a decision-making tool. Having said all of this, however, it should be stressed that classification of cities is useful for urban administrators in several ways.

First, it helps to bring some order out of a seemingly incomprehensible mass of national, state, metropolitan, and local data. It shows that data need critical analysis in their selection as well as their use, that it may help to concentrate on a few readily identifiable items in the interest of economy and time.

For example, a city may be classified M123 (using the Forstall classification referred to in the first chapter of this volume), which means that it is a city in the Midwest; an independent, nonsuburban city; a city with below average socioeconomic status and a considerably older population; and a city with a high percentage of the labor force in manufacturing. The city manager or city planning director, for purposes of developing the budget, can compare his city with other midwestern cities that are in groups M10, M12, M13, and perhaps M15 and M18. He does not need to limit his review to cities that are in his own classification but can look also at other independent cities in his part of the country.

Turning inward, the city manager or city planner can look at the data and give practical consideration to the changes that have occurred through annexation, the growth of shopping centers outside the city, industrial development inside and outside the city, and the effects of a highway bypass that skirts the city limits.

It should be stressed that the description of a city as "low average" in socioeconomic status does not refer to an absolute scale but simply to the city's position in relation to other cities, particularly those in the same geographic region.

Second, classification may help identify phenomena of local origin. Take, for example, a relatively small independent city with both above-average status and older population (classification 11). This classification, which includes many college towns and some resorts, will not explain why this specific city is losing population despite its seemingly high standing on socioeconomic status. The explanation may be that the educational institution is not enough of a pull and that the city is deficient in other environmental and amenity elements.

Better understanding of local phenomena is extremely helpful to the city administrator, the city planning agency, the city council, and citizen groups in defining realistic objectives for the community and developing feasible means of attaining those objectives.

Stated in a broader framework, for example, significant industrial development is a hopeless objective for many cities. Recognition of this limitation, always within the broader framework of what citizens want their community to be, is the first and indispensable step toward realistic development of a better (not necessarily richer or larger) community.

Third, classification helps in the isolation of influential variables. This is most easily done in those cities that either have an unusual proportion of nonwhite population, special economic activities such as mining, college, or military, or a relatively large proportion of the labor force in manufacturing. Particularly important in the Forstall classification are those cities with an unusual proportion of nonwhite population.

Let us take an example of a city in the Midwest that has the classification of 109 (average level in socioeconomic status and stage in life cycle and 11% or more of the population nonwhite). The first question is: Is the nonwhite ratio still an influential variable? Has the ratio increased or decreased since the last census? What is the nonwhite ratio within the city in comparison with the urban fringe outside the city? How has employment changed in recent years for the nonwhites as compared with the whites?

Answers to these and similar questions can be found in most cities without overwhelming time and effort, and the conclusion may be that the nonwhite population is not an influential variable. Then the city administrator, the planning director, and others can begin to look elsewhere for information on what is influencing the social, physical, cultural, and economic development of the city.

Fourth, the classification provides the indispensable data framework for continuing analysis. It is the checkpoint for population estimates, health statistics, employment statistics, local government expenditures (city, county, school district), educational level, fire losses, crime statistics, and many others.

The administrator can look for the seemingly contradictory phenomena. Why is the crime rate rising in a city of affluence? Why is a city of below average socioeconomic status gaining in population? Why does a city of average socioeconomic status and a high proportion of the work force engaged in manufacturing have both high unemployment and a high job-vacancy ratio? Why does a city with a high educational level have trouble securing passage of bond issues for schools?

Fifth, classification, within carefully prescribed limits, can be used as an element of governmental decision-making. In Chapter 11 Alford very effectively points out that classification, as a specific, decision-making tool, is of little use. He points to the need for a broader range of data to be included and for analysis of variations within major types of cities to make classification a decision-making tool. Until this is done, however, the administrator must work with what he has, which means that he must develop the missing information, particularly local government and cultural characteristics, and then check them out against the classification to see what is likely to happen.

Good administrators always have attempted to predict events wherever possible. It is a part of their professional obligation to apprise the city council of things that are likely to happen, the consequences that will follow on certain decisions. Classification will help them to appraise their information, to consider a wider range of tangible and intangible influences, to look for information that is not obvious on the surface, and thus to be better prepared for the future.

URBAN INFORMATION FRAMEWORK

For the urban administrator classifications of cities are one part of an urban information framework within which administrative analysis, research, budgeting, programming, and planning can be operational. It is neither necessary nor desirable to include a highly centralized and automated records center, but it does require judicious selection of information with continual testing for usefulness. At the start a data-base inventory should be taken to decide what is needed and where it can be found. Both public and private information sources should be reviewed.

To be of greatest usefulness the information framework should be built on operating data from city departments and agencies, especially planning, police, fire, and assessment records. Health, welfare, and education records are equally important; in many cities, these data are compiled by counties, school districts, and other governments. Of necessity, the data compilation should start out on a modest scale and then be modified on the basis of experience.[12]

For medium-size and large cities (perhaps those of 25,000 population or more) small-area data by census tracts and other geographic units should be built into the information framework. It has been predicted that small-area coding will become commonplace following the 1970 censuses of population and housing. The small-area coding will facilitate the summarization and use of municipal operating records by providing a geographic common denominator. The U.S. Bureau of the Census will be offering address coding

---

[12] For a starting point see *Performance Reports for the Chief Administrator* (Washington, D.C.: International City Managers' Association, 1963), 66 pages.

guides, computer tapes, an information center, and other practical aids for local government use of the 1970 census.[13]

The urban information framework should be enlarged eventually to cover governmental decision-making. Major administrative and political acts are too descriptive and generative a portion of the information process to be omitted. Chapter 11 documents the case persuasively.

This, of course, is far more easily said than done, but a start must be made somewhere. Voting statistics fascinate political scientists and sociologists, but for the local administrator they only tell him things he already knows. Perhaps one way to start would be for the city manager, the planning director, the mayor, or some other person close to the administrative process to write brief case histories of major decisions. It would not be an onerous task to dictate summaries of events leading up to two or three major decisions that are made every year that have long-range consequences for the community. Although the information would be too unstructured for use in classifications, it will provide a good checkpoint for other data. The planning director and the chief administrator are particularly well suited to maintain this surveillance because they constantly deal with decision-making in zoning, land subdivision, appointment of personnel, urban renewal, and other sensitive areas.

ORGANIZATION FOR INFORMATION

In an information-oriented society, it is evident that large cities, and many medium-sized ones as well, will need to establish an organizational location for the urban information framework that has been outlined above.

For most cities the most logical place to assign responsibility is with the city budget agency. In larger cities a department or division—variously titled administrative management, budget and research, administrative planning and analysis, etc.—should be established with responsibilities for operating and capital budgets, administrative planning, organization studies, work simplification, and the urban information framework. The purview of such an agency might also include development of standards for data processing, office layout, records management, and internal and external forms and records.

[13] Management responsibilities, the nature of useful data, availability of data, and data management are covered clearly and concisely by Richard Hanel in *Management, Systems Analysis and Urban Data* (Washington, D.C.: International City Managers' Association, 1969), Management Information Service Report, Vol. 1, No. L-2.

The budget agency usually is the best choice because it is at the heart of the decision-making process, is responsible for citywide activities dealing in information in many forms, and is directly responsible to the chief administrator.

A radically different approach would be to integrate information, communications, and public relations in a municipal division on operational effectiveness:

Merging existing administrative analysis and public relations sections, the new staff unit would be manned by assistants trained in the social and behavioral disciplines, including organization theorists, administrative analysts, and those having social survey, statistical, and journalistic skills. Concerned primarily with applied organizational and behavioral research, including community analysis to ascertain attitudes and reactions, the resources of the new unit would enhance the totality of management decisions and actions.

For planning and evaluation purposes an operations analyst would probe public opinions, attitudes, and reactions of those concerned with organizational goals, policies, and procedures. The proposed operational effectiveness division would identify current public issues and problems, derive data, and analyze and propose alternative policy and procedural recommendations regarding the environment in which governmental units operate, the degree and extent of program achievement, and the effectiveness of existing organizational arrangements. While such research, fact-finding, and analysis would be carried on centrally, the information should be made available, with follow-up counsel, to operating officials where training programs and procedures modification are most effective.[14]

The proposed division on operational effectiveness is an organizational focus of communications and decision-making research, but the logical corollary is for the information framework to be assigned there also.

A more specialized approach to organization is to establish a statistical data section or unit in the office of the chief administrator to be concerned only with data compilation and analysis. As a practical matter, it probably is the best first step to be taken toward the municipal division of operational effectiveness.[15]

---

[14] Desmond L. Anderson, Chapter 2, "Public Relations and the Administrative Process," in *Municipal Public Relations* (Washington, D.C.: International City Managers' Association, 1966), pp. 35 and 36.

[15] The value of centralization, professionalism, and orientation toward operating records was set forth by Albert Mindlin, Chief Statistician, Government of the District of Columbia, in an address on October 2, 1969, before the Intergovernmental Seminar on Federal Statistics for Local Government Use, sponsored by the U.S. Bureau of the Census. Mindlin indicated that at least three local governments have made a good start in this direction: District of Columbia; Alexandria, Virginia; and Alameda County, California.

Only a handful of the 18,000 incorporated municipalities in the United States are prepared to undertake a comprehensive, locally operated information system. In any case the system generally will serve better when organized on a metropolitan-area basis. Coordination of information is a function particularly suited for councils of governments. Information is one of the first functions that all councils have undertaken, and a logical extension is to coordinate the work and provide the professional supervision that member jurisdictions cannot do alone. Rapid payoff could be obtained from intergovernmental development of uniform data area boundaries, uniform time periods, and uniform data definitions.

As Chapter 1 shows, intrametropolitan characteristics of classification are much more important in a nation that is heavily metropolitanized. In some of the standard metropolitan statistical areas (SMSAs), and in most of the urban areas outside them, the information coordination can be achieved through city–county cooperation, joint committees, a city–county planning commission, or other formal devices.

CONCLUSIONS

Classifications of cities have changed significantly, even dramatically, over the past generation, as this volume so abundantly shows. The most significant changes are the following:

1. Classifications are regarded as being developed to serve different purposes. A single classification will not suffice for all purposes.
2. Classifications are constantly evolving as a process that is adapted to particular needs at particular times.
3. Classification is striving for better descriptive powers through searching out the underlying dimensions of cities and other urban areas.[16]

Future classifications will include more social data, partly because of the great public interest in problems of poverty, minority-group relationships, inadequate education, and other manifestations of urbanism, and partly because it makes classifications themselves more descriptive.

[16] A compilation made by Brian J. L. Berry on factorial studies of the dimensionality of urban systems showed that the earliest analysis, based on 1930 U.S. census data, covered 93 cities of over 100,000 inhabitants, introduced 15 variables, and came up with 4 factors relating to size, socioeconomic status, family structure, and economic base. Since that pioneering analysis, more than a dozen factorial studies have been made in the United States, Canada, the United Kingdom, Australia, Yugoslavia, India, and the Soviet Union. It is truly an international interest.

Indicative of this interest is the recommendation of the Advisory Commission on Intergovernmental Relations (ACIR) for the establishment "of a national system for the collection, analysis, and dissemination of social statistics, with full participation by federal, state, and local governments, with special emphasis upon the development of such data for sub-state geographic areas (major cities, counties, and SMSAs) as well as state and national aggregates."[17]

Particularly important, according to the ACIR, is a much greater effort to develop employment, income, health, mobility, school enrollment, union membership, voting participation, and other social indicators for smaller areas, right down to the subareas of cities. The need is both for more frequent data gathering and for data for smaller areas.

Future classifications will be more closely geared to data from metropolitan areas and regions. National classifications, except for relatively simple indicators, will be of decreasing importance.

As Berry points out, classifications will help provide community profiles. Cities that are well above or below average in status, family size, percentage of foreign-born inhabitants, population-growth rate, and other indicators have measures of local characteristics that should be explored in community planning and in the development of municipal budgets.

Classifications increasingly will be used as a tool of urban planning, partly because of substantial changes that have taken place in the scope of urban planning in recent years. Increasingly viewed as an integrated and comprehensive profession, urban planning now concerns itself with social welfare, employment, economic development, education, public housing, and citizen participation. It no longer is an "add-on," concerned only with highways, the civic center, and other kinds of physical development. Rather, its range of interest and influence has spread so that planning is right at the heart of the governmental process.

Urban planning that is responsive to human needs requires social and economic information of a quality and scope surpassing the perfunctory projections and outdated census and employment data typical of "comprehensive" plans.[18]

---

[17] Advisory Commission on Intergovernmental Relations, *Fiscal Balance in the American Federal System,* Vol. 2, *Metropolitan Fiscal Disparities* (Washington, D.C.: U.S. Government Printing Office, 1967), pp. 23–25.

[18] See Doris B. Holleb, *Social and Economic Information for Urban Planning* (Chicago: Center for Urban Studies, University of Chicago, 1969). Two volumes. Volume I discusses information systems for urban planning for metropolitan areas and nonmetropolitan cities, reviews analytic techniques and urban statistics, provides a brief summary of data sources, and describes the information process for residential neigh-

Classifications are fluid rather than final and will change as methodologies are improved through future research, as better quality data become available, and as urban characteristics, both properties and their relationships, change over time.

The justifications for classification of cities can be elegant, rational, and logical (as they should be!), but they are also of practical necessity. They provide the framework for better understanding of urban phenomena that are susceptible to quantitative measurement and the checkpoints for comparison, compilation, and evaluation of information. Mayors, city managers, and other chief administrators must take a greater personal interest in and responsibility for information; if they do not, it is inevitable that other governments will step in to do the job.

Too many urban problems are national problems for a localized analysis to be satisfactory. The local information system—whether termed the statistical data center, the division of operational effectiveness, or the data bank —within a relatively few years will have to mesh with metropolitan and national data sets. The warnings are clear:

The heat is on—both nationally and locally—for more knowledge and more answers in all the critical areas of human and social values.[19]

. . .

Local officials should be aware that the construction of such systems [comprehensive data gatherings systems] is both technically feasible and inevitable. The question is really whether local governments want to control or shape them. If not, they will be controlled by state, federal, or regional entities.[20]

Classifications of cities are adaptive and facilitate the broader framework of data gathering, compilation, and analysis. Information is at the heart of governmental decision-making, although not all of it when one considers political and other "irrational" elements. An impressive beginning has been made with the multivariate approach to classifications, increasing recognition of the limitations as well as the uses of data, and the larger range and higher quality of data being generated. The challenge now is for urban management to conceptualize the information for planning and programming governmental services.

borhoods. Volume II is a directory of data sources, including general statistical sources, the decennial censuses of housing and population, the urban Negro American, and such specific data areas as population and vital statistics, housing, transportation, social welfare, education, and environmental quality.

[19] Hanel, *Management, Systems Analysis and Urban Data,* p. 6.
[20] John K. Harris, "Long-Range Planning and Information-Gathering Systems," paper presented at the Conference on Systems Applications in Local Government Operations, sponsored by Texas Christian University, Arlington, Texas, January 9, 1969, p. 8.

Index

Abler, Ronald, 1
Abu-Lughod, Janet L., 154, 295
Adams, John S., 1
Adrian, Charles R., 6, 247-250, 252, 256, 259
Advisory Commission on Intergovernmental Relations, 376
Affluence, and the congressional vote, 110
  as a factor in voting behavior, 119, 123
  and the presidential vote, 108ff
Africa, contemporary cities of, 252
Aggregate analysis, utility of, 114ff
Agricultural processing, 47
Agriculture, as a dominant factor in American history, 363
Ahmad, Qazi, 55, 181, 182, 211
Aiken, Michael, 174, 347, 350
Air travel as measure of interurban flows, 195
Akron, Ohio, 217, 221
Alabama, 82, 89
Alameda County, California, statistical data section established in, 374
Alexandersson, Gunnar, 125
Alexandria, Virginia, statistical data section established in, 374
Alford, Robert L., 3, 6, 115, 174, 251, 347, 350, 358, 369, 371
Alienation, as aspect of social change, 366
Alker, Hayward R., Jr., 278
Allentown, Pennsylvania, 134, 219, 220, 223
"Amenities," role of in locational choice, 365
"Amenities" cities, 253ff
"Amenities" government, 247, 248
"Amenity resources," 364
American and British factorial ecologies,

key elements in, 294
American and Canadian urban systems, similarities in, 6, 203
American cities, factorial ecologies for, 283
  factor structure of, 16, 294
  interrelationships of policies in, 346, 348, 349
  political structure of, 343, 344
  studies of, 50ff, 200, 293
  voting turnout in, 343, 344
American communities, factor analysis of, 162
  studies of decision-making in, 159
American factorial studies, comparison of, 201
American Indians, discrimination against, 80
American Manufacturing Belt, 364
American suburbs, diversity among, 97
American urban system, evolution of, 363
  latent dimensions of, 16
Amherst, Nova Scotia, 193
Anderson, Desemond L., 374
Ann Arbor, Michigan, 127
Apartment neighborhoods, 24
Apparel industry, 76
"Arbiter" cities, 253ff
"Arbiter" government, 250
Area, "underbounded," 226
Area labor market trends, 214
Arkansas, 89
Arnold, David S., 3, 6, 100
Arvida, Quebec, 193
Asia, 189
  contemporary cities of, 252
  immigrants from to Canada, 199
Asiatic and Slavic cultural components, 52
Atchley, Robert C., 125, 126
Atlanta, Georgia, 217

379

Atlantic Provinces, 197, 200
  analysis of, 199
  as slow postwar growth centers, 200
  opportunities for agriculture and industry
    in, 189
At-large elections for councilmen, 255
Attleboro, Massachusetts, 98
Automobile centers of Michigan, 221
Automobile industry, 90

Bailey, D. E., 115
Baker, A. M., 181, 199, 200
Baltimore, Maryland, 217, 221
Banbury, Oxfordshire, 270
Banfield, Edward C., 121, 251, 256, 261
Banovetz, James M., 367
Bartholemew, Harland, 368
Bedroom suburbs, 24
Behavior and environment, link between,
  279
Bell, Wendell, 183, 274-279, 281, 286, 287
Bensman, Joseph, 259, 261
Berry, Brian J. L., 3, 15-17, 19, 24, 47, 50,
  51, 54, 61, 84, 104, 155, 162, 165,
  181-183, 200, 267, 288, 289, 295,
  296, 298, 299, 304, 306, 310, 331-
  335, 339-341, 363-366, 375, 376
Bethlehem, Pennsylvania, 134, 219, 220,
  223
Billingsley, Andrew, 92
Birmingham, Alabama, 221, 286
Black Americans, 131
  diversity among, 92, 93
  employment characteristics of, 88
  housing characteristics of, 88
  rates of unemployment of, 88
  socioeconomic status of, 63
Black "ghettos," dissimilarity of, 92
Black migration patterns, 82
  from the South, 1910-30, 81
  to Texas, 89, 90
Blacks, abandonment of central city to, 127
  discrimination against, in Oklahoma, 80
    in Texas, 80
  socioeconomic status of, 64
Blalock, Hubert M., Jr., 156
Bloom, Harold, 159
Blue-collar workers, 114
Board of Inland Revenue, 229
Bogue, Donald J., 156

Bombay, India, 56
Bonjean, Charles M., 154, 162, 175
"Booster" cities, 253ff
"Booster" government, 247
  image defined, 248
Border South (U.S.), 286
Borgatta, E. F., 51, 125, 153, 158, 181,
  183, 200, 211
Borts, G. H., 217
Boston (Mass.), area, 365
  description of, 5
  ethnicity in, 292
  and Helsinki (Finland), social and factori-
    al, ecologies of, 291, 292
  study of, 293
Boudon, Raymond, 156, 165
Bowen, Don R., 158, 260
Brazilian cities, factorial ecologies for, 283
Britain, 56
  correlations among land uses in, 241
  industrial land uses in, 234
  "industrial suburb" in, 245
  land-use patterns in, 234
  number of persons per, industrial estab-
    lishment in, 236
  office in, 236
  "other commercial" establishment in,
    236
  shop in, 235
  number of residents per housing unit in,
    235
  per capita income in 1965, 288
  relationships of land uses in, 240ff
  urban dimensions of land uses in, 234
British cities, factorial ecologies for, 283
  studies of, 293
British Columbia, 189, 194, 197
  cities, 200
    concentration of Asian and Scandinav-
      ian immigrants in, 199, 202
    type, 52, 189, 190
British towns, 225, 244, 245, 294
  characteristics of, 235, 237-240
  dimensions and classifications of, 232ff
  Moser and Scott's multivariate urban stud-
    ies of, 52ff, 333
Brookline, Massachusetts, 98
Budget expenditures, 176
  explanations of, 175
  governmental, 174

Buffalo, New York, 364
Bunting, T., 181, 199, 200
Burgess, Ernest W., hypothesis of, 135
   index of, 141
   work of, 305
Business cycle analysis, spatial dimension
   of, 224
Business cycles, interregional transmission
   of, 217

Cairo, Egypt, 294
   study of, 295
Calcutta, India, 56, 294-296, 298, 299
   social space of, 299
   studies of, 301
Calgary, Alberta, 194, 195
California, 24, 99, 273
Camden (London), Metropolitan Borough
   of, 301
Camilleri, Santo F., 156, 279
Campaign speeches, analysis of, 258
Campbell, Angus, 115, 116
Campbell, Donald T., 165
Canada, 56, 245, 246, 288
   center-periphery contrasts in urbanization
      of, 200
   English-French contrasts in, 57
   ethnometropolitan centers in, 196
   French minority group in, 201
   immigration as role in urban growth of,
      199
   importance of cultural differences in, 199
   per capita income in 1965 in, 288
   peripheral centers in, 195
   postwar growth centers in, 193
   process of urbanization in, 189, 193
Canadian, cities, analysis of socioeconomic
      characteristics of, 181
   center-periphery distribution of, 195
   cultural diversity of, 185
   functional classification of, 196
   with high proportions of craftsmen, 196
   list of, 207-210
   Slavic component in, 187
   socioeconomic dimensions of, 184ff
   space-economy dimensions in, 202
   strong regionalism in, 199
   studies of, 193
   factorial studies, comparison of, 197ff
   heartland, manufacturing belt in, 200, 202

metropolitan areas, immigrants in, 194
metropolitan centers, hierarchy of, 195
studies, center-periphery factors identified
   in, 202
urban dimensions, recent analysis of, 183
urban system, ethnometropolitan component in, 194
   studies of, 52
Canadian and American, city types, similar-
      ity of, 6
   urban centers, analysis of, 183
   urban dimensions, comparison of, 197ff
Capecchi, V., 156
Cardiff, Wales, study of, 293
"Caretaker" cities, 253ff
"Caretaker" government, 249
Carpenters, percentage of male labor force
   employed as, 189
Casetti, E., 212
Cattell, Ramond B., 117, 118, 211, 213
   matrix formula given by, 223
"Causal analysis," 155
Causal interpretation of regression, 155
Census of Canada, 1961, 189
Center for Urban Studies, 3, 281
Center-periphery contrasts in Canada, 196,
   197
Centers, urban, functional size of, 18
   hierarchy of, 56
Centerville, Illinois, 201
Central cities, abandoned to blacks, 127
   abandonment of by high-status persons,
      144
   aging housing stock of, 127
   concentrations of industry within, 139
   functional classifications of, 131
   major, 24
   manufacturing ratios of, 131, 138
   nonwhite population in, 131
   unattractiveness of to high-status persons,
      143
Central Falls, Rhode Island, 106
Central Mortgage and Housing Corporation,
   7
Central-place theory, 17
Champaign-Urbana, Illinois, 127
Chapin, F. Stuart, Jr., 90
Chattanooga, Tennessee, 217
Chelsea, Massachusetts, median family income for, 97

Chester, Pennsylvania, 98
Chicago, Illinois, 68, 92, 195, 217, 261,
    296, 298, 299, 364
  analysis of, 302
  and Calcutta, social areas of mapped, 300
  classification of community areas of, 273
  North Shore of, 24
  Rees's study of, 292
  reevaluation of community boundaries of,
    306
  retailing centers of, 267
  social space of, 298
  studies of, 301, 306, 308-311
Chicago-Northwestern Indiana Standard
    Consolidated Area, 134
Childs, Richard S., 255, 256
Chile, 56
  analysis of data on, 54ff
Chilton, Roland, 158
Chinese, in South San Francisco, 122
Cities, aggregate economic power of, 17
  analysis of amount and nature of land-use
    in, 225ff
  areal functional organization of, 303ff
  British Columbia type of, 189
  changing ethnic composition of, 127
  changing nature of, 363ff
  classes, areal classes, 271
  classification of subareas within, 6
  definitions of, 265ff
  Democratic, 343
  economic classification of, 17
  economic specialities of, 11
  ethnicity of related to political character-
    istics, 346
  factor scores for, 14
  forces influencing size and growth of, 351
  formation of ethnic character of, 352
  functional sizes of, 17
  future changes in land use in, 367
  grouping of, 4
    in terms of cyclical response, 214
  industrial, 72
  influence of function on residential choice,
    127ff
  large industrial, essence of, 365
  with large Japanese, Chinese, and Filipino
    populations, 66, 68
  manufacturing, 127
  observed or manifest similarities of, 12

"overbounded," 226
  political characteristics of, 343ff
  political images of, 6
  "postindustrial," 364, 365
  prairie type, 187
  size of related to sizes of government labor
    force and city council, 346
  social areas within, 273ff
  socioeconomic, characteristics of, 339
    and political environments of, 350ff
  "truebounded," 225
  types, culture-bound, 262
    time-bound, 262
City classification, alternative approach to,
    212
  application and potential extension of, 6
  central issues in, 15
  classical taxonomic approach to, 12
  developing a new approach to, 2
  future changes predicted in, 375, 376
  most significant changes in, 375
  from a nonwhite perspective, 61
  problem of, reconsidered, 12
  purposes of, 367ff
    for policymakers and social scientists,
      335, 336
  traditional taxonomic process of, 13
  two major conclusions about, 357, 358
  use of land-use and valuation data in, 6
City Councils, 255ff
City hall, analysis of outputs from, 258
City of London, 232, 236, 245
City Rating Guide, 17
Civic disorders, 251
Civic voluntary organizations, activities in,
    166, 167
Civil War, 89
Clark, Colin, 17
Clark, Terry N., 6, 15, 153, 154, 159, 160,
    162, 175, 186
Classifications, based on economic functions,
    47
  basic definitions of and procedures in,
    266ff
  definition of, 362
  functional, 11, 139
  as help in providing community profiles,
    376
  links between within-city and city, 306
  of possible future value, 368

of property, 229
purpose of, 1ff
role of location in, 313
schemes of, functional, 124ff
social area of, 277
as tool of urban planning, 376
uses of, 369ff
within-city, 303ff
Clauber, Robert R., 157
Cleveland, Ohio, 364
Cliffe-Phillips, Geoffrey, 289, 291
Clifton, New Jersey, 219, 223
Cluster analysis, 274, 280
Cluster search methods, 213
Coleman, James S., 154
Colleges, 47
College towns, 37, 41, 43
Collins, Herbert, 132
Collver, Andrew, 2, 124
Communities, bibliography of studies on,
    260
  decisional outputs of, 159
  decision-making patterns of, 158
  differentiation of, 19
  highest status, 19
  life-cycle stage in residents of, 24, 25
  lowest status, 24, 27
  median educational level of, 166
  militarily specialized, 170
  nation's highest and lowest status, 23
  nonwhite population in, 27
  older family, 24
  per capita expenditures by, 260
  profiles of, 16, 47-49
  retirement, 24, 26, 47
  socioeconomic status of residents of, 22
  structure as related to decision-making
    patterns of, 159
Community Chest, 346, 347, 349, 354
Community types, rank-order scales of, 254
Commuting, interstate, 37
  in metropolitan centers, 21
Company town, 251
Comparative urban analysis, statistical tech-
    niques applied to, 244
Computer technology, 155
"Conditional regression analysis," 157
Conflict, minimization of, 368
Congressional elections (U.S.), 99, 110
Conurbation, English concept of, 232

Copenhagen, Denmark, Pedersen's study of,
    292
Correlation analysis, limitations of tradition-
    al, 117
Correlation matrix, zero-order, 163
Cosman, Bernard, 123
Coulter, M. A., 213
Council-manager plan, 256
Councilmen, 255ff
  at-large elections for, 255
  elected by wards, 251
County and City Data Book, 134
Covariance analysis, 15
Cowhig, James, 304
Cox, Kevin R., 158, 278
Cross-tabulation, 15
Crown property, 234
Cultural components, Asiatic and Slavic, 52
Cultural diversity as aspect of human devel-
    opment, 366
Cultural ties, power of, 120
Czechoslovakian origin, persons of, 119

Data as political weapon, 363
Davidowicz, Lucy C., 121
Davis, Allison, 90
Davis, Kingsley, 225, 228, 232
Dayton, Ohio, 217, 221
Decentralization, index of, 160, 161
Decision-making, causes of decentralized,
    170
  centralized patterns of, 170, 172, 178
  index of decentralization of, 160
  measure of centralization of, 174
  variations in centralization of, 161
Decision-making patterns of community,
    158
Decision-making structure, 168
  decentralized, 171
Deep South (U.S.)., 90, 143, 145, 149, 286
  defined, 89
Delhi, India, 56
Democratic party, 109
Democratic suburbs, 109ff
Democratic voting, 346
Denmark, per capita income in 1965, 288
Detroit, Michigan, 71, 135, 136, 364
  distribution of educational categories for,
    135
"Dichotomous division," 272

Differentiation, intermetropolitan and intrametropolitan, 47
life-cycle, 24
socioeconomic, 47
Direct oblimin approach, 214
Direct oblimin solution, 216
District of Columbia, statistical data section established in, 374
Diversified cities, 136, 137
Diversity, among American suburbs, 97
among black Americans, 92, 93
Dobriner, William T., 113
Dogan, Mattei, 154
Dollard, John, 90
Dormont, Pennsylvania, 98
Drummond, J. M., 229
Dubin, Robert, 152
Duncan, Beverly, 82, 83, 125, 145, 304
Duncan, Otis Dudley, 82, 125, 145, 151, 153, 156, 165, 276
Duncan-Reiss typology, 126
Dye, Thomas F., 332

Easton, Pennsylvania, 219, 220, 223
East Peoria, Illinois, 49
Economic achievement, aggressive pursuit of, 14
Economic activities, 44
Economic base, differences in, 16
"Economic Classification of Cities," 361, 362
Economic forecasting, urban, 6
Economic power, aggregate, of cities, 17
Edmonton, Alberta, 195
Education, 101, 102
centers of, 127
future changes in, 367
Educational classes, residential distribution of, 136
Egypt, per capita income in 1965, 288
Eisenhower, Dwight D., 108, 109
suburban votes for in 1956, 116
Elazar, Daniel J., 123
Elderly males in labor force, 38
Election, unrepresentative nature of an, 116
Electoral behavior patterns, explanations of, 119
measures of, 98
Electrical machinery industry, 76
Elyria, Ohio, 219, 220, 223

Employment, characteristics of among black Americans, 88
expansion of, 27, 31
levels of among females, 32
recent growth in, 32, 35
England, 52, 226, 246
analysis of urbanism in, 227
land-use patterns in, 230
standard classes for assessing residential properties in, 240
English cities, 187
English-French and Ontario-Quebec contrasts, 186ff
English-French contrasts in Canada, 188, 201, 202
Environment, link with behavior, 279
pollution of, 365, 368
Ethnic composition, changing, of city, 127
Ethnic groups, data on, 119
Ethnicity, potency of in political behavior, 120, 121
Ethnometropolitan centers, 195, 196
Eulau, Heinz, 115
Europe, 291
contemporary cities of, 252
immigration from, 189
European cities, link with North American cities, 291
medieval, 252
Evenson, Philip C., 128
Ewy, Douglas P., 158
Export-base approach to study of regional business cycles, 217

Factor ambiguity, 177
Factor analysis, 3, 4, 14-16, 49, 61, 62, 97, 98, 118, 164, 177, 185, 203, 245, 279, 281, 291, 334, 335, 337-339, 347
of American communities, 162
application of techniques of, 155
assessment of ability of, 331ff
assumptions of, 332ff
centroid method of, 213
claims made for, 155
as classification procedure, 213
of intercorrelation matrix, 103
major purposes of, 339
as means of replicating relationships, 178
multivariate approach to, 211

principal-axis method of, 213
standard oblimin, 216
techniques of, 154, 155
of time-series data, 224
Factor-analysis studies, major factors discovered by, 356
Factorial, dimensions, use of in within-city classifications, 296
ecology, 313
classification of variables employed in, 285
invariance, 182
methods, limitations of, 6
studies, international interest in, 375
Factors, as solutions to multicollinearity, 117
Family types, intermetropolitan distribution of, among blacks, 82
Farming states, service workers in, 76, 78, 80
Farrar, Donald E., 157
Features of social class differentiation, in cities and suburbs, 129ff
Federal Government, nation's largest producer of data, 363
Federal poverty programs, 346
Female employment, levels of, 32
role of in labor force, 33, 36
Ferber, Robert, 157
Finland, studies of cities in, 293
Swedish-speaking population in, 292
Firestine, Robert, 6
Fisher, Jack C., 54
Fisher, R. A., 158
Fishermen, percentages of male labor force employed as, 189
Flin Flon, Manitoba, 191, 193
Florida, 24, 89, 90, 99
movement of employment to, 364
Fluoridation, 346, 347, 349, 354
Forbes, Hugh D., 117
Foreign-born population, in British Columbia cities, 202
in Prairie cities, 202
Form, William H., 304
Forstall, Richard L., 2-4, 11, 17, 49, 124
classification developed by, 126, 131, 139, 140, 370, 371
economic typology developed by, 151
Four Cities, 260

France, data from, 159
Frankenberg, Ronald, 270
Frazier, E. Franklin, 62
Fredericton, New Brunswick, 194, 197
French cities, 187
French minority group in Canada, 201
Friedmann, John R. P., urban field concept of, 265
Frisch, Ragnar, 156
Fuchs, Lawrence H., 121
Functional classification schemes, 124ff
Furniture and textile industries, 90

Galle, Omer R., 125
Galt, John E., 304
Gans, Herbert J., 270
Gardner, Burleigh B., 90
Geographical Review, 361
Georgia, 82, 89
German and American immigration to Canada, 187
Ghana, per capita income in 1965, 288
study of urban systems of, 55, 56
"Ghettos," black, dissimilarity of, 92
Giggs, J. A., 294
Gittus, Elizabeth, 294
Glaab, Charles N., 368
Glace Bay (Canada), 193
Glass, Ruth, 300
Glazer, Nathan, 83, 121
Glenn, Norval D., 122
Goheen, Peter, 310
Goldberger, Arthur S., 156
Gold, David, 108, 109, 116
Goldstein, Harold, 310
Goldstein, Leon T., 121
Goldwater, Barry M., 108, 109
Goodale, D. W., 213
Goodman, Leo A., 156
Gordon, Robert A., 158
Gould, Peter, 1
Government, "Amenities" type of, 247
"Arbiter" type of, 248
"Booster" type of, 247
budget expenditures of, 174
"Caretaker" type of, 248
centers of, 127
English system of local, 229
images of, 247ff
utility of images of, 250

Great Britain, 246
Greater London Council, 231
Greek Orthodox religion, 187
Greenwich, London, 232
Greer, Scott, 278, 305
Greer-Wootten, Bryn, 289, 291
Grigg, David, 85, 266, 272, 300
Griliches, Zvi, 158
Grosse Pointe Park, Michigan, 98
Grouping, basic purpose of, 4
Growth measure, new housing as a, 129

Hadden-Borgatta typology, 126
Hadden, J. K., 51, 125, 153, 181, 183, 200, 211
Hahn, Harlan D., 251
Halifax, Nova Scotia, 189, 197
Hanel, Richard, 373, 377
Harbaugh, John W., 281
Harmon, Harry H., 61, 214, 216
Harris, Chauncy D., 11, 125, 362
  pioneering economic classification of, 3, 361
Harris, John K., 377
Harrisburg, Pennsylvania, 90
Hart, John Fraser, 11
Hatt, Paul K., 272, 273
Hauser, Philip M., 82, 83, 226
Havighurst, Robert J., 153
Hawley, Amos H., 276
Helsinki and Boston, social and factorial ecologies of, 291, 292
  study of, 293
Helsinki, Finland, career women in, 292
Henderson, Cyril McC., 3
Henkel, Ramon E., 165
Herbert, D. T., studies of Cardiff and Swansea by, 293
High-status persons, abandonment of central city by, 143, 144
Himmelfarb, Milton, 121
Hodge, Gerald, 49-51, 53, 56, 181-183, 199, 200, 202
Hofstaetter, Peter R., 50, 51
Holland, 187
Holleb, Doris B., 376
Honolulu, Hawaii, 92
Hoover, Edgar M., 106
Horton, Frank, 17, 19, 24
Housing, aging stock of in central city, 127

characteristics of among black Americans, 88
intermetropolitan distribution of among blacks, 82
multidwelling characteristic of, 74
new, as growth measure, 129
units of, percentage sound, 131
Housing Act of 1949, 347
Howard, Nigel, 300
Hunter, Allan, 307
Hydro power, 364
Hypothesis-testing, 15

Ideal community, 256
Immigration, in Canadian metropolitan areas, 194
to Canada, 199
from Europe, 189
German and American to Canada, 187
India, 56
  analysis of largest cities of, 55
  factorial ecologies for cities of, 283
  per capita income in 1965, 288
Industrial city, 72, 302-303
Industrialization in United States, from mid-nineteenth century on, 364
Industrial land uses in Britain, 234
Industrial-mix approach, 217
Industrial prominence (early) of New England and Middle Atlantic cities, 74
"Industrial suburb" in Britain, 245
Industries, "footloose," 364
  hazards of concentration of, 127, 139
  heavy, 106
  unattractive features of, 138, 140
Information, organized location for, 373, 374
Inner London, 232-234, 236, 237
  number of persons per shop in, 235
  typology of, 301
Inner London Educational Authority, 228, 231, 232
  analysis of, 245
Integration, racial and ethnic as aspect of human development, 367
International City Management Association, 2-4, 17, 361, 362
Interstate commuting, 37
Interurban flows, air travel as measure of, 195

Iowa, 80
Iron ore, production and shipment of, 193
Italians, 122
Italian suburbs, characteristics of, 121
Italy, per capita income in 1965, 288
Ivory Coast, per capita income in 1965, 288

Jambrek, Peter, 159
Janowitz, Morris, 123
Jansen, Anton J., 153
Janson, Carl-Gunnar, 154
Jeffrey, Douglas, 6, 7, 212
Jennings, Kent, 121
Jennrich and Harman, direct oblimin approach of, 214
Jennrich, R. I., 216
Jerovsek, Janez, 159
Jewish vote, the, 121, 122
Johnson, Charles S., 62
Johnson, Lyndon B., 108, 109
Johnston, J., 156, 157
Jones, F. Lancaster, 298
Jones, Victor, 2, 3, 11, 124
Journey-to-work trips, 304
Jureen, Lars, 157

Kansas, 80
Kaplan, Howard B., 51
Kasahara, Yoshiko, 194
Kendall, M. G., 158
Kennedy, John F., 108, 109
Kerner Commission, 251
Key, V. O., Jr., 115, 116
King, Leslie J., 3, 6, 7, 52, 181, 199, 200, 202, 212
Kitagawa, Evelyn M., 273
Kneedler, Grace, 124
Knight, Richard V., 17
Kornblum, William, 159
Kube, Ella, 278
Kukawka, Pierre, 159
Kutzbach, J. E., 224

Labor force, elderly males in, 32, 38
  female participation in, 31, 33, 36
Lake Michigan, 299
Lampard, Eric, 226
Lancashire, England, 236
Lander, Bernard, 158
Land use, analysis of, 246

classification of, 228
intensity of, 226
patterns of, in Britain, 234
  in England, 230
  in Wales, 230
urban dimensions of, in Britain, 234
Lankford, Philip M., 85
Lansing, Michigan, within-city classification approaches as applied to, 304
Las Vegas, Nevada, 127
Latent dimensions, search for, 14
Latent structure, generality of, 49
  universality of in urban systems, 17
Latin American urban research, 1
Lazarsfeld, Paul F., 156
League of Women Voters, 161, 166
Lee, Eugene C., 255
Lenski, Gerhard, 123
Lewis, Hylan, 83
Lewisham, England, 232
Lieberson, Stanley, 125
Life cycle, extremes of stages in, 26
Lineberry, Robert L., 154, 162, 175
Lipset, Seymour M., 114
Literacy index, 288
Lloyd's of London, 268
Local Community Factbook, 273
Local government, proper tasks of, 247
Loggers, percentage of male labor force employed as, 189
London, England, 195, 227, 228, 230, 231, 233, 234, 236-238, 245
  Inner Boroughs of, 228
  Northwest, 301
London County Council, 228
Longshoremen, percentage of male labor force employed as, 189
Lorain, Ohio, 219, 220, 223
Los Angeles, California, 135, 136, 275, 277, 279, 311
Louisiana, 82, 89
Lower Mississippi Valley (U.S.), 217
Lynch, Kevin, 368
Lynd, Helen M., 261
Lynd, Robert S., 261

Mabogunje, Akin, 55
McCannell, Earle, 281
McCaskell, Murray, 186
McEntire, David, 83

McNulty, Michael L., 55
MacRae, Duncan, 155
Madras, India, 56
Maidan (in Calcutta), 299
Male labor force, carpenters in, 189
  the elderly in, 32, 37
  loggers in, 189
  longshoremen in, 189
Malinvaud, E., 157
Manifest variables, factor loadings for, 14
Manufacturing, 131
  cities, predominantly, 33, 39, 40, 136,
    137, 346
    concentration of low-status people in,
    127
  ratios of, 137, 139, 145
  regions, predominantly, 27, 33, 69, 202,
    217
Marble, Duane F., 267
Maritime Provinces, 194, 196, 197
Markets, national, 44
Masotti, Louis H., 158, 260
Maxwell, J. W., functional classification of
    Canadian cities by, 196
Mayer, Harold M., 3, 51
Megalopolis cities, short-term economic
    forces affecting, 223
Melbourne (Australia) study, 301
Memphis, Tennessee, 217
Mercer, John, 289, 291
Merit system, 258
Merriam, Daniel E., 281
Metropolises, largest in national "social
    space," 313, 314
Metropolitan areas, outward movement in,
    366
Metropolitan centers, 47
  commuting areas of, 19, 21
  dominant dimensions of, 51
  preeminence of in Canada, 200
  spatial distribution of, 19
Metropolitan Chicago, 312
Metropolitanism, indicators of, 195
Metropolitan network (U.S.) in 1960, 20
Metropolitan New York Region, 106
Metropolitan Toronto, 302
Mexicans, 122
Mexico, 24
Meyer, David R., 5, 47
Meyerson, Martin, 261

Miami, Florida, 286
Michelson, William, 102
Michigan, automobile centers of, 221
  study of four cities of, 247
Middle Atlantic States, 128
Middle class, suburbanization of, 127, 130,
    139
Middlesex County, New Jersey, 226
The Middle South (U.S.), 143, 145
Middletown, Ohio, 261
Migration-interaction model, 189
Migration of blacks, 82
Militarily specialized communities, 170
Military bases, 47
Military communities, 172
Military-industrial complex, 170
Military installations, 41, 44, 45, 170, 178
Miller, John, 265
Mindlin, Albert, 374
Mineral resources, 364
Mingasson, Christian, 159
Minneapolis, Minnesota, 134
Mobility, geographic, 24
  social, 19
  trends of intercity, 366
Model cities program, 346, 347, 349, 354
Model muddling, 177
Montreal, 195, 200, 202, 288, 289
  European immigrants to, 291
  social geography of, 290
Montreal Island, Quebec, 185
Morrison, Denton E., 165
Moser, C. A., 52-54, 181, 182, 211, 225,
    227, 228, 333, 334
Moser, Ruth, 159
Moynihan, Daniel P., 121
Multicollinearity, 118, 156, 157, 162, 177
  direct solution to, 158
Multifamily housing in northeast United
    States, 72, 74
Multivariate analysis, 138, 157, 245
Multivariate classification problem, 16, 17
Muncie, Indiana, 270
Municipal Year Book, 2, 4, 49, 100, 126,
    160, 256
Murdie, Robert A., 6, 182, 289, 301, 302
Muslim concentrations, 296
Myrdal, Gunnar, 80-82, 90

"National business centers," 17

National economy, trends and oscillations in, 214
National markets, 44
National Opinion Research Center, 160
National Science Foundation 7
Natural area concept, 272
Natural gas, extraction of, 37
Natural region, 272
Nebraska, 80
Needham, Massachusetts, median family income for, 97
Neely, Peter, 84, 85
Neff, P., 217
Negroes, 127, 309
   communities of, 309
   concern with economic equality of, 201, 202
   as minority group in United States, 201
Neighborhood-limited algorithm, 84
Neighborhoods, classification of, 253
   predominantly apartment, 24
Neils, Elaine, 47, 50, 51, 363-366
Nelson, Howard J., 11, 125, 126, 161, 170
New England, 74, 99, 128
   data from communities in, 18, 159
New Jersey, 74
New Waterford, Nova Scotia, 191, 193, 197
New York, New York, 48, 68, 92, 135, 195
New York State, 74, 364
New York-Northeastern New Jersey Standard Consolidated Area, 134
Niagara Falls, New York, 195
Nigeria, study of urban systems of, 55, 56
1970 Census of Population, 366
Nixon, Richard M., 108, 109, 116
Nobbe, Charles E., 68
Nolting, Orin F., 100
Non-American cities, factorial ecologies for, 287ff
Non-London area, 233, 236
Non-Western cities, factor analysis applied in studies of, 294ff
Nonwhites, intermetropolitan differentiation of, 61, 62, 92
   population of in communities, 27
   status differentiation of, 64, 66
Noranda, Quebec, 193
Norman, Peter, 298, 300, 301
Norsworthy, David R., 90
North, The (U.S.), 286, 353, 354

cities of, 341-343
defined, 80
industrial cities of, with old housing and high unemployment, 71
North American cities, link with European cities, 291
North Carolina, 89, 90, 217
North Central States (U.S.), 68, 99
Northeast, The (U.S.), 68, 74, 151
   multifamily housing in, 72, 74
Northern Ontario, 200
Nova Scotia, 199
Numerical taxonomy, development of a classification using, 5

Oblique factor analysis, 212, 214, 224
Oblique rotation, 106
Ogburn, William F., 124
Ohio, 90
   steel centers of, 221
Oklahoma, 80
Older family communities, 24
Ontario, 194, 199
Operational taxonomic units (OTUs), 265ff
Orcutt, Guy H., 157
Oromocto, Atlantic Provinces, 193, 197
Oshawa, Ontario, 196
Osofsky, Gilbert, 81
Ottawa, Ontario, 194, 195
Overlapping variables, redundancies of, 49

Pacific Coast (U.S.), 66
Pacific Coast (U.S.) SMSAs, 91, 92
Palm Springs, California, 49
Park Forest, Illinois, 261
Passaic, New Jersey, 219, 223
Paterson, New Jersey, 219, 223
Patronage system, 258
Patterson, Samuel C., 122
Pedersen, Poul O., 292
Pennsylvania, 90
   steel centers of, 221
Performance Reports for the Chief Administrator, 372
Perle, Sylvia M., 50
Perloff, Harvey S., 74, 88
Petroleum, extraction of, 37
Philbrick, Allen K., 303
Physical density as measure of intensity of land use, 226ff

Piedmont area (U.S.), 44
Piedmont Crescent (U.S.), 90
Pinkerton, James R., 125
Pittsburgh, Pennsylvania, 71
Police force, 259
Policy development, future changes in, 367
Policy makers, questions of interest to, 336
Polish origin, persons of, 119
Political behavior, potency of ethnicity in, 121
Political outputs, range of, 6
Political units, overlay on urban systems, 19
Polk, Kenneth, 278
Polsby, Nelson W., 159
Population, density of in British towns, 233
  foreign-born or foreign stock, 27, 28, 30
  with high educational levels, 14
  growth of, 27, 31, 34
  nonwhite, 27
Port Colborne, Ontario, 196
Poverty, rural, 24, 47
Pownall, L. L., 11
Prairie cities (in Canada), 52, 187-189, 199
  foreign-born population in, 202
Prairie Provinces, 194, 196, 197, 200
Presidential elections (U.S.), 99, 108, 110
Press, Charles, 256, 260
Price, Daniel O., 50, 51
Prince Edward Island (Canada), 199
Principal-axis factor analysis, 15
Principal-components analysis, 103
Professional planning activities, 257
Professional workers, 14
Property classification, 229
Property taxation, American system of, 229
Protestant affiliation, 187
Psychological stress, 365
Public housing, 346, 347, 354
Public Opinion Quarterly, 115
Public transportation, increased government
  commitment to, 367
Pyle Gerald F., 296

Quebec City, Quebec, 191, 194, 199, 200

Rabinowitz, Francine F., 1, 358
Race, southern (U.S.) polarization over, 122
Racial segregation, 151
Rand McNally and Company, 3
Rand McNally's hierarchical ratings, 17

"Rateable values," meaning of, 228ff
Ray, D. Michael, 6, 16, 52
Recent-growth factor, 104
  and the congressional vote, 113, 114
  and the presidential vote, 111ff
Rees, Philip H., 6, 47, 154, 183, 295, 296,
  298, 299, 307, 368, 369
  Chicago study of, 291, 292
Reform government, 166, 172
  causes of, 168
  index of, 161, 169
  in the South and North (U.S.), 343
  structures of, 178
Reform movements of the twentieth cen-
  tury (U.S.), 255, 256
Regionalism as a factor in voting behavior,
  122, 123
"Regression analysis, conditional," 157
Regression causal interpretation of, 155
  equations for, 139
  statistical aspects of, 156
Reiss, Albert J., Jr., 125
Reno, Nevada, 127
Republican party, 109, 116
Republican suburban vote, 109ff, 117
Residential densities, increasing in cities,
  138, 367
Residential distribution of social classes,
  151
Residential location of social classes, 134ff
Residential segregation, 143
Residents per housing unit in Britain, 235
Resort and recreation centers, 127
Resources, for the future, 3
  waste of, 365
Retail trade, 131, 136
  centers, 136, 137
    low-status people in, 127
Retirement communities, 24, 26, 47
Rimouski, Quebec, 191
River Rouge, Michigan, family incomes for,
  98
Riviere-du-Loup, Quebec, 191
Robinson, W. S., 100
Robson, Brian, 293
Rohlf, F. J., 213
Roig, Charles, 159
Rokkan, Stein, 154
Roman Catholic Church, 161
Roman Catholic population, 174

Rootlessness, as aspect of social change, 366
Rossi, Peter, 130
Rummell, Rudolph J., 155, 185

Sacks, Seymour, 6
Saint John, New Brunswick, 195
Sampling, 15
Sampson, P. F., 216
San Francisco, California, 277, 279
  homogenity assumption tested for, 275
San Francisco Bay area, 275, 365
Sarnia, Ontario, 193
Sault Ste. Marie, Ontario, 195, 196
Scandinavia, 189
Scandinavian immigrants to Canada, 199
Schmid, Calvin F., 68, 279
Schnore, Leo F., 5, 62, 123, 128, 130-132,
  226
School trips, 304
Scoble, Harry M., 369
Scott, Richard W., 125
Scott, Wolf, 52-54, 181, 182, 211, 225, 227,
  228, 300, 333, 334
Segal, David R., 123
Segregation, nonwhite residential, 143
  racial, 151
  by socioeconomic status, 151
Selective suburbanization, interaction of
  with racial segregation, 143
Sellers, Charles, 116
Sept-Iles (Canada), 192
Service centers, 44, 46, 190, 191
Service sector, 364
Service workers in farming states, 76, 78,
  80
Shevky, Eshref, 183, 274-277, 279, 284,
  287
Shevky-Bell patterns, 280
Shopping trips, 304
Shreveport, Lóuisiana, 286
Simmons, J. L., 122
Simon, Herbert, 155
Simpson, David, 288
Simpson, Richard L., 90
Single communities, studies of, 270
Sixty-six Chicago suburbs, relations between
  national and metropolitan factor
  scores of, 307
Slavic origin, persons of, 119
Smith, Joel, 132, 304

Smith Robert H. T., 3, 11, 12
Smith, T. Lynn, 82
SMSAs (Standard Metropolitan Statistical
    Areas)
  characteristics of nonwhite populations in,
    5, 61
  classification of, 84ff
  declining industrial and young-family in-
    dustrial, 91
  high proportions of service workers in, 78,
    79
  high socioeconomic status, 66, 67
  low socioeconomic status, 63-65
  multifamily dwelling, 74, 75
  old housing and high unemployment in,
    72, 73
  in upper levels of urban hierarchy, 77, 78
  young family, 69, 70
Sneath, P. H. A., 213
Social area analyses, 274, 313
  consolidated list of, 315ff
  selected bibliography of, 325ff
Social area framework, uses of, 278ff
Social classes, city function as influence in
    residential location of, 127ff
  high, 14
  residential, distribution of, 151
    location of, 5, 134ff
  spatial sifting and sorting of, 151
Social elite, movement of to suburbs, 127,
    139
Social mobility process, 19
Social organizational areas, hierarchy of,
    305
Social participation, 304
Social reorganization, 251
Society, culturally heterogeneous, 56
Sociocultural factors, system-wide, 16
Socioeconomic differentiation, 47
  principal dimensions of, 56
Socioeconomic status, of blacks, 63, 64
  measurement of, 134ff
  variations in among nonwhite groups, 80ff
Sokal, R. R., 213
Somerset County, New Jersey, 226
South Carolina, 82, 89, 217
South San Francisco, California, large minor-
    ities in, 122
South, the (U.S.), 68, 143, 172, 342, 353,
    354

textile towns in, 32
Southern California areas, 365
Southern Ontario, 197
Southern (U.S.) cities, 27, 341-343
   authoritarian, 172
Southwest, the (U.S.), movement of
   employment to, 364
Southwestern Ontario, role of immigration
   in growth of cities in, 189
Space, local government control of, 367
Space economy, dimensions of, 190
Spanish-speaking people, 122
Spear, Allan H., 81
Springdale, Arkansas, 261
St. Paul, Minnesota, 134
Stages in life cycle, 104
   of nonwhites, 68ff
Stanback, Thomas M., Jr., 17
Standard Land Use Coding Manual, 368
State College, Pennsylvania, 49
State legislature, degree of centralization of
   decision-making in, 353-355
*Statistical Abstract of the United States,
   1968,* 202
Statistical techniques applied to comparative
   urban analysis, 244
Status, as a factor in voting behavior, 123
Steel centers, of Indiana, 217
   of Ohio, 217, 221
   of Pennsylvania, 217, 221
Steigenga, William, 11
Stein, Maurice R., 270
Stevenson, Adlai E., 108, 109
Stinchcombe, Arthur L., 152
Stokes, Donald, 116
Stone, Gregory P., 304
Stone, J. R. N., 158
Stone, Leroy O., 195
Strong-mayor system, 251
Stuart, Alan, 158
Suburban characteristics, correlations with
   voting behavior, 5
Suburbanization, selective, 142, 143, 147,
   149, 151
   correlations among indices of, 148
   two-stage model of, 150
Suburban voting, 108
Suburbs, bedroom, 24
   Democratic and Republican, 109
   Eisenhower landslide in, 116

movement of middle class and social elite
   to, 127
"reluctant," 113
social and economic characteristics of,
   100
variety of, 5
Suits, Daniel B., 128
Sunderland, England, study of, 293
Suttles, Gerald, 270
Swansea, Wales, study of, 293
Sweden, per capita income in 1965, 288
Sweetser, Dorrian Apple, 291
   study of Helsinki (Finland) and Boston
   (Massachusetts) by, 293
Sweetser, Frank L., 183, 291, 292, 294
   study of Helsinki and Boston by, 293
Swift Current, Saskatchewan, 191

Taeuber, Alma F., 62, 68, 83, 286
Taeuber, Karl E., 62, 83, 273, 286
   segregation index of, 68
Tax and Land-use measure, 257
Taxonomic analysis, 313
Taxonomy, numerical, development of a
   classification using, 5
Taylor, Peter J., 268, 281, 300, 313
   typology of grouping techniques by, 269
Telser, Lester, 158
Tennessee, 89
Texas, 24, 80, 90, 99
   black migrants to, 89, 90
   discrimination against blacks in, 80
Textile and furniture industries, 90
Textiles, 47
Theil, Henri, 158
"The Third Survey of London Life and
   Labor," 300
Thompson, Robert A., 83
Thompson, Wilbur R., 19, 71, 72
Thorndike, E. L., 50, 51
Tiger Bay, Wales, multiracial society of, 293
Time dimension, 211
Time-series data, 212
Timmins, Ontario, 191
Tobias, Susan, 159
Toledo, Ohio, 217
   sample factorial ecology summary for,
   282, 283
Toronto, Ontario, 195, 196, 200, 202, 288,
   289, 301

factorial ecologies developed in, 368
foremost center for postwar immigrants, 194
Toronto (Ontario) Metropolitan Planning Board, 288
Tourist industry, 90
Towns, child-rearing, 26
    college, 37, 41, 43
    functional types of, 32
    manufacturing, 33, 39, 40
    mining, 32, 37, 40, 42
    textile, 32
Traffic congestion, 139
Trail, British Columbia, 193
Transgenerated variables, list of, 205, 206
Transportation, evolving system of, 127
Tropman, John E., 51
Trueblood, Felicity M., 1
Truro, Nova Scotia, 193
Tryon, Robert C., 115, 274, 275, 280, 281
Tucker, L. R., 224
Tucson, Arizona, 135
Tufte, Edward R., 117
Typologies, role of in development theory, 152ff

"Underbounded" area, 226
Unemployment, data, as index of cyclical response, 214
    rates, for all major labor market areas, 214
    of among black Americans, 88
United Kingdom, 187
United Nations, 358
United States, 56, 226, 245, 246, 266
    internal ethnic differences identified as Negro concentrations, 201
    Negro minority group in, 201
    per capita income in 1965 in, 288
    process of urbanization in, 193
    space-economy dimensions in cities of, 202
United States Bureau of the Census, 372
    urbanized area concept of, 265
United States census, political influences on, 334
University of Chicago, 3, 281, 361
Urban, analysis, attempts at measuring factorial invariance in, 182
    centers, classification of, 11

economic base of, 56
    variables for predicting growth or decline of, 182
    variation of, 57
    characteristics, valuation density as measure of, 245
    classification, development of principles of, 347
    economy, base of, 16
    forecasting of, 6
    environments, quality of, 51
    government images, fourfold typology of, 247
    hierarchy, black, 76
        position in, 83
        status of towns within, 17
    information framework, development of, 372, 373
    and regional development theory, development of, 182
    research, in Latin America, 1
    residential patterning, 314
    studies of British towns, 52ff
    systems, latent structure of, 56
        overlay of political units on, 19
Urban Data Service 1971, 4, 49
Urbanism, analysis of, in England and Wales, 227
    definition of, 228
Urbanization, measures of, 233
    spatial nature of, 231
Urbanized areas, 133, 134
    nature of, 132ff
Urban renewal, 346, 354
    expenditures for, 173, 174
    variance in, 174

Valuation densities, 236
    as measure of land-use intensity and urbanization characteristics, 227, 245
Van Arsdol, Maurice, 279, 281
Vance, Rupert B., 90
Vancouver, British Columbia, 195
Verdoorn, P. J., 157
Vernon, Raymond, 106
Vidich, A. J., 259, 261
Vining, R., 217, 219
"Voluntary" trips, 304
Voter-turnout patterns, 259
Voting, suburban, 108

Voting behavior, 278
  affluence as factor in, 119, 123
  regionalism as factor in, 122, 123
  status as factor in, 123
Voting data, 98ff

Wales, 52, 226, 246
  analysis of urbanism in, 227
  land-use patterns in, 230
  standard classes for assessing residential
    properties in, 240
Walter, Benjamin, 5
Warkentin, John, 186
War on Poverty, 347, 349
Washington, D.C., 127, 217
Weaver, Robert C., 83
Weifenbach, A., 217
Weiss, Shirley F., 90
Welland, Ontario, 196
Weslaco, Texas, 49
West Africa, 56
Western Canada, economic opportunities in,
  189
  metropolitan centers in, 194
West Germany, 245
West, the (U.S.), 60, 68, 143, 286
  movement of employment to, 364
Westminster, England, 232, 236
White-collar strata, 130
White-collar workers, 14, 114
Whitehead, Alfred North, 155
Wholesale trade, 131
Whyte, William H., Jr., 261
Williams, Marianne, 274-276, 279, 284

Williams, Oliver P., 247-250, 252, 256, 259
Williams, R. M., 217
Wilson, James Q., 251, 256
Winch, Robert G., 165
Windsor, Ontario, 195, 200
Winnipeg, Manitoba, 195
Winsborough, Hal H., 5, 125, 130
Wirt, Frederick M., 3, 5, 97, 116, 166
Wold, Herman, 155, 157
Wolfe, Roy I., 195
Wolfinger, Raymond E., 121
Wood, Robert C., 15
Woofter, T. J., Jr., 62, 81
Workers, blue-collar, 114
  white-collar, 114
World War I, 82
World War II, 273, 364
Wright, Sewall, 156

Yeung, Yue Man, 289, 291
Yiddish-speaking people, 122
Yorkshire, England, 236
Youngstown, Ohio, 219, 223
Youngstown-Warren (Ohio) area, 219, 223
Yugoslavia, 56
  data from, 159
  urban centers in, 54
Yugoslavian origin, persons of, 119

Ziegler, Harmon, 121
Zero-order correlation matrix, 163
Zetterberg, Hans L., 152
Zikmund, Joseph, 97, 123
Zorbaugh, Harvey W., 272

7230 272